# History of New Testament Literature

# History of New Testament Literature

## Georg Strecker

*Translated by*

Calvin Katter

*With the assistance of*

Hans-Joachim Mollenhauer

**Trinity Press International**
**Harrisburg, Pennsylvania**

Translated from the German *Literaturgeschichte des Neuen Testaments,* published
in 1992 by Vandenhoeck & Ruprecht, Göttingen, Germany

© Vandenhoeck & Ruprecht 1992
Translation © Calvin Katter 1997

Trinity Press International, P.O. Box 1321, Harrisburg, PA 17105
Trinity Press International is a division of the Morehouse Group

Library of Congress Cataloging-in-Publication Data

>Strecker, Georg, 1929-
>>[Literatürgeschichte des Neuen Testaments. English]
>>History of New Testament Literature / Georg Strecker; translated
>by Calvin Katter with the assistance of Hans-Joachim Mollenhauer.
>>>p.    cm.
>>Includes bibliographical references and index
>>ISBN 1-56338-203-2 (pbk. : alk. paper)
>>1. Greek literature--Relation to the New Testament. 2. Bible
>N.T.--Criticism, interpretation, etc.   I. Title.
>BS2364.2.S85513  1997
>225.6'6--dc21                                                    97-12971
>                                                                 CIP

Printed in the United States of America

97  98  99  00  01   5  4  3  2  1

# Table of Contents

# Preface

How are the New Testament writings related to ancient literature? To what degree are literary forms and genres of the non-Christian tradition taken up and reworked in them, and to what extent can we speak of genuine Christian literary genres? These questions have been raised and answered in very disparate ways. Even if we accept the judgment of Rudolf Bultmann that no comprehensive history of New Testament literature can be produced, given the relatively modest literary basis, it should still be possible to distinguish the New Testament literary forms and their particular literary characteristics, and to show their correspondences and special features relative to contemporary non-Christian literature.

This process occurs when we set boundaries for the New Testament canon, without thereby assuming a special position for the writings summarized in the canon in relationship to other early Christian literature. On the contrary, the works of Martin Dibelius and Philipp Vielhauer on the history of New Testament literature have exemplified that, from the point of view of literary criticism, the boundaries of the New Testament canon are not stable. Thus is not possible to make a basic distinction between the New Testament and the contemporary and subsequent development of early Christian literature. Even for the later period such a distinction can only be carried through in an artificial manner, so that the restriction to canonical writings can at least claim to be pragmatic.

It need not be specifically demonstrated that a history of New Testament literature is an urgent *desideratum* for contemporary research. Only a few areas of New Testament research are currently being studied with the same intensity. Literary concepts and structures for the interpretation of the New Testament are being used in a scarcely understandable manner: in varied and often mutually exclusive textual, structural, linguistic, and other types of literary approaches. This work attempts to describe various new methodologies as they apply to the New Testament writings, to present their significance for research, and at the same time to deal with them critically. The dynamic relationship of synchronic and diachronic analysis is especially emphasized. It is of basic significance for the understanding of the New Testament writings which are formally as well as materially molded by their literary associations. It also provides access to the New Testament forms and genres.

For this book I have had the support of numerous friendly assistants. In the first place, without the indefatigable and unselfish help of Michael Labahn, cand. theol., this book would not have been written. Thanks also to my student assistants, Woldemar Flake, Frank Kleinschmidt, and Jörg Sievert, and to my wife, for their help in proofreading and preparing the index. Finally, thanks to Pastor Klaus Fricke, retired, who proofread the entire manuscript. Ms. Margaret Lessner oversaw the final version of the galley proofs, earning the gratitude of the readers, along with those mentioned earlier.

Göttingen, November 20, 1991                                        Georg Strecker

# Translator's Note

The English language version of Georg Strecker's *Literaturgeschichte des Neuen Testaments* for the most part follows the formatting conventions of the German original. Sections within chapters are arranged in numerical fashion. A smaller typeface within the body of the text indicates supplementary material. Notes are placed at the bottom of each page, and, with a few noted exceptions, follow Strecker's enumeration.

I have attempted to indicate English equivalents, where readily available, for works which Strecker cites in German. While listing the English volume or page numbers, I have retained the details of the original German citation as well.

It is my hope that the English language version of this work will further enhance the memory and reputation of Georg Strecker in the English-speaking world.

Chicago, July 8, 1997                                          Calvin Katter

# Abbreviations

| | |
|---|---|
| *AcOr* | *Acta orientalia* |
| AnBib | Analecta biblica |
| *ANRW* | *Aufsteig und Niedergang der römischen Welt* |
| ATANT | Abhandlungen zur Theologie des Alten und Neuen Testaments |
| *ATR* | *Anglican Theological Review* |
| *AusBR* | *Australian Biblical Review* |
| BAGD | W. Bauer, W.F. Arndt, F.W. Gingrich. F.W. Danker, *Greek-English Lexicon of the New Testament* |
| *BASOR* | *Bulletin of the American Schools of Oriental Research* |
| BBB | Bonner biblische Beiträge |
| BBET | Beiträge zur biblischen Exegese und Theologie |
| BDF | F. Blass, A. Debrunner, and R.W. Funk, *A Greek Grammar of the NT* |
| BDR | F. Blass, A. Debrunner, and F. Rehkopf, *Grammatik des neutestamentlichen Griechisch* |
| BETL | Bibliotheca ephemeridum theologicarum lovaniensium |
| BEvT | Beiträge zur evangelischen Theologie |
| BHT | Beiträge zur historischen Theologie |
| *Bib* | *Biblica* |
| BibB | Biblische Beiträge |
| *BibLeb* | *Bibel und Leben* |
| BibOr | Biblica et orientalia |
| *BJRL* | *Bulletin of the John Rylands University Library of Manchester* |
| *BK* | *Bibel und Kirche* |
| *BR* | *Biblical Research* |
| *BTZ* | *Berliner Theologische Zeitschrift* |
| *BVC* | *Bible et vie chrétienne* |
| BWANT | Beiträge zur Wissenschaft vom Alten und Neuen Testament |
| *BZ* | *Biblische Zeitschrift* |
| BZNW | Beihefte zur ZNW |
| CBC | Cambridge Bible Commentary |
| *CBQ* | *Catholic Biblical Quarterly* |
| CBQMS | Catholic Biblical Quarterly Monograph Series |
| CGTC | Cambridge Greek Testament Commentaries |
| *CH* | *Church History* |
| *CIG* | *Corpus inscriptionum graecarum* |
| *CJT* | *Canadian Journal of Theology* |
| CNT | Commentaire du Nouveau Testament |
| ConB | Coniectanea biblica |
| ConBNT | Coniectanea biblica, New Testament |
| *CP* | *Classical Philology* |
| CQR | Church Quarterly Review |
| CRINT | Compendia rerum iudaicarum ad novum testamentum |

| | |
|---|---|
| CSEL | Corpus scriptorum ecclesiasticorum latinorum |
| *DTT* | *Dansk teologisk tidsskrift* |
| EB | Echter Bibel |
| Ebib | Etudes bibliques |
| EKKNT | Evangelish-katholischer Commentar zum Neuen Testament |
| *EKL* | *Evangelisches Kirchenlexikon* |
| ErFor | Erträge der Forschung |
| *ETL* | *Ephemerides theologicae lovanienses* |
| *ETR* | *Etudes théologiques et religieuses* |
| ETS | Erfurter theologische Studien |
| EvK | Evangelische Kommentare |
| *EvT* | *Evangelische Theologie* |
| FB | Forschung zur Bibel |
| FBBS | Facet Books, Biblical Series |
| FC | Fathers of the Church |
| FFNT | Foundations and Facets: New Testament |
| FRLANT | Forschungen zur Religion und Literatur des Alten und Neuen Testaments |
| GCS | Griechischen christlichen Schriftsteller |
| GNT | Grundrisse zum Neuen Testament |
| GTA | Göttinger theologische Arbeiten |
| HKNT | Handkommentar zum Neuen Testament |
| HNT | Handbuch zum Neuen Testament |
| HNTC | Harper's NT Commentaries |
| HTKNT | Herders theologischer Kommentar zum Neuen Testament |
| *HTR* | *Harvard Theological Review* |
| HTS | Harvard Theological Studies |
| HUT | Hermaneutische Untersuchungen zur Theologie |
| *IB* | *Interpreter's Bible* |
| ICC | International Critical Commentary |
| *IDB* | *Interpreter's Dictionary of the Bible* |
| *IDBSup* | Supplementary volume to *IDB* |
| *JAAR* | *Journal of the American Academy of Religion* |
| JAC | Jahrbuch für Antike und Christentum |
| *JBL* | *Journal of Biblical Literature* |
| *JBR* | *Journal of Bible and Religion* |
| *JEH* | *Journal of Ecclesiastical History* |
| *JHS* | *Journal of Hellenic Studies* |
| *JSJ* | *Journal for the Study of Judaism in the Persian, Hellenistic and Roman Period* |
| *JSNT* | *Journal for the Study of the New Testament* |
| JSNTSup | Journal for the Study of the New Testament–Supplement Series |
| *JTC* | *Journal for Theology and the Church* |
| *JTS* | *Journal of Theological Studies* |
| *KD* | *Kerygma und Dogma* |
| KlT | Kleine Texte |
| *LB* | *Linguistica Biblica* |

| | |
|---|---|
| LCC | Library of Christian Classics |
| LCL | Loeb Classical Library |
| LD | Lectio Divina |
| *LR* | *Lutherische Rundschau* |
| *LS* | *Louvain Studies* |
| *LTK* | *Lexicon für Theologie und Kirche* |
| MeyerK | H.A.W. Meyer, Kritisch-exegetischer Kommentar über das Neue Testament |
| MNTC | Moffatt NT Commentary |
| *MScRel* | *Mélanges de science religieuse* |
| MTZ | Münchener theologische Zeitschrift |
| *Mus* | *Muséon* |
| *NetTTs* | *Nederlands theologisch tijdscrift* |
| *Neot* | *Neotestamentica* |
| *NKZ* | *Neue kirchliche Zeitschrift* |
| *NorTT* | *Norsk Teologisk Tidsskrift* |
| *NovT* | *Novum Testamentum* |
| NovTSup | Novum Testamentum, Supplements |
| *NRT* | *La nouvelle revue théologique* |
| NTAbh | Neutestamentliche Abhandlungen |
| NTD | Das Neue Testament Deutsch |
| NTF | Neutestamentliche Forschungen |
| NTL | New Testament Library |
| NTOA | Novum Testamentum et Orbis Antiquus |
| *NTS* | *New Testament Studies* |
| NTTS | New Testament Tools and Studies |
| *Numen* | *Numen: International Review for the History of Religions* |
| ÖBO | Österreichische biblische Studien |
| OBT | Overtures to Biblical Theology |
| *PG* | J. Migne, *Patrologia graeca* |
| *PL* | J. Migne, *Patrologia latina* |
| PW | Pauly-Wissowa, Real-Encyclopädie der classischen Altertumswissenschaft |
| PWSup | Supplement to PW |
| QD | Questiones disputatae |
| *RAC* | *Reallexikon für Antike und Christentum* |
| *RB* | *Revue biblique* |
| *RBén* | *Revue bénédictine* |
| *RE* | *Realencyklopädie für prostentantische Theologie und Kirche* |
| RechBib | Recherches bibliques |
| *RevScRel* | *Revue des sciences religieuses* |
| *Rev Thom* | *Revue thomiste* |
| *RGG* | *Religion in Geschichte und Gegenwart* |
| RNT | Regensburger Neues Testament |
| SANT | Studien zum Alten und Neuen Testament |
| SB | Sources bibliques |
| *SBAW* | *Sitzungsberichte der bayerischen Akademie der Wissenschaften* |

| | |
|---|---|
| SBB | Stuttgarter biblische Beiträge |
| SBLDS | SBL Dissertation Series |
| SBLMS | SBL Monograph Series |
| SBLSBS | SBL Sources for Biblical Study |
| SBLSP | SBL Seminar Papers |
| SBM | Stuttgarter biblische Monographien |
| SBS | Stuttgarter Bibelstudien |
| SBT | Studies in Biblical Theology |
| SC | Source chrétiennes |
| *SE* | *Studia Evangelica I,II, III* |
| *SEÅ* | *Svensk exegetisk årsbok* |
| *SJT* | *Scottish Journal of Theology* |
| SNT | Studien zum Neuen Testament |
| SNTSMS | Society for New Testament Studies Monograph Series |
| SO | Symbolae osloensis |
| SPAW | Sitzungsberichte der preussischen Akademie der Wissenschaften |
| StudBib | Studia Biblica |
| Stud Neot | Studia neotestamentica |
| SUNT | Studien zur Umwelt des Neuen Testaments |
| SymBU | Symbolae biblicae upsalienses |
| *TBei* | *Theologische Beiträge* |
| *TBl* | *Theologische Blätter* |
| TBü | Theologische Bücherei |
| TCGNT | B.M. Metzger, *A Textual Commentary on the Greek New Testament* |
| TDNT | G. Kittel and F. Friedrich (eds.), *Theological Dictionary of the New Testament* |
| *TF* | *Theologische Forschung* |
| *TGl* | *Theologie und Glaube* |
| THKNT | Theologischer Handkommentar zum Neuen Testament |
| *ThStud* | *Theologische Studiën* |
| *TLZ* | *Theologische Literaturzeitung* |
| *TRE* | *Theologische Realenzyklopädie* |
| *TRev* | *Theologische Revue* |
| *TRu* | *Theologische Rundschau* |
| *TS* | *Theological Studies* |
| *TSK* | *Theologische Studien und Kritiken* |
| *TT* | *Teologisk Tidsskrift* |
| TU | Texte und Untersuchungen |
| *TWNT* | G.Kittel and G. Friedrich, *Theologisches Wörterbuch zum Neuen Testament* |
| *TZ* | *Theologisches Zeitschrift* |
| UBSGNT | United Bible Societies Greek New Testament |
| UNT | Untersuchungen zum Neuen Testament |
| *VC* | *Vigiliae christianae* |
| *VD* | *Verbum domini* |
| *VF* | *Verkündigen und Forschung* |

| | |
|---|---|
| VS | Verbum salutis |
| *WD* | *Wort und Dienst* |
| WMANT | Wissenschaftliche Monographien zum Alten und Neuen Testament |
| WUNT | Wissenschaftliche Untersuchungen zum Neuen Testament |
| *ZKG* | *Zeitschrift für Kirchengeschichte* |
| *ZKT* | *Zeitschrift für katholische Theologie* |
| *ZNW* | *Zeitschrift für die neutestamentliche Wissenschaft* |
| *ZTK* | *Zeitschrift für Theologie und Kirche* |

# 1 The Development and Task of the History of New Testament Literature

## 1.1 Historical Overview

### 1.1.1 The Beginnings of the History of New Testament Literature[1]

Although the literary-historical investigation of the NT is primarily a work of the nineteenth and twentieth centuries, literary questions were already being considered in the ancient church. Particularly for apologetic motives, specific authors were interested in literary comparisons of biblical writings with one another and with ancient classical literature, as well as in their literary forms.

The comments of Papias of Hierapolis concerning the Gospel of Mark, which are possibly anti-Marcionite and which assume categories of ancient rhetoric, exemplify this interest.[2] If the assertion that specific rhetorical categories underly these literary characterizations demands critical analysis, so much more justified is

---

[1]The following data refer to witnesses with a literary-historical approach which show that "in the service of exegesis individual scholars of the ancient church were interested in the form of the NT writings, but this interest was guided by the categories of ancient rhetoric. Their works were influential through the medieval era" (R. Bultmann, "Literaturgeschichte, Biblische 3. Literaturgeschichte des NT." *RGG2*, 1929, 3:1682; cf. also his *Die Exegese des Theodor von Mopsuestia,* posthumously edited by H. Feld, et al., 1984, pp. 64ff. [on "Explaining the form of the Scripture as a whole" in Adrian, Junilius, and Theodore]). The depiction takes into account texts and questions which are taken up for consideration in contemporary research (e.g., the issue of rhetoric).

[2] "Mark wrote down *the words and deeds of the Lord* (τὰ ὑπὸ τοῦ Χριστοῦ ἢ λεχθέντα ἢ πραχθέντα), which he *remembered* (ἐμνημόνευσεν) as Peter's interpreter, *accurately* (ἀκριβῶς), but not in order (οὐ μέντοι τάξει). For he had not heard or accompanied the Lord, but later, as mentioned, he followed Peter, who arranged his teaching according to need (πρὸς τὰς χρείας), but not so that he had given a connected account of the Lord's sayings (σύνταξιν τῶν κυριακῶν λόγων). It is therefore no error on Mark's part (ἥμαρτεν) if he wrote down matters as he remembered them (ἀπεμνημόνευσεν). For to one thing he gave special care, to omit (παραλιπεῖν) nothing that he had heard, and not to be guilty of any falsehood (ψεύσασθαι) in his report" (Eusebius, E.H. III 39,15). On this cf. E. Güttgemanns, "In welchem Sinn ist Lukas 'Historiker?' Die Beziehungen von Lk 1,1-4 und Papias zur antiken Rhetorik," *LB* 54 (1983): 23-25; D.E. Aune, *The New Testament in Its Literary Environment,* Library of Early Christianity (1987) 66f.; and D. Dormeyer, *Evangelium als literarische und theologische Gattung,* EdF 263 (1989) 8f. J. Kürzinger also attempts to show that Papias utilizes ancient rhetorical concepts. Cf. "Die Aussage des Papias von Hierapolis zur literarischen Form des Markusevangeliums" (first published in 1977), now in his *Papias von Hierapolis und die Evangelien des Neuen Testaments. Gesammelte Aufsätze. Neuausgabe und Übersetzung der Fragmente. Kommentierte Bibliographie,* Eichstätter Materialien 4 (1983) 43-67.

the assumption that the concept utilized by Papias is to be explained as analogous to the meaning of the ancient chreia genre.[3]

Justin's classification of the Gospels as *apomnemoneumata* deserves special attention. "For the apostles have passed on, in the *apomnemoneumata* (ἀπομνημονεύμασιν) derived from them, called Gospels,[4] that the following instructions were given to them; . . . (Apol I 66,3)." Both the meaning and the function of *"apomnemoneumata"* are disputed. Although K.L. Schmidt found the motive for this description in the Gospels' classification as *memoria* within *Hochliteratur,*[5] the term is more comprehensively defined as "the recording of 'reminiscences'."[6]

Further proof of interest in the literary form of the New Testament writings is their interpretation by the church fathers with the aid of the rhetorical style of the *"sermo humilis."*

---

[3] Cf. E. Güttgemanns, *LB* 54 (1983): 25; "'ethical' illustrations by means of episodes;" J. Kürzinger, "Das Papiaszeugnis und die Erstgestalt des Matthäusevangeliums" (1960), in his *Papias von Hierapolis und die Evangelien,* 9-32; for a different point of view cf. U.H.J. Körtner, *Papias von Hierapolis. Ein Beitrag zur Geschichte des frühen Christentums.* FRLANT 133 (1983): 158, who falls back on the significance of "need." Nevertheless, it is difficult to infer a clear relation to a literary genre from the expressions of Papias.

[4] Since A. von Harnack this relative clause has been suspected of being a gloss. Cf. "Evangelium: Geschichte des Begriffs in der ältesten Kirche," in his *Entstehung und Entwicklung der Kirchenverfassung und des Kirchenrechts in den ersten zwei Jahrhunderten* (1910, 199-239), 225, n. 1. Cf. also W. Bousset, *Die Evangeliencitate Justins des Märtyrers in ihrem Wert für die Evangelienkritik* (1891), 17. L. Abramowski presumes its genuineness in "Die 'Erinnerungen der Apostle' bei Justin," in *Das Evangelium und die Evangelien: Vorträge vom Tübinger Symposium 1982,* ed. Peter Stuhlmacher. WUNT 28: 341-353 (1983), 341 *The Gospel and the Gospels* (1991), 323; as does H. Koester in ANRW II 25.2: 1467. On the basis of Justin's further employment of "apomnemoneumata" and "gospel," especially in the Dialogue with Trypho, the identification of the two concepts seems certain [cf. D. Dormeyer, *Evangelium als literarische und theologische Gattung,* ErFor 263 (1989), 11f.].

[5] K.L. Schmidt "Die Stellung der Evangelien in der allgemeinen Literaturgeschichte," (first published in 1923) reprinted in his *Neues Testament– Judentum–Kirche: Kleine Schriften,* ed. G. Sauter. TBü 69:37-130 (1981): 45. M. Dibelius, *Die Formgeschichte des Evangeliums.* 6th ed. (1971), 2f. ; *From Tradition to Gospel* (1935, repr. 1965), 2-4. Note also the translation "memoirs of the apostles," by P. Vielhauer in his *Geschichte der urchristlichen Literatur: Einleitung in das Neue Testament, die Apokryphen und die Apostolischen Väter,* 2nd ed. (1987 (=1975), 254; by M.J. Suggs, in "Gospel, Genre," *IDBSup* 370-372); and others. In favor of this interpretation is Justin's own acquaintance with the memorabilia literature and his citation of the ʾΑπομνημονεύματα Σωκράτους at Apology II, 11.

6 Dormeyer, *Evangelium,* 12 (the term defines not the final form of the gospels, but is intended to prove that the data they contain is historical); K. Berger in ANRW II 25.2: 1246f.; N. Hyldahl, "Hegesipps Hypomnemata," *ST* 14 (1960): 70-113, 80; H. Koester, *Ancient Christian Gospels* (1990), 39f.: "But what is of primary importance is the fact that the use of this term advertises the written gospels as replacement for the older oral traditions under apostolic authority."

This expression corresponds to ancient rhetoric's distinguishing levels of style (χαρακτῆρες/*genera dicendi*). Lower or plain style (χαρακτὴρ ἰσχνός/*genus subtile*) was set off from the intermediate (χαρακτὴρ μέσος/*genus medium*) and high styles (χαρακτὴρ μεγαλοπρεπής/*genus sublime*). The purpose of the speech and its style were in mutual correspondence (cf. the following table[7]).

| Style | Function | Characteristics |
|---|---|---|
| Plain Style | Private business, objects of every-day life, etc. | Simplicity and clarity. Conspicuous embellishments and artistic periods are avoided. |
| Intermediate Style | Public entertainment. | Many tropes and figures. Some rhythmic structure to periods. |
| High Style | Significant oratorical objectives (e.g., matters of life and death). | Artistic style, using figures and pronounced rhythmic periods. |

In ancient rhetoric the boundaries between these levels of style had absolute validity.[8]

If, on the other hand, leaders of the ancient church referred to the lowly style of the sacred scriptures along with their content of highest truth[9]—a mixed style which these authors also claimed for their own writings—this is due either to an

---

[7] Cf. M. Fuhrmann, *Die antike Rhetorik: Eine Einführung*. 3rd ed. (1990), 144f. Also Augustine, *de doctr*. 4, 12ff: which compares selections of Christian literature (e.g., from the Pauline letters) with ancient rhetorical stylistic genres.

[8] For the whole, cf. Fuhrmann, 143-145; H. Lausberg, *Elemente der literarischen Rhetorik: Eine Einführung für Studierende der klassischen, romanischen, englischen und deutschen Philologie*, 3rd ed. (1967), §§ 465-469; J. Martin, *Antike Rhetorik: Technik und Methode*, Handbuch der Altertumswissenschaft II.3 (1974), 329-345; J. Zmijewski, *Der Stil der paulinischen "Narrenrede." Analyse der Sprachgestaltung in 2 Kor 11,1-12,10 als Beitrag zur Methodik von Stiluntersuchungen neutestamentlicher Texte*, BBB 52 (1978): 428.

[9] E.g., Augustine, *de doctr* 2,41-42; 4,18; also *conf*. vi,5; Ep. 137,18. Cf. E. Auerbach, *Mimesis: Dargestellte Wirklichkeit in der abendländischen Literatur* (1946), 76, 150; *Mimesis: The Representation of Reality in Western Literature* (1968), 74, 155f.; *Literatursprache und Publikum in der lateinischen Spätantike und im Mittelalter* (1958), 30-53 (with further references); "Sacrae scripturae sermo humilis," in his *Neue Dantestudien*, Istanbuler Schriften 5 (1944): 1-10, 4ff. Cf. also J. Zmijewski, *Stil*, 429, who emphasizes the patristic motif of the scriptures' general accessibility.

apologetic motive, confronting the objection of educated unbelievers that the Christian scriptures were composed in a modest style, or to an emphasis on the theological motif of humility.[10] That a rhetorical approach has been taken to the biblical texts since the earliest Christian authors does not impede this understanding.[11]

An apologetic interest is also characteristic of Jerome's *de viris illustribus*,[12] described by O. Stählin as "the first survey of early Christian literature."[13] Dependent on Eusebius' *Ecclesiastical History*,[14] it begins with Peter and reaches all the way to Jerome himself, though it contains many inaccuracies with respect to the authors cited and their works. Jerome cites a list of 135 authors and their writings (among them the Jewish authors Philo, Josephus, and Justus, as well as Seneca and other Stoics) to prove that the church had produced well-educated persons, philosophers, orators, and teachers.[15] Questions of literary form are subordinate both to this goal and to the sequential character of the work.

---

[10] With respect to the theological and historical understanding of humility in the ancient church, cf. S. Rehrl, "Demut IV. Alte Kirche," *TRE* 8 (1981): 465-468 (with bibliography).

[11] Cf. footnote 9 above and C.J. Classen, "Paulus und die antike Rhetorik," *ZNW* 82 (1991): 2, n. 5 (bibliography) and 15f.

[12] Text: *Hieronymus und Gennadius: De viris inlustribus,* ed. C.A. Bernoulli, Sammlung ausgewählte alter kirchen- und dogmengeschichtlicher Quellenschriften 11 (1895).

[13] O. Stählin, "IV. Christliche Schriftsteller," *Geschichte der griechischen Literatur: Die nachklassische Periode der griechischen Literatur von 100 bis 530 nach Christus,* Handbuch der Altertumswissenschaft VII/2.2, 6th ed. (1924), 1112.

[14] On *E.H.* 1-78: for the literary-critical problem see S. von Suchowski, "Hieronymous als Litterarhistoriker. Eine quellenkritische Untersuchung der Schrift des hl. Hieronymus 'De viris illustribus'," *Kirchengeschichtliche Studien,* ed. A. Knöpfler et al. II/2 (1984), 19, 21; C.A. Bernoulli, *Der Schriftstellerkatalog des Hieronymus. Ein Beitrag zur Geschichte der altchristlichen Literatur* (1985); H. Hagendahl, Latin Fathers and the Classics: a Study of the Apologists, Jerome and other Christian Writers, SGLG 6 = GUA 64.2 (1958): 93f, 139ff. Literary-historical aspects were also emphasized in Eusebius' Ecclesiastical History (excerpted by Jerome), as the citation from Papias (cf. this chapter n. 2) indicates.

[15] Note the prologue of the work, lines 40-42: *"Discant igitur Celsus, Porphyrius et Iulianus, rabidi adversum Christum canes, discant sectatores eorum qui putant ecclesiam nullos philosophos et eloquentes, nullos habuisse doctores, quanti et quales uiri eam fundauerint exstruxerint adornauerint et desinant fidem nostram rusticae tantum simplicitatis arguere, suamque potius imperitiam recognoscant."* ["Let them learn—Celsus, Porphyry, and Julius, mad dogs, adversaries of Christ, and their followers who think that the Church could never boast of any profound thinkers, eloquent spokesmen, and learned teachers—let them learn of the greatness and quality of the men who laid the church's foundations, who built it up and adorned it and let them stop arguing that our faith is the faith of unlettered peasants, and let them recognize instead their own ignorance."]

Humanist and Reformation interpreters were also interested in the relationship between rhetoric and scriptural literature,[16] e.g., Philipp Melanchthon's 1532 commentary on Romans.[17] Melanchthon proceeded on the presupposition that Romans was written on the basis of rhetorical and dialectical rules,[18] and that it should be interpreted with the assistance of a corresponding methodology.[19] His organization of Romans using rhetorical terminology, as practiced in the narrow sense in his exegesis of Romans 1:8-5:11, is especially interesting to contemporary researchers.[20] By this, in express juxtaposition to scholastic methods of

---

[16] Cf. the references in H.D. Betz, "The Problem of Rhetoric and Theology According to the Apostle Paul," in *L'Apôtre Paul: Personnalité, style et conception du ministère*, ed. A. Vanhoye, BETL 73 (1986): 17, nn. 5-7; and C.J. Classen, *ZNW* 82 (1991): 2, n. 5 (bibliography).

[17] P. Melanchthon, *Römerbrief-Kommentar 1532*, with G. Ebeling ed. by R. Schäfer, Melanchthons Werke V (1965); note also the new edition of the commentary: *Commentarii in epistolam ad Romanos hoc anno M.D. XL. recognitii et locupletati, 1540*, published in Corpus Reformatorum 15.

[18] We can trace the beginnings of his attempt to interpret Romans on a rhetorical basis to 1519, cf. E. Bizer, *Theologie der Verheissung. Studien zur theologischen Entwicklung des jungen Melanchthon 1519-1524*, (1964), 132f.; B. Moeller, "Philipp Melanchthon," in *Luther kontrovers*, ed. H.J. Schultz (1983), 201; W. Maurer, Der junge Melanchthon zwischen Humanismus und Reformation. Vol. I, Der Humanist (1967), 171ff, esp. 184-186 (also deals with the development and significance of rhetoric for scriptural interpretation); note also the comments and further attempts at a rhetorical interpretation of Romans by R. Schäfer in "Melanchthons Hermeneutik im Römerbrief-Kommentar von 1532," *ZTK* 60 (1963): 217f. C.J. Classen offers numerous comments on Melanchthon's evaluation and employment of rhetoric in his "Paulus und die antike Rhetorik," *ZNW* 82 (1991): 1-33, esp. 16-26 (including comments on Melanchthon's exegesis of Galatians and 1 Corinthians).

[19] Cf. R. Schäfer in *P. Melanchthon, Römerbrief-Kommentar 1532*, 18, see also 15f.; also *ZTK* 60 (1963): 216f. According to G. Ebeling, "Hermeneutik," *RGG3* 3 (1959): 252, among the reformers Melanchthon's hermeneutic was most strongly oriented toward rhetoric and dialectic, placing him in danger of reading foreign speech and thought patterns into the biblical writings.

[20] Cf. R.Schäfer, *P. Melanchthon, Römerbrief-Kommentar 1532*, 19 and Appendix I, 373-378 (for his analysis of the structure, see also *ZTK* 60 (1963): 220-226). According to Melanchthon, Romans belonged to a fourth rhetorical genre (on the three rhetorical *genera*, see chapter three, below), the διδασκαλικόν (Römerbrief 32, 14) or *genus doctrinae* (cf. his comments to 10:26 at 58). With regard to this genus inferred by Melanchthon, cf. the definition in the Elementorum Rhetorices in Corpus reformatorum 13: 421: *"Ego addendum censeo* διδασκαλικὸν *genus, quod etsi ad dialecticam pertinet, tamen, ubi negociorum genera recensentur, non est praetermittendum, praesertim, cum hoc tempore ad maximam usum in Ecclesiis habeat, ubi non tamtum suasoriae conciones habendae sunt, sed multo saepius homines dialecticorum more, de dogmatibus religionis docendi sunt, ut ea perfecte cognoscere possint."* Cf. C.J. Classen, *ZNW* 82 (1991): 16, with n. 54. ["I propose that a *doctrinal genre* be added. This genre is not to be ignored when the genres of public affairs are reviewed, even though this genre belongs to the study of logic. This inclusion is particularly important since at this point in time it is put to extensive use in the churches, not only in the case of public debate, but also where the doctrines of religion are being taught by teachers

interpretation, Melanchthon attempted to understand the relationships of individual sections of the letter to one another.[21] Noteworthy is the comment that Paul was basically *"illiteratus,"* although Melanchthon had already discarded this opinion before the publication of his commentary.[22] It corresponds to the modern distinction between nonliterary occasional writings and literary epistles.[23]

## 1.1.2    History of New Testament Literature and Introduction to the New Testament[24]

*Literature*

Baur, F.C., "Die Einleitung in das Neue Testament als theologische Wissenschaft. Ihr Begriff und ihre Aufgabe, ihr Entwicklungsgang und ihr innerer Organismus," *ThJb* [T] 9 (1850): 463-566; 10 (1851): 222-253; 291-329. Bleek, F. *Einleitung in die Heilige Schrift. Part Two. Einleitung in das Neue Testament,* 3rd ed. overseen by W. Mangold (1875). Credner, K.A., *Einleitung in das Neue Testament. Part One* (1836). Hupfeld, H. *Ueber Begriff und Methode der sogenannten biblischen Einleitung nebst einer Uebersicht ihrer Geschichte und Literatur* (1844); "Noch ein Wort über den Begriff der sogenannten biblischen Einleitung," *TSK* 34 (1861): 3-28. Reuss, E., *Die Geschichte der Heiligen Schriften Neuen Testaments* ([1]1842 [6]1887).

Hermann Hupfeld, a scholar of the Hebrew Scriptures and successor to Wilhelm Gesenius at Halle beginning in 1843, introduced the concept "history of biblical literature" in a discussion with Karl August Credner.[25]    Though he

---

who adopt the style of the rhetoricians in order that their teaching may be clearly understood."] In light of his consistent understanding of Paul from a rhetorical point of view, Melanchthon draws examples out of the Pauline letters in his discussion of rhetorical theory, cf. Classen, p. 1.

[21] Melanchthon himself suggests this in the dedicatory letter to his *"Dispositio orationis in epistola Pauli ad Romanos"* of 1529 (Corpus Reformatorum 1, 1043-1045; for the *dispositio* itself see Corpus Reformatorum 15, 443-492).

[22] Melanchthon deleted this remark from later editions, cf. Classen, *ZNW* 82 (1991)1 n. 3 (Corpus Reformatorum 1, 1044f.).

[23] As with A. Deissmann, *Licht vom Osten. Das Neue Testament und die neuentdeckten Texte der hellenistisch-römischen Welt,* 4th ed. (1923), 193-198; *Light from the Ancient East: The New Testament Illustrated by Recently Discovered Texts of the Greco-Roman World* (1927), 227-230; *Bibelstudien. Beiträge zumeist aus den Papyri und Inschriften, zur Geschichte der Sprache, des Schrifttums und der Religion des hellenistischen Judentums und des Urchristentums* (1895), 187-252; *Bible Studies: Contributions Chiefly from Papyri and Inscriptions to the History of the Language, the Literature, and the Religion of Hellenistic Judaism and Primitive Christianity* (1901), 173-267.

[24] On the history of NT Introduction, cf. W.G. Kümmel, "Einleitungswissenschaft II. Neues Testament," *TRE* 9 (1982): 469-482.

[25] Cf. Credner's definition of "introduction" as "a critical history of the NT collection from its first beginnings to the present, with respect to its parts as well as to

recognized the pronounced differences between the Hebrew and Christian Scriptures, Hupfeld felt that separate histories of the two were not advisable. These writings were produced by one people and the New Testament "was the final stage of that singular development of religious spirit begun in the Old Testament."[26] Of course, with this conception comprising the whole Bible, Hupfeld lagged behind earlier works which had clearly distinguished the Hebrew and Christian Scriptures. Eduard Reuss[27] of Strasbourg made this necessary distinction in his *Geschichte der heiligen Schriften Neuen Testaments,* [28] followed in 1881 by his *Geschichte der Schriften Alten Testaments.*[29] In the developing discussion about the nature and method of "introductions," he sought to recognize this field as a historical discipline and to protect it from the domination of dogmatic viewpoints.

Hupfeld defined "history of biblical literature" *methodologically* as occupied with three issues: the origins of the writings, their collection, and history of their preservation, dissemination, and revision. Thus he still remains within the boundaries of a conventional introduction. But his goal of determining the process which he expressed as "historical succession and development" went beyond these boundaries.[30] "Historical pragmatism," i.e., examining and describing the interconnections and development of phenomena,[31] was to be based on critical research which would compensate for missing evidence on the basis of internal grounds and analogies from ancient literature.

Alongside the question of the relationship to contemporary literature, E. Reuss also emphasized that of a writing's place of origin within early Christian history.[32] The outlook of the apocryphal literature, the depiction of which is indispensable for understanding the history of the canon, is oriented toward the future.[33]

This conception of a history of literature as "Introduction to the New Testament" encounters criticism from Ferdinand Christian Baur, the principle

---

the whole" (2). For Credner this historical task led to a study of canonicity, i.e. to the question of the apostolocity of the NT writings, as it later did for F.C. Baur (see below, and Kümmel, *TRE* 9: 474.).

[26] H. Hupfeld, *Ueber Begriff und Methode,* 35; here he sets for himself the task of supplanting, as he sees it, the inappropriate and unscientific concept of "introduction."

[27] On E. Reuss see now J.M. Vincent, *Leben und Werk des frühen Eduard Reuss. Ein Beitrag zu den geistesgeschichtlichen Voraussetzungen der Bibelkritik im zweiten Viertel des 19. Jahrhunderts,* BEvT 106, 1990. On the history of the "Heiligen Schriften Neuen Testaments," cf. esp. 322-327.

[28] Cf. also F. Bleek who regarded "the history of the writings collected in the NT" as "part of the history of Christian literature."

[29] For the significance of Reuss to the history of the Hebrew scriptural literature, cf. O. Kaiser, "Literaturgeschichte. I. AT," *TRE* 21 (1991): 306-337.

[30] Hupfeld, *Ueber Begriff und Methode,* 10.

[31] Hupfeld, *Ueber Begriff und Methode,* 14f.

[32] "The spiritual and theological development of the church" forms "both the background and the physiognomy of the history of NT literature." The history of literature which began with Jesus is to be portrayed in light of the place which any text "occupies in the general intellectual current of its time."

[33] Hupfeld, *Ueber Begriff und Methode,* 4.

representative of the "Tübingen school." For him there was no controversy about the necessity of a historical approach in the field of introduction. Baur himself emphasized this approach, referring to external influences and internal motivations of composition, i.e., the historical setting of a writing.[34] Of course, for him the important matter was not the history of literature, but the question of the historical origin of the writing, its apostolicity, and with this the essential goal of New Testament introduction, i.e., research on the canon. This goal alone determines the historical investigation.

In his reply to various critical reactions in 1861 Hupfeld conceded to Baur that a restriction to canonical writings could "be advisable on practical grounds, but that it could not be proved to be the only justified or necessary approach." He based his objection on the recognition that the biblical writings should be regarded as "national literature," i.e., within the stream of their historical development, and should not be wrested out of this connection.[35] Even at this early period, the history of literature approach pressed for a consideration of extra-canonical literature, finally discrediting canonical considerations as obstacles to investigation of early Christian writings. (On this see also the following section.)

### 1.1.3   The History of Literature Approach as a Critique of Canonical Boundaries

*Literature*

Bousset, W. "Zur Methodologie der Wissenschaft vom neuen Testament," *TRu* 2 (1899): 1-15. Krüger, G. *Das Dogma vom neuen Testament,* 1896; *Geschichte der altchristlichen Litteratur in den ersten drei Jahrhunderten,* Grundriss der theologischen Wissenschaft II/3 ([12]1895), *Nachträge* (1897). van Manen, W.C. "Old Christian Literature," *Encyclopedia Biblica,* ed. Cheyne and Black, 3 (1902): 3471-3495. Wrede, William, review of A. Jülicher's *Einleitung in das Neue Testament,* Grundriss der theologischen Wissenschaft 3.1 ([12]1894), in *Göttingische Gelehrte Anzeigen* 158 (1896): 513-531; "Über Aufgabe und Methode der sogennanten neutestamentlichen Theologie" (1897), in *Das Problem der Theologie des Neuen Testaments,* ed. G. Strecker, Wege der Forschung 367 (1975): 81-154.

Albert Eichhorn[36] included in his 1886 thesis which qualified him for university lecturing the phrase "3. New Testament introduction must be a history of early Christian literature."[37] This shows that the examination of the New

---

[34] F.C. Baur, *Theologische Jahrbücher [Tübingen]* 9 (1850): 482f.; 10 (1851): 297.

[35] H. Hupfeld, *TSK* 34 (1861): 11.

[36] On Eichhorn, cf. Hugo Gressmann, *Albert Eichhorn und Die Religionsgeschichtliche Schule,* 1914.

[37] Published in E. Barnikol, *Albert Eichhorn (1856-1926). Sein "Lebenslauf," seine Thesen 1886, seine Abendmahlsthese 1898 und seine Leidensbriefe an seinen Schüler Erich Franz (1913/1919) nebst seinen Bekenntnissen über Heilige Geschichte und Evangelium, über Orthodoxie und Liberalismus,* Wissenschaftliche Zeitschrift

Testament from the perspective of the history of literature owes a significant part of its impulse and progress to the history of religions school.[38] The idea of the history of New Testament literature at this time essentially applied to the canon. But the form critical approach, introduced by Franz Overbeck (see the next section), also received increasing attention.

The church historian Gustav Krüger from Giessen, in connection with his thesis that "the existence of a New Testament field of study . . . as a special theological and historical discipline was an obstacle to productive . . . examination . . . of primitive Christianity and therefore of the New Testament itself,"[39] defended the assertion that a history of primitive Christian literature should supplant introductions to the New Testament.[40] As there was a consensus about the necessity of understanding writings historically, "in terms of their time and place," Krüger argued against treating the New Testament writings in an isolated manner.[41] In his *Literaturgeschichte,* Krüger himself treats both the canonical and non-canonical writings according to their literary genres.

In his *Zur Methodologie der Wissenschaft vom Neuen Testament,* which assisted both Krüger (*Das Dogma vom Neuen Testament,* 1896) and Wrede ("Über Aufgabe und Methode der sogenannten neutestamentllichen Theologie," 1897) in their discussions of methodology, Wilhelm Bousset expressly associated himself with the demand to transcend canonical limitations. Willem Christiaan van Manen, who had been public professor of Old and New Testament literature at Leiden since 1885, also moved across canonical boundaries in his article "Old-Christian Literature" of 1902. As van Manen programmatically wrote, "The old distinction between canonical and non-canonical books as regards this literature

---

(Halle-Wittenberg). Gesammelte Schriften IX (1960): 141-152, cf. 144; cf. also Gressmann, *Eichhorn,* 8f.

[38] On the history of religions school see (among others) W.G. Kümmel, *Das Neue Testament. Geschichte der Erforschung seiner Probleme,* OA III/3, 1970[2], 310-357; *Die Religionsgeschichtliche Schule in Göttingen. Eine Dokumentation,* ed. G. Lüdemann and M. Schroeder, 1987 (with bibliography); G. Lüdemann, "Die religionsgeschichtliche Schule," in *Theologie in Göttingen. Eine Vorlesungsreihe,* ed. B. Moeller, Göttinger Universitätsschriften A/1 (1987): 325-361.

[39] Krüger, *Das Dogma vom Neuen Testament* (1896), 4f. Krüger's assertion should be evaluated against the background of his understanding of the "history of religions" method, by which "the Christian religion should be examined according to the same methods as other religions. . . ." (In his letter to Adolf Jülicher, dated October 30, 1901, published in H. Rollmann, "Theologie und Religionsgeschichte. Zeitgenössische Stimmen zur Diskussion um die religionsgeschichtliche Methode und die Einführung religionsgeschichtlicher Lehrstühle in den theologischen Fakultäten um die Jahrhundertwende," ZTK 80 (1983): 69-84, cf. p. 2f. and Rollmann's remarks on p. 78.

[40] Krüger, *Dogma,* 37.

[41] Krüger, *Dogma,* 5f.; see also his *Litteraturgeschichte,* 9. With reference to P. de Lagarde, *Deutsche Schriften,* 1886, 55 (= 1920[5], 47f.) W. Wrede agrees, remarking that "the boundary between the canonical literature and that which follows it . . . is very unstable ("Über Aufgabe und Methode," 85-91, citation 85).

must be abandoned; NT Introduction and Patristic must no longer be separate studies, they must be amalgamated in that of Old-Christian literature."[42]

Van Manen set off this old-Christian literature from that which followed it through its temporal relationship to the writings of the New Testament. Once these were treated as authoritative for faith and action, i.e., as "Holy Scripture," the break between earlier and later become evident. Van Manen dates this to about 180 CE,[43] and his article treats Christian literature before this time by its literary form.[44]

William Wrede also reflected on primitive Christian literature and its classification according to form in his extensive and basically sympathetic review of A. Jülicher's *Einleitung in das Neue Testament.* Wrede began with Jülicher's definition of introduction as "a branch of historical, more specifically literary-historical, New Testament research.[45] He then set down his own conception of a history of primitive Christian literature. "The Pauline letters, because they are not yet literature . . . , have their place in a history of apostolic times or a biography of Paul. The majority of the New Testament books are literature and accordingly belong in a primitive Christian–not New Testament–history of literature...." Wrede also addressed questions of form and genre. "It must be asked how they (i.e., the genres) and only they arose in earliest Christianity, and how they are related to the forms of contemporary and especially Jewish literature...." [46] Here Wrede shows an openness to literary-historical comparisons transcending the boundaries drawn by Overbeck.

## 1.1.4    Literary History of New Testament and of Greco-Roman Literature

*Literature*

von Christ, W. *Geschichte der griechischen Litteratur* ([4]1904). Deissmann, A. *Licht vom Osten. Das Neue Testament und die neuentdeckten Texte der hellenistisch-römischen Welt* ([4]1923); *Light from the Ancient East: The New Testament Illustrated by Recently Discovered Texts of the Greco-Roman World* (1927). Dihle, A. *Die griechische und lateinische Literatur der Kaiserzeit. Von Augustus bis Justinian* (1989); *Greek and Latin Literature of the Roman Empire from Augustus to Justinian* (1994). Heinrici, C.F.G. *Der litterarische Charakter der neutestamentlichen Schriften* (1908). Norden, E. *Die antike Kunstprosa vom VI. Jh. vor Christus bis in die Zeit der Renaissance*, 2 vols. ([5]1958); *Agnostos Theos. Untersuchungen zur Formengeschichte religiöser Rede* (1913). von Soden,

---

[42] W. van Manen, in *Encyclopedia Biblica,* ed. Cheyne and Black, 3: 3473.

[43] van Manen, 3474f.

[44] van Manen, 3475: ". . . to classify the writings according to their different literary forms."

[45] A. Jülicher, *Einleitung in das Neue Testament,* Grundriss der theologischen Wissenschaft 3.1, ([1, 2]1894) 1; revised with E. Fascher ([7]1931) 2.

[46] Wrede, Willliam, review of A. Jülicher's *Einleitung in das Neue Testament,* Grundriss der theologischen Wissenschaft 3.1, 1894[1] and 2, in *Göttingische Gelehrte Anzeigen* 158 (1896): 527-530.

H. *Urchristliche Literaturgeschichte [die Schriften des Neuen Testaments]* (1905). Stählin, O., IV. "Christliche Schriftsteller," in *Geschichte der griechischen Litteratur. Die nachklassische Periode der griechischen Litteratur von 100 bis 530 nach Christus,* HAW VII/2.2 (⁶1924 = reprint 1961), 1105-1492 [Introduction: 1105-1121; New Testament: 1122-1184]. Stemberger, G. *Geschichte der jüdischen Literatur. Eine Einführung.* Beck'sche Elementarbücher (1977). Wendland, P. *Die urchristlichen Literaturformen,* HNT 1/3 (²1912). von Wilamowitz-Moellendorff, U., "Die griechische Literatur des Altertums," in *Kultur der Gegenwart* I/8. *Die griechische und lateinische Literatur und Sprache,* ed P. Hinneberg (³1912), 3-318.

With the questions posed above, literary research bloomed, dedicated to the problems of language, form, and style of the New Testament writings. Of particular importance were the contributions of *Adolf Deissmann, C.F. Georg Heinrici, Eduard Norden, Hermann von Soden, and Paul Wendland.*

Literary-historical research is indebted for inspiration and significant contributions to comparative analyses which elaborated the relationships between early Christian and Hellenistic writings. Adolf Deissmann cited inscriptions, papyri, and ostraca. His distinction between letters and epistles in light of ancient correspondence is especially important.[47] C.F.G. Heinrici identified the conditions under which the New Testament writings were produced, and their literary forms and means of expression.[48] Eduard Norden showed the connection between passages such as Acts 17:22-31 and Hellenistic as well as Jewish and Christian religious propaganda literature.[49] He also significantly influenced New Testament form criticism.

H. von Soden's work, *Early Christian Literary History,* lagged behind the efforts of Krüger and others. It restricted its presentation to the writings of the New Testament, doubting the religious value of extracanonical early Christian literature.[50] As to cultural influences of the milieu, this work expressly orients itself not to the "intellectual world of these books" but to "the books, which record this intellectual world and convey it to us."[51]

Paul Wendland formulates the literary-historical problem in a more advanced and precise manner in his contribution to the *Handbuch des Neuen Testaments,* identifying numerous correspondences between ancient and early Christian literature. "Strictly observing aspects of form, which has not been attempted until now, determines the scope of the problem. In this approach the theological standpoint of the author is only considered to the extent that it influenced the form of presentation. Dealing with the Gospels, the existence of oral tradition, at the first more influential on the forms than literary personalities, is

---

[47] Cf. below, 3.2.1. In his research A. Deissmann called attention to the correlation between literary form and social context.

[48] Cf. Bultmann's review in *Christliche Welt* 22 (1908): 378.

[49] Norden, *Agnostos Theos,* 1-140; cf. also below, n. 76.

[50] H. von Soden, 3f.

[51] von Soden, 5.

carefully considered."[52] This approach joined earlier references to the oral pre-history of the New Testament (J.G. Herder)[53] and to the significance of form for literary history (F. Overbeck)[54] and presented them in connection with literature contemporary to the New Testament. Form history and literary history were connected, rightly claiming special attention in further research (cf. 1.1.5).

If parallels and connections can be drawn between early Christian literature and the writings of its milieu, the relationship of the early Christian writings to that literature deserves consideration. Emphasizing that the New Testament writings come out of the Jewish tradition[55] excessively reduces the general, especially the Greek and Hellenistic, background. Such an approach also overlooks the specific Christian influences which extensively modified and powerfully affected early Christian genres.[56]

The association of early Christian writings with contemporary culture and literature also includes accounts which present them as part of Greek and Hellenistic literature. Intentionally opposing *Wilhelm von Christ's* restricted presentation in the first four editions of the *Geschichte der griechischen Literatur* in HAW[57], O. Stählin considered (early) Christian literature as "an essential component of the whole of Greek literature. Just as Christian literature, detached from the Hellenistic milieu in which it grew up, cannot be rightly understood and evaluated, so neither would the picture of Hellenistic literature which lacked the strand of Christian writings be complete."[58]

But Stählin added a double caveat. First, ancient Christian literature was drawn back from Greek and Hellenistic influence, because "the consciousness of having

---

[52] P. Wendland, P. *Die urchristlichen Literaturformen,* HNT 1/3, 1912², 257. In carrying out this program, Wendland insisted that canonical boundaries had to be transcended, since they thwarted understanding literary history. His presentation was organized by literary genres and he added "Christian Apologetic" to Gospels, Acts, Letters, and Apocalypse.

[53] Cf. 1.1.5.

[54] Cf. 1.1.5

[55] As does G. Stemberger, 65: "The New Testament grew wholly out of Judaism of the first and early second centuries and stands in the rich tradition of Judaism. . . . Its individual writings disclose the varied literary genres of Hellenistic Judaism, though in more specifically developed form."

[56] Compare, e.g., the categorization of the gospels as essentially a genre *sui generis* (see below, 4.1.2.1). Likewise the Johannine Apocalypse, while sharing numerous formal characteristics with Jewish apocalypses, is most deeply shaped by the Christian message.

[57] In this work (early) Christian literature received limited treatment, and only in an appendix. This corresponds to his verdict against its portrayal: "Since Hellenism was opposed by early Christianity, and after a century-long battle succumbed to the power of Christianity's ethical ideals, *the works of Christian authors in and of themselves do not belong within the framework of the history of Greek literature.*" Parallels to Greek literature are more the result of the assimilation of Greek culture in Christian writings as well as references there to profane Greek writers (912f., emphasis by author).

[58] O. Stählin, 1106. U. von Wilamowitz-Moellendorff even more decisively supports the presentation of Christian writings almost undifferentiated within the framework of Greek and Hellenistic literature, 317.

new life and the need to express it" led "to a powerful break with all literary traditions and to a new beginning even in the realm of form."[59] He emphasized the correctness of treating early Christian literature separately, since "the development of Christian literature best shows itself when considered on its own."[60] Stählin alluded to influences other than the development of Hellenistic literature: connection with Jewish culture; struggle against opponents (Jews, Gnostics, etc.); needs of the community. A second argument is that Christian writings have a common content which stands over against that of Greek literature.[61]

So the significance of the individual authors "with their total literary activity" was stressed over against a literary history based simply on form.[62]

Albrecht Dihle, the classical philologist from Heidelberg, treated New Testament literature in connection with the Flavian era in his 1989 work, *Die griechische und lateinische Literatur der Kaiserzeit. Von Augustus bis Justinian* [English translation, *Greek and Latin Literature of the Roman Empire from Augustus to Justinian* (1994)].[63] Subsumed under the rubrics 'Letters' and 'Gospels,'[64] he considered their relation to Greek literature in terms of form, style, and function.

---

[59] Stählin, 1106.

[60] Stählin, 1107.

[61] Stählin, 1108.

[62] Stählin, 1115f. In not conceding what went before when considering form in the context of early Christian literature, despite his important insight that New Testament forms were also found outside the canon, Stählin treated New Testament writings separately from the "apocryphal" (cf. pp. 1122f.), although here it is not a question of authorial personalities being responsible for the different writings (compare below, the end of section 4.2.2). This must be considered a retrograde step with respect to literary-historical study of the canon. Cf. also G. Krüger, review of O. Stählin, *Geschichte der griechischen Literatur*, in *TLZ* 39 (1914): 617-619.

[63] Pp. 216-224[English 203-212]; the presentation is not restricted to the New Testament, but open to any early Christian literature of like form. Connections are blurred, however, due to the treatment of the literature by epochs. Thus most of the non-canonical writings are relegated to the period of the "adoptive emporer." (Cf. pp. 305ff. [English 295ff.] The Didache is covered in treatments of both the earlier and later periods, but Hermas, 1 Clement, and the letters of Ignatius only in the later period.)

[64] This division into only two classes poses problems. E.g, under "Gospels" Acts is treated as the second half of the Lucan history (p. 223; for the necessary distinction in genre between Luke and Acts, cf. below, section 5.2). Dihle also refers to the genres of apocalypse (The Revelation of John) and community codes (Didache), cf. pp. 224 and 308.

## 1.1.5    Literary History and Form Criticism

*Literature*

Bultmann, R. "Neues Testament. Einleitung II," *TRu* 17 (1914): 79-90; "Ein neuer Zugang zum synoptischen Problem" (in English, 1926), in *Zur Formgeschichte des Evangeliums,* ed. F. Hahn, Wege der Forschung 81 (1985), 233-255; "Literaturgeschichte, Biblische 1. Methodologisch und wissenschaftsgeschichtlich. 3. Literaturgeschichte des NT," *RGG²* 3 (1929): 1675-1677, 1680-1682; "Die Erforschung der synoptischen Evangelien" (first published in 1961), in *Glauben und Verstehen. Gesammelte Aufsätze* 4 (1965): 1-41. Fascher, E. *Die formgeschichtliche Methode. Eine Darstellung und Kritik. Zugleich ein Beitrag zur Geschichte des synoptischen Problems.* BZNW 2 (1924). Gunkel, H. "Die Lieder in der Kindheitsgeschichte Jesu bei Lukas," in Festgabe A. von Harnack (1921), 43-60. Herder, J.G. "Von Gottes Sohn, der Welt Heiland. Nach Johannes Evangelium. Nebst einer Regel der Zusammenstimmung unsrer Evangelien aus ihrer Entstehung und Ordnung" (first in 1797), in *Herder SW* 19, ed. B. Suphan (1880): 253-424; "Vom Erlöser der Menschen. Nach unsern drei ersten Evangelien" (first in 1796), in Suphan 135-252. Jordan, H. *Geschichte der altchristlichen Literatur* (1911). Merk, O. "Aus (unveröffentlichten) Aufzeichnungen Rudolf Bultmanns zur Synoptikerforschung," in *Jesu Rede von Gott und ihre Nachgeschichte im frühen Christentum. Beiträge zur Verkündigung Jesus und zum Kerygma der Kirche.* FS W. Marxsen, ed. D.-A. Koch *et al.* (1989), 195-207. Overbeck, F. "Über die Anfänge der patristischen Literatur," *Libelli* 15 (1954) [first in *Historische Zeitschrift* 48 (1882): 417-472; cf. also *Overbeckiana. Übersicht über den Franz-Overbeck-Nachlass der Universitätbibliothek Basel. II. Teil. Der wissenschaftliche Nachlass Franz Overbecks,* described by M. Tetz (1962), 160-164 (Studien zur Geschichte der Wissenschaften in Basel XIII)]; *Christentum und Kultur. Gedanken und Anmerkungen zur modernen Theologie.* Aus dem Nachlass ed. C.A. Bernoulli (1919). Schmidt, K.L. *Der Rahmen der Geschichte Jesu. Literarkritische Untersuchung zur ältesten Jesusüberlieferung* (1919, new editions 1964 and subsequently); "Formgeschichte" (first in 1928), in *Zur Formgeschichte des Evangeliums,* ed. F. Hahn, Wege der Forschung 81 (1985), 123-126. Weiss, J. *Beiträge zur Paulinischen Rhetorik* (1897, offprint); *Die Aufgaben der Neutestamentlichen Wissenschaft in der Gegenwart* (1908); "Literaturgeschichte, Christl. IA. Literaturgeschichte des NT," in *RGG¹* 3 (1912): 2175-2215. *Zur Formgeschichte des Evangeliums,* ed. F. Hahn, Wege der Forschung 81 (1985).

*Johann Gottfried Herder's* thesis that the roots of the Gospels should be sought in oral preaching is widely recognized.[65] It is especially influential with respect to the development and understanding of form criticism.[66] Nor have his

---

[65] Cf. J.G. Herder, *Regel* 381-384, 416-417 and *Erlöser* 196-199, etc.

[66] Cf. H. Koester, "Formgeschichte/Formenkritik. II. Neues Testament," in *TRE* 11 (1983): 286-299.

reflections on the literary character of the Gospels remained without effect.[67] Herder thus rejected the comparison with ancient literature on the basis of the romantic and idealistic conception of a relatively isolated and original literature as it was first differentiated through research in the history of religions. "Are the Gospels *history* or *biography* according to Greek or Roman ideals? No. . . ." In contrast to the ancient historical writing, the "historical style of the Hebrews. . . , as their poetry" belongs "to the childhood of the human race, and is an expression of that childhood . . . ." Thus it follows for Herder that they are independent over against ancient literature. "Forgetting everything foreign, we must subject ourselves to the character of a nation which *knows no alien literature and which lives in its old sacred books* . . . as in *the sanctuary of all wisdom.*"[68]

Without reference to Herder, Franz Overbeck also separated early Christian literature from that of the environment. In his *On the Origins of Patristic Literature,* labelled by *Adolf von Harnack* "prolegomena to any future history of ancient Christian literature,"[69] Overbeck took the position that even patristic literature should be marked off from that of the New Testament. This corresponded to his basic definition of the history of literature as a history of its forms. "A literature has its history in its forms; every true history of literature is therefore a history of its forms." [70]

---

[67] C.F.G. Heinrici expressly cites Herder's method in his *Der litterarische Charakter der neutestamentlichen Schriften,* 1908, 4. Cf. also M. Dibelius, *Die Formgeschichte des Evangeliums,* [6]1971, 4.

[68] Herder, *Erlöser,* 194, 195, 196.

[69] A. (v.) Harnack, ZKG 6 (1884): 120. But note Overbeck's critical remarks on Harnack's evaluation in *Overbeckiana* 161-163. He intends no program for ancient Christian literature, but simply a clear demarcation between New Testament or the earliest Christian literature on the one hand and patristic literature on the other.

[70] F. Overbeck, *Anfänge* 12. Overbeck's conception of form relates not to the forms contained *in* the works, but to the writings themselves. M. Rese seeks to show that, with his conception of form, Overbeck methodologically joined together "that which we in this century have called the study of literary tendency (Tendenzkritik) and what in the second half of our century has again been taken up under the name of redaction or composition criticism" ("Fruchtbare Missverständnisse. Franz Overbeck und die neutestamentliche Wissenschaft," in *Franz Overbecks unerledigte Anfragen an das Christentum,* ed. R Brändle et al. 1988, 211-226, esp. 225.) While for the "fathers" of form criticism the authors were played down as collectors of tradition (cf. Dibelius, *Formgeschichte,* 1), Overbeck was interested in these authors and what they formulated (cf. J.-C. Emmelius, "Tendenzkritik und Formgeschichte. Der Beitrag Franz Overbecks zur Auslegung der Apostelgeschichte im 19. Jahrhundert," *FKDG* 27 (1975): 89-92). On the other hand Overbeck explicitly used the expression "literary forms" (*Christentum* 24 and *Anfänge* 13, etc.), and concentrated on the writings more than on content and author (cf. above 1.1.4, for the interconnectedness of arguments on form and content); yet in such a way that "form is the product of a literary work's origin" (M. Tetz, "Altchristliche Literaturgeschichte–Patrologie," *TRu* 32 (1967): 1-47, 11, against a formal-aesthetic interpretation of Overbeck's use of "form"). On the meaning and development of comments on form criticism in Overbeck's theology cf. M. Tetz, "Über Formengeschichte in der Kirchengeschichte," *TZ* 17 (1961): 413-431. P. Vielhauer has emphasized Overbeck's influence on New Testament form criticism in "Franz Overbeck

Here Overbeck notes the differences in form.  While the (genuine) Letters of the New Testament share the common form of Christian writers, they do not belong to literature,[71] and the forms which do belong to literature (the Catholic Epistles, Gospels, Apostolic History, and Apocalypse[72] ) are forms which from the time of canon building have been missing in the church.[73] These moribund forms are counted as a part of "early Christian literature."[74]  The Apostolic Fathers, Hegesippus' Hypomnemata, and Papias' Exegeses also belong here, though this list is not exhaustive.[75]  This is "a literature which Christianity, so to speak, created out of its own means, insofar as it grew up totally on the ground and in the interest of the Christian community before its mingling with the world around it."[76]  Overbeck did not mean that Christianity always utilized new literary forms; just that it used only the religious forms of earlier times and not the secular forms of world literature.[77]  Precisely because this literature comes from the earliest period of Christianity, appealing "immediately to a faith which it shares with its intended readers and they with it," and renouncing "all literary artistry," it is separated from later readers and subsequent Christian literature.[78]  This is especially true of the Gospels, which in the final analysis "are the single original form with which Christianity enriched literature."[79]

In his work treating "ancient Christian literature" down to the sixth and seventh centuries *Hermann Jordan* describes the goal of a literary history to show "how in origin and development a literature has evolved and branched out under the influence of other literatures and of the spiritual and cultural milieu, through the original force of creative personalities."[80]  Jordan taught church history in Erlangen, beginning in 1907.  Since he distinguished himself, on the one hand, from those

---

und die neutestamentliche Wissenschaft," in "Aufsätze zum Neuen Testament," *TB* 31 (1965): 235-252 (cf. 246-252), first published in 1950/51.

[71] Overbeck, *Anfänge*, 18-22.

[72] *Anfänge*, 22-23.

[73] *Anfänge*, 23, 29-30.

[74] *Anfänge*, 22 and often elsewhere.  This is an expression which Overbeck wanted to promote not only as a chronological but also a qualitative concept.  Cf. also his *Christentum*, 23.

[75] *Anfänge*, 32-35.

[76] *Anfänge*, 36.  E. Norden opposed this thesis, differentiating his own  viewpoint on the isolation of early Christian literature from genuine literature (*Kunstprosa*, literary prose) from that of Overbeck, on whom he was dependent.  (Cf. Norden, *Die Antike Kunstprosa*, [2]1958, 1:479f.  But Norden, in contrast to Overbeck, here draws Acts and the letters of Paul into the orbit of "Hellenistic sensitivities," cf. pp. 481 and 492.) Referring expressly to Overbeck, Norden states, "But I now know that the evidence, which for the Pauline writings and Acts is, in any case, a failure, can only be regarded as provided for the gospels if the concept of literature is derived from the canon of Hellenistic genres.  But it is clear that no such derivation is justified" (*Agnostos Theos*, 306f.).

[77] *Anfänge*, 36.

[78] *Christentum*, 24.

[79] *Anfänge*, 36.  This thesis of Overbeck has enjoyed considerable acceptance into the present and limits the search for potential analogies.  Cf. the remarks by D. Dormeyer, Erträge der Forschung 263 (1989), passim.

[80] Hermann Jordan, *Geschichte der altchristlichen Literatur*, 1911, 6.

who understood the history of literature as a history of its contents, themes, and ideas, and, on the other hand, from those who took it as a history of authors, he understood it as a history of forms,[81] which joined him with Overbeck.[82] Like Overbeck he oriented the conception of form (and with it what is represented) to literary form. "Therefore a history of literature has its history in the first place in its forms; i.e., first in its form as a whole, in what the Greeks called εἶδος or γένος . . ."[83]

*Johannes Weiss's* article on the *History of NT Literature* in the first edition of *RGG* essentially treats the literary character of the New Testament, since he presents the forms in context. He does not thematically take up the questions of introduction. In this a different understanding of the history of literature appears from what was first associated with the concept (cf. 1.1.2). Even if the results of introductory research are assumed to be obvious, they are not in and of themselves objects of a literary-historical presentation.

The Gospels depend on older materials, traditions, and notes. Beginning with the presentation of the words and deeds of Jesus from a form-critical viewpoint,[84] Weiss demonstrates that New Testament literature has its roots in oral tradition. Weiss's definition of the problem in his *Die Aufgaben der neutestamentlichen Wissenschaft* of 1908,[85] shows that he is indebted to the history of religions approach. Weiss recognizes that his presentation is incomplete in the necessarily short and sketchy delineation of the "Question of Old Testament and Hellenistic precedents."[86] Nevertheless he refers to both the Jewish and Hellenistic contexts of the New Testament writings.[87] He especially finds traces of rhetorical education in the authors of the letters.[88]

Paul Wendland's formulation that "examining the earlier stratum of the oral tradition and its individuality...is an essential presupposition for understanding the later literary product"[89] agreed with Weiss's outlook. This same insight is

---

[81] Jordan, 6-8.

[82] Cf. Overbeck, *Anfänge*, 23f.

[83] Jordan, 6.

[84] J. Weiss presents the "New Testament writings essentially from a literary viewpoint, i.e., above all with respect to their forms." His intention is "to picture the earliest Christian literature in its forms and according to the motifs of its development" (*RGG*[1] 3:2175). Accordingly W. Schmithals has correctly evaluated this article as "a relatively complete program for form criticism, as Bultmann would describe it" ("Johannes Weiss als Wegbereiter der Formgeschichte," *ZTK* 80 (1983): 389-410, 404). Cf. also B. Lannert, "Die Wiederentdeckung der neutestamentlichen Eschatologie durch Johannes Weiss," TANZ 2 (1989), to the *RGG*[1] article, esp. pp. 60f.

[85] Weiss, *Aufgabe*, 35: "It is not only the literary form of the gospels as a whole which is to date an unsolved problem, but even more so the individual narratives and collections of material. It is essential that this material be compared in terms of its content and formal structure with precedents from the Old Testament and with anything else accessible of similar form. . . ."

[86] Weiss, *RGG*[1], 3:2175.

[87] Compare especially his comments on the miracle narratives, *RGG*[1], 3:2188.

[88] *RGG*[1], 3:2203f. 2211; cf. also his *Beiträge zur paulinischen Rhetorik*.

[89] P. Wendland, *Die urchristlichen Literaturformen*, HNT 1/3, [2]1912, 261.

shared in varying form by Karl Ludwig Schmidt, Rudolf Bultmann, and Martin Dibelius, whose works profitably applied the literary-historical theories of Hermann Gunkel[90] to New Testament exegesis.[91]

H. Gunkel himself produced a contribution to the history of New Testament literature in his study *Die Lieder in der Kindheitsgeschichte Jesu bei Lukas.* Through a "literary-historical treatment,"[92] i.e., through comparing forms in light of the results of his research on the Psalms, he described these songs as "eschatological hymns" of a Jewish author writing in a Semitic language.[93] They were arranged in their present context by a Christian writer. Thus Gunkel always insisted on the study of the genres and the specific language of their forms.

K.L. Schmidt took up the study of the Gospels in his *Der Rahmen der Geschichte Jesu* and *Die Stellung der Evangelien in der allgemeinen Literaturgeschichte,* important both for form and literary criticism. The latter addressed the question of the Gospels' literary character. Schmidt saw them as "cultic pamphlets" as found in "minor literature" (*Kleinliteratur*).[94] In his work on the "framework" of the Gospels he sought to contribute to the solution of the problem of distinguishing between traditional materials and their redaction, a basic

---

[90] For the theory, cf. H. Gunkel, "Die Grundprobleme der israelitischen Literaturgeschichte," in his *Reden und Aufsätze,* 1913, 29-38; "Die israelitische Literatur," in *Kultur der Gegenwart,* ed. Paul Hinneberg, Vol I,7: *Orientalische Literaturen,* [2]1925, 53-112 (unchanged but separately paginated reprint, 1963). These observations are spelled out in the introduction to sagas in his Commentary on Genesis (*Genesis,* HK I/1, [3]1910 = [8]1969), in his research on the genres of the Psalms (Gunkel/J. Begrich, *Einleitung in die Psalmen. Die Gattungen der religiösen Lyrik Israels,* 1933), and on tales in the Hebrew Scriptures (*Das Märchen im Alten Testament,* reprint with an afterword by H.J. Hermisson, 1987). On the expression and conception of the setting in life (*Sitz im Leben*) to which each form is adapted, cf. his "Formen der Hymnen," *TR* 20 (1917): 265-304 (p. 269: "It belongs to the concept of an ancient genre that it has a very specific *Sitz im Leben*"). For Gunkel's significance to literary-historical research, cf. O. Kaiser, "Literaturgeschichte. I. AT," *TRE* 21 (1991) and H.-J. Kraus, *Geschichte der historisch-kritischen Erforschung des Alten Testaments,* [3]1982 ([4]1988), 341-347.

[91] This is true despite H. Gunkels own negative yet isolated judgment about his "New Testament students" in a letter of September 9, 1925 to Adolf Jülicher. "...it seems to me, however, that my New Testament students have blurred the clear lines which I so laboriously worked out" (printed in *ZTK* 78 (1981): 276-288, 285; cf. also H Rollmann's remarks in the same article, 285, n. 19). The three New Testament scholars named above heard Gunkel in Berlin, and Dibelius and Bultmann had a close personal relationship with him. Cf. W. Klatt, *Hermann Gunkel. Zu seiner Theologie der Religionsgeschichte und zur Entstehung der formgeschichtliche Methode.* FRLANT 100 (1969): 168, nn. 13 and 14. On the relationship between Gunkel and Bultmann cf. M. Evang, *Rudolf Bultmann in seiner Frühzeit.* BHT 74 (1988): 13f., 17f. Bultmann's *curriculum vitae* of 1910 is especially significant: Gunkel is the only teacher named from Bultmann's year of study in Berlin (cf. M. Evang's comments in the work just cited, 17f.). Bultmann dates his personal acquaintance with Gunkel first to 1908 (cf. Evang, 17.).

[92] Gunkel, *Lieder* 44.

[93] *Lieder* 53.

[94] On this see below, section 4.1.2.1; cf. also E. Fascher 128-131.

assumption of form critical work.[95] He began with the question as posed in research on the life of Jesus, where it raised the problem of the setting and the duration of Jesus' ministry. He showed that the geographical and chronological presentation of the ministry (the "framework") could not be used for a historical reconstruction of the career of Jesus.

"The oldest tradition of Jesus is a tradition of 'pericopes,' i.e., of individual scenes and sayings, which for the most part were passed on in the community without firm chronological or topographical indications. Much of that which appears to be chronological or topographical is only the framework later added to these individual pictures."[96] Instead, the spatial and temporal settings for the individual pericopes are added to the traditional material according to the laws of popular storytelling. Against a widespread viewpoint in the interpretation of especially Mark's Gospel, these notices are not the work of the evangelists, but were added as secondary "ornamentation" in the course of the tradition before their time. They were taken over without hesitation by the evangelists, or sometimes first created by them (especially Matthew and Luke) in the interest of connecting their narrative. The Gospels are therefore "collective works" in which entirely different individual bits and pieces of tradition which once circulated separately are loosely connected with one another.

Rudolf Bultmann distinguished between the history of New Testament literature in the general and in "the true" sense, identifying the former with introduction to the New Testament. According to Bultmann, literary-historical work in "the true sense" is impossible for the New Testament.[97] It can first be accomplished after Christianity has become culturally unified. Furthermore, the materials collected in the New Testament must be classified chronologically and in terms of their content in order to develop a history of literature. Despite these difficulties with respect to the literary-historical analysis of the New Testament, "it is possible for the materials of the synoptic tradition to distinguish some specific literary forms with their own stylistic laws."[98] He also emphasizes that "the literary expressions of primitive Christianity . . . are presented mainly in fixed forms." Thus they can only be understood, "when one knows the genres, their forms and laws of tradition."[99] If the literary-historical approach is thus challenged, yet for Bultmann the more modest role of "genre-historical research on the New Testament" is still a possibility.[100]

---

[95] K.L. Schmidt in *Zur Formgeschichte des Evangeliums*, ed. F. Hahn. Wege der Forschung 81 (1985), 124.

[96] Schmidt, *Rahmen* v.

[97] Bultmann, in *TRu* 17 (1914): 79.

[98] Bultmann in Wege der Forschung 81 (1985), 239.

[99] Bultmann, "Literaturgeschichte, Biblische 3. L. G. des NT," *RGG*[2] 3 (1929), 1680. This corresponds to his fundamental remarks on "the form critical approach" (Wege der Forschung 81: 239), "This method begins with the realization that all literary formulations, especially in primitive cultures and in the ancient world, follow relatively fixed forms." Cf. also his "Die Erforschung der synoptischen Evangelien," (first published in 1961) in *Glauben und Verstehen. Gesammelte Aufsätze* 4 (1965), 1-41, 11.

[100] Literaturgeschichte 1681. Cf. also Erforschung 6: ". . . a literary-historical approach, which we designate as form criticism." Likewise *RGG*[3] 4:399, under *Literaturgeschichte, biblische*, refers in parts I and II to forms and genres.

## 1.1.6   Histories of New Testament Literature (M. Dibelius and P. Vielhauer)

*Literature*

Dibelius, M. "Zur Formgeschichte des Neuen Testaments (ausserhalb der Evangelien)," *TRu* 3 (1931): 207-242; *Geschichte der urchristlichen Literatur. Neudruck der Erstausgabe von 1926 unter Berücksichtigung der Änderungen der englischen Übersetzung von 1936*, ed. F. Hahn. Theologische Bücherei 58 (1975) = Kaiser Taschenbücher 89 (³1990); Aufsätze zur Apostelgeschichte, ed. H. Greeven, FRLANT 68 (³1957); *Studies in the Acts of the Apostles* (1956). Hahn, F. "Vorwort" to Dibelius/Hahn *Geschichte.* Kümmel, W.G. "Review of P. Vielhauer, Geschichte der urchristlichen Literatur," *TLZ* 102 (1977): 879-894. Vielhauer, P. *Geschichte der urchristlichen Literatur. Einleitung in das Neue Testament, die Apokryphen und die Apostolischen Väter,* (²1978=1975).

As early as the summer semester of 1915 Martin Dibelius delivered his first lecture on the history of early Christian literature.[101] In 1926 he published his *Geschichte der urchristlichen Literatur,* directed to a wider audience. Unrestricted by canonical limits,[102] like his teacher H. Gunkel[103] he studied oral tradition. The question as to how the tradition included in the writings had arisen is to be answered just as is the problem "how from these beginnings books ensued."[104] This minor literature (*Kleinliteratur,* i.e., writings intended for a specific group) should be studied in terms of its literary history: the history of its forms and genres.[105] To reconstruct the forms contained in this literature Dibelius recommended a history of religions *(religionsgeschichtlich)* approach, i.e., the use of parallels from the history of religions for the discovery and explanation of primitive Christian traditional fragments.[106] Summarizing his task, Dibelius wrote: "The historian of early Christian literature who would make the emergence of these writings understandable must show how the first Christians came to this literary activity and in what manner these books mirror the uniqueness of their authors and the influence of the conditions under which they were written."[107] An

---

[101] F. Hahn in M. Dibelius, *Geschichte der urchristlichen Literatur. Neudruck der Erstausgabe von 1926 unter Berücksichtigung der Änderungen der englischen Übersetzung von 1936,* ed. F. Hahn. Theologische Bücherei 58 (1975), 12.

[102] Dibelius, *Geschichte* 20f.

[103] Gunkel, "Die Grundproblem der israelitischen Literaturgeschichte," in his *Reden und Aufsätze,* 1913, 33ff.; and "Die israelitische Literatur," in *Kultur der Gegenwart,* ed. Paul Hinneberg, Vol I,7: *Orientalische Literaturen,* ²1925, esp. 55.

[104] Dibelius, *Geschichte* 17f.; also *Formgeschichte* 1f.

[105] Dibelius, *Geschichte* 21.

[106] Dibelius, *TRu* 3 (1931): 211.

[107] Dibelius, *Geschichte* 15 and *TRu* 3 (1931): 241.

extensive history of the literature of primitive Christianity in the context of the "new theological situation" can no longer be realized.[108]

In his foreword to a new edition of Dibelius's *Geschichte der urchristlichen Literatur* in 1975, over against customary introductions which "onesidedly proceed from the literary form of the writings and from literary-critical questions," Ferdinand Hahn suggests an approach analogous to that of Dibelius, taking into account the problem of oral tradition.[109]

This conception, dedicated to the traditional demand to replace New Testament introduction with a history of New Testament literature, is realized by *Philipp Vielhauer's Geschichte der urchristlichen Literatur*. Vielhauer emphasizes the continuity of his idea with the earlier work of Overbeck and Dibelius.[110] Over and above the work of Dibelius, Vielhauer presents the literary genres in a historical series,[111] and in this, like Dibelius, stepping outside canonical boundaries. It is no judgment against the value and significance of this work to say with *Werner Georg Kümmel*[112] that, despite the constant reflection of "literary character," Vielhauer has not produced and has not intended to produce a "history of literature 'in the true sense.'"[113]

## 1.1.7 Recent Sketches and Reflections on the History of Early Christian Literature

*Literature*

Aune, D.E. *The New Testament in its Literary Environment.* Library of Early Christianity 8 (1987). Berger, K. *Exegese des Neuen Testaments. Neue Wege vom Text zur Auslegung.* Uni-Taschenbücher 658 (1977, ²1984); *Formgeschichte des Neuen Testaments* (1984); *Einführung in die Formgeschichte.* Uni-Taschenbücher 1444 (1987). Betz, H.D. "Review of P. Vielhauer's *Geschichte der urchristlichen Literatur,*" *SEÅ* 43 (1978): 128-132. Koester, H. "Literature, Early Christian," in *IDBSup* (1976), 551-556. Paulsen, H. "Literaturgeschichte 2. Neues Testament," *EKL³* 3 (1992): 133-138.

In his review of Vielhauer's *Geschichte der urchristlichen Literatur,* Hans Dieter Betz goes beyond the conclusions of Overbeck, Deissmann, and Dibelius.

---

[108] Cf. P. Vielhauer, "Einleitung in das Neue Testament," *TRu* 31 (1965/66): 97-155 and 193-231, 216. See also the remarks of H. Greeven in the foreword to M. Dibelius, *Aufsätze zur Apostelgeschichte,* 7. There also are Dibelius's comments on Acts with respect to the prospective history of early Christian literature.

[109] *Geschichte* 12f.

[110] P. Vielhauer, *Geschichte der urchristlichen Literatur. Einleitung in das Neue Testament, die Apokryphen und die Apostolischen Väter* (²1978).

[111] Vielhauer, *Geschichte* 8; cf. H. Conzelmann's review of Vielhauer's book in *TRu* 42 (1977): 273f., 274.

[112] W.G. Kümmel, Review of Vielhauer's *Geschichte* in *TLZ* 102 (1977): 879-884, cf. 880-882. See also H. D. Betz's review of the same work in *SEÅ* 43 (1978): 128-132.

[113] Vielhauer, *Geschichte,* 6.

He critiques not only the separation of actual letters and epistles[114] and the demarcation of patristic literature on the bais of Scripture as canon,[115] but especially calls into question the strict divorce between New Testament and Hellenistic literature.[116] Correspondingly, he suggests that future literary-historical research should utilize the terminology of ancient literary theory and convention.[117] "Rhetorical criticism," a method inaugurated by Betz for the interpretation of the New Testament letters (cf. 3.2.3.2), fits with these reflections. This method was preceded by earlier attempts to utilize ancient rhetoric for the understanding of New Testament writings.[118]

One year after the first edition of Vielhauer's *Geschichte der urchristlichen Literatur* Helmut Koester's article on "Early Christian Literature" appeared in the *IDB Supplement Volume*. Koester shares with Vielhauer the approach of consistently stepping over canonical boundaries. But unlike Vielhauer, he does not make problems of New Testament introduction part of his presentation. Yet, as corresponds to a "history of literature in the true sense,"[119] they are presupposed. After reflections on language, textual tradition, and cultural context, Koester discusses the relationship of literature and oral tradition and the significance of the latter for the former. He goes his own way in the arrangement of "wisdom books," "apocalyptic literature," "aretalogy, biography, romance," and "passion narrative and 'gospel,'"[120] corresponding to his approach that sees four original gospel genres underlying our Gospels. This approach is problematical even on grounds of its terminology.[121] Likewise for "aretalogy:" not only the evidence for the so-called aretalogical collections (cf. 4.2.2.; 4.4.1.1) but even the concept of such a genre (cf. 4.1.2.4) should be questioned. Yet Koester's article presents a consistent if limited realization of a history of literature as Dibelius had intended, centering on the oral tradition.

Research is indebted for critical stimulation to the detailed work of Klaus Berger. He understands form criticism as "the literary history of the individual genres" as well as the "history of the relationship between genres and their historical sequence." Thus it becomes "actual community history."[122] The literary form of the text is (as for Bultmann) the point of departure for determining the genre. The oral pre-history of the text is not described, in contrast to earlier

---

[114] Betz, review of Vielhauer's *Geschichte*, 130.

[115] Betz, 131.

[116] Betz, 131.

[117] Betz, 131.

[118] C.G. Wilke's *Neutestamentliche Rhetorik* appeared as early as 1843, defined by its subtitle as "a companion on the grammar of New Testament verbal idiom." Note also C.L. Bauer's studies on Pauline argumentation and rhetoric, *Logica Paulina* of 1774 and *Rhetoricae Paullinae,* 2 volumes, 1782.

[119] See above, section 1.1.5, page 19.

[120] H. Koester, "Literature, Early Christian," *IDBSup* (1976), 553-555.

[121] See below, chapter 4, n. 26.

[122] K. Berger, *Formgeschichte des Neuen Testaments* (1984), 12, cf. also 10, and his *Exegese des Neuen Testaments. Neue Wege vom Text zur Auslegung.* Uni-Taschenbücher 658 (1977, ²1984), 111-127.

form criticism and to literary criticism, which valued the oral tradition as a foundation and presupposition of the literary genres.[123]   Berger grants ancient rhetoric a more influential role in form and literary criticism.   His form criticism rests on a communication theory of genre, and its primary descriptive categories correspond to rhetorical situations as these can be discovered from ancient rhetoric. Berger accordingly distinguishes symbuleutic, epideictic, and dikanic texts;[124] comparable to the deliberative, epideictic, and forensic rhetorical genera.[125]   This organizational schema, however, does not suffice for all the New Testament materials.   Berger's classification must employ the category "miscellaneous genres" (Sammelgattungen), where he classifies analogical and figurative texts (e.g., parables), sentences, etc.

David Aune's work, *The New Testament in its Literary Environment,* compares the New Testament literary genres with those of the ancient Mediterranean, and especially the Hellenistic, world.[126]   Since Aune attempts to understand the formal and stylistic characteristics of New Testament genres against the backdrop of ancient Mediterranean literature and presupposes the results of New Testament introductory research, his presentation is close to a "history of literature in the true sense."[127]   Aune expressly relativizes the absolute distinction between cultivated and minor literature, which would hinder this comparison.   In light of recent research these should only be regarded as ideal types.   This does not mean that all forms of cultivated literature are to be claimed for minor literature.   Note however, the general continuity of literary conventions.   ". . . there are some basically similar literary and rhetorical patterns and genres found in all strata of ancient society."[128]   The forms of cultivated literature transmitted among the upper levels of society influenced the "literary" productions of other social classes.[129] Aune gives little place to pre-literary forms, which he nevertheless regards as constitutive elements of the literary genres.[130]   Discussion of the genre of the Sayings Source (Q, the existence of which is presupposed[131]) is unrightly sacrificed to Aune's concentration on the larger genres.   Since Aune regularly steps outside of

---

[123] Berger, *Formgeschichte,* 11, 12, 13-16.; *Einführung in die Formgeschichte.* Uni-Taschenbücher 1444 (1987), 103-129.   For a critique cf. F. Hahn, "Die Formgeschichte des Evangeliums. Voraussetzungen, Ausbau und Tragweite," in *Zur Formgeschichte des Evangeliums,* ed. F. Hahn. Wege der Forschung 81 (1985), 427-477, 476f. and G. Strecker, "A. Neues Testament," in G. Strecker and Johann Maier, "Neues Testament – Antikes Judentum," *Grundkurs Theologie* 2 (1989): 50f.

[124] Cf. esp. *Formgeschichte,* 16f.

[125] On the ancient rhetorical genres cf. below, section 3.2.3.2, note 141.

[126] D.E. Aune, *The New Testament in its Literary Environment.* Library of Early Christianity 8 (Philadelphia: Westminster, 1987), 12.

[127] See above, page 19.

[128] Aune, *Literary Environment,* 13.

[129] *Literary Environment,* 12f.

[130] *Literary Environment,* 50-52.

[131] *Literary Environment,* 19f., 52.

canonical boundaries, Q is mentioned in reference to texts of similar genres (such as the Gospel of Thomas, cf. 4.2.3.2).[132]

Henning Paulsen's article offers a look at the present status of research. In a penetrating evaluation of the methodological presuppositions of New Testament literary history, he refers not only to the necessity of giving up the restriction to canonical boundaries,[133] but also poses the question of the relationship between synchronic and diachronic treatments of the forms. Paulsen sees the first issue as closely connected to the definition of the history of literature.[134] Along with this he emphasizes the significance of a synchronic consideration as a "descriptive approach to forms, genres and texts," without dealing with the specific themes of this classification.[135] Thus he takes into account the methodology of K. Berger. Corresponding to the inclination of contemporary research, he perceives contact with literature contemporary to the New Testament as significant, and hence seems to have overcome earlier restraints on the history of literature.[136] While identification of oral tradition with the concept of "pre-literary" may be questioned,[137] this could be seen as true of tradition with relatively fixed forms.[138] However, his accompanying challenge "that the differentiation within materials between the oral and written has been worked through"[139] is to be doubted. This issue of the relationship of the two types of tradition is still up for intensive discussion in present research (cf. 4.3).

## 1.2   Defining the Task

The historical study of New Testament literature must be defined in contrast to form and literary criticism. Form criticism works with the forms of the oral tradition.[140] Literary criticism is concerned with written sources and

---

[132] *Literary Environment,* 71f.

[133] H. Paulsen, "Literaturgeschichte 2. Neues Testament," in *EKL*[3] (1992) 3:133-138.

[134] Paulsen understands literary history as a description of "the circumstances and conditions under which the literature of the early Christian community originated." This implies reflection on "the derivation and development of the forms and genres," and ought to occur along with observation of "their effects and the process of their reception in the history of the church" (cf. p. 133).

[135] Paulsen, 134.

[136] Paulsen, 134.

[137] Paulsen, 134.

[138] As does Willi Marxsen, "Literaturgeschichte: II. Das NT," in *EKL*[2] (1962) 2:1127. "On the grounds of its formation according to certain laws (in this restricted sense)," the oral tradition should be "considered as literature."

[139] Paulsen, 135.

[140] On the task and function of form criticism, cf. Koester's article "Formgeschichte/Formenkritik. II. Neues Testament," in *TRE* (1983) 11:286f., as well as G. Strecker and U. Schnelle, *Einführung in die neutestamentliche Exegese.* Uni-Taschenbücher 1253 ([3]1989), 72ff.

precedents. The history of New Testament literature utilizes the results of these efforts on the New Testament text, relating the various New Testament literary forms to one another, and placing them wherever possible within a framework of historical development.

## 1.2.1    The Concept of a *History* of Early Christian Literature

It is appropriate to the search for the historical origins of the New Testament writings to consider also the pre-literary forms. They must be acknowledged as preliminary stages and presuppositions of the process in which the tradition became literature. Since they have found such considerable access into early Christian literature, they must be considered a part of its history.

The depiction of this history is based mainly on the chronological succession of its literary genres, which in some cases have assimilated older forms and genres as well as older sources (esp. the Sayings Source, (Q), cf. 4.2.3). This is as necessary for historical research as considering the significance of common theological and historical locations (schools, circles) for the origin and development of New Testament literature (cf. 3.5; 4.4.2; 6.4), as is consideration of religious-historical or literary analogies, or of questions about cultic or sociological backgrounds (older form criticism's question about the *Sitz im Leben*), to the extent that these are justified by the text.[141] The value of the latter is in its specifying the sociological and economic presuppositions of the New Testament, widening the perspective of form criticism. Yet historically verifiable results can only be reached on the basis of historical-critical methods.[142]

The history of New Testament literature presupposes the perspectives and conclusions of New Testament introduction. But this denies authority of the methodological dictate that introductory studies be carried out in light of a conception of "early Christian literature" based on fundamentalistic restrictions. The cultural milieu of early Christianity cannot be delineated in detail, but provides the background for this presentation. Further particulars and evidence may be found in the cited literature.[143]

---

[141] Psychological questions should also be considered, to the relatively small degree that they can be answered from the New Testament texts. (On the limits of psychological studies on the New Testament, cf. the critical comments in Strecker and Schnelle, *Exegese*, 155-158.)

[142] Unfortunately, this often remains without emphasis in sociological interpretation, which likewise disregards the pronounced refusal of New Testament faith to absolutize immanent reality. Cf. Strecker and Schnelle, *Exegese,* 140-144, with bibliography.

[143] On the "religious and cultural history of the Hellenistic and Roman eras," cf. esp. H. Koester, *Einführung in das Neue Testament im Rahmen der Religionsgeschichte und Kulturgeschichte der hellenistischen und römischen Zeit,*1980 (English version, *Introduction to the New Testament, volume one: History, Culture, and Religion of the Hellenistic Age,* 1982). On Jewish religious, cultural, and literary history up to 70 CE cf. J. Maier, *Zwischen den Testamenten. Geschichte und Religion in der Zeit des zweiten Tempels,* Neue Echter Bibel, Kommentar zum AT, Supplement Volume 3 (1990). *Greco-Roman Literature and the New Testament*

A project such as this must have limits, so it is hardly possible to provide a history in the sense of stringent linear development of the forms. Rudolf Bultmann referred earlier to the quantitative problem:[144] of some literary forms or genres there are only a few or perhaps only one example in early Christian literature.[145] Assigning New Testament or early Christian literature to specific chronological periods[146] is also difficult. For example, only in a qualified sense do the deutero-Pauline writings form a break in the New Testament epistolary literature, since the pseudepigraphical Pauline letters are to be understood as having a relatively close connection to Paul's genuine letters.[147] On the other hand, the true letter genre–although not in the Pauline form–appears later on in Christian literature (with 2 and 3 John, cf. 3.1.1). The genre represented by the Sayings Source (Q) does not disappear with the writing of the Gospels, but is substantiated anew by the gnostic Gospel of Thomas. Moreover, traditions and pictures from the Jesus tradition formally corresponding to synoptic materials continue to circulate after the Gospels are written.[148] Early Christianity itself does not develop in a

---

(SBLSBS 21, 1988), edited by D.E. Aune, offers ancient parallels to specific New Testament forms.

[144] See above, p. 19.

[145] Note canonical Acts (cf. chapter 4), which should be distinguished from the apocryphal acts, and thus stands alone in early Christian literature.

[146] For instance, cf. the categories of H. Paulsen in "Literaturgeschichte 2. Neues Testament," in *EKL*[3] (1992) 3:135-138. 1. *Beginnings:* characterized by a rich variety of forms. To this period belong the formula traditions, the beginnings of the Jesus tradition, and the Pauline letters. 2. The *second period* is marked less by the introduction of new forms than by the "hardening of those generic possibilities already present in the earlier period" (p. 137). To this period belong the deutero-Pauline writings, and reformulations of the sayings source among which are numbered the Synoptic Gospels. 3. In the *concluding period* come the John's Gospel and the Johannine apocalypse. In addition to the collection of the Pauline letters, this period also sees an increased incliniation toward the world and a resultant introduction of new forms (e.g., apologetics).

[147] In his treatment of the Pauline corpus in *Geschichte der urchristlichen Literatur,* Vielhauer also includes the deutero-Pauline writings. Note especially the significance of the Pauline school for the existence of the deuteropauline literature (cf. below, section 3.5).

[148] Cf. H. Koester, "Gnostic Writings as Witnesses for the Development of the Sayings Tradition," in *The Rediscovery of Gnosticism 1: The School of Valentinus,* ed. by B. Layton. Numen Supplement 41 (1980): 239-261; and *ANRW* II 25.2 (1984), 1463-1542, among others. Examples are the fragments from Papias' five treatises  on the "Interpretation of the Oracles of the Lord" (Λογίων κυριακῶν ἐξήγησις συγγράμματα πέντε, in Eusebius, Ecclesiastical History III 39,1), based primarily on oral tradition, sometimes characterized as "wild tradition" (e.g. the grotesque report on the end of Judas). Cf. Vielhauer, *Geschichte,* 760. For texts, cf. E. Preuschen, *Antilegomena. Die Reste der ausserkanonischen Evangelien und urchristlichen Überlieferungen* ([2]1905), 91-99, with German translations on pp. 195-202. See also J. Kürzinger, *Papias von Hierapolis und die Evangelien des Neuen Testaments. Gesammelte Aufsätze. Neuausgabe  und Übersetzung der Fragmente. Kommentierte Bibliographie,* Eichstätter Materialien 4 (1983): 89ff.. Note also the secondary passages in the New Testament, such as Luke 6:5 in D and John 7:53-8:11, the Gospel of Thomas, and passages in the fathers.

unilinear fashion and is incapable of a simple periodic arrangement in which the individual writings have only to be assigned places. Even the sequence of early Palestinian and Hellenistic Christian communities (as Acts suggests it) is a questionable criterion for the age of traditions[149] or the disjunction of epochs (illustrated by the difficulty of defining the exact chronological boundary of so-called "early catholicism"[150]).

## 1.2.2  The Concept of Literature and the History of Literature as a History of its Genres

The concept of genre relates not to aesthetic considerations, restricted to describing and classifying  literary materials,[151] but to formal characteristics of individual forms, seeking to reconstruct their relationships and development.[152] Pure genre,[153] as well as pure form,[154] is unachievable. In the New Testament writings, rather, faith in Christ is expressed in various ways, powerfully influencing the genres. Sociological, cultic, and cultural factors as well as the historical situation have also had their influence, motivating the individual witnesses and finding expression in them. Postulating purity of form presupposes an ideal which gives as little credit to these influences as to an individual's living contact with all those genres around him or her, well known from the history of literature. Therefore description of a genre is based on further defining characteristics. The section on letters especially illustrates this. When the selected letters are depicted there, no

---

[149] Cf. D. Lührmann, "Erwägungen zur Geschichte des Urchristentums," *EvT* 32 (1972): 452-467, 459 and W. Schneemelcher, *Das Urchristentum.* Urban Taschenbücher 336 (1981), 14.

[150] Cf. the excursus on early catholicism ("Frühkatholizismus") in G. Strecker, *Die Johannesbriefe.* Kritisch-exegetischer Kommentar 14 (1989), 348-354, *The Johannine Letters,* Hermeneia (1996), 244-249, with bibliography, and H. Paulsen, *EKL*[3] (1992) 3:135.

[151] See also section 4.3, pages 131f., below.

[152] Form criticism or the history of genres understood in this sense can be carried out independently of the question as to whether the New Testament writings should be regarded as literature. Thus refusing to regard the New Testament as literature poses no objection to literary-historical research on the New Testament (against W. Marxen, "Literaturgeschichte II. Das NT," *EKL*[2] (1962) 2:1126). Moreover, it is becoming increasingly common in modern literary scholarship to regard "even practical and documentary writings as worthy of the name of literature" (C. Christandl *et al. Die römische Literatur. Ein Überblick über Autoren, Werke und Epochen von den Anfängen bis zum Ende der Antike,* ed. R. Seroner. Bech'sche Elementarbücher (1981), 163). In addition, since the popular writings (*"'Klein'-Literatur"*) of the New Testament utilize the forms of secular literature, they can hardly be denied literary research.

[153] With respect to affirming purity of genre, K.M. Fischer ("Zum gegenwärtigen Stand der neutestamentlichen Einleitungswissenschaft," *VF* 24/1 (1979): 3-35, 10) explains that a history of literature as suggested by F. Overbeck and M. Dibelius is "unwritable."

[154] See below, section 4.3, p. 133.

attempt is made to reduce the specific distinction between genuine letters and literary epistles,[155] but rather to agree with the claim of these writings to be letters, following a widely disseminated ancient convention to stylize writings of various forms as letters.[156]

## 1.2.3    Limitations

Although the forms and genres found in the New Testament are not restricted to it, and numerous examples of them are found outside the canon, for the most part this work will cover only New Testament writings.[157]    This is due mainly to practical considerations.[158]    It is methodologically impossible to go back behind the "fundamental opening up the New Testament canon,"[159] as literary-historical and religious-historical research have shown and P. Vielhauer's *Geschichte der urchristlichen Literatur* has impressively explained.

Limiting this study to New Testament writings relieves us from methodological reflections on the boundary between early Christian and patristic literature, which represented the starting point for F. Overbeck's observations.    The difficulty of drawing a clear boundary line between the two has been rightly noted,[160] related to the complexity of historical development which comes to a real turning point with the closing of the canon.

## 1.2.4    History of Literature: the Present Formulation of the Question

Questions about the necessity for a survey of New Testament literary history in the present situation are answered by reference to the many new studies which have been published since the work of P. Vielhauer.    Many new studies on ancient analogies to New Testament forms and genres need to be assessed, as does the almost explosive acceptance and usage of rhetorical concepts and structures.[161] The goal of our discussion is to advance methodological discussion.    To the extent that this is possible within the given framework, approaches from the perspectives of

---

[155] See below, section 3.2.1, pp. 44f.

[156] Cf. D.E. Aune, *Literary Environment,* 158.

[157] On the so-called New Testament apocryphal literature, besides P. Vielhauer, Geschichte, see the revised edition of the standard work in two volumes, edited by W. Schneemelcher and translated by R. McL. Wilson, *New Testament Apocrypha* (1991/1992).    This latter examines not only the literary form but also the historical relationships of these writings.    On the concept of apocryphal writing or apocrypha, cf. W. Schneemelcher's general introduction to the two volume work, 1:9-75. Cf. also K. Rudolph, "Die Gnosis: Texte und Übersetzungen," *TRu* 55 (1990): 113-152, 152.

[158] See also below, section 7, p. 224

[159] See G. Strecker in *Grundkurs Theologie* 2 (1989): 36.

[160] Cf. H. Paulsen, *EKL*[3] (1992) 3:135.

[161] Cf. the bibliography on the rhetorical analysis of New Testament letters at section 3.2.3.3. See also section 4.5.

textual theory, structual analysis, linguistics,[162] and literary criticism must all be utilized.[163] But they must be utilized critically. They have sometimes been indiscriminately combined in New Testament research. The absolutizing of synchronic factors, as often occurs in newer methodologies, is especially to be questioned. While the synchronic approach characterizes an aspect of exegesis which ought not to be overlooked, and which can serve to resolve structural problems of New Testament texts, context within the history of tradition should not be neglected.

---

[162] Cf. Strecker in *Grundkurs Theologie* 2 (1989): 127-130 (bibliography).

[163] Hermeneutical issues are taken up only occasionally. (Cf. comments on the parables of Jesus at section 4.3.1e.) in *Grundkurs Theologie* 2 (1989): 36.

# 2 The New Testament Writings

## 2.1 The Text

*Editions*[1]

Aland, K., M. Black, C.M. Martini, B.M. Metzger, A. Wikgren, *Greek New Testament*, ([3]1975, rev. ed. 1983) [text-critical data only where relevant to the translation]. *The New Testament in Greek II: The Gospel According to St. Luke,* ed. by the American and British Committees of the International Greek New Testament Project. 2 vols. (1984 and 1987).[2] Huck, A., H. Greeven, *Synopse der drei ersten Evangelien mit Beigaben der johanneischen Parallelstellen* ([13]1981) [independent edition of the text]. Nestle, E., K. Aland, *Novum Testamentum Graece* ([26]1979, rev. 1983, [27]1993).

*Literature*

Aland, B., "Neutestamentliche Textkritik heute," *VF* 21 (1976): 3-22. Aland, K., C. Hannick, K. Junack,"Bibelhandschriften II. Neues Testament," *TRE* 6 (1980): 114-131. Aland K. and B. Aland, *Der Test des Neuen Testaments. Einführung in die wissenschaftlichen Ausgaben sowie in Theorie und Praxis der modernen Textkritik* ([2]1989); *The Text of the New Testament: an Introduction to the Critical Editions and to the Theory and Practice of Modern Textual Criticism* (1987). Borger, R., "NA[26] und die neutestamentliche Textkritik," *TRu* 52 (1987): 1-58, 326. Elliot, J.K., "Textkritik heute," *ZNW* 82 (1991): 34-41. Greeven, H., "Text und Textkritik der Bible II. Neues Testament," *RGG[3]* 6 (1992): 716-725. Koester, H., *Einführung in das Neue Testament im Rahmen der Religionsgeschichte und Kulturgeschichte der hellenistischen und römischen Zeit* (1980), 444-475; *Introduction to the New Testament, volume two: History and Literature of Early Christianity* (1982), 15-43. Lietzmann, H., "Textgeschichte und Textkritik," in his *Kleine Schriften II,* ed. by K. Aland, TU 68 (1958): 15-250. Metzger, B.M. *The Text of the New Testament: Its Transmission, Corruption, and Restoration,* [2]1968; *A Textual Commentary on the New Testament* ([3]1971). Strecker, G. and U. Schnelle, *Einführung in die neutestamentliche Exegese,* Uni-Taschenbücher 1253, ([3]1989), 25-42. Zimmermann H., *Neutestamentliche Methodenlehre. Darstellung der historisch-kritischen Methode,* rev. K. Kliesch ([7]1982), 28-76.

---

[1] On older editions, cf. G. Strecker "Neues Testament," in Strecker and Johann Maier, *Neues Testament—Antikes Judentum,* Grundkurs Theologie 2 (1989): 10f.; Kurt and Barbara Aland, *Der Text des Neuen Testaments. Einführung in die wissenschaftlichen Ausgaben sowie in Theorie und Praxis der modernen Textkritik,* [2]1989.

[2] On the text-critical method of the "executive editor," cf. J.K. Elliot, "Textkritik heute," *ZNW* 82 (1991): esp. 39.

The text of the New Testament, extant in about five thousand manuscripts,[3] is more extensively attested than any other ancient or early Christian literature. Texts are classified according to the materials on which they are written, as papyri or parchments, and by the style of writing, as uncials and minuscules.

The oldest New Testament texts are papyri, extant only in fragments. Their name stems from the material on which they are written, papyrus, a marsh plant growing chiefly in the Nile delta. The earliest extant papyrus fragments of the New Testament date from the second century.[4] The great uncial manuscripts of the fourth and fifth centuries are written in capital letters and mainly in continuous script, and on parchment from the hides of small or young animals: goats, sheep, or asses.[5] The majority of manuscripts are minuscules, of which the earliest (#461) is to be dated in the ninth century.[6] These present the text in small cursive letters and with accentuation.[7]

No original manuscripts of any New Testament writings are extant. In the process of transmission the text was liable to scribal errors and conscious corrections in vocabulary and style, but also to harmonizing and dogmatic alterations. Textual criticism attempts to reconstruct the earliest possible text.[8] Modern editions of the Greek New Testament are the products of these efforts and the basis for New Testament exegesis.

The copious text-critical apparatus of the *Novum Testamentum Graece* (currently in its 27th edition) equips the reader for an independent assessment on the reconstruction of the text. Although the text-critical judgments of the editors may be questioned in specific cases[9] and criticism of their arrangement of hymnic passages is necessary, the 26th and 27th go beyond all previous editions, yet do not ignore the conclusions of earlier manuscripts or editors, but include them in appendices.

---

[3] J.K. Elliot, 37.

[4] Currently the oldest papyri are $P^{46}$, $P^{52}$, $P^{66}$, and $P^{75}$.

[5] The most important and well known uncials are: Codex Sinaiticus (ℵ, 01) Codex Alexandrinus (A, 02), Codex Vaticanus (B, 03), Codex Ephraemi (rescriptus; C, 04), and Codex Bezae Cantabrigensis (D, 05).

[6] Cf. K. and B. Aland, *Der Text des Neuen Testaments,* [2]1989, 145, 149. For an illustration of a miniscule page, cf. p. 148.

[7] For lectionaries used in worship services, cf. H. Greeven, "Die Textgestalt der Evangelienlektionare," *TLZ* 76 (1951): 513-522 and K. and B. Aland, *Text,* 172-178, 326. For ancient versions and the evidence from the church fathers, cf. K. and B. Aland, 181-226.

[8] On the history, task, and methodology of text criticism, cf. G. Strecker and U. Schnelle, *Einführung in die neutestamentliche Exegese.* Uni-Taschenbücher 1253, [3]1989, 25-42; K. and B. Aland, Text; H. Greeven, "Text und Textkritik der Bible II. Neues Testament," *RGG³* 6 (1992): 717-719; Zimmermann H., *Neutestamentliche Methodenlehre. Darstellung der historisch-kritischen Methode,* rev. K. Kliesch, [7]1982, 28-76.

[9] It should be noted that the Nestle-Aland 26th and 27th editions do not free the reader from making his or her own text-critical judgments. See also the comments of R. Borger, "NA²⁶ und die neutestamentliche Textkritik," *TRu* 52 (1987): 15: "No single edition can claim a monopoly. A monopolistic text would serve neither the church nor research."

## 2.2    The Language of the New Testament

*Literature*

Bauer, W. "Zur Einführung in das Wörterbuch zum Neuen Testament," (first published in 1928 and expanded in 1955) in *Aufsätze und Kleine Schriften,* ed. G. Strecker (1967), 61-90; "An Introduction to the Lexicon of the Greek New Testament," in Bauer, Arndt, Gingrich, Danker, *A Greek-English Lexicon of the New Testament and Other Early Christian Literature* (1979), xi-xxviii). Blass, F., A. Debrunner, F. Rehkopf, *Grammatik des neutestamentlichen Griechisch* ($^{16}$1984, $^{17}$1990);[10] English translation of the 9th and 10th German editions by Robert Funk, *A Greek Grammar of the New Testament and Other Early Christian Literature* (1961). Beyer, K., *Semitische Syntax im Neuen Testament,* Vol. 1, Satzlehre Part 1. SUNT 1 (1962, $^{2}$1968). Conzelmann, H. and A. Lindemann, *Arbeitsbuch zum Neuen Testament.* Uni-Taschenbücher 52 ($^{9}$1988), 19-22. Dahl, N.A. "Griechisch," in *BHH* 1 (1962): 610-611. Deissmann, A. "Hellenistisches Griechisch (with special reference to the Greek Bible)," in *RE* 7 (1899): 627-639. Friedrich, G. "Pre-History of the Theological Dictionary of the New Testament," trans. G.W. Bromiley *TDNT* 10 (1976): 613-661. Koester, H., *Einführung in das Neuue Testament im Rahmen der Religionsgeschichte und Kulturgeschichte der hellenistischen und römischen Zeit* (1980), 103-117; *Introduction to the New Testament. Vol. I, History, Culture, and Religion of the Hellenistic Age* (1982), 101-113. Kümmel, W.G. "Bibel IIC. Sprache und Schriftzeichen des NT," in *RGG*$^{3}$, 1 (1957): 1138-1141. Michaelis, W., "Der Attizismus und das Neue Testament," *ZNW* 22 (1923): 91-121. Moulton, J.H., *A Grammar of New Testament Greek. Vol. I, Prolegomena* ($^{3}$1908). Radermacher, L., *Neutestamentliche Grammatik. Das Griechisch des Neuen Testaments im Zusammenhang mit der Volkssprache.* HNT 1 ($^{2}$1925). Rehkopf, F. "Griechisch (des Neuen Testaments)," in *TRE* 14 (1985): 228-235. Ros, J., *De studie van het Bijbelgrieksch van Hugo Grotius tot Adolf Deissmann* (1940). Rüger, H.P. "Aramäisch II. Im Neuen Testament," in *TRE* 3 (1978): 602-610. Schwyzer, E. *Griechische Grammatik auf der Grundlage von Karl Brugmanns Griechischer Grammatik.* Handbuch der Altertumswissenschaft II, 1, 1-4 ($^{5}$1977, $^{4}$1975, 1980 [=$^{2}$1960], 1971). Strecker, G. "Walter Bauers Wörterbuch in neuer Auflage," *TLZ* 116 (1991): 81-92. Thumb, A. *Die griechische Sprache im Zeitalter des Hellenismus. Beiträge zur Geschichte und Beurteilung der KOINH* (1901).

In general, the language of the New Testament may be included within the Koine (named from ἡ κοινὴ διάλεκτος), i.e., the common language of the Hellenistic era[11] as it was spoken in the Roman empire in New Testament times.

---

[10] Abbreviated as BDR (German) and BDF (English), with references to numbered paragraphs.

[11] Koine Greek is distinguished from classical by a series of changes: simplified declensions, conjugation, and syntax; changes in pronunciation (sometimes seen in papyri and inscriptions as well); vocabulary changes (newly built words; the acceptance of foreign words, especially in realms of the military [e.g., κεντυρίων in Mark

But there are differences in the specifics. The New Testament writings display variations in the structure of their grammar and the quality of their vocabulary,[12] corresponding to distinctions in ethnic background, level of education, and faithfulness to tradition.

A. Deissmann's judgment that "the Greek gospels" are " . . . essentially monuments to the speech of their environments," and that Paul spoke the language of the "common people" of Ephesus and Corinth,[13] a generally negative assessment of New Testament literary quality, has not caught on. The language of Luke-Acts[14] and Hebrews[15] can been regarded as very carefully crafted.[16] Paul's letters are elevated above the other writings at very least by a sort of rhetorical and stylistic artistry, and show a "sometimes refined Greek."[17] The thesis that the Gospel of Mark is written in "Jewish Greek" is likewise unsupported. In some passages close verbal parallels to popular Greek literature are evident. Thus it is much more a matter of "*literary* style . . . , which throughout is separated from living and spoken language, even if Mark does not soar to the highest levels of the so-called literary koine."[18]

But Deissmann found agreement when he critically scrutinized the hypothesis of an alleged "biblical Greek."[19] This harmonized with the goal of W.

---

15:39], commerce, and administration; names [E.g., Παῦλος; for a list of Aramaic foreign words cf. H.P. Rüger in *TRE* 3]; and a preference for composite words); less precise use of prepositions and failure to preserve distinctions in meaning; greatly restricted usage of the optative; and others. On the Koine cf., BDR/BDF §3; Conzelmann and Lindemann, *Arbeitsbuch*, 20-21; Koester, *Introduction* 1:101-107; Radermacher, *Grammatik*, 1ff.; Rehkopf in *TRE* 14: 230f. The papyri and private inscriptions display non-literary Koine. Polybius and Epictetus use literary Koine, as do Hellenistic Jewish authors such as Philo, Josephus, etc. Atticism represents a counter movement of educated authors, but mainly restricted to literature (e.g., Dionysius of Halicarnassus, cf. A. Dihle, *Die griechische und lateinische Literatur der Kaiserzeit. Von Augustus bis Justinian*, 1989, 62-72). Atticizing tendencies in the New Testament may be regarded as corrections by later scribes, as the textual tradition indicates (cf. W. Michaelis, *ZNW* 22).

[12] Corresponding to the "numerous linguistic levels and distinctions" in secular Koine. Cf. Rehkopf in *TRE* 14:229.

[13] Deissmann in *RE* 7:639.

[14] Koester, *Introduction* 1:108, with examples.

[15] Some affinities to artistic Attic prose have even been claimed, cf. Koester 107.

[16] BDR/BDF §3.

[17] BDR/BDF §3.

[18] M. Reiser, *Syntax und Stil des Markusevangeliums im Licht der hellenistischen Volksliteratur*, WUNT II 11, 1984, citation 166. Cf. also Reiser's "Der Alexanderroman und das Markusevangelium," in *Markus-Philologie. Historische, literargeschichtliche und stilistische Untersuchungen*, ed. H. Cancik. WUNT 33 (1984): 131-163. For a different viewpoint cf. P. Dschulnigg, "Sprache, Redaktion und Intention des Markus-Evangelium und ihre Bedeutung für die Redaktionskritik," SBB 11 (²1986): 274-276. Dschulnigg attributes to the author of the second Gospel a style influenced by Semitic Greek, "mirroring contemporary popular language, close to the Greek of those without literary education" (275).

[19] Cf., e.g., H. Cremer, Biblisch-theologisches Wörterbuch der Neutestamentlichen Grazität, ed. J. Kögel, [10]1915, xx, "Christianity brought the conceptual world of Israel and its own new conceptual world to the Greeks, speaking to them in their own language and yet in a foreign tongue." Cf. also *xv-xviii* and *xix-xx*.

Bauer's lexical research, providing secular evidence to understand New Testament vocabulary on the basis of everyday Greek.[20]

The attempt to prove *Semitisms* (distinguishing Aramaisms and Hebraisms) in New Testament Greek[21] demands critical examination case by case. The argument for Semitisms in Acts must be seen as unpersuasive.[22] Here it is rather a matter of Acts reflecting the Septuagint, itself semitically influenced.[23] This same factor accounts for most of the other New Testament Semitisms.[24] But it still must be shown that any particular example should always be regarded as a Semitism.[25]

An early Aramaic text may sometimes underlie the Aramaisms. But the evidence is seldom unambiguous. While Jesus and the earliest community spoke Aramaic, the process of translation soon began. At an early date, already in the stage of oral tradition, it led to the transformation of the old Aramaic materials into Greek.

E.g., the attempt to find a mistranslation of Aramaic קְדִישָׁא in Matt 7:6a, which could be translated as either "the holy" or "the ring," is not very helpful.[26] The same is true of the hypothesis which finds a reference to the παῖς θεοῦ concept of Isaiah 53 in the double meaning of טַלְיָא (lamb, child/servant) in John 1: 29 and 36.[27] Likewise, valid objections have been raised[28] against the derivation of the tradition in 1 Cor 15:3b-5a from an earlier Aramaic examplar.[29]

---

[20] W. Bauer, "Introduction" *xix*, "The experience of how our advancing knowledge has freed one after another of these words from their isolation and demonstrated that they were part of the living language forces upon us the conclusion that the great mass of biblical words for which we do not yet have secular evidence also belong to that language." Cf. also *xxi-xxii*, and L. Radermacher, *Neutestamentliche Grammatik*, 19ff. It is regrettable that in the newer editions of Bauer's Lexicon revised by Kurt and Barbara Aland the goal of reducing the number of Semitisms to an indisputable minimum through citing secular Greek parallels has not really been pursued.

[21] On the history of this question, cf. G. Friedrich, *TDNT* 10:634-637 and 653-660.

[22] See below, section 5.2, pp. 188f.

[23] On Hebraisms in the Septuagint, cf. e.g., I. Soisalon-Soininen, "Zurück zur Hebraismenfrage," in *Studien zur Septuaginta--Robert Hanhart zu Ehren*, ed. D. Fraenkel, *et al*. Mitteilungen des Septuaginta Unternehmens 20 (1990), 35-51, esp. 38ff; by the same author *Die Infinitive in der Septuaginta*, Annales Academiae Scientiarum Fennicae, Series B 132, 1 (1965); A. Aejmelaeus, *Parataxis in the Septuagint. A Study of the Renderings of the Hebrew Coordinate Clauses in the Greek Pentateuch*, Annales Academiae Scientiarum Fennicae, Dissertationes humanarum litterarum 31 (1982); R. Sollamo, *Renderings of Hebrew Semiprepositions in the Septuagint*, Annales Academiae Scientiarum Fennicae, Dissertationes humanarum litterarum 19 (1979), esp. 298-301.

[24] On "Septuagintalisms," cf. F. Rehkopf, *TRE* 14: 223f.

[25] BDR/BDF §4.

[26] E.g., J. Jeremias, "Matthäus 7:6a" (first published in 1963), now in his *Abba. Studien zur neutestamentlichen Theologie und Zeitgeschichte* (1966), 83-90; G. Schwarz, "Matthäus vi 6a. Emendation und Rückübersetzung," *NT* 14 (1972): 18-25.

[27] As does J. Jeremias, "'Αμνὸς τοῦ θεοῦ - παῖς θεοῦ," *ZNW* 34 (1935): 115-123.

[28] E.g., H. Conzelmann, *Der erste Brief an die Korinther*, ($^{2(12)}$1981), 307-309 (English: *1 Corinthians*. Hermeneia (1975), 251-254).

[29] Cf. J. Jeremias, *Die Abendmahlsworte Jesu* ($^4$1967), 95-99; *The Eucharistic Words of Jesus* (1966), 101-105; "Artikelloses Χριστός. Zur Ursprache von 1 Cor

Hebraisms, which are seldom exactly distinguishable from Aramaisms, are usually the result of scriptural citations or allusions. It is therefore advisable to be cautious about appraising New Testament language as evidence for "Jewish Greek." We cannot share the assertion that "most New Testament authors (though not all) Hebraize in some manner, since Aramiac was their mother tongue,"[30] given its incorrect presupposition.

---

15,3b-5," *ZNW* 57 (1966): 211-215; and "Nochmals: Artikelloses Χριστός in 1 Cor 15,3," *ZNW* 60 (1969): 214-219; B. Klappert, "Zur Frage des semitischen oder griechischen Urtextes von 1 Kor XV.3-5," *NTS* 13 (1966/67): 168-173.

[30] As in L. Radermacher's unjustly neglected *Grammatik des neutestamentlichen Griechisch,* 29, which is especially concerned with the relationship of New Testament to secular Greek. Cf. also BDR/BDF §7.

# 3 Letters

*Literature*

Andresen, C. "Zum Formular frühchristlicher Gemeindebriefe," *ZNW* 56 (1965): 233-259. *L'apôtre Paul. Personnalité, style et conception du ministère*, by A Vanhoye, BETL 73 (1966). Becker, J. *Paulus. Der Apostel der Völker* (1989); *Paul: Apostle to the Gentiles* (1993). Berger, K. "Apostelbrief und apostolische Rede/Zum Formular frühchristlicher Briefe," *ZNW* 65 (1974): 190-231. Bultmann, R. "Briefliteratur, Urchristliche, formgeschichtlich," in *RGG²*, 1 (1927): 1254-1257. Conzelmann, H. *Der erste Brief an die Korinther.* Kritisch-exegetischer Kommentar 5 (²⁽¹²⁾1981); *I Corinthians.* Hermeneia (1975). Cugusi, P. *Evoluzione e forme dell'epistolografia latina. Nella tarda repubblica e nei primi due secoli dell'impero con cenni sull'epistolografia preciceroniana* (1983). Dahl, N.A. "Letter," in *IDBSup* (1976), 538-541. Deissmann, A. *Bibelstudien. Beiträge zumeist aus den Papyri und Inschriften, zur Geschichte der Sprache, des Schrifttums und der Religion des hellenistischen-Judentums und des Urchristentums* (1895); *Bible Studies: Contributions Chiefly from Papyri and Inscriptions to the History of the Language, the Literature, and the Religion of Hellenistic Judaism and Primitive Christianity* (1901); *Paulus. Eine kultur- und religionsgeschichtliche Skizze* (²1925); *Paul. A Study in Social and Religious History* (1926). Doty, W.G. "The Epistle in Late Hellenism and Early Christianity. Developments, Influences, and Literary Form." Ph.D. diss., U. of Wisconsin (1966); "The Classification of Epistolary Literature," *CBQ* 31 (1969): 183-199; *Letters in Primitive Christianity.* Guides to Biblical Scholarship: NT Series 1 (³1979). Exler, F.X.J. "The Form of the Ancient Greek Letter. A Study in Greek Epistolography," Ph.D. diss. Washington (1923). Fascher, E. "Briefliteratur, urchristliche, formgeschichtlich," in *RGG³* 1 (1957): 1412-1415. Fitzer, G. "Brief," in *BHH* 1 (1962): 272f. Hercher, R. *Epistolographi Graeci* (1873). Kim, C.H., *Form and Structure of the Familiar Greek Letter of Recommendation*, SBLDS 4 (1972). Kostenniemi, H. *Studien zur Idee und Phraseologie des griechischen Briefes bis 400 n. Christus,* Annales Academicae Scientiarum Fennicae, Series B, 102,2 (1956). Luke, G., "Brief und Epistel in der Antike," *Das Altertum* 7 (1961): 77-84. Peter, H., *Der Brief in der römischen Literatur. Literaturgeschichtliche Untersuchungen und Zussamenfassungen,* Allgemeines Gelehrten-Lexicon XX/3, (1901, reprint 1965). Rigaux, B. *Paulus und seine Briefe. Der Stand der Forschung.* Biblische Handbibliothek 2 (1964). Schmidt, P.L., "Epistolographie," in *Der kleine Pauly* 2 (1967): 324-327. Schneider, J., "Brief," in *RAC* 2 (1954): 564-585. Stowers, S.K., *Letter Writing in Greco-Roman Antiquity,* Library of Early Christianity 5 (1986). Strecker, G., "Paulus in nachpaulinischer Zeit," (first published in 1970), now in Strecker, *Eschaton und Historie. Aufsätze* (1979), 311-319. Sykutris, I., "Epistolographie," in PWSup 5 (1931): 185-220. Thraede, K., "Einheit—Gegenwart—Gespräch. Zur Christianisierung antiker Brieftopoi," Diss. theol., Bonn (1968); *Grundzüge griechisch-römischer Brieftopik,* Zetemata 48 (1970). Weiss, J. "Die paulinischen Briefe. Einleitung," in Schriften des Neuen Testaments 2

(³1917): 1-5. White, J.L. ed., *Studies in Ancient Letter Writings,* Semeia 22 (1982); "Saint Paul and the Apostolic Letter Tradition," *CBQ* 45 (1983): 433-444; "New Testament Epistolary Literature in the Framework of Ancient Epistolography," in *ANRW* II 25.2 (1984): 1730-1756; *Light from Ancient Letters,* FFNT (1986); "Ancient Greek Letters," in *Greco-Roman Literature and the New Testament: Selected Forms and Genres,* ed. David Aune, SBLSBS 21 (1988): 85-105.

# 3.1 The New Testament Data

## 3.1.1 A Survey of the New Testament Letters and their Authors[1]

Letters are the most common literary form in the New Testament and most varied in terms of breadth, content, and design. It is the oldest form[2] and is present in the latest strata of the New Testament, 2 Peter being probably its latest composition.

With respect to authorship, New Testament Letters fall into three classes.
1. Letters whose sender is an historical person from New Testament times: e.g. the Letters of Paul (1 Thessalonians, 1 and 2 Corinthians, Galatians, Romans, Philippians, Philemon[3]) and Letters of the Elder (2[4] and 3 John–these Letters are the oldest witnesses to a Johannine school).[5]

---

[1] On specific issues see the relevant introductions and commentaries.

[2] According to G. Lüdemann, the earliest writing found in the New Testament is 1 Thessalonians, independently of questions about the exact circumstances of its authorship. So he concludes (in *Paulus, der Heidenapostel, Bd. 1. Studien zur Chronologie,* FRLANT 123, 1980, 272) on the basis of his analysis of Gal 1:6-2:14. He regards 1 Thessalonians as written before the Apostolic Council of 41 CE. It lacks any mention of the Pauline collection, which we encounter in Paul from the time of 1 Cor 16:1ff. But the customary dating of the Letter to 49-52 CE, after the council, can appeal to the uncertainty of a mission in Greece before the council (e.g., cf. T. Holtz, *Der erste Brief an die Thessalonicher,* MeyerK 13, 1986, 21f.; "Die Bedeutung des Apostelkonzils für Paulus," *NT* 16 (1974): 110-148). J. Becker's idea that 1 Thessalonians is a "witness to Antiochene mission theology" (*Apostel* 138; *Apostle* 130f.) would be supported by a date close to Paul's time in Antioch. Yet we have little historical data on the relationship between the Antioch community and the Pauline mission. (On the so-called Antiochene source in Acts, cf. below, section 5.3.1.)

[3] In probable order of authorship, cf. G. Strecker, "New Testament," in Strecker and Johann Maier, *Neues Testament—Antikes Judentum,* Grundkurs Theologie 2, 1989, 77f.; on 2 Cor cf. below, section 3.1.2.

[4] 2 John is not a fictional Letter attributed to the elder; cf. H. Thyen "Johannesbriefe," in *TRE* 17 (1988): 186-200, 187; G. Strecker, *Die Johannesbriefe,* MeyerK 14 (1989) 313; *The Johannine Letters: A Commentary,* Hermeneia (1996), 217. Bultmann sees 2 John as a fictional Letter which utilizes both 1 and 3 John (*Die drei Johannesbriefe,* MeyerK 14, ²⁽⁸⁾1969, 103); cf. also G. Schunack, *Die Briefe des Johannes,* Zürcher Bibelkommentar, NT 17, 1982, 108f., etc.

[5] Strecker, *Johannesbriefe* 357.

2.  Pseudepigraphical Letters which stand in the tradition of a "school,"[6] and written in the name of the school's founder: 2 Thessalonians, Colossians, Ephesians, 1 and 2 Timothy, Titus; probably also 1 John, Hebrews, and Revelation. 1 John and Hebrews appeared first as anonymous works, transmitted wihout data as to their writers. Yet 1 John may be considered "pseudo-apostolic" in a further sense. It marks its author, who is somehow connected to the Johannine school, with the fictive claim of being an eyewitness to Jesus (cf. 1 John 1:1-4[7]). The author appears to regard this fiction as appropriate to strengthen the authority of his Letter and with it his position against Docetic opponents. Hebrews was numbered with the Pauline Letters on the basis of its (secondary) appendix, 13:(18) 22-25[8] (cf. 13:23, "Timothy"). The Apocalypse not only contains letters (the "seven" of 2:1-3:20), but itself has a weak literary framework.[9] "John" is a pseudonym, possibly added so that the work could be understood as an independent representative of the Johannine school (cf. 6:4).

3.  Pseudepigraphical Letters which address various communities or the whole church in the name of a famous personality: James 1 and 2 Peter, Jude.

Some of the Letters show a close literary dependence on others: e.g., Ephesians on Colossians; 2 Thessalonians on 1 Thessalonians; 2 Peter on Jude.[10]

Almost all New Testament Letters (excepting 3 John) are addressed to a (limited) public; not only to be read at worship (cf. 1 Thess 5:27), but to have a wider distribution (cf. 2 Cor 1:1 and Col 4:16).

## 3.1.2    The Literary Integrity of the Pauline Letters

*Literature*[11]

Aejmelaeus, L., *Streit und Versöhnung. Das Problem der Zusammensetzung des 2. Korintherbriefes,* Suomen Eksegeettisen Seuran julkaisuja 46 (1987). Aland, K., "Der Schluss und die ursprüngliche Gestalt des Römerbriefes," in his

---

[6] On the Pauline school see below, section 3.5; on the Johannine school, section 4.4.2.

[7] Cf. Strecker, *Johannesbriefe* 55ff.; *The Johannine Letters,* 8ff.

[8] For a different viewpoint, cf. H.W. Attridge, *The Epistle to the Hebrews,* ed. H. Koester. Hermeneia, 1989, 404-410.

[9] On the relationship of the framework and the genre of Revelation, see below, section 6.1.3.

[10] On the basis of his literary analysis, P. Vielhauer calls these Letters "fictional" in terms of both form (on James, see below, p. 49) and authorship. This last judgment is not often questioned in contemporary research, though time and again attempts are made to prove that James was written by Jesus' brother (e.g., M. Hengel, "Der Jakobusbrief als antipaulinische Polemik," in *Tradition and Interpretation in the New Testament. Festschrift for E.E. Ellis,* ed. G.F. Hawthorne *et al.,* 1987, 248-278, 252).

[11] On the literary-critical issues see also the various introductions to the New Testament, the commentaries, the relevant articles in *TRE,* and descriptions of the current status of research in *ANRW* II 25.4 (J.D.G. Dunn on Romans; G. Sellin on 1 Corinthians; G. Dautzenberg on 2 Corinthians; A. Suhl on Galatians; W. Schenk on Philippians; and W. Trilling on 1 and 2 Thessalonians).

*Neutestamentliche Entwürfe,* TBü 63 (1979), 284-301. Betz, H.D., "2 Cor 6:14-7:1: An Anti-Pauline Fragment?" *JBL* 92 (1973): 88-108. Bornkamm, G., "Die Vorgeschichte des sogenannten Zweiten Korintherbriefes" (first published in 1961), now in *Geschichte und Glaube II. Gesammelte Aufsätze IV,* BEvT 53 (1971), 162-194; "Der Philipperbrief als paulinische Briefsammlung" (first published in 1962), in BEvT 53 (1971), 195-205. Borse, U., *Der Standort des Galaterbriefes,* BBB41 (1972). Bultmann, R. "Glossen im Römerbrief" (first published in 1947), now in his *Exegetica. Aufsätze zur Erforschung des Neuen Testaments,* ed. E. Dinkler (1967), 278-284; "Exegetische Probleme des 2. Korintherbriefes," (first published in 1947), in *Exegetica* 298-322. Clemen, C. *Die Einheitlichkeit der paulinischen Briefe an der Hand der bisher mit bezug auf die aufgestellten Interpolations- und Compilationshypothesen* (1894). Eckart, H.-G., "Der zweite echte Brief des Apostels Paulus an die Thessalonicher," *ZTK* 58 (1961): 30-44. Elliot, J.K., "The Language and Style of the Concluding Doxology of the Epistle to the Romans," ZNW 72 (1981): 124-130. Friedrich, G., "1. Thessalonicher 5,1-11, der apologetische Einschub eines Späteren" (first published in 1973), now in his *Auf das Wort kommt es an. Gesammelte Aufsätze. Zum 70. Geburtstag,* ed. J.H. Friedrich (1978), 251-278. Garland, D.E., "The Composition and Unity of Philippians: Some Neglected Literary Factors," *NovT* 27 (1985): 141-173. Hausrath, A., Der Vier-Capitelbrief des Paulus an die Korinther (1870). Horn, F.W., "1 Korinther 15,56—ein exegetischer Stachel," *ZNW* 82 (1991): 88-105. Hübner, H. "Glossen in Epheser 2," in *Vom Urchristentum zu Jesus.* Festschrift J. Gnilka, ed. H. Frankemölle, *et al.,* (1989), 392-406. Kümmel, W.G., "Das literarische und geschichtliche Problem des ersten Thessalonicherbriefes," in his *Heilsgeschehen und Geschichte. Gesammelte Aufsätze 1933-1964,* ed. E. Grässer, et al. Münchener theologischer Studien 3 (1965): 406-416. Lambrecht, J. , "The Fragment 2 Cor VI 14 - VII 1. A Plea for its Authenticity," in *Miscellanea Neotestamentica,* vol. 2, ed T. Baarda *et al.,* NovTSup 48 (1978): 143-161. Mengel, B. *Studien zum Philipperbrief. Untersuchungen zum situativen Kontext unter besonderer Berücksichtigung der Frage nach der Ganzheitlichkeit oder Einheitlichkeit eines paulinischen Briefes,* WUNT II 8 (1982). Merklein, H., "Die Einheitlichkeit des ersten Korintherbriefes, " in his *Studien zu Jesus und Paulus,* WUNT 43 (1987), 345-375. Murphy-O'Connor, J. "Interpolations in I Corinthians," *CBQ* 48 (1986): 81-94. Ollrog, W.-H., "Die Abfassungsverhältnisse von Römer 16," in *Kirche.* Festschrift G. Bornkamm, ed. D. Lührmann, et al., (1980), 221-244. Pearson, B.A. "I Thessalonians 2:13-16: A Deutero-Pauline Interpolation," *HTR* 64 (1971): 79-94. Schenk, W. "Korintherbriefe," in *TRE* 19 (1990): 620-640. Schmidt, D., "I Thess 2:13-16: Linguistic Evidence for an Interpolation," *JBL* 102 (1983): 269-279. Schmithals, W., *Der Römerbrief als historisches Problem,* SNT 9 (1975). Schnelle, U. "1 Kor 6,14: Eine nachpaulinische Glosse," *NovT* 25 (1983): 217-219. Stowers, S.Kl, *"Peri men gar* and the Integrity of 2 Cor. 8 and 9," *NovT* 32 (1990): 340-348. Thrall, M.El, "The Problem of II Cor. VI. 14 —VII. 1 in some recent Discussion," *NTS* 24 (1978): 132-148. Weiss, J. *Der erste Korintherbrief,* MeyerK 5 (⁹1910, reprint 1977).

It is the object of literary criticism to discover if the current form of the Pauline Letters is their original form. Glosses have been supposed and are probable, although nineteenth century Netherlands conjectural criticism[12] went beyond responsible limits.[13]    Interpolations,[14] i.e., intentional additions to the text, are also to be expected. For example, 2 Cor 6:14-7:1 is apparently a secondary and non-Pauline insertion into the text directed against "unbelievers."[15] It has been suggested that 1 Cor 14:33b-36 should be removed from the Pauline Letter corpus on grounds it is an interpolation,[16] but without persuasive detailed evidence. The same is true for 1 Thess 2:(13-)15f.[17] and 5:1-11.[18]   Appendices are also secondary, subsequently added to the body of the Letter. Thus the concluding doxology of Romans (16:25-27) occurs in various places in different textual traditions: after 14:23, 15:33, or 16:23[24]; after both 14:23 and 15:33; or in some cases not at all.[19]   The case of Rom 16:1-23 (24) is different.    Pauline authorship is

---

[12] Cf. C. Clemen's overview and critical evaluation of nineteenth century interpolation hypotheses on the Pauline and Deuteropauline Letters.

[13] Yet, on Romans cf. R. Bultmann, Glossen, 278f.   Bultmann interprets 7:25b and 8:1 as "secondary glosses" and has had a lasting influence on subsequent exegesis. For additional material on glosses in contemporary research, cf. Bultmann, Glossen, 280ff. on Romans 2:1; 2:16; 6:17f.; 10:17; 13:5; and W. Schmithals in SNT 9, 202-209 on 1 and 2 Corinthians; cf. also W. Schenk in *TRE* 19:621f.; J. Murphy-O'Connor in CBQ 48:81-94; on 1 Cor 6:14, U. Schnelle in *NovT* 25:217; on 1 Cor 15:56, F.W. Horn in ZNW 82:88-105; on Phil 1:1c, W. Schenk, *Der Philipperbrief des Paulus. Kommentar,* 1984, 78-82 and 334; on Ephesians 2, Hübner in the Gnilka Festschrift, etc.

[14] Interpolations are found not only in the New Testament Letters.   The Gospels display the same sort of additions. Cf. e.g., Matt 13:14-15, a citation of the LXX agreeing with Acts 28:26-27, but which ought to be attributed to neither a pre-Matthean collection of testimonia nor to the Evangelist himself, as the introductory formula for the citation indicates.

[15] Cf. R. Bultmann, Exegetische Probleme, 307, n. 17 and H.D. Betz in JBL 92:88-108.   Betz sees this un-Pauline paraenesis intended for Jewish Christians as an anti-Pauline polemic the *Sitz im Leben* of which he identifies with the Antiochene incident described in Gal 2:11-14.   Cf. also his comments in "Korintherbriefe," EKL³ 2 (1989): 1452.   On the side of genuineness, cf. J. Lambrecht in NovTSup 48. For a survey of the discussion, cf. M.E. Thrall in *NTS* 24:132-148.

[16] As by Conzelmann, MeyerK 5 ²(12)1981, 298f.

[17] E.g., B.A. Pearson and D. Schmidt.   W.G. Kümmel lists older literature and refers to further interpolations in 1 Thessalonians in his *Problem des ersten Thessalonicherbriefes* 407 n. 5.   See also references and evaluation in T. Holz, MeyerK 13 (3 n. 2) 25-29 and in G. Lüdemann, *Paulus und das Judentum* (1983), 25-27.

[18] Cf. G. Friedrich, "1. Thessalonicher 5,1-11, der apologetische Einschub eines Späteren." Against this viewpoint, cf. A Lindemann, *Paulus im ältesten Christentum. Das Bild des Apostels und die Rezeption der paulinischen Theologie in der frühchristlichen Literatur bis Marcion,* BHT 58 (1979), 29f.

[19] Cf. W.G. Kümmel, *Einleitung in das Neue Testament* (²¹1983), 275-277; *Introduction to the New Testament* (²1975), 315-317; U. Wilckens, *Der Brief an die Römer,* MeyerK 6.1, (²1987), 22-24; K. Aland, "Glosse, Interpolation, Redaktion und Komposition in der Sicht der neutestamentlichen Textkritik" in his *Studien zur Überlieferung des Neuen Testaments und seines Textes,* ANTF 2 (1967), 46-48; cf. also his *Neutestamentliche Entwürfe,* TBü 63 (1979), 287-289 (a different survey of the

generally no longer doubted. Its place in the text of Romans is almost undisputed.[20] Yet it does not seem to fit its current context. It is surprising that Paul would greet so many people in a church he had never visited, and their names are doubtful for the Roman church.

Accordingly the whole chapter is often explained as accompanying a copy of the Roman Letter sent to Ephesus.[21] Yet the chapter is not a unity. Only 16:1-2 touch expressly on the commendation of our "sister Phoebe" of Cenchrea. The list of those greeted (16:3-16) contains names that to some extent point to Ephesus (esp. 16:3, "Prisca and Aquila;" and 16:5, "Epaenetos, who was the first convert in Asia"). The list of Paul's co-workers who send their greetings (16:21-23) could imply Corinth as the place of authorship (cf. 1 Cor 1:14, "Gaius") and thus would fit a letter to Rome. Yet the polemic of 16:17-20 lacks any connection with its context, and is surprising in a letter to a church which Paul had never visited.

Even though recent research is more inclined to regard Romans 16 as an original part of the Letter,[22] the chapter's lack of unity and its tension with the situation and context of the Letter's authorship should not be dismissed in favor of its originality.

The so-called "Comma Johanneum" in 1 John 5:7-8, found almost exclusively in Latin texts,[23] is a later dogmatic addition. It was taken up in the official Catholic edition of the Vulgate text, the (Sixto-) Clementine of 1592, with the in the following wording (in italics):

[7]　　Quoniam tres sunt, qui testimonium dant
*in caelo: Pater, Verbum, et Spiritus Sanctus*
*et hi tres unum sunt*
[8]　　*Et tres sunt, qui testimonium dant in terra*
Spiritus et aqua et sanguis,
et he tres unum sunt.

---

textual data). On problems of tradition-history cf. E. Kamlah, "Traditionsgeschichtliche Untersuchung zur Schlussdoxologie des Römerbriefs" (theological dissertation, Tübingen, 1955).

[20] Except, e.g., for Marcion, whose edition of Romans comprised 1:1-14:23.

[21] P. Vielhauer, *Geschichte der urchristlichen Literatur*, 188-190. Further bibliography in W.H. Ollrog, "Die Abfassungsverhältnisse von Römer 16," in the Bornkamm Festschrift, 223 nn. 12ff. In SNT 9 (1975), 128, W. Schmithals emphasizes that the passage is an independent letter.

[22] E.g., U. Schnelle, *Gerechtigkeit und Christusgegenwart. Vorpaulinische und paulinische Tauftheologie*, GTA 24 ([2]1986), 65; P. Stuhlmacher, *Der Brief an die Römer*, NTD 6 ([1(14)]1989), 215f.; J. Becker, *Paulus. Der Apostel der Völker* (1989), 359f.; *Paul: Apostle to the Gentiles* (1993), 340f.; Ollrog, "Abfassungsverhältnisse," 230-234 (who excludes the polemic against false teaching as an interpolation).

[23] It is also found in eight Greek miniscules, none of which date from before 1400 CE. On the textual evidence and historical effects of the passage, cf. the excursus "Die Textüberlieferung des 'Comma Johanneum'" in G. Strecker, *Die Johannesbriefe*, 279-283; *The Johannine Letters*, 188-191, including bibliography. Cf. also J.J. Klauck, *Die Johannesbriefe*, ErFor 276 (1991), 11-13.

Erasmus and the reformers already opposed this passage, and its secondary character has been regarded as proved within Protestantism since the time of J.S. Semler.[24]

The inner unity of the Letters has also been called into question.[25] It is commonly thought that 2 Corinthians is a collection of Letters,[26] but there is no general agreement on the number of fragments involved or on their historical place within the Corinthian correspondence.[27]

From the reports in Paul's extant Letters to Corinth and the rifts and abrupt transitions of 2 Corinthians itself we may reconstruct the following sequence of events:

> *Letter A* (cf. 1 Cor 5:9f.) is not extant.  It included instructions for the community.
> The sending of Timothy (1 Cor 4:17; 16:10) in connection with changes to the travel plans communicated in Letter A.  The new plans aimed at maintaining closer contact with the Corinthian community.
> *Letter B* = 1 Cor 1:1-16:24.
> Paul's second visit ἐν λύπῃ (2 Cor 2:1-11; 7:12; 10:1, 10).
> *Letter C* = 2 Cor 10-13: the "letter of tears"[28] which is not completely extant.[29]

---

[24] This insight could not be realized in Catholicism before our century, since previously such questioning was forbidden by official restrictions.  In 1927 the Holy Office allowed discussion of such issues.

[25] Cf. K. Aland's remarks, made on the basis of text criticism, against extensive literary critical hypotheses and dividing up the Letter into separate documents, in his "Glosse, Interpolation, Redaktion und Komposition in der Sicht der neutestamentlichen Textkritik" in *Studien zur Überlieferung des Neuen Testaments und seines Textes,* ANTF 2 (1967), 35ff. Yet textual history is not absolutely dependable as an argument, since alterations to the text might have been made in the earliest period, before a work was widely distributed.  John 21, with its unified manuscript tradition, but which on grounds of content is regarded as secondary, shows the limitations of text critical arguments.

[26] But cf. W.G. Kümmel, *Einleitung,* 252ff; *Introduction,* 288ff.; C. Wolff, *Der zweite Brief an die Korinther,* HTKNT 8 (1989), 2f. U Borse, *Der Standort des Galaterbriefes,* BBB41 (1972), 6f., 114-119, accepts a longer period of time between the authorship of 2 Cor 1-9 and 10-13. Against Borse, U. Schnelle, *Gerechtigkeit und Christusgegenwart. Vorpaulinische und paulinische Tauftheologie,* GTA 24 (²1986), 35-37, places the writing of Galatians not between 2 Cor 1-9 and 10-13, but immediately before the writing of Romans (cf. also 53f.).

[27] On various hypotheses partitioning 2 Corinthians, cf. L. Aejmelaeus, *Streit und Versöhnung. Das Problem der Zusammensetzung des 2. Korintherbriefes,* Suomen Eksegeettisen Seuran julkaisuja 46 (1987).  H.D. Betz's commentary *2 Corinthians 8 and 9,* Hermeneia (1985) takes into account the Letter's lack of unity through partitioning the commentary.  (On this cf. S.K. Stowers review in JBL 106 (1987): 727-730, esp. 727f.)  Cf. also Bultmann's commentary on 2 Corinthians, *Der zweite Brief an die Korinther,* ed. E. Dinkler, MeyerK Sonderband (1976, ²1988), likewise structured with the help of partition hypotheses. Cf. further, V.P. Furnish, *II Corinthians,* AB 32A, (²1985).

[28] Already postulated by H. Hausrath in 1870.  Cf. also F. Lang, *Die Brief an die Korinther,* NTD 7 (1(16)1986), 13f., 326; F. Watson, "2 Cor. x-xiii and Paul's Painful Letter to the Corinthians," *JTS* NS35 (1984): 324-346; etc.  For older research cf. H. Windisch, Die zweite Korintherbrief, MeyerK 6, ed. G. Strecker (reprint 1970=1924),

Announcement of a third visit (2 Cor 12:14; 13:1).
*Letter D* = 2 Cor 1:1-7:16; 8; 9(?):[30] the conciliatory letter.

We do not have the same degree of unanimity with respect to arranging the various fragments of other Pauline Letters as we have for 2 Corinthians. Controversy surrounds both the issue of their integrity as well as the quantity and content of the alleged fragments. W. Schmithals has attempted to reconstruct a number of original letters on the basis of abrupt literary transitions.[31] Yet the generally complex interweaving and numerous strata of the reconstructed fragments strain his hypothesis. Moreover, literary-critical criteria of differences in vocabulary and content between sources and their reworking apply only in a limited manner here. The various letters all presuppose Paul as their author, and it cannot be shown from their language that any redactor has edited them. This applies in essentials also to other partition hypotheses popular among researchers; to 1 Corinthians,[32] going back mainly to the observations of J. Weiss,[33] to 1 Thessalonians,[34] and to Philippians.[35]

---

12f.   Windisch claims that 2 Cor 10-13 represents a later stage of the Corinthian correspondence (16-18).

[29] It lacks not only a prescript introducing the context but also concrete data and discussion (e.g., a demand for discipline of those in the wrong).

[30] S.K. Stowers stresses the immediate connection of 2 Cor 8:24 and 9:1-4 (in *NovT* 32: 346: "9:1-4 provides a warrant and explanation for the exhortation in 8:24"). Yet chapter 9 is more likely a doublette of chapter 8, written to accompany those gathering up the collection in Achaia. It is possible that it was originally enclosed as an appendix to, or was also a later addition to, chapter 8.

[31] Cf. the TRE articles as well as the commentaries on the individual Letters; e.g., W. Schmithals, *Der Römerbrief. Ein Kommentar* (1988). Note the critique by H. Hübner, *Das Gesetz bei Paulus. Ein Beitrag zum Werden der paulinischen Theologie*, FRLANT 119 (²1980), 58-60; and U. Wilckens, *Der Brief an die Römer*, MeyerK 6.1, (²1987), 28f.

[32] J. Weiss, MeyerK 5⁹, xl-xlii.

[33] Cf. the survey and critique by H. Merklein, "Einheitlichkeit," 348ff., and W.G. Kümmel, *Einleitung*, 238-241; *Introduction*, 276-278. W. Schenk renews the plea for the Letter's lack of unity in *TRE* 19.

[34] K.-G. Eckart, who is decisively opposed by W.G. Kümmel, "Problem des ersten Thessalonicherbriefs," and others.

[35] E.g., cf. G. Bornkamm, "Philipperbrief," 195ff; W. Schenk on Philippians in *ANRW* II 25.4. For the opposite view cf. D.E. Garland in NovT 27: 141-173, who fully cites the literature and gives a tabular presentation of partition hypotheses of Philippians (155). Cf. also B. Mengel, Philipperbrief, 314-316 and D.F. Watson, "A Rhetorical Analysis of Philippians and its Implications for the Unity Question," *NovT* 30 (1988): 57-88.

## 3.2    Letters as a Literary Genre in Ancient Letter Writing and Contemporary Research

### 3.2.1 The Literary Character of New Testament Letters

*Literature*

Baasland, E., "Literarische Form, Thematik und geschichtliche Einordnung des Jakobusbriefes," in *ANRW* II 25.5 (1988), 3646-3684. Bornkamm, G. "Der Römerbrief as Testament des Paulus," in his Geschichte und Glaube II, Gesammelte Aufsätze IV, BEvT 53 (1971), 120-139. Bultmann, R., "Die kirchliche Redaktion des ersten Johannesbriefes" (first published in 1951), in *Exegetica. Aufsätze zur Erforschung des Neuen Testaments*, ed. E. Dinkler (1967), 381-393. Burggaller, E., "Das literarische Problem des Hebräerbriefes," *ZNW* 9 (1908): 110-131. Cross, F.L., *I Peter: A Paschal Liturgy* (²1957). Feld, H. "Der Hebräerbrief," in *ANRW* ii 25.4 (1987), 3522-3601. Filson, F.V., *"Yesterday:" A Study in Hebrews in the Light of Chapter 13*, SBT 2.4 (1967). Frances, F.O., "The Form and Function of the Opening and Closing Paragraphs of James and I John," *ZNW* 61 (1970): 110-126. Hengel, M., *The Johannine Question* (1990). Klauck, H.-J. *Die Johannesbriefe*, ErFor 276 (1991). Perdelwitz, R., "Das literarische Problem des Hebräerbriefes," *ZNW* 11 (1910): 59-78, 105-123; *Die Mysterienreligion und das Problem des I Petrusbriefes. Ein literarischer und religionsgeschichtlicher Versuch*, Religionsgeschichtliches Versuche und Vorarbeiten XI.3 (1911). Slot, W.L., *De letterkundige vorm van den Brief aan de Hebreër* (1912). Swetman, J., "On the Literary Genre of the 'Epistle' to the Hebrews," *NovT* 11 (1969): 261-269. Trilling, W., *Untersuchungen zum 2. Thessalonicherbrief*, ETS 27. Übelacker, W.G., *Der Hebräerbrief als Appell. I. Untersuchungen zu* exordium, narratio *und* postscriptum *(Hebr 1-2 und 13:22-25)*, ConBNT Series 21 (1989). Vouga, F. "La réception de la théologie johannique dans les épîtres," in *La communauté johannique et son histoire. La trajectoire de l'évangile de Jean aux deux premiers siècles*, by J.-D. Kaestli/J.-M. Poffet/ J. Zumstein, Le monde de la bible (1990), 283-302. Wolter, M., *Die Pastoralbriefe als Paulustradition*, FRLANT 146 (1988). Wrede, W. *Das literarische Rätsel des Hebräerbriefs*, FRLANT 8 (1906).

Deissmann[36] distinguished between genuine letters (which were without literary value or pretensions;[37] and therefore 'occasional' correspondence "sent from one or more authors to a certain person or group [e.g., a community]; intended only for these and not for publication...as it were a halved 'conversation' which can be understood only when we know the reader's situation..."[38]) and artistic letters, for

---

[36] *Licht vom Osten* (⁴1923),193-198; *Light from the Ancient East* (1927), 227-233.
[37] Cf. also his *Bibelstudien* (1895), 187-252; *Bible Studies* (1901), 1-59.
[38] R. Bultmann, "Briefliteratur," in *RGG²* 1 (1927): 1254-1257. Cf. also Deissmann, *Paulus. Eine kultur- und religionsgeschichtliche Skizze* (²1925), 8-10; *Paul. A Study in Social and Religious History* (1926), 7-11; G. Luck, "Brief und Epistel in der Antike,"

which Deissmann utilized the expression 'epistle.' But against such a clear distinction stands the variety found within the letter form. Genuine letters show themselves as living beings. Using rhetorical devices, which ancient letters commonly display (cf. 3.2.3), they sometimes deal with general concerns transcending their immediate situation.[39]

According to objective and audience, they may be characterized more as letters (the majority[40]) or as homilies and tractates.

*a. Homilies*

1 John.

R. Rothe suggests that several factors point to letter form despite the lack of letter framework: the "visualization of specific readers and their situation, the not infrequent address in genuine letter style together with the dominant use of the second person plural, and finally the loose connection of thought: a presentation which suggests, sets forth, and repeats itself."[41] But such a style more likely intimates preaching.[42] F.O. Francis has renewed the effort to support 1 John and also James as having the form of letters. He attempts to prove this with the assistance of the form "secondary letters . . . which for one reason or another lack situational immediacy."[43] K. Berger likewise ponders the compatibility of 1 John 1:1ff. with the introductions to other New Testament Letters.[44] But we cannot overlook the fact that the most important formal characteristics of a letter such as

---

*Das Altertum* 7 (1961): 77-84; J. Weiss, "Die paulinischen Briefe. Einleitung," in *Schriften des Neuen Testaments* 2 (³1917): 1f.

[39] As already in Bultmann, "Briefliteratur," 1255; cf. also N.A. Dahl, "Letter," in *IDBSup*, 540; W.G. Doty, "The Classification of Epistolary Literature," *CBQ* 31 (1969): 183-199; Koskenniemi, H. *Studien zur Idee und Phraseologie des griechischen Briefes bis 400 n. Christus*, Annales Academicae Scientiarum Fennicae, Series B, 102,2, (1956), 88-91; S.K. Stowers, *Letter Writing in Greco-Roman Antiquity*, Library of Early Christianity 5 (1986): 19f.; I. Sykutris, "Epistolographie," in PWSup 5 (1931): 187; P.L. Schmidt, "Epistolographie," in *Der kleine Pauly* 2 (1967): 325f.

[40] On the problem of classifying actual letters in ancient epistolography, cf. below, section 3.2.3.3.

[41] R. Rothe, *Der erste Brief Johannis praktisch erklärt*, ed. K Mühlhäusser (1978), 1f.

[42] H.-J. Klauck gives a historical survey of the questioning of 1 John as a Letter in *Die Johannesbriefe*, ErFor 276 (1991), 69.

[43] *ZNW* 61 (1970): 111.

[44] "Apostelbrief und apostolische Rede/Zum Formular frühchristlicher Briefe," *ZNW* 65 (1974): 203, n. 59; cf. also 218. On the letter form cf. also F. Vouga, *Die Johannisbriefe*, HNT 15/III (1990); M. Hengel, *The Johannine Question* (1990), 47f. (which sees 1 John as an "admonitory circular to different house communities); G. Schnauk, *Die Brief des Johannes*, Zürcher Bibelkommentar, NT 17 (1982), 8-11 (examining the communication in its specific situation, calls it "letter-like"); H.-J. Klauck, *Johannesbriefe*, 70-74 (the prescript and conclusion of the Letter are sacrificed to imitation of the prologue and original conclusion to the Fourth Gospel); according to Klauck, 74, the "paraenetic Letters" represent the closest analogy to ancient epistolography.

prescript, proem, and concluding greeting are missing. Despite the direct address to the reader, 1 John lacks the necessary information about the sender and the addressees conventional in ancient letters.[45] R. Bultmann regarded 1 John 5:13 as an imitation letter postscript.[46] But this viewpoint is unacceptable, since elements of a typical letter conclusion such as greetings and a blessing are missing.

On the other hand, characterizing 1 John as a "tractate"[47] or a "instructional handbook"[48] does not do justice to the situation of direct address which is presupposed. The style of 1 John, which is very difficult for research to associate with the arrangement of this writing, makes its characterization as preaching more likely, and goes back to the connection between letter and sermon.[49] Thus 1 John may be considered a "homily in letter form" or just a homily.[50]

### Hebrews

The literary classification of Hebrews depends on the evaluation of 13:18-25 or 13:22-25. The interpretation of Hebrews as a genuine letter, as was widely presupposed at the end of the nineteenth century,[51] was based on this passage understood formally as letter conclusion. Because it betrayed no concrete setting, A. Deissmann understood Hebrews as a "document of Christian literary art;" and on the grounds of its conclusion in 13:22-25 (= "ornament") as an artistic letter (= an epistle).[52] H. Braun regards Hebrews as both a letter and a homily.[53] But classifying Hebrews as a homily[54] or tractate[55] is more appropriate formal

---

[45] On the sources and redaction of 1 John, cf. below, section 4.4.1.1.

[46] In MeyerK 2(8)14: 3, n. 4; cf. also his "Die kirchliche Redaktion des ersten Johannesbriefes" 382.

[47] M. Dibelius, *Geschichte der urchristlichen Literatur*, TBü 58 (1975), 136; P. Vielhauer, *Geschichte*, 462; H. Windisch/H. Preisker, Die katholischen Briefe, HNT 15, ³1951, 107.

[48] K. Grayston, *The Johannine Epistles*, NCB (1984), 4.

[49] The objection of M Hengel, *The Johannine Question* (1990), 46 and H.-J. Klauck, *Die Johannesbriefe* (1991), 70, that the expression "ταῦτα γράφομεν ἡμεῖς" (1 John 1:4, cf. also 2:7, 8, 12, etc.) speaks against the genre "homily" is not persuasive. Rather the expression results fromt he fact that the homily is communicated through a literary medium. Hengel opposes his own position when he writes that the work "was written to be read, *like a sermon*, in the services of the communites" (48, author's emphasis).

[50] As in G. Strecker, *Die Johannesbriefe*, 49, *The Johannine Letters*, 3; and "Johannesbriefe," in *EKL³* 2 (1989): 838. E. Lohmeyer also classified 1 John as a homily in his "Über Aufbau und Gliederung des ersten Johannesbriefes," *ZNW* 27 (1928): 258. D.E. Aune calls it a "deliberative homily" (*The New Testament in its Literary Environment* (1987), 218; and C.H. Dodd an "informal tract or homily" in *The Johannine Epistles*, MNTC (³1953), xxi.

[51] So still E. Riggenbach, *Der Brief an die Hebräer*, Kommentar zum Neuen Testament 14 (2.31922), XII-XVII; now with reference to F.V. Filson, who considers Hebrews a community Letter, cf. H Feld in *ANRW* ii 25.4 (1987), 3540.

[52] *Licht vom Osten*, 207; *Light from the Ancient East*, 243f.

[53] H. Braun, *An die Hebräer*, HNT 14 (1984), 1f.

[54] E.g., E. Burggaller, "Das literarische Problem des Hebräerbriefes," *ZNW* 9 (1908): 110-131, esp. 123-130; H Thyen, *Der Stil der Jüdisch-Hellenistischen Homilie*,

definition. Classifying it as an "appeal"[56] fails to take seriously the obvious theoretical character of the work, but characterizing it as a tractate would. Theoretical reflection is presented through typological and allegorical interpretation of the Hebrew Scriptures. Along with early Christian tradition, this use of scripture is doubtlessly an essential factor in the formation of Hebrews. Accordingly, F. Schröger calls the author of Hebrews an interpreter of the Hebrew Scriptures.[57] But Hebrews cannot be explained satisfactorily in terms of form as "interpretation of scripture."[58] The literary character and personal address of the writing (cf. Hebrews 3:12; 5:11f.; 6:9;[59] etc.) as well as the primacy of speaking over writing style[60] strengthens Hebrews' sermonic character. As a homiletic strategy, the interchange between dogmatic and paraenetic passages emphasized by A. Vanhoye[61] and I. Goldhahn-Müller[62] can be understood as a structural characteristic of Hebrews.[63]

---

FRLANT 65 (1955), 16f.; J. Swetnam, "On the Literary Genre of the 'Epistle' to the Hebrews," *NovT* 11 (1969): 261-269; A. Vanhoye, "Hebräerbrief," in *TRE* 14 (1955): 494-505, 498; D.E. Aune, *Literary Environment,* 212-214 (Hebrews is a "hortatory sermon"); W.L. Slot, *De letterkundige vorm van den Brief aan de Hebreër* (1912); similarly already W. Wrede in *Das literarische Rätsel des Hebräerbriefs,* FRLANT 8 (1906), 73 who calls it "a combination of treatise and sermon." G.W. Buchanan's description as "homiletical midrash based on Ps 110" (*To the Hebrews,* AB 36 (1972), XIX, can only be regarded as a constriction. While Ps 110 is significant throughout Hebrews, it is not the only text underlying Hebrews.

[55] H. Conzelmann/A. Lindemann, *Arbeitsbuch zum Neuen Testament,* Uni-Taschenbücher 52 ([9]1988), 325, calls it "a tractate or written preaching."

[56] W.G. Übelacker, *Der Hebräerbrief als Appell. I. Untersuchungen zu* exordium, narratio *und* postscriptum *(Hebr 1-2 und 13:22-25),* ConBNT Series 21 (1989).

[57] F. Schröger, *Der Verfasser des Hebräerbriefes als Schriftausleger,* Biblische Untersuchungen 8 (1968).

[58] H. Zimmermann, *Das Bekenntnis der Hoffnung. Tradition und Redaktion im Hebräerbrief,* BBB 47 (1977), 8f.

[59] Note the distinction between the "we" of the author and the ἀγαπητοί who are addressed.

[60] E. Grässer, *An die Hebräer,* EKKNT XVII/1 (1990), 16. R. Perdelwitz, "Das literarische Problem des Hebräerbriefes," *ZNW* 11 (1910): 59-78, 105-123, calls Hebrews a "speech." H. von Soden, *Hebräerbrief, Briefe des Petrus, Jakobus, Judas* ([3]1899), 6f., terms it a "written lecture" constructed by the rules of Greek rhetoric.

[61] *La structure littéraire de l'Epître aux Hébreux,* StudNeot 1 ([2]1976); "Discussions sur la structure de l'Epître aux Hebreux," *Bib* 55 (1974): 349-380; "Literarische Struktur und theologische Botschaft des Hebräerbriefs," *Studien zum Neuen Testament und seiner Umwelt, Series A* 4 (1979): 119-147; 5 (1980): 18-49.

[62] *Die Grenze der Gemeinde. Studien zum Problem der Zweiten Busse im Neuen Testament unter Berücksichtigung der Entwicklung im 2. Jahrhundert bis Tertullian,* GTA 39 (1989), 78, n. 175.

[63] 1 John is also organized on the basis of alternating theological teaching and moral exhortation. cf. T. Häring, *Die Johannesbriefe* (1927), 9; G. Strecker, *Die Johannesbriefe,* 30f.; *The Johannine Letters,* xlii-xliv; "Johannesbriefe," in *EKL[3]* 2 (1989): 838.

1 Peter

We grant homiletical features to 1 Peter if, with R. Perdelwitz , we identify 1 Pet 1:3-4:11 as an "ancient Christian casual address," carried further in 1:1-2 and 4:12-5:14 as "written comfort and exhortation."[64]

Understanding 1 Peter from the perspective of worship has been carried through in different ways. It cannot be proved a baptismal service[65] nor a Passover and baptismal ritual.[66] Such speculations indicate redaction-critical problems. Yet the work displays no comprehensive unity. The author uses "extensive traditional materials of paraenetic, and probably also of homiletical and liturgical, character."[67] Thus we should think of individual bits of tradition, e.g., as in the hymnic passages (1:18-21; 3:18-22: cf. 3.3.3) or the socio-ethical instructions (2:13-3:7; cf. 3.4).

Considering the prescript, postscript and general character, 1 Peter may be considered an "encyclical letter."[68] But it is still questionable whether this is a genuine[69] or fictive[70] letter. This depends primarily on our reconstruction of the letter's situation. In the case of a broadly circulated work, there may be little distinction between the two possibilities.

*b. Tractates*

Ephesians

While the deutero-Pauline Colossians and 2 Thessalonians[71] take over the literary conventions of the genuine Pauline Letter style, Ephesians (dependent on Colossians, cf. 3.1.1) displays greater distance from the genuine Pauline Letters. Removing the secondary "in Ephesus" of 1:1, one could regard this as a "Catholic

---

[64] R. Perdelwitz, *Die Mysterienreligion und das Problem des I Petrusbriefes. Ein literarischer und religionsgeschichtlicher Versuch,* Religionsgeschichtliche Versuche und Vorarbeiten XI.3 (1911), 19, 16. Cf. also P. Vielhauer, *Geschichte,* 585.

[65] H. Windisch/H. Preisker. F.L. Cross considers it a baptismal liturgy with a bishop as celebrant.

[66] A. Strobel, "Zum Verständnis von Mt XXV 1-13," *NovT* 2 (1958): 199-227, 221, n.1.

[67] N. Brox, *Der erste Petrusbrief,* EKKNT 21 ($^3$1989), 23.

[68] D.E. Aune, *The New Testament in its Literary Environment* (1987), 221f.; H. Frankenmölle, *1. Petrusbrief, 2. Petrusbrief, Judasbrief,* Neue Echter Bibel. Kommentar zum NT 18, 20 (1987), 11; N. Brox, *Der erste Petrusbrief,* 23; L. Goppelt, *Der erste Petrusbrief,* ed. F. Hahn, MeyerK 12/1 ($^{1(8)}$1978), 45; F.-R. Prostmeier, *Handlungsmodelle im ersten Petrusbrief,* Forschungen zur Bibel 63 (1990), 120 (who calls 1 Peter a "encyclical writing in Letter form").

[69] As H. Frankenmölle, *1. Petrusbrief, 2. Petrusbrief, Judasbrief,* 13-20, maintains, without asserting Petrine authorship.

[70] With N. Brox, *Der erste Petrusbrief,* 23; H. Gunkel, "Der erste Brief des Petrus," in Schriften des Neuen Testaments$^3$ 3 (1917): 248-292, 248. Cf. also M. Dibelius, *Geschichte,* 121-123, who calls it a "treatise in the form of a Letter."

[71] According to W. Trilling, *Untersuchungen zum 2. Thessalonicherbrief,* ETS 27, 157, 2 Thessalonians is not "a Letter to a specific community," but a general "apostolic" admonitory and instructional Letter.

Letter"[72] of the later Pauline school (cf. section 3.5, below).[73]  The predominance of its theological pretensions and content give it the character of a tractate.[74]

James

Although James has the prescript of a genuine letter,[75] its form and content permit designating it a tractate with paraenetic objectives.[76]

Jude

Given its framework of prescript and concluding doxology, H. Paulsen designates Jude as a letter, with reference to Rom 16:25-27.[77]  But the secondary concluding doxology of Romans (cf. 3.1.2) carries no weight in determining the genre of Jude.  Since there is no indication of relationship between the author and readers, "anti-heretical leaflet"[78] or preferably "tractate for a specific situation"[79] are better categorizations.

*c.  Testament*

2 Peter

The same may be said for 2 Peter, which is dependent on Jude (cf. 3.1.1). While it may be described as "a contemporary anti-heretical document,"[80] the fiction that it is a legacy of Peter written shortly before his death justifies the categorization "testament in letter form"[81] over that of "tractate."  The same would apply to 2 Timothy.[82]

---

[72] P. Vielhauer, *Geschichte*, 213.

[73] But R. Schnackenburg (*Der Brief an die Epheser*, MeyerK 10 (1982), 19) describes Ephesians as a "theologically based, pastorally organized Letter."

[74] Cf., e.g., E. Lohse, *Die Entstehung des Neuen Testaments*, Theologische Wissenschaft 4, [4]1983, 58.  This might also suggest classifying it as a homily, e.g., P. Pokorny, "Epheserbrief und gnostische Mysterien," ZNW 53 (1962): 160-194, 178, who calls it a "baptismal homily."  Similarly, H. Schlier, *Der Brief an die Epheser. Ein Kommentar* ([4]1963), 21, terms it a "mystery address" or a "wisdom address."

[75] Cf. further E Baasland, *ANRW* II 25,2, 4654: "a didactic wisdom sermon in Letter form for public reading."  Cf. also F.O. Francis,"The Form and Function of the Opening and Closing Paragraphs of James and I John," *ZNW* 61 (1970): 110-126.

[76] Cf. G. Strecker, "Jakobusbrief," in *EKL*[3] 2 (1989): 794f.  For recent considerations on the paraenetic orientation of James, cf. below, section 3.4.

[77] "Judasbrief," in *TRE* 17 (1988): 307-310, 307.

[78] K.H. Schelke, *Die Petrusbriefe — Der Judasbrief*, HTKNT XIII.2 ([2]1964), 137.

[79] M. Dibelius, *Geschichte der urchristlichen Literatur*, TBü 58 (1975), 133ff.

[80] P. Vielhauer, *Geschichte*, 595.

[81] Cf. Vielhauer, *Geschichte*, 595.

[82] On a closer definition of the literary character of 2 Timothy, cf. M. Wolter, *Die Pastoralbriefe als Paulustradition*, FRLANT 146 (1988), 226ff, who terms it "an admonitory speech in the form of a testament."

Romans has been designated a "Testament of Paul."[83]  This is not so much a literary classification, as G. Bornkamm himself remarks, but a historical description which may be granted with relative accuracy. But this presupposes Romans as the final work of the Pauline corpus.[84] Philippians and the subsequent Philemon can better make this claim. In addition, this foundational work betrays the purpose of preparing for Paul's intended visit to Rome, indicating the situation of a genuine letter.[85]

## 3.2.2   Construction and Structure

*Literature*

Arzt, P., "'Ich danke meinem Gott allezeit . . .' Zur sogennanten 'Danksagung' bei Paulus auf dem Hintergrund griechischer Papyrusbriefe," in *Ein Gott — eine Offenbarung. Festschrift Notker Füglister OSB,* ed F.V. Reiterer (1991), 417-437. Bahr, G.J. "The Subscriptions in the Pauline Letters," *JBL* 87 (1968): 27-41. Bjerkelund, C.J., *PARAKALO. Form, Funktion und Sinn der parakalo-Sätze in den paulinischen Briefen,* Bibliotheca theologica Norvegica 1 (1967). Boers, H., "The Form Critical Study of Paul's Letters: I Thessalonians as a Case Study," NTS 22 (1976): 140-158.   Dahl, N.A., "Adresse und Proömium des Epheserbriefes," *TZ* 7 (1951): 241-264. Friedrich, G., "Lohmeyers These über das paulinische Briefpräskript kritisch beleuchtet" (first published in 1956), in his *Auf das Wort kommt es an. Gesammelte Aufsätze. Zum 70. Geburtstag,* ed. J.H. Friedrich (1978), 103-106. Funk, R.W., "The Apostolic Parousia: Form and Significance," in *Christian History and Interpretation: Festschrift John Knox,* ed. W.R. Farmer *et al.,* (1967), 249-268 (reprinted as "The Apostolic Presence: Paul," in Funk's *Parables and Presence: Forms of the New Testament Tradition* (1982), 81-102); "The Form and Structure of II and III John," *JBL* 86 (1967): 424-430 (reprinted as "John the Elder," in *Parables,* 103-110).   Lambrecht, J., "Thanksgivings in I Thessalonians 1-3," in *The Thessalonian Correspondence,* ed. R.F. Collins, BETL 87 (1990), 183-205. Lieu, J.M., "'Grace to You and Peace:' The Apostolic Greeting," *BJRL* 68 (1985/86): 161-178. Lohmeyer, E., "Briefliche Grussüberschriften" (first published in 1927), in his *Probleme paulinischer Theologie* (1954), 7-29. Mullins, T.Y., "Petition as a Literary Form," *NovT* 5 (1962): 46-54; "Disclosure: A Literary Form in the New Testament," *NovT* 7 (1964/65): 44-50; "Greeting as a New Testament Form," *JBL* 87 (1968): 418-426; "Formulas in New Testament Epistles," *JBL* 91 (1972): 380-390; "The Thanksgivings of Philemon and Colossians," *NTS* 30 (1984): 288-293. O'Brien, P.T., "Thanksgiving and the Gospel of Paul," NTS 21 (1975): 144-155; *Introductory Thanksgivings in the Letters of Paul,* NovTSup 49 (1977). Parkin,

---

[83] G. Bornkamm, "Der Römerbrief als Testament des Paulus," in his *Geschichte und Glaube II. Gesammelte Aufsätze IV,* BEvT 53, 1971, 120-139; cf. also his *Paulus,* Urban-Taschenbuch 119, ⁵1983 (⁶1987), 103-111; *Paul* (1971), 88-96; J. Becker, *Paulus. Der Apostel der Völker* (1989), 351ff.; *Paul: Apostle to the Gentiles* (1993), 333ff.

[84] As, e.g., in Bornkamm, *Paulus,* 245, *Paul,* 241f.

[85] Which also applies to P. Stuhlmacher's description of Romans as a "report," cf. *Der Brief an die Römer,* NTD 6 (¹⁽¹⁴⁾1989), 13.

V. "Some Comments on the Pauline Prescripts," *International Bibliography of Sociology* 8 (1986): 92-99. Richards, E.R., *The Secretary in the Letters of Paul,* WUNT II 43 (1991). Roberts, J.H., "Pauline Transitions in the Letter Body," in *L'apôtre Paul. Personnalité, style et conception du ministère,* ed. A. Vanhoye, BETL 73 (1966), 93-99; "The Eschatological Transitions to the Pauline Letter Body," *Neot* 20 (1986): 29-35. Robinson, J.M., "Die Hodajot-Formel in Gebet und Hymnus des Frühchristentums," in *Apophoreta. Festschrift E. Haenchen,* BZNW 30 (1964), 194-235. Roller, O., *Das Formular der paulinischen Briefe. Ein Beitrag zur Lehre vom antiken Briefe,* BWANT IV H.6 (1933). Sanders, J.T., "The Transition from Opening Epistolary Thanksgiving to Body in the Letters of the Pauline Corpus," *JBL* 81 (1962): 348-362; "Hymnic Elements in Ephesians 1-3," *ZNW* 56 (1965): 214-232. Schnider, F./Stenger, W., *Studien zum neutestamentlichen Briefformular,* NTTS 11 (1987). Schubert, P., *Form and Function of the Pauline Thanksgivings,* BZNW 20 (1939). Stecker, A., "Formen und Formeln in den paulinischen Hauptbriefen und den Pastoralbriefen," Diss theol. Münster (1966). Steen, H.A., "Les clichés épistolaires dans les lettres sur papyrus grecques," Classica et mediaevalia 1 (1938): 119-176. White, J.L., "The Structural Analysis of Philemon: A Point of Departure in the Formal Analysis of the Pauline Letters," SBLSP 1 (1971): 1-47; "Introductory Formulae in the Body of the Pauline Letter," JBL 90 (1971): 91-97; *The Form and Function of the Body of the Greek Letter: A Study of the Letter-Body in the Non-Literary Papyri and in Paul the Apostle,* SBLDS 2 ($^2$1972); "Epistolary Formulas and Cliches in Greek Papyrus Letters," SBLSP 14,2 (1978): 289-319. Zmijewski, J., "Beobachtungen zur Struktur des Philemonbriefes," *BibLeb* 15 (1974): 273-296.

Formally, early Christian letters utilize "the epistolary conventions of the surrounding world."[86] Letters are divided into three parts: prescript (not the same

---

[86] P. Vielhauer, *Geschichte,* 64. When A. Dihle [in his *Die griechische und lateinische Literatur der Kaiserzeit. Von Augustus bis Justinian* (1989), 218] emphasizes, with reference to formal details, the special status of the Pauline Letters, this pertains to the expansion of characteristic Pauline features and early Christian elements in comparison with ancient epistolary conventions. But this comparison also indicates that Paul's Letters reflect ancient conventions of letter writing, although in freely varied form. While Paul borrows elements from the tradition of Jewish letters, the numerous parallels to Hellenistic epistolography indicate that recourse to Jewish letter-writing contributes little to our understanding of early Christian letters (against E. Peterson, "Das Praescriptum des 1. Clemens-Briefes," in his *Frühkirche Judentum und Gnosis* (1959), 129-136, 129). Cf. also I. Taatz, "Frühjüdische Briefe. Die paulinischen Briefe im Rahmen der offiziallen religiösen Briefe des Frühjudentums," NTOA 16 (1991), 110-114. On p. 111 Taatz mentions the taking over of "Judaism's practice of instructing communities via letter." Texts of ancient letters are available as photographic plates, transcriptions, and translations in A. Deissmann, *Licht vom Osten* ($^4$1923); *Light from the Ancient East* (1927). Texts and English translations of Cynic philosophic letters are found in *The Cynic Epistles: A Study Edition,* ed. A.J. Malherbe, SBLSBS 12 (1977). Further translations are given in C.K. Barrett, *The New Testament Background: Selected Documents* (rev. ed. 1987), 28-31; *Texte zur Umwelt des Neuen Testaments,* ed. C.-J. Thornton, Uni-Taschenbücher 1591 ($^2$1991), 38-40; J. Leipoldt and W. Grundmann, eds., *Umwelt des Urchristentums* 1 ($^8$1990), 64f.; S.K. Stowers, *Letter Writing in Greco-*

as the address), body, and conclusions. Standard formulae were utilized in the introductions and conclusions.

The Greek letter *prescript* (generally subdivided into *superscriptio, adscriptio, and salutatio*: the name of the sender, the reader(s) in the dative case, joined by χαίρειν[87]) occurs in James 1:1:

> *James, a servant of God and of the Lord Jesus Christ,*
> *To the twelve tribes in the Dispersion*
> *Greetings.*

It is also found in Acts 15:23 and 23:26.

E. Lohmeyer[88] noted the influence of Near Eastern epistolary style for Pauline Letter prescripts. Their essential characteristic is that they are in two parts.[89] The first vests the writer and reader(s) with various attributes. The second breaks into the sentence construction with a religious or everyday blessing in direct address (e.g. 1 Cor 1:1-3):

> *Paul, called to be an apostle of Christ Jesus by the will of God, and our brother Sosthenes, to the church of God that is in Corinth, to those who are sanctified in Christ Jesus, called to be saints, together with all those who in every place call on the name of our Lord Jesus Christ, both their Lord and ours:*[90]
> > *Grace to you and peace from God our Father and the Lord Jesus Christ.*[91]

---

*Roman Antiquity*, Library of Early Christianity 5 (1986). On Hebrew and Aramaic letters cf. J.A. Fitzmyer, "Aramaic Epistolography" (first published in 1974), in his *A Wandering Aramean: Collected Aramaic Essays*, SBLMS 25 (1979), 183-204 (and re-edited for *Semeia* 22); P.S. Alexander, "Remarks on Aramaic Epistolography in the Persian Period," *JSS* 23 (1978): 155-170; D. Pardee, "An Overview of Ancient Hebrew Epistolography," *JBL* 97 (1978): 321-346; I. Taatz in NTOA 16 (1991): 18-101; D.E. Aune, *The New Testament in its Literary Environment*, Library of Early Christianity 8 (1987), 174-176. On Hellenistic-Jewish letters cf. Aune, 177-179.

[87] Less frequently letters utilize a form of the prescript which begins with the *adscriptio*. This form is used with great regularity in petitions or in other official documents (J.L. White, *ANRW* II 25.2: 1734), but is not found in the New Testament. On the Greek prescript, cf. also J.M. Lieu, "'Grace to You and Peace:' The Apostolic Greeting," *BJRL* 68 (1985/86): 162f.

[88] "Briefliche Grussüberschriften," in his *Probleme paulinischer Theologie* (1954), 7-29. Cf. also H. Lietzmann, "Einführung in die Textgeschichte der Paulusbriefe," *An die Römer*, HNT 8 ([5]1971), 22f.

[89] Cf. also J.M. Lieu in *BJRL* 68 (1985/86): 165-167.

[90] On the issue of the "ecumenical outlook," cf. H. Conzelmann, *Der erste Brief an die Korinther.* MeyerK 5 ([2(12)]1981), 41; *I Corinthians.* Hermeneia (1975), 23.

[91] Cf. also 2 Cor 1:1-2. Here Christian formulation, perhaps liturgical usage, may be at work. Cf. R. Deichgräber, "Formeln, Liturgische II. Neues Testament und Alte Kirche 1-4," *TRE* 11 (1983): 256-263, 258, and J.L. White in *ANRW* II 25.2: 1740. But G. Friedrich, "Lohmeyers These über das paulinische Briefpräskript kritisch beleuchtet," in *Auf das Wort kommt es an. Gesammelte Aufsätze. Zum 70. Geburtstag*, ed. J.H. Friedrich, 1978, 103-106, disagrees. K. Berger emphasizes the distinctiveness of the

Specific to Pauline introductions is the naming of Paul's coworkers as fellow senders, and the recipients as a community rather than as individuals.[92]

With χάρις, which he wishes for his readers, Paul Christianizes the greeting formula of the Greco-Roman letter. εἰρήνη, which accompanies it, is reminiscent of the Hebrew שלום (Rom 1:7; 1 Cor 1:3, 2 Cor 1:2; Gal 1:3, Phil 1:2, etc.[93]). In the wished blessing of the Pauline Letters, Hellenistic and Jewish elements are joined together.

In the NT and Apostolic Fathers, only 3 John 2 has a "conventional health wish."[94] While this corresponds to secular Greek tradition, here it should be taken theologically.[95]

Akin to secular letter style, the *proömium* [proem] follows as a standard component of Pauline Letters.[96] As in secular praxis, thanksgivings became prevalent in letters.[97] The language of the proem less closely follows secular conventions.[98] Paul includes here not only the language of Jewish prayers,[99] but also of early Christian worship and apostolic preaching.[100]

In the Pauline corpus two forms of thanksgiving predominate. One is a) εὐχαριστῶ τῷ θεῷ with ὅτι (1 Cor 1:4ff.) or with a participle construction following (Phlm 4ff.; Phil 1:3-6, cf. also Col 1:3-6 and Eph 1:15ff). Rom 1:8ff, 1 Thess 1:2-5, 2 Thess 1:3ff. are mixed forms. The second is b) εὐλογητὸς ὁ θεός (2 Cor 1:3; Eph 1:3-14; cf. 1 Pet 1:3-5). Nils Dahl saw Eph 1:3ff as an introductory eulogy, "a Jewish analogy to the thanksgiving in Hellenistic letters."[101] In this

---

apostolic letters in "Apostelbrief und apostolische Rede/Zum Formular frühchristlicher Briefe," *ZNW* 65 (1974): 196f., as does J. Roloff, Der erste Brief on Timotheus, EKKNT 15 (1988), 53, n. 1. Cf. also J.M. Lieu in *BJRL* 68 (1985/86).

[92] But note the ancient parallels in philosophical letters to the schools.

[93] Cf., e.g., H.D. Betz, *A Commentary on Paul's Letter to the Galatians*, Hermeneia (1979), 40f., Der Galaterbrief. Ein Kommentar zum Brief des Apostels Paulus an die Gemeinden in Galatien (1988), 93. But P. Vielhauer, in *Geschichte* 65, refers the two Pauline expressions back to the Jewish greeting "mercy and health." Cf. also T. Holtz, *Der erste Brief an die Thessalonicher*, EKK 13 (1986), 39. On the Pauline greeting in general cf. G. Ebeling, *Die Wahrheit des Evangeliums. Eine Lesehilfe zum Galaterbrief* (1981), 35ff.

[94] R.W. Funk, *JBL* 86 (1967): 424f.

[95] G. Strecker, *Die Johannesbriefe*, 360f.; *The Johannine Letters*, 256f.

[96] The Pauline proömium consists of thanksgiving, intercession, and remembrance; cf. P. Vielhauer, *Geschichte* 65f. Galatians lacks a proem, but not 1 Peter. Also on proems, cf. P. Schubert, *Form and Function of the Pauline Thanksgivings*, BZNW 20 (1939); E. Lohse, *Die Briefe an die Kolosser und an Philemon*, MeyerK IX/2 (²1977), 40f., with examples from Hellenistic letters.

[97] P. Schubert 27: "Their province is to indicate the occasion for and the contents of the letters which they introduce."

[98] So P. Schubert.

[99] J.M. Robinson, "Die Hodajot-Formel in Gebet und Hymnus des Frühchristentums," in *Apophoreta. Festschrift für E. Haenchen*, BZNW 30 (1964), 201f.

[100] Cf. P.T. O'Brien, *Introductory Thanksgivings in the Letters of Paul*, NTSup 49 (1977), 264 and his "Thanksgiving and the Gospel of Paul," *NTS* 21 (1975): 147f.

[101] Despite the elevated style of the eulogy, the attempt to prove that Ephesians 1:3-14 is a well organized hymn sung at worship is unpersuasive (e.g., E. Lohmeyer, *TBl* 5). Cf. the critique by J.T. Sanders in *ZNW* 56 (1965): 223-229. It is better considered "a

praise of God's actions, determined by the specific situation of the letter, author and recipients are bound together.[102]

1 Thess 1:2-3:13 is the longest Pauline thanksgiving.[103] Since it is followed by paraenesis in 4:1-5:22, 1 Thessalonians lacks the body typical of other Pauline Letters.

Ephesians is also distinct in that the whole first part of the Letter (1:3-3:21) may be seen as proem.[104] Along with the eulogy which introduces the Letter it contains the keyword εὐχαριστῶν (1:15ff.). This doubling shows the author's efforts to leave out no essential aspect of a Pauline Letter.[105] This large proem, utilizing communal and liturgical traditions (e.g., 1:20-23; 2:4-10, 14-18, 19-22), gives the author opportunity for various observations about Christ and about the origin and unity of the church.

2 and 3 John use the formula ἐχάρην λίαν (also found in the papyri[106]) in place of the thanksgiving (2 John 4; 3 John 3).

The body of the letter,[107] as in Greek private letters, contains the specific and often complex content. Despite varying scope (cf. the brevity of Philemon as compared with Romans), Pauline Letters in general distinguish themselves from brief Greek private letters by their length. Paul's Letters take up orally transmitted information as well as written questions from the community addressed (introduced by περὶ δέ + gen., cf. 1 Cor 7:1; 7:25, etc.).

---

unified, hymn-like, ad hoc passage in rhythmic artistic prose," with H. Schlier, *Der Brief an die Epheser. Ein Kommentar* (⁴1963), 41. Cf. also R. Schnackenburg, "Die grosse Eulogie Eph 1,3-14. Analyse unter textlinguistischen Aspekten," *BZ*, N.F. 21 (1977): 67-87. Schnackenburg provides bibliography in his *Der Brief an die Epheser*, MeyerK 10 (1982), 42. Ephesians 1:3-14 reflects the Christ hymn of Colossians 1:15-20 in detail; thus the latter is important for the interpretation of the former.

[102] N.A. Dahl, "Adresse und Proömium des Epheserbriefes," *TZ* 7 (1951): 250-251, citation 251, which is taken from R. Deichgräber, *Gotteshymnus und Christushymnus in der frühen Christenheit. Untersuchungen zu Form, Sprache und Stil der frühchristlichen Hymnen*, SUNT 5 (1967), 64ff.

[103] Cf. P. Schubert, *Pauline Thanksgivings* 9, 17; P. Vielhauer, *Geschichte* 84ff.; T. Holtz, *Der erste Brief an die Thessalonicher*, MeyerK 13, 1986, 29-31. For a different viewpoint cf. e.g., J.T. Sanders, who understands 1:2-10 as the first and 2:13-3:13 as a second song of thanksgiving surrounding the corpus of 2:1-10 *(JBL* 81 [1962]: 356). H. Boers, after removing 2:13-16 (cf. 3.1.2 above), characterizes 2:17-3:13 not as a thanksgiving but as "apostolic parousia" following the "apostolic apology" of 2:1-12; cf. "The Form Critical Study of Paul's Letters: 1 Thessalonians as a Case Study," *NTS* 22 (1976): 140-158.

[104] P. Vielhauer, *Geschichte* 203f.; cf. also M. Dibelius, *Geschichte der urchristlichen Literatur*, ed. F. Hahn (1975), 121.

[105] P. Schubert, *Pauline Thanksgivings* 44; M. Dibelius/H. Greeven, *An die Kolosser, Epheser. An Philemon*, HNT 12 (³1953), 63. On the literary character of Ephesians, cf. section 3.2.1 above.

[106] Cf. Deissmann, *Licht vom Osten*, 150, 152 n. 7; *Light from the Ancient East*, 184, 185 n. 6.

[107] Cf. J.L. White, *The Form and Function of the Body of the Greek Letter*, SBLDS 2 (²1972), 47. White distinguishes Pauline Letters from Greek papyrus letters in that the Pauline letter bodies are divided into "theoretical" and "practical" sections. Cf. below, section 3.4.

Some have sought to identify transitional formulae standing between the thanksgiving, which not seldom concludes with an eschatological outlook (1 Thess 1:10; 1 Cor 1:8; Phil 1:10f.; as well as 2 Thess 1:10),[108] and the letter body, introducing the latter.[109] W.G. Doty[110] and D.E. Aune[111] have attempted to identify specific forms in the letter corpus. For example, the form "apostolic parusia" has been cited as a concluding formula which specifies the place of writing, the relationship with the addressed community, and the apostle's plans for future visits.[112] But these passages are less a *form* and more a *topos*[113] with these characteristic motifs, comparable to the *topoi* found in letters of friendship.[114]

Letters (except for Galatians) customarily conclude with greetings (ἀσπάζεσθαι[115]) from the writer and his associates to the recipient along with relatives and friends: cf. 1 Thess 5:26; Rom 16:3-16; 1 Cor 16:19f.:

> *The churches of Asia send greetings. Aquile and Prisca, together with the church in their house, greet you warmly in the Lord. All the brothers and sisters send greetings. Greet one another with a holy kiss.*

A concluding wish follows. The secular ἔρρωσο/ἔρρωσθε[116] is reflected in Acts 15:29 (and in the variant at 23:30). This wish or blessing receives a

---

[108] Cf. P. Schubert, *Pauline Thanksgivings* 4-9. In a different manner J.H. Roberts sees the "eschatological climax" as a transitional formula in the body of the Letter, serving the important rhetorical function of pointing out the eschatological expressions ("The Eschatological Transitions to the Pauline Letter Body," in *Neot* 20 [1986]: 29-35). But since an eschatological outlook implies no special function for literary transitions, it is better to interpret these eschatological expressions in connection with the thanksgivings and the settings which they reflect for the Letters.

[109] J.T. Sanders, "The Transition from the Opening Epistolary Thanksiving to the Body in the Letters of the Pauline Corpus," *JBL* 81 (1962): 348-362; T.Y. Mullins (cf. the bibliography for this section); J.H. Roberts, "Pauline Transitions;" C.J. Berkelund, *PARAKALO. Form, Funktion und Sinn der parakalo-Sätze in den paulinischen Briefen* (1967), 139, 146, 189, etc., in connection with the παρακαλῶ formula. J.L. White, in comparison with ancient papyri, identifies six categories of formulas: *Disclosure Formula, Request Formula, Joy Expression, Expression of Astonishment, Statement of Compliance, Formulaic Use of the Verb of Hearing or Learning.*

[110] W.G. Doty, *Letters in Primitive Christianity*. Guides to Biblical Scholarship: NT Series 1, (³1979), 35ff.

[111] D.E. Aune, *The New Testament in Its Literary Environment* (1987), 188-191.

[112] R.W. Funk, "The Apostolic Parousia: Form and Significance," in *Christian History and Interpretation: Festschrift for John Knox* (1967), 249-268; J.L. White, *The Form and Function of the Body of the Greek Letter*, SBLDS 2 (21972), 59ff.

[113] Cf. D.E. Aune, 190.

[114] On letters of friendship, cf. below, section 3.2.3.3, pp. 67f, n. 182. On differentiating "form" and "topos," cf. D.E. Aune, *The New Testament in Its Literary Environment,* 173.

[115] Cf. J.L. White, ANRW II 25.2, 1735. On the form of the greeting cf. T.Y. Mullins, "Greeting as a New Testament Form," *JBL* 87 (1968): 418-426.

[116] Cf. H. Koskenniemi, *Studien zur Idee und Phraseologie des griechischen Briefes bis 400 n. Christus,* Annales Academicae Scientiarum Fennicae, Series B, 102,2, 1956, 151-154; J.L White in ANRW II 25.2, 1734.

religious content from the Hebrew and Jewish "peace" (1 Pet. 5:14; 3 John 15) and in the variable Pauline blessings as at 1 Thess 5:28:

> *The grace of our Lord Jesus Christ be with you.*

Note also Rom 16:20; 1 Cor 16:23; etc., the deutero-Pauline 1 Tim 6:21; 2 Tim 4:22; etc., and also Heb 13:25.

Since Paul apparently dictated his Letters to amenuenses (Romans, cf. 16:22[117], but probably not Philemon[118]), he ends 1 Corinthians (16:21f.) and Galatians (6:11) with an analogy to the Hellenistic "illiteracy formula,"[119] finishing them in his own hand (cf. also Col 4:18 and 2 Thess 3:17).

### 3.2.3  Style, Epistolography, and Rhetoric

*Literature*

Betz, H.D., "The Problem of Rhetoric and Theology According to the Apostle Paul," in *L'apôtre Paul. Personnalité, style et conception du ministère,* by A. Vanhoye, BETL 73 (1966), 16-48. Bünker, M., *Briefformular und rhetorische Disposition im 1 Korintherbrief,* Göttinger theologische Arbeiten 28 (1984). Classen, C.J. "Paulus und die antike Rhetorik," *ZNW* 82 (1991): 1-33. Forbes, C. "Comparison, Self-Praise and Irony: Paul's Boasting and the Conventions of Hellenistic Rhetoric," *NTS* 32 (1986): 1-30. Hübner, H., "Der Galaterbrief und der Verhältnis von antiker Rhetorik und Epistolographie," *TLZ* 109 (1984): 241-250. Klauck, H.-J., "Hellenistische Rhetorik im Diasporajudentum. Das Exordium des vierten Makkabäerbuchs (4 Makk 1.1-12)," *NTS* 35 (1989): 451-465; "Zur rhetorischen Analyse der Johannesbriefe," *ZNW* 81 (1990): 205-224. Schoon-Janssen, J., *Umstrittene "Apologien" in den Paulusbriefen. Studien zur rhetorischen Situation des 1. Thessalonicherbriefes, des Galaterbriefes und des Philipperbriefes,* Göttinger theologischer Arbeiten 45 (1991). Watson, D.F., *Invention, Arrangement, and Style: Rhetorical Criticism of Jude and 2 Peter,* SBLDS 104 (1988); "The New Testament and Greco-Roman Rhetoric: a

---

[117] E.R. Richards attempts to clarify the significance of the actual writer in both ancient and Pauline Letters.

[118] The personal explanation in Philemon 19 does not come in the conclusion of the Letter, nor is a repeated change of writers likely. Cf. P. Stuhlmacher, *Der Brief an Philemon,* MeyerK 18 (1975) (³1989), 50, n. 122; E. Schweizer, *Theologische Einleitung in das Neue Testament,* Grundrisse zum Neuen Testament 2 (1989), 54; but for a different viewpoint W.G. Doty, *Letters in Primitive Christianity.* Guides to Biblical Scholarship: NT Series 1, (³1979), 41.

[119] J.L. White, ANRW II 25.2, 1735, 1740: in official letters touching juristic circumstances this formula is used where those who have written the letters give their names instead of those of the senders, whose names are sometimes added. Cf. G.J. Bahr, "The Subscriptions in the Pauline Letters," *JBL* 87 (1968): 27-41, who calls this formula a "subscription;" and F. Schnider/W. Stenger, *Studien zum neutestamentlichen Briefformular,* NTTS 11 (1987), 142ff, who consider it a "secretarial mark."

Bibliography," *JETS* 31 (1988): 470-472 (bibliography). Wuellner, W.H., "Where is Rhetorical Criticism Taking Us?" *CBQ* 49 (1987): 448-463.

### 3.2.3.1 Observations on Style, Theory of Argumentation, and Structure

*Literature*

Bujard, W. *Stilanalytische Untersuchungen zum Kolosserbrief als Beitrag zur Methodik von Sprachvergleichen,* SUNT 11 (1973). Bultmann, R. Der Stil der paulinischen Predigt und die kynisch-stoische Diatribe. Mit einem Geleitwort von H. Hübner, FRLANT 13 (reprint 1984 = first edition of 1910). Charles, J.D., "Literary Artifice in the Epistle of Jude," *ZNW* 82 (1991): 106-124. Gieger, L.G., "Figures of Speech in the Epistle of James: A Rhetorical Analysis," Ph.D. diss., Southwestern Baptist Theological Seminary (1981). Malherbe, A.J., "M H ΓΕΝΟΙΤΟ in the Diatribe and Paul," *HTR* 73 (1980): 231-240. Schmeller, T., *Paulus und die "Diatribe." Eine vergleichende Stilinterpretation,* NTAbh. Neue Folge 19 (1987). Schneider, N. *Die rhetorische Eigenart der paulinischen Antithese,* HUT 11 (1970). Siegert, F., *Argumentation bei Paulus gezeigt an Röm 9-11,* WUNT 34 (1985). Stowers, S.K., *The Diatribe and Paul's Letter to the Romans,* SBLDS 57 (1981); "Paul's Dialogue with a Fellow Jew in Romans 3:1-9," *CBQ* 46 (1984): 707-722; "The Diatribe," in *Greco-Roman Literature and the New Testament,* ed. David Aune, SBLSBS 21 (1988), 71-83. Watson, D.F., "I John 2:12-14 as Distributio, Conduplicatio, and Expolitio: A Rhetorical Understanding," *JSNT* 35 (1989): 97-110; "I Corinthians 10:23-11:1 in the Light of Greco-Roman Rhetoric: The Role of Rhetorical Questions," *JBL* 108 (1989): 301-318. Weiss, J. *Beiträge zur Paulinischen Rhetorik,* (1897, offprint). Wischmeyer, O., *Der höchste Weg. Das 13. Kapitel des 1. Korintherbriefes,* SNT 13 (1981). Wuellner, W.H., "Paul as Pastor: The Function of Rhetorical Questions in First Corinthians," in *L'apôtre Paul. Personnalité, style et conception du ministère,* by A Vanhoye, BETL 73 (1966), 49-77. Zmijewski, J., *Der Stil der paulinischen "Narrenrede." Analyse der Sprachgestaltung in 2 Kor 11,1-12,10 als Beitrag zur Methodik von Stiluntersuchungen neutestamentlicher Texte,* BBB 52 (1978).

*Literature on the Catologues of Hardships*

Berger, K., *Formgeschichte des Neuen Testaments* (1984), 225-228. Fitzgerald, J.T., *Cracks in an Earthen Vessel: An Examination of the Catalogues of Hardships in the Corinthian Correspondence,* SBLDS 99 (1988). Fridrichsen, A., "Zum Stil des paulinischen Peristasenkatalogs 2. Cor 11,23ff.," *Symbolae Osloenses* 7 (1928): 25-29; "Peristasenkatalog und Res gestae. Nachtrag zu 2. Cor 11,23ff.," *Symbolae Osloenses* 8 (1929): 78-82. Hodgson, R. "Paul the Apostle and First Century Tribulation Lists," *ZNW* 74 (1983): 59-80. Schrage, W., "Leid, Kreuz und Eschaton. Die Peristasenkataloge als Merkmale paulinischer theologia crucis und Eschatologie," *EvT* 34 (1974): 141-175.

The New Testament Letters are distinguished in specific details by considerable formal variety.[120] They utilize formal rhetorical devices commonly recognized in ancient letters. They employ dialogue style in which the sender enters into conversation with the audience (utilizing ethos and pathos, contemporizing and communicating figures, etc.[121]).

J. Weiss[122] and R. Bultmann (in his dissertation *Der Stil der paulinischen Predigt und die kynisch-stoische Diatribe*) called attention to rhetorical training and especially to the significance of diatribe style[123] for the Pauline Letters.[124]

Diatribe style is widely varied and imitates a presentation intended to teach or admonish (primarily in the realm of ethics). It is simple and sharp, often paratactical and with catechetical questions and answers (cf. Epict. I, 28, 21), but related to a rich variety of terms and concepts. The presentation is often interrupted by interlocutary interchanges and challenges, anecdotes, sentences, jokes, poetic citations, historical examples, etc. Rhetorical marks of diatribe style are word plays, rhetorical questions (e.g., Seneca, *epist* 14.15), parallelism (e.g., Epictetus, III 24, 10ff.), antitheses, paradoxes, similes, and metaphors (e.g., Epictetus I 3,7). Imperatives are frequent;[125] repetitions and doublets are favorite marks of the style. Possible questions and objections from fictive

---

[120] This corresponds to the formal diversity characteristic of the ancient letter in general.

[121] Cf. the style-critical research of W. Bujard, C. Forbes, N. Schneider, O. Wischmeyer, W. Wuellner in BETL 73, J. Zmijewski, etc.

[122] J. Weiss, *Beiträge*. Previously C.F.G. Heinrici, *Der erste Brief an die Korinther*, MeyerK 5, [8]1896, VI.32f.; *Der litterarische Charakter der neutestamentlichen Schriften* (1908), 58; and *Erklärung der Korintherbriefe in zwei Bänden. Bd. 2. Das zweite Sendschreiben des Apostle Paulus an die Korinther* (1887), 403, assumed Paul utilized the "method of an ancient apology."

[123] On the form of the diatribe style, cf. D.E. Aune, The New Testament in its Literary Envionment (1987), 200-202; R. Bultmann, *Der Stil der paulinischen Predigt und die kynisch-stoische Diatribe*, 10-64; W. Capelle/H.I. Marrou, "Diatribe," in *RAC* 3 (1957), 990-1009; A. Dihle, Die griechische und lateinische Literatur der Kaiserzeit. Von Augustus bis Justinian (1989), 95f.; E.G. Schmidt, "Diatribai," in Der kleine Pauly 2 (1967), 1577f.; S.K. Stowers, *The Diatribe and Paul's Letter to the Romans*, SBLDS 57 (1981), 7-78 (for the description of the diatribe and bibliography); Stowers, "The Diatribe," in *Greco-Roman Literature and the New Testament*, ed. David Aune, SBLSBS 21 (1988), 71-83; "Paul's Dialogue with a Fellow Jew in Romans 3:1-9," *CBQ* 46 (1984): 707-722.

[124] According to H. Thyen, *Der Stil der Jüdisch-Hellenistischen Homilie*, FRLANT 65 (1955), 63, and cf. also 119f., the diatribe style was mediated to Paul through the Hellenistic synagogue, so that Paul is "an admittedly secondary witness for the style of the Jewish and Hellenistic homily." Yet we cannot get beyond probabilities in this matter, since there was always the possibility of encountering the diatribe style in Hellenistic cities through the frequent public speeches and lectures. S.K. Stowers's suggestion that the *Sitz im Leben* of the diatribe was the lecture of the teacher in the (philosophical) schools should be taken seriously, while it contradicts Bultmann's thesis which identifies the diatribe as the "style of Cynic-Stoic popular preaching" (*Der Stil der paulinischen Predigt und die kynisch-stoische Diatribe*, 3).

[125] Bultmann, *Der Stil*, 32f.

opponents may occur (e.g., Dio Chrys. 74,8,23).[126] These easily controverted objections may be repudiated through exclamations (e.g., μὴ γένοιτο;[127] οὐδαμῶς, etc.). In the New Testament it is particularly Paul (especially in Romans 1-11) and James[128] who know and use the diatribe style.[129]

The "catalogues of hardships" (περιστάσεις) pose a special problem.[130] Besides simple enumerations (e.g., 2 Cor 6:4b-5, 11:23b-29, 12:10; Rom 8:35) Paul also has antithetical lists (e.g., 1 Cor 4:10-13; 2 Cor 4:8f., 6:8-10; Phil 4:12). In his study of diatribe style, Bultmann sought to explain them in connection with the catalogues of

---

[126] Bultmann, *Der Stil*, 10f. Yet it may be questioned whether the transfer of the diatribe stylistic method to Romans sufficiently takes into account the determination of the argument through issues of Pauline theology which are independent of the local Roman situation.

[127] Cf. A. Malherbe, "MH ΓΕΝΟΙΤΟ in the Diatribe and Paul," *HTR* 73 (1980): 231-240 for a comparative study of this usage in Paul and Epictetus.

[128] Cf. J. Geffcken, *Kynika und Verwandtes*, 1909. M. Dibelius also noted elements of the diatribe style in James, cf. *Der Brief des Jakobus*, revised ed. H. Greeven, MeyerK 15[5(11)], 1964, 56f. and often elsewhere.

[129] Cf. Schoon-Janssen, J., *Umstrittene "Apologien" in den Paulusbriefen. Studien zur rhetorischen Situation des 1. Thessalonicherbriefes, des Galaterbriefes und des Philipperbriefes*, Göttinger theologischer Arbeiten 45 (1991), passim; and S.K. Stowers, *The Diatribe and Paul's Letter to the Romans*, SBLDS 57 (1981), 57. Schmeller, T., *Paulus und die "Diatribe." Eine vergleichende Stilinterpretation*, NTAbh. Neue Folge 19 (1987), 430f., treats "Pauline analogies to the diatribe" differently, suggesting that they were at least partly examples of Paul utilizing what he found in the context which he was addressing. Thus the supposition of oral diatribe style influencing the Letters is reduced to "letter-sections 'resembling the diatribe' with themes of mission preaching" (435, 414ff.). A. Dihle, *Die griechische und lateinische Literatur der Kaiserzeit* (1989), 218f., reduces the significance of the diatribe style. "The ancillary, erratic, immediate qualities which are associated with the so-called diatribe style are in Paul less to be explained as purposive formulations than by Paul's character as a person of uncommon richness of thought and powerful temperament, which the rhetorical and philosophical training of educated Greeks lacked." While it is correct to question the degree to which Paul had *specific* rhetorical knowledge as contained in the rhetorical handbooks (e.g., Quintilian), a *general* acquaintance may be presupposed. It is recognizable in the figures and details of rhetorical style. With regard to these, Paul's formative activity ought not to be underestimated (cf. section 3.2.3.3 below). Paul's own conceptualizing ought not to be advanced against the supposition that he was influenced by diatribe style, for that style was not only extremely variable but also widely disseminated and not restricted to the usage of a specific philosophical school. Caution is advisable against a psychologizing appeal to the person of Paul and his "temperment." Malherbe's research on the usage of μὴ γένοιτο indicates rather that, "It would not appear that there Paul felt less need to confirm his propositions intellectually than Epictetus did or that he was more indebted to experience and intuition than the teacher of Nicopolis" ("MH ΓΕΝΟΙΤΟ in the Diatribe and Paul," *HTR* 73 (1980): 240).

[130] Cf. the survey of research in J.T. Fitzgerald, *Cracks in an Earthen Vessel: An Examination of the Catalogues of Hardships in the Corinthian Correspondence*, SBLDS 99 (1988), 7-31.

virtues and vices.[131] A. Fridrichsen regarded them at first as a sort of *cursus honorum;* then later as a portrayal of oneself in "I-form," imitating the *res gestae.* W. Schrage, while not entirely rejecting Stoic influence, thought apocalyptic was their primary background.[132] Picking up on more ancient considerations, R. Hodgson and K. Berger turn again to the Hellenistic background. They seek to refer the hardship catalogues back to the Heracles tradition, which brings us "clearly to recognize . . . the inner affinity of deeds and suffering."[133] J.T. Fitzgerald sets them in a wider context, referring to descriptions of sufferings of the wise or philosophers.[134] Paul interprets these in light of traditions about the sufferings of the righteous and the prophets in the Hebrew Scriptures as well as in connection with the cross of Christ.[135]

The suffering of Christ on his cross is really the decisive influence on Paul's concept of suffering as it comes to expression in his catalogues of suffering. Paul does not alleviate his adversity as do comparable Stoic catalogues, where suffering is enhanced through considerations drawn from natural law and one's self-consciousness achieved thereby. Nor is suffering experienced as "a station along the way to a new world."[136] Instead, Paul understands and bears his weakness as a participation in the sufferings of Christ (2 Cor 1:5ff.; Gal. 6:17). Suffering does not point to the person of the apostle himself as an example of one who is wise, but beyond the person of the apostle himself, contributing, in the "word of the cross" (1 Cor 1:18), to the unity of the proclaimer and the community (2 Cor 11:29).

Given the importance of this style-critical evidence,[137] structural[138] and argumentation-theoretical[139] analyses are also important for clarifying the situation and intention of the author. Insofar as redaction-critical reflection on the relationship between tradition and redaction declines in favor of synchronic analyses these approaches become questionable. But at least the differences between ancient rhetorical tradition and modern linguistic theory remain significant.[140]

---

[131] *Der Stil,* 19. For a survey of other exegetes with similar opinions, cf. W. Schrage, "Leid, Kreuz und Eschaton. Die Peristasenkataloge als Merkmale paulinischer theologia crucis und Eschatologie," *EvT* 34 (1974): 142 and n. 2.

[132] *EvT* 34 (1974): 143-145, 147.

[133] K. Berger, *Formgeschichte des Neuen Testaments* (1984), 226.

[134] Fitzgerald, SBLDS 99 (1988), 47-116.

[135] Fitzgerald 207.

[136] W. Schrage, "Leid, Kreuz und Eschaton. Die Peristasenkataloge als Merkmale paulinischer theologia crucis und Eschatologie," *EvT* 34 (1974): 165.

[137] In ancient rhetoric there are references to stylistic discussions in the *elocutio.* (Cf. below, p. 182.)

[138] D. Patte.

[139] F. Siegert.

[140] Cf. G. Strecker, "Neues Testament," in *Neues Testament — Antikes Judentum,* ed. Johann Maier, Grundkurs Theologie 2 (1989), 82.

### 3.2.3.2 Ancient Rhetorical and Epistolographic Models for New Testament Letters: H.D. Betz's New Approach

*Literature*

Aune, D.E., Review of Hans Dieter Betz, *Galatians: A Commentary on Paul's Letter to the Churches in Galatia,* Hermeneia (Philadelphia, 1979) in *RSR* 7 (1981): 323-328. Betz, H.D., *Der Apostel Paulus und die sokratische Tradition. Eine exegetische Untersuchung zu seiner "Apologie" 2 Korinther 10-13,* BHT 45 (1972); "The Literary Composition and Function of Paul's Letter to the Galatians," *NTS* 21 (9175): 353-379; *2 Corinthians 8 and 9: A Commentary on Two Administrative Letters of the Apostle Paul,* Hermeneia (1985); "Hellenismus," *TRE* 15 (1986): 19-35; *Galatians: A Commentary on Paul's Letter to the Churches in Galatia,* Hermeneia (1979); *Der Galaterbrief. Ein Kommentar zum Brief des Apostels Paulus an die Gemeinden in Galatien* (1988); "Korintherbriefe," *EKL³* 2 (1989): 1448-1453. Hansen, G.W., *Abraham in Galatians: Epistolary and Rhetorical Contexts,* JSNTSup 29 (1989). Smit, J., "The Letter of Paul to the Galatians: A Deliberative Speech," *NTS* 35 (1989): 1-26. Standaert, B., "La rhétorique antique et l' epître aux Galates," *Foi et vie* 84, no. 5 (1985): 33-40. Vouga, F., "Zur rhetorischen Gattung des Galaterbriefes," *ZNW* 79 (1988): 291f.

Recent discussion has concentrated on models from ancient rhetoric (divided between forensic, deliberative, and epideictic)[141] and epistolography[142] (especially related to the issue of letter type).[143] This interest originated with the work of H.D. Betz.[144]

Betz began by interpreting 2 Cor 10-13 as a "Pauline apology."[145] Standing in the Socratic tradition, Paul explains that he relinquishes defending himself before the Corinthians (2 Cor 12:19).[146] Yet, renouncing sophistic and rhetorical means, he uses

---

[141] Cf. H. Lausberg, *Handbuch der Literarischen Rhetorik. Eine Grundlegung der Literaturwissenschaft* (²1973) 1:123-129; J. Martin, *Antike Rhetorik. Technik und Methode,* HAW II.3 (1974); M. Fuhrmann, *Die antike Rhetorik. Eine Einführung* (³1990); D.E. Aune, *The New Testament in its Literary Environment* (1987); G. Kennedy, *The Art of Rhetoric in the Roman World: 300 B.C.—A.D. 300* (1972), 7-23.

[142] On the structuring of Letters cf. below, section 3.2.2.

[143] Cf. H.D. Betz, "Hellenismus," *TRE* 15 (1986): 30.

[144] James Muilenberg, in "Form Criticism and Beyond," *JBL* 88 (1969): 1-18, put forward a similar pioneering effort to make "rhetorical analysis" fruitful in the realm of research on the Hebrew Scriptures. In *Invention, Arrangement, and Style: Rhetorical Criticism of Jude and 2 Peter,* SBLDS 104, 1-28 D.F. Watson gives a survey of research and an introduction to the application of "rhetorical criticism." Cf. also the analysis of the current situation for research posed by the method of "rhetorical criticism" in the context of the "new rhetoric" and modern linguistics in W. Wuellner, "Where is Rhetorical Criticism Taking Us?" CBQ 49 (1987): 448-463. Cf. also B.L. Mack, *Rhetoric in the New Testament,* Guides to Biblical Scholarship, New Testament Series, 9ff. and 19ff.

[145] H.D. Betz, *Der Apostel Paulus und die sokratische Tradition. Eine exegetische Untersuchung zu seiner "Apologie" 2 Korinther 10-13,* BHT 45 (1972), 45.

[146] BHT 45 (1972): 14-18.

the apologetic possibilities available to a philosopher against his opponents' charge of sorcery, magic, or finesse (γοητεία).[147] In light of Demetrius' τύποι ἐπιστολικοί ("epistolary categories"), Betz identifies this apology as a letter of defense.[148] From Paul's defense Betz identifies the approach introduced by his opponents: γοήτων φωρά ("detection of sorceries").[149] Yet Betz stops short of seeing Paul in the "sorrowful letter" regarding himself as as a defendent. It is not the accusations of the opponents but the authority of the apostle and of his apostolicity which is primary. Both of these are based on an appeal to the risen Lord (cf. 2 Cor 10:7-8, 17-18).[150]

In his presentation, "The literary composition and function of Paul's Letter to the Galatians," at the twenty-ninth annual meeting of the S.N.T.S. in Sigtuna (Sweden), 1974, Betz sought to demonstrate the same genre, "apologetic letter," for Galatians.[151] The attempt to divide the Letter so designated according to the structural elements of an ancient speech is decisive:

| | |
|---|---|
| *exordium* | Gal 1:6-11 |
| *narratio* | 1:12-2:14 |
| *propositio* | 2:15-21 |
| *probatio* | 3:1-4:31 |
| *exhortatio* | 5:1-6:10 |

The letter introduction (1:1-5) provides the prescript and the conclusion (6:11-18) the *conclusio*.[152]

G.A. Kennedy regards Galatians as deliberative rather than forensic rhetoric. "The Letter looks to the immediate future, not to judgment of the past, and the question

---

[147] BHT 45 (1972): 18-26. For examples of defense against accusations of sorcery (γοητεία) cf. Philostratus, Life of Apollonius VII,17-VIII,5 (the trial), and VIII,7 (the defense); and Apuleius' Apology. Such speeches display as a topos the tendency to picture the accusation as against true philosophy and the point of the accusation as directed against famous philosophers (cf. pp. 29-31).

[148] Ἀπολογητικὸς δέ ἐστιν ὁ πρὸς τὸ κατηγορούμενα τοὺς ἐναντίους λόγους μετ' ἀποδείξεως εἰσφέρειν, cited by Betz, BHT 45 (1972): 40. Betz makes reference to H. Windisch, *Der zweite Korintherbrief,* MeyerK 6, ed. G. Strecker (reprint 1970 = 1924), 8f., and Plato, *ep.* 3, as well as J.A. Goldstein, *The Letters of Demosthenes* (1968), 97ff.

[149] BHT 45 (1972): 41. This would stand in an ancient tradition (also Jewish) of the struggle against "religious and philosophical sorcery or finesse" (cf. pp. 31-39).

[150] Cf. G. Strecker,, "Die Legitimität des paulinischen Apostolates nach 2 Korinther 10-13," *NTS* 38 (1992): 566-586 (with bibliography).

[151] Here Betz was building on evidence from A. Momigliano, *The Development of Greek Biography* (1971), 58-62, who considers "autobiography" and "apologetic speech" as presuppostions for the genre of "apologetic letter" which arose in the fourth century B.C.E.. Cf. also Plato's *ep* 7. Momigliano mentions Epicurus, Seneca, and Paul as followers in the tradition of Socratic letters; Betz adds the Cynic letters ("The Literary Composition and Function of Paul's Letter to the Galatians," *NTS* 21 (1975): 354f.).

[152] Betz, *NTS* 21 (1975): 354; *Galatians: A Commentary,* passim, esp. 14-23. For a critique, cf. C.J. Classen, "Paulus und die antike Rhetorik," *ZNW* 82 (1991): 13-15; J. Schoon-Janssen, *Umstrittene "Apologien" in den Paulusbriefen. Studien zur rhetorischen Situation des 1. Thessalonicherbriefes, des Galaterbriefes und des Philipperbriefes,* Göttinger theologischer Arbeiten 45 (1991), 72-78; S.K. Stowers, *Letter Writing in Greco-Roman Antiquity* (1986), 173.

to be decided by the Galatains was not whether Paul had been right in what he had said or done, but what they themselves were going to believe and to do."[153]   D.E. Aune suggests a change in the rhetorical character of the Letter. "Paul turns from forensic oratory in Gal 1-2 to deliberative oratory in Gal 3-4."[154]   Betz himself, in the expanded forward to the German edition of his comentary on Galatians, does not exclude elements of deliberative rhetoric for an apologetic letter.[155]

Betz applies the same rhetorical approach to 2 Corinthians 8 and 9,[156] as well as to 1 Corinthians.[157]

### 3.2.3.3. Rhetorical Analysis and Epistolography

*Literature*

Alexander, L., "Hellenistic-Letter Forms and the Structure of Philippians," *JSNT* 37 (1989): 87-101. Fitzgerald, J.T., "Paul, The Ancient Epistolary Theorists, and 2 Corinthians 10-13: The Purpose and Literary Genre of a Pauline Letter," in *Greeks, Romans, and Christians: Essays in Honor of A.J. Malherbe,* ed. D.L. Balch *et al.* (1990), 190-200. Jewett, R., *The Thessalonian Correspondence: Pauline Rhetoric and Millenarian Piety,* FFNT (1986). Klauck, H.-J., *Die Johannesbriefe,* ErFor 276 (1991), 75-87. Lührmann, D., "Freundschaft trotz Spannungen. Zu Gattung und Aufbau des Ersten Korintherbriefs," in *Studien zum Text und zur Ethik des Neuen Testaments. Festschrift H. Greeven,* ed. W. Schrage, BZNW 47 (1986), 298-314. Malherbe, A.J., "Ancient Epistolary Theorists," *Ohio Journal of Religious Studies* 5.2 (1977): 3-77 (reprinted as *Ancient Epistolary Theorists,* SBLSBS 19 [1987]); "Exhortation in First Thessalonians," *NovT* 25 (1983): 238-256. Propst, H., *Paulus und der Brief. Die Rhetorik des antiken Briefes als Form der paulinischen Korintherkorrespondenz,* WUNT II 45 (1991). Schüssler-Fiorenza, E., "Rhetorical Stiuation and Historical Reconstruction in 1 Corinthians," *NTS* 33 (1987): 386-403. Wickert, U., "Der Philemonbrief — Privatbrief oder apostolisches Schreiben," *ZNW* 52 (1961): 230-238.

---

[153] G.A. Kennedy, *New Testament Interpretation through Rhetorical Criticism,* Studies in Religion (1984), 146. Cf. also F. Vouga, "Zur rhetorischen Gattung des Galaterbriefes," *ZNW* 79 (1988): 292; B. Standaert, "La rhétorique antique et l' epître aux Galates," *Foi et vie* 84, no. 5 (1985): 36f.; and J. Smit, "The Letter of Paul to the Galatians: A Deliberative Speech," *NTS* 35 (1989): 1-26.

[154] D.E. Aune, in his review of Betz's commentary on Galatians in RSR 7 (1981): 325. G.W. Hansen claims a similar change of rhetorical genus: Galatians is forensic up through 4:11, but from 4:12 on it becomes deliberative (*Abraham in Galatians: Epistolary and Rhetorical Contexts,* JSNTSup 29 (1989), 58-60.

[155] Betz, *Der Galaterbrief* 2.

[156] Betz, *2 Corinthians.*

[157] Betz, "Korintherbriefe," *EKL³* 2 (1989): 1450f. Compare also W. Schenk, "Korintherbriefe," *TRE* 19 (1990): 620-640, who divides up the Corinthian correspondence on the basis of rhetorical aspects.

*A selection of articles, monographs, etc., which utilize "rhetorical analysis" to interpret New Testament passages or whole Letters against the background of ancient rhetoric:*[158]

Church, F.F., "Rhetorical Structure and Design in Paul's Letter to Philemon," *HTR* 71 (1978): 17-33. Holland, G.S., *The Tradition that You Received from Us: 2 Thessalonians in the Pauline Tradition,* HUT 24 (1988). Hughes, F.W., Early Christian Rhetoric and 2 Thessalonians, JSNTSup 30 (1989); "The Rhetoric of 1 Thessalonians," in *The Thessalonian Correspondence,* ed. R.F. Collins, BETL 87 (1990), 94-116. Jewett, R., *The Thessalonian Correspondence: Pauline Rhetoric and Millenarian Piety,* FFNT (1986). Lindars, B., "The Rhetorical Structure of Hebrews," NTS 35 (1989): 382-406. Mitchell, M.M., *Paul and the Rhetoric of Reconciliation: An Exegetical Investigation of the Language and Composition of I Corinthians,* HUT 28 (1991). Schenk, W., "Korintherbriefe," in *TRE* 19 (1990): 620-640. Vouga, F., "Römer 1,18-3,20 als narratio," *TGl* 77 (1987): 225-236; "La réception de la théologie johannique das les épîtres," in *La communauté johannique et son histoire. La trajectoire de l'évangile de Jean aux deux premiers siècles,* by J.-D. Kaestli/J.-M. Poffet/ J. Zumstein, Le monde de la bible (1990), 288-291. Watson, D.F., *Invention, Arrangement, and Style: Rhetorical Criticism of Jude and 2 Peter,* SBLDS 104 (1988); "A Rhetorical Analysis of 2 John According to Greco-Roman Convention," *NTS* 35 (1989): 104-130; "A Rhetorical Analysis of 3 John: A Study in Epistolary Rhetoric," *CBQ* 51 (1989): 479-501.

Analyzing the Pauline Letters on the basis of rhetorical criteria is especially characteristic of American New Testament research. R. Jewett applies these methods to 1 and 2 Thessalonians (cf. his arrangements of 1[159] and 2 Thessalonians[160]). F.F. Church structured Philemon according to the genre of "deliberative rhetoric."[161] Further studies followed, some dedicated to letters outside the Pauline corpus.[162] They express current New Testament exegesis' strong interest in the rhetorical approach.

---

[158] Cf. also the literature to 3.2.3.2. Further bibliography is cited by J. Lambrecht, "Rhetorical Criticism and the New Testament," *Bijdragen* 50 (1989): 239-253; C.J. Classen, "Paulus und die antike Rhetorik," *ZNW* 82 (1991): 27f., n. 92.

[159] R. Jewett, *Thessalonian Correspondence* 72-76: it is close to a "praising letter" or "thankful letter," i.e., epideictic rhetoric. But A.J. Malherbe classifies the Letter differently in *Moral Exhortation, A Greco-Roman Sourcebook,* Library of Early Christianity 4 (1986), 80 and in "Exhortation in First Thessalonians," *NovT* 25 (1983): 238-256, as does S.K. Stowers in *Letter Writing in Greco-Roman Antiquity* (1986), 96, 42. They place 1 Thessalonians among the "paraenetic" or "hortatory letters."

[160] R. Jewett, *Thessalonian Correspondence,* 82-85 calls 2 Thessalonians a "mixed letter" and deliberative rhetoric. G.S. Holland (HUT 24) and F.W. Hughes (JSNTSup 30, 51-74) structure 2 Thessalonians in correspondence with deliberative rhetoric.

[161] *HTR* 71:19f.: "The key is to demonstrate love of friendship and to introduce sympathy or goodwill, in order to dispose the hearer favorably to the merits of one's case."

[162] Cf. e.g., F. Vouga in *TGl* 77: Romans as apology. D.F. Watson (*NTS* 35) sees 2 John as a "paraenetic-advisory letter" in deliberative rhetoric. In *CBQ* 51 he regards

To the extent that a text is understood as a direct answer to a specific historical situation, rhetorical analysis or criticism should lead to a determination of the historical background of this individual work. The decisive criterion of rhetoric is not aesthetic, but practical.[163]

Deissmann regarded the Pauline Letters as lacking a definite arrangement.[164] Against this, rhetorical analysis attempts to provide such an inner structure, though the problems in doing so are not to be overlooked. Specific points of demarcation between individual sections remain questionable.[165] Furthermore, the paraenetic section beginning at 1 Thessalonians 4:1 can only with diffiiculty be included in the *probatio*.[166]

A schematizing application of rhetorical analysis on the basis of the theories from ancient rhetorical handbooks, as is from time to time attempted by researchers, fits neither ancient nor New Testament Letters.[167] Primary significance belongs to the actual structure and argumentation of individual authors based on the analysis of their work.[168]

---

3 John as a mixed form of friendship, petition, and paraenesis in the form of epideictic rhetoric. Cf. also Watson's work on Jude and 2 Peter in SBLDS 104, etc.

[163] E. Schüssler-Fiorenza, NTS 33:387f. Cf. also F.W. Hughes, JSNTSup 30, 30.

[164] *Paulus. Eine kultur- und religionsgeschichtliche Skizze* ($^2$1925), 11; *Paul. A Study in Social and Religious History* (1926), 14: "... all this, too, mostly without any careful arrangement, unconsciously passing from one thing to the other, often indeed jumping. The longer Letteres, too, show clearly the often abrupt change of mood while he was dictating."

[165] The *narratio* of Galatians should begin at 1:13 instead of 1:12, and the *exhortatio* with 5:13 rather than 5:1. Cf. H. Hübner, "Galaterbrief," *TRE* 12 (1984), 5; *TLZ* 109: 244, 245f., 249; J. Becker, Paulus, *Der Apostel der Völker* (1989), 291f.; *Paul: Apostle to the Gentiles* (1993), 275f. The conceptual *narratio* is not clear. Cassiodor uses the term in the genral sense of "section." Melanchthon, however, uses it for the *pars ovationis* between the *exordium* and *confirmatio*. Cf. C.J. Classen, "Paulus und die antike Rhetorik," *ZNW* 82 (1991): 16, 20.

[166] Cf. on the relationship between rhetoric and paraenesis cf. D.E. Aune's review of Hans Dieter Betz, *Galatians: A Commentary on Paul's Letter to the Churches in Galatia*, Hermeneia (Philadelphia, 1979) in *RSR* 7 (1981): 325. "Parenesis was part of what may be broadly designated as 'philosophical rhetoric,' but the relationship between that setting of paraenesis, epistolary parenesis, and the parenetical sections of the Pauline Letters remains a subject for investigation." Cf. also S.K. Stowers, *Letter Writing in Greco-Roman Antiquity* (1986), 42f., 91ff. (with sources). Stowers agrees with the classification of philosophical "hortatory letters" for paraenesis in the New Testament Letters, but has some disagreements with Aune. Cf. also A.J. Malherbe, *Moral Exhortation, A Greco-Roman Sourcebook* (1986), 79-85; H.-J. Klauck in *ZNW* 81:212; J. Schoon-Janssen, *Umstrittene "Apologien" in den Paulusbriefen. Studien zur rhetoricshen Situation des 1. Thessalonicherbriefes, des Galaterbriefes und des Philipperbriefes,* Göttinger theologischer Arbeiten 45 (1991), 80f.

[167] Cf. the reference of M. Fuhrmann, *Die antike Rhetorik. Eine Einführung* ($^3$1990), 78f., to the speeches of Cicero.

[168] Emphasized by C.J. Classen, "Paulus und die antike Rhetorik," *ZNW* 82 (1991): 27f.: "that exegesis must proceed from the specific literary (or subliterary) work, from its genre, author, time, and audience, etc., and also from the structure, argumentation, vocabulary; text should be studied in light of theory and where possible data and theory

While letters may substitute for actual conversation, given spatial separation of the parties,[169] the distinction between speeches and letters is of foundational significance for ancient rhetoric.[170]

Hence it is questionable that apostolic letters should be considered "literarily fixed, addressed apostolic speeches."[171] A. Dihle[172] conceives of the Pauline Letters as "evidence of continuing or incipient preaching and pastoral care over a distance."[173] If the concept of preaching is not understood in the narrow sense of the genre "homily," Paul's Letters should obviously be understood as a part of his proclamation of the gospel. This occurs in letter form, which also gives Paul the opportunity to answer questions from the communities,[174] to remark on specific situations, for instruction and admonition, for confronting opponents, and for commenting on the legitimacy of his own apostleship (2 Cor 10-13).

It is also worth asking how Paul might have acquired the specific knowledge and insight into ancient rhetoric which is presupposed in rhetorical analysis. That Paul received a certain rhetorical education,[175] perhaps in Tarsus,[176]

---

should be qualified by one another, so to ascertain the intention of the whole work. . . Even if many of the data correspond to the norms of the theory, it is nevertheless not permissible to conclude that other norms should also be applied." Cf. also the judgment of H.-J. Klauck, *ZNW* 81:224: "Finding a balance between the typical generic pattern and the individual text is a continual task of literary criticism. . . . Previous rhetorical analyses of the Johannine Letters have hardly solved this problem more satisfactorily than other approaches." The same may be said for rhetorical analyses of the other Letters.

[169] Cf. H. Koskenniemi, *Studien zur Idee und Phraseologie des griechischen Briefes bis 400 n. Christus,* Annales Academicae Scientiarum Fennicae, Series B, 102,2 (1956), 38. J.L. White (*ANRW* II 25.2, 1731) lists as further concerns of the letter the communication of or request for information as well as wishes for or demands on the recipient(s). Cf. also N.A. Dahl, *IDBSup,* 539.

[170] Cf. H. Koskenniemi, *Studien* 43 with references. Cf. also C.J. Classen, "Paulus und die antike Rhetorik," *ZNW* 82 (1991): 5f., 13; S.K. Stowers, *Letter Writing in Greco-Roman Antiquity* (1986), 52. D.E. Aune refers to distinctions in vocabulary, style, and structure (*The New Testament in its Literary Environment* [1987], 159). In ZNW 81:208 H.-J. Klauck leaves open the question, "to what extent rhetoric on the level of macrostructure applies to the writing of other sorts of texts, whether it ought without qualification be carried over to letters." Cf. also his comments in *Erträge der Forschung* 276:77, 87.

[171] K. Berger, *ZNW* 65:231, cf. also 219; V. Stolle, "Apostelbriefe und Evangelien als Zeugnisse für den urchristlichen Gottesdienst. Zu den neutestamentlichen Grundlagen und Kriterien des christlichen Gottesdienst," in *LTK* 12 (1988): 51.

[172] A. Dihle, *Die griechische und lateinische Literatur der Kaiserzeit* (1989), 217; *Greek and Latin Literature of the Roman Empire* (1994), 205.

[173] Cf. Dihle, *Literatur,* 218; *Literature,* 205: "the synthesis of instruction, pastoral care, and personal communication on the basis of a bond of common worship between the sender and the addressees."

[174] Cf. above, p. 54.

[175] On the relationship between the writing of letters, rhetorical knowledge, and social status in Hellenistic education, cf. S.K. Stowers, *Letter Writing in Greco-Roman Antiquity* (1986), 32ff.

[176] As C. Forbes suggests in "Comparison, Self-Praise and Irony: Paul's Boasting and the Conventions of Hellenistic Rhetoric," *NTS* 32 (1986): 22f. Public speeches and lectures gave frequent opportunities for contact with ancient rhetoric (cf. above note

is likely in light of the use of Hellenistic rhetoric throughout disapora Judaism.[177] Questions about Paul's specific education and the extent of his rhetorical knowledge can only be answered on the basis of his Letters. The perplexity mentioned earlier with respect to our knowledge of ancient letter theory presents an additional difficulty. We should be sceptical about presuming for Paul a specialized rhetorical knowledge, as detailed in ancient or modern rhetorical handbooks. We cannot prove he had such knowledge.

Despite intensive efforts, especially in English language works, there is as yet no persuasive classification of the New Testament Letters in comparison with ancient letters.[178]

A.J. Malherbe has done important preparatory work in collecting texts on the theory of ancient letter writing and translating them into English,[179] as has S.K. Stowers in editions of ancient letters classified by their different types.[180] Since the question of letter types was debated already in the ancient tradition,[181] extreme caution must be exercised in any attempts at an exact typology of ancient letters today. Alongside the question of literary character, that of function or intended objective will probably be most productive.

Despite these as yet unsatisfactorily clarified preliminary questions, letter models from antiquity have increasingly been put forward as instructive for our understanding New Testament Letters (e.g. the genres of friendship letters[182] or

---

124). C.J. Klassen refers to contact through the written word, "Paulus und die antike Rhetorik," *ZNW* 82 (1991): 4.

[177] Cf. H.-J. Klauck, *ZNW* 81:207 with reference to 4 Maccabees. Cf. also his "Hellenistische Rhetorik im Diasporajudentum. Das Exordium des vierten Makkabäerbuchs (4 Makk 1.1-12)," *NTS* 35 (1989): 451-465.

[178] Cf. the still relevant judgment of A.J. Malherbe, "Ancient Epistolary Theorists," *Ohio Journal of Religious Studies* 5.2 (1977): 3 (reprinted as *Ancient Epistolary Theorists*, SBLSBS 19 [1987]): "Nor has any successful attempt been made to place letter writing in its exact context in rhetorical theory or in school instruction."

[179] Cf. "Theorists," 19-77, where special attention is given letters of recommendation. Cf. C.W. Keyes, "The Greek Letter of Introduction," *AJP* 56 (1935): 28-44; C.H. Kim, *Form and Structure of the Greek Letter of Recommendation*, SBLDS 4 (1972); H.M. Cotton, "Greek and Latin Epistolography: Some Light on Cicero's Letter Writing," *AJP* 105 (1984): 409-425.

[180] S.K. Stowers, *Letter Writing in Greco-Roman Antiquity* (1986), 49ff.: *Letters of friendship; family letters; letters of praise and blame; letters of exhortation and advice* with seven subtypes; *letters of mediation; accusing, apologetic and accounting letters.* D.E. Aune, *The New Testament in its Literary Environment* (1987), 162-169 has a different classification: *private or documentary letters; official letters; litarary letters.*

[181] Cf. the differentiation of 21 letter types in Pseudo-Dionysius and 41 in Pseudo-Libanius. For the texts cf. Malherbe, "Theorists," 28-39 and 62-69.

[182] M. Bünker, D. Lührmann in "Freundschaft trotz Spannungen. Zu Gattung und Aufbau des Ersten Korintherbriefs," in *Studien zum Text und zur Ethik des Neuen Testaments.* Festschrift H. Greeven, ed. W. Schrage, BZNW 47 (1986), 298-314; K. Thraede in *Grundzüge griechisch-römischer Briefoptik*, Zetemata 48 (1970); and J. Schoon-Janssen, *Umstrittene "Apologien" in den Paulusbriefen. Studien zur rhetorischen Situation des 1. Thessalonicherbriefes, des Galaterbriefes und des Philipperbriefes*, Göttinger theologischer Arbeiten 45 (1991), 39-47 (on

family letters[183]). Other attempts at classification refer to Jewish prophetic letters.[184] M. Wolter, orienting himself to the "communicative model of the letter or letter-like instructional writings widely substantiated in Hellenistic and Roman antiquity," characterizes 1 Timothy and Titus as *Mandata principis,* i.e., "on the basis of their mandates as instructions for those who have authority or commission to issue directives."[185]

Rhetorical analysis and epistolographic comparison can only lead to persuasive conclusions in harmony with other measures of the historical-critical method. We must always remember that the authors of New Testament Letters were expressing issues of Christian faith, which in the final analysis can be satisfactorily interpreted only in coordination with a system of New Testament theology.

## 3.3    Traditional Material

*Literature*

Von Campenhausen, H., "Das Bekenntnis im Urchristentum," *ZNW* 63 (1972): 210-253. Deichgräber, R., *Gotteshymnus und Christushymnus in der frühen Christenheit. Untersuchungen zu Form, Sprache und Stil der frühchristlichen Hymnen,* SUNT 5 (1967). Delling, G., *Der Gottesdienst im Neuen Testament* (1952), esp. 60-76 on forms and 77-88 on creeds and hymns; *Worship in the New Testament* (1962), 55-76 and 77-87. Rese, M., "Formeln und Lieder im Neuen Testament. Einige notwendige Anmerkungen," *VF* 15 (1970): 75-95. Seeberg, A., *Der Katechismus der Urchristenheit. Mit einer Einführung v. F. Hahn,* TBü 26 (1966). Wengst, K., *Christologische Formeln und Lieder des Urchristentums,* SNT 7 (1972).

---

1 Thessalonians), as well as others, understand the Pauline Letters as influenced by the topoi of ancient letters of friendship. So does S.K. Stowers, *Letter Writing in Greco-Roman Antiquity* (1986), 60. Though he refuses to carry this genre over as a whole, he sees some elements of it taken up in the New Testament; e.g. the motif of "absent in the body, but present in spirit in 1 Cor 5:3 (not 2 Cor 5:3; Stowers 60); 2 Cor 10:1f.[?]; Col 2:5; 1 Thess 2:17.

[183] L. Alexander, "Hellenistic-Letter Forms and the Structure of Philippians," *JSNT* 37 (1989): 87-101, regards Philippians as a family letter, yet in the New Testament Letters the familiar address in the most genuine sense is lacking. ἀδελφός in Phil 1:12, as mostly elsewhere, means fellow Christians; cf. Phil 4:21.

[184]  Cf. K. Berger, "Apostelbrief und apostolische Rede/Zum Formular frühchristlicher Briefe," *ZNW* 65 (1974): 190-231. Berger sees a relationship also to the testament genre and to the Apocalypse.

[185] M. Wolter, *Die Pastoralbriefe als Paulustradition,* FRLANT 146 (1988), 164-170 and often throughout. Cf. citations 180 and 196. Cf. similarly N.A. Dahl, "Letter," in *IDBSup,* 1976, 540: "mandates for ministers of the church."

Early Christian formulaic materials with independent histories are demonstrable in the New Testament Letters.[186] These varied traditions and their scholarly discussion can only be sampled here.

A. Seeberg's attempt to reconstruct a primitive Christian catechism from these various individual texts is unpersuasive, given the complexity of the oral tradition. It is preferable to begin with the individual traditions[187] which, bound to their present contexts, are adapted to their needs. This redactional interest is to be ascertained from these connections and taken into account in the reconstruction of the tradition.[188] In this sense the redactional activity of Paul demands the same sort of study as that of the Evangelists.

### 3.3.1 Confessional Formulas

*Literature*

Conzelmann, H. "Was glaubte die frühe Christenheit?" (first published in 1955), in his *Theologie als Schriftauslesung. Aufsätze zum Neuen Testament,* BEvT 65 (1974), 106-119. Cullmann, O., *Die ersten christlichen Glaubensbekenntnisse,* Theologische Studien 15 (1943). Hoffmann, P. "Auferstehung Jesu Christi II/1. Neues Testament," *TRE* 4 (1979): 478-513. Kamlah, E., "Bekenntnis II. Im NT," *RGG³* 1 (1957): 991-993. Kramer, W., *Christos Kyrios Gottesohn. Untersuchungen zu Gebrauch und Bedeutung der christologischen Bezeichnungen bei Paulus und den vorpaulinischen Gemeinden,* ATANT 44 (1963). Neufeld, V.H., *The Earliest Christian Confessions,* NTTS V (1963). Schnelle, U., *Gerechtigkeit und Christusgegenwart. Vorpaulinische und paulinische Tauftheologie.* Göttinger Theologische Arbeiten 24 (²1986). Wengst, K., "Glaubensbekenntnis(se) IV. Neues Testament," *TRE* 13 (1984): 392-399.

Identification and specific dimensions are disputed. The distinction between credo-formulae (Conzelmann) or pistis-formulae (W. Kramer) and homologies is artificial. According to this distinction, credo and pistis formulae begin with a form of the verb πιστεύειν ("believe") and center on the resurrection of

---

[186] N.A. Dahl (*IDBSup* 539) refers to secular (papyrus) letters as formal analogies. They reflect the human condition through the use of traditional materials such as proverbs, quotations, historical examples, and rules.

[187] On criteria for reconstructing traditional materials cf. M. Dibelius in *TRu* 3:210f.; G. Strecker and U. Schnelle, *Einführung in die neutestamentliche Exegese,* Uni-Taschenbücher 1253 (³1989), 95. On the problem of such qualifications and the resultant procedures, cf. U. Schnelle, *Gerechtigkeit und Christusgegenwart. Vorpaulinische und paulinische Tauftheologie,* Göttinger Theologische Arbeiten 24 (²1986), 33f.; and M. Rese, "Formeln," *VF* 15 (1970): 93-95.

[188] E.g., in the Jewish Christian tradition utilized in Rom 3:25, which utilizes the conception of a vicarious sacrifice to describe the saving death of Christ as a demonstration of the righteousness of God, it can be shown that Paul inserted the phrase "through faith." Thereby, as in Rom 3:21f., Paul emphasizes the means by which salvation is appropriated (cf. G. Schnelle, *Gerechtigkeit* 67-72). Cf. also comments on the hymn in Philippians 2 below at 3.3.3.

Jesus from the dead and along with it his saving work (e.g., Rom 4:25, etc.). The homologies begin with a form of the verb ὁμολογεῖν ("confess") and appeal to the risen Lord (e.g., Phil. 2:11, etc.). Given that both verbs are used in the *parallelismus membrorum* in Rom 10:9, this thesis is not persuasive.[189] It is due to a schematic contraction that 1 Thess. 1:9f. lacks the "credo" terminology, since reference to the resurrection should not be excluded here.[190] The distinction between single, exclusively Christological (e.g., 1 Thess 4:14), double (Rom 15:6; 1 Cor 8:6; 1 Thess 1:9b-10; 1 Tim 2:5f.), and (occasionally) triple formulae (2 Cor 13:13; Matt 28:19) is more clear.

The oldest Christian traditional materials are found in confessional formulae which relate the death[191] and/or resurrection of Jesus.[192] Those traditions which exalt Jesus as Kyrios (Rom 10:9; Phil 2:11, cf. 3.3.2), or as Son of David or Son of God (Rom. 1:3f.) are also ancient. The pre-Pauline baptismal traditions in 1 Cor 1:30, 6:11, etc., are also important.[193]

These confessions have various settings in the life of the ancient church.[194] This is true despite the objections of H. von Campenhausen, according to whom confessions "in the early Christian communities generally were not tied to a specific place or text, but generally were everywhere at home, so to speak."[195]

### 3.3.2   Liturgical Formulas

*Literature*

Bornkamm, G., "Das Anathema in der urchristlichen Abendmahlsliturgie," (first published in 1950), now in his *Das Ende des Gesetzes. Paulusstudien. Gesammelte Aufsätze I*, BEvT 16 (⁵1966), 123-132. Deichgräber, R., "Formeln, Liturgische II. Neues Testament und Alte Kirche 1-4," *TRE* 11 (1983): 256-263. Hahn, F. *Der urchristliche Gottesdienst*, SBS 41 (1970). Käsemann, E., "Formeln II. Liturgische Formeln in NT," *RGG³* 2 (1958): 993-996. Klauser, T., "Akklamation," *RAC* 1 (1950): 216-223. Martin, R.P., "Liturgical Materials,

---

[189] Against H. Conzelmann, "Was glaubte," 109 and P. Vielhauer, *Geschichte der urchristlichen Literatur,* 13ff. For the critique cf. G. Strecker, "Befreiung und Rechtfertigung. Zur Stellung der Rechtfertigungslehre in der Theologie des Paulus," (first published in 1976), now in his *Eschaton und Historie. Aufsätze* (1979), 229-259, 238, with n. 26.

[190] But for a different outlook cf. D.-A. Koch, "Zum Verständnis von Christologie und Eschatologie im Markusevangelium. Beobachtungen aufgrund von Mk 8,27-9,1," in *Jesus Christus in Historie und Theologie. Festschrift H. Conzelmann,* ed. G. Strecker (1975), 395-408, 400 with n. 16.

[191] On the basis of the verb used, formulae about Jesus' "dying" are distinguished from those about his "giving up his life," the latter sometimes giving a positive meaning to that death by using ὑπέρ with the genitive or an equivalent prespositional expression.

[192] P. Hoffmann, "Auferstehung," 479-481; classically: 1 Cor 15:3b-5a.

[193] Cf. U. Schnelle, *Gerechtigkeit.*

[194] O. Cullmann, *Glaubensbekenntnisse,* 13, lists: baptism, catechizing, worship, exorcism, persecution, polemics against heresy.

[195] H. von Campenhausen, *ZNW* 63:231.

NT," *IDBSup* (1976), 556f. *ΕΙΣ ΘΕΟΣ. Epigraphische, formgeschichtliche und religionsgeschichtliche Untersuchungen,* FRLANT 41 (1926). Stolle, V. "Apostelbriefe und Evangelien als Zeugnisse für den urchristlichen Gottesdienst. Zu den neutestamentlichen Grundlagen und Kriterien des christlichen Gottesdienstes," *Lutherische Theologie und Kirche* 12 (1988): 50-65. Wengst, K., "Glaubensbekenntnis(se) IV. Neues Testament," *TRE* 13 (1984): 396f.

At least one confessional formula was used in worship. The petition "maranatha"[196] (1 Cor 16:22, cf. Rev 22:20) certainly comes from the worship of the Aramaic-speaking communities. Paul himself recognizes the constituting words of the Lord's Supper in 1 Cor 11:23-25 as traditional. Their oldest form is to be discovered in comparison with Mark 14:22-25.[197]

The "acclamation" also belongs to liturgy; to be regarded as "public, inspired, and a legally binding petition."[198]   Such acclamations are the exclamations κύριος' Ιοοῦς (Rom 10:9; 1 Cor 12:3; in extended form, Phil 2:11), ἀββὰ ὁ πατήρ (Gal 4:6; Rom 8:15[199]), and the εἶς acclamations (e.g., 1 Cor 8:6, 1 Tim 2:5f., Eph 4:5).[200]   (Further acclamations are "amen" (cf. 1 Cor 14:16), "hallelujah," and "hosanna.")

The κύριε σῶσον and κύριε ἐλέησον formulae of Matthew's Gospel may reflect acclamations of the Matthean community.[201]

In addition, doxologies (e.g., Rom 11:36b; Phil 4:20 1 Tim 1:17; and greatly expanded in Rom 16:25-27) and eulogies (cf. Rom 1:25; 2 Cor 11:31) which often conclude sections of the Letters, have their origins in early Christian worship (note also the introductory eulogies in the Letters[202]).

Doxologies are usually tripartite in form. First, the person praised is named, usually in the dative case. The word of praise follows, generally expressed with δόξα. The doxology concludes with a temporal formula, often with "amen" added: ᾧ τῷ αὐτῷ σοὶ (seldom with the genetive σοῦ) ἡ δόξα εἰς τοὺς αἰῶνας (ἀμήν).[203]

---

[196] H.P. Rüger, "Aramäisch II. Im Neuen Testament," *TRE* 3 (1978): 607.

[197] Outside the Letters, the baptismal formula of Matt 28:19b should be classified with liturgical formulae, cf. G. Strecker, *Der Weg der Gerechtigkeit. Untersuchung zur Theologie des Matthäus,* FRLANT 82 (³1971), 210.

[198] E. Käsemann in *RGG³* 2:993.

[199] This address ought not to be identified as a prayer (the beginning of the Lord's Prayer), following the formal analysis of A. Seeberg (*Der Katechismus der Urchristenheit,* 240-243). Cf. E. Käsemann, *An die Römer,* HNT 8a⁴, 220; H. Paulsen, *Überlieferung und Auslegung in Römer 8,* WMANT 43 (1974), 88-94 with bibliography; R. Gebauer, *Das Gebet bei Paulus. Forschungsgeschichte und exegetische Studien* (1989), 150 (n. 348 for bibliography), 156. But Gebauer's evaluation of ὁ πατήρ as a Pauline interpretive expression (149, n. 340 with bibliography and 156) is dubious, given the unified tradition in Romans and Galatians.

[200] On all of these cf. E. Peterson, *ΕΙΣ ΘΕΟΣ;* K. Wengst, *SNT* 7:131ff.

[201] Cf. also V. Stolle, "Apostelbriefe und Evangelien," 58. For a different viewpoint, cf. U. Luz, *Das Evangelium nach Matthäus. Mt 1-7.* EKKNT I/1 (²1989), 60. Luz finds here the language of the Psalms, which he explains on the basis of worship experience.

[202] See above, pp. 53f.

[203] Cf. R. Deichgräber, SUNT 5, 25.

Formulas of blessing and cursing, as Paul already knows them (1 Cor 16:22: ἤτω ἀνάθεμα) should be regarded as derived from worship, thus the "anathema" formula in connection with the Lord's Supper (Didache 10:6).[204]

From time to time the greetings of Paul's Letters are also attributed to liturgical tradition.[205]

Even though early Christian prayer was not restricted to worship services, prayers inscribed in the New Testament are influenced by the liturgy. The Lord's Prayer was first composed in Aramaic (or Hebrew) and used by the primal community. In its earliest form it goes back to Jesus himself. But the version found in Matthew 6:9-13 was probably taken by Matthew from the tradition and mirrors the liturgical practice of the Matthean community.[206] It has already been explained that the ἀββὰ ὁ πατήρ formula cannot be accounted for on the basis of the Lord's Prayer. Prayer-like components of New Testament Letters were formulated in reaction to each epistolary situation. (Even the prayer of Acts 4:24b-25 was not traditional, but written by Luke.[207])

Others have attempted to derive longer sections of New Testament Letters from early Christian liturgy. G. Holtz sought to prove "that chapters 2 and 3 [of 1 Timothy] reflected eucharistic liturgy from late in Paul's lifetime."[208]    While the Pastorals doubtlessly make use of liturgical materials,[209] the idea that they contain longer liturgical units remains hypothetical. Such units really cannot be extracted from the Letters. Referring for support to later liturgical texts is also questionable, since one cannot simply presuppose the continuity between earlier and later Christian worship.

In general, we should be cautious about deriving texts from early Christian worship, since aside from occasional formulas and a few songs (cf. 3.3.3) there are hardly any data on which to reconstruct their order and extent.[210]

---

[204] Cf. G. Bornkamm, "Das Anathema," 123-125, and with respect to this F. Hahn, *Der urchristliche Gottesdienst,* 64 and 42f., where this formula is seen as "early tradition of the Palestinian church." I. Goldhahn-Müller sees the Pauline *Sitz im Leben* of this formula as the "proclamation of apostolic judgment" (*Die Grenze der Gemeinde. Studien zum Problem der Zweiten Busse im Neuen Testament unter Berücksichtigung der Entwicklung im 2. Jahrhundert bis Tertullian,* GTA 39 [1989], 153). But according to K. Berger [*Formgeschichte des Neuen Testaments* (1984), 181] the formula reflects a phenomenon related to the paraenesis at the conclusion of a letter.

[205] Cf. E. Lohmeyer, "Briefliche Grussüberschriften" (first appeared in 1927), in his *Probleme paulinischer Theologie* (1954), 7-29; F. Hahn, *Gottesdienst,* 64; R.P. Martin in *IDBSup* 557, etc. See also above, pp. 52f.

[206] Cf. U. Luz, *Matthäus,* 59f.; G. Strecker, *Der Weg der Gerechtigkeit³,* 18.

[207] Cf., e.g., M. Dömer, *Das Heil Gottes. Studien zur Theologie des lukanischen Doppelwerkes,* BBB 51 (1978); 63f.

[208] G. Holtz, *Die Pastoralbriefe,* THKNT 13 (⁴1986), 96.

[209] For 1 Timothy cf., e.g., J. Roloff, *Der erste Brief an Timotheus,* EKKNT 15 (1988), 41.

[210] On 1 Peter, see above, p. 48.

### 3.3.3 Hymns and Songs

*Literature*

Bauer, W. "Der Wortgottesdienst der ältesten Christen," (first published in 1930) in his *Aufsätze und Kleine Schriften,* ed. G. Strecker (1967), 155-209. Bornkamm, G. "Das Bekenntnis im Hebräerbrief," (first published in 1942) in his *Studien zu Antike und Christentum. Gesammelte Aufsätze II,* BEvT 28 ($^3$1970), 188-203. Bultmann, R. "Bekenntnis- und Liedfragmente im ersten Petrusbrief," (first published in 1947) in his *Exegetische. Aufsätze zur Erforshung des Neuen Testaments,* ed. E. Dinkler (1967), 285-297. Burger, C. *Schöpfung und Versöhnung. Studien zum liturgischen Gut im Kolosser- und Epheserbrief,* WMANT 46 (1975). Jeremias, G. "Hymnus 2. Neues Testament," in *EKL³* 2 (1989): 588-590. Käsemann, E., "Eine urchristliche Taufliturgie," (first published in 1949) in his *Exegetische Versuche und Besinnungen* I (1964): 34-51; "A Primitive Christian Baptismal Liturgy," in his *Essays on New Testament Themes,* SBT 41 (1964), 149-168. Riesenfeld, H., "Unpoetische Hymnen im Neuen Testament? Zu Phil 2,5-11," in *Glaube und Gerechtigkeit. In Memoriam R. Gyllenberg,* ed. J. Külunen, *et al.,* Suomen Eksegeettisen Seuran julkaisuja 38 (1983), 155-168. Robinson, J.M. "A Formal Analysis of Colossians 1:15-20," JBL 76 (1957): 270-287. Sanders, J.T. *The New Testament Christological Hymns: Their Historical Religious Background,* SNTSMS 15 (1971). Schille, G. *Frühchristliche Hymnen* (1962). Stenger, W., *Der Christushymnus 1 Tim 3,16. Eine strukturanalytische Untersuchung,* Regensburger Studien zur Theologie 6 (1977).

*Literature on Philippians 2:6-11 (a selection)*

Bornkamm, G. "Zum Verständnis des Christus-Hymnus Phil 2,6-11," in his *Studien zu Antike und Christentum. Gesammelte Aufsätze II,* BEvT 28 ($^3$1970), 177-187. Feuillet, A., "L'hymne christologique de l'epître aux Philippiens (II,6-11)," *RB* 72 (1965): 352-380, 481-507. Georgi, D., "Der vorpaulinische Hymnus Phil 2,6-11," in *Zeit und Geschichte. Dankesgabe an R. Bultmann,* ed. E. Dinkler (1964), 263-293. Habermann, J., *Präexistenzaussagen im Neuen Testament* (1990). Hofius, O., *Der Christushymnus Philipper 2,6-11. Untersuchung zu Gestalt und Aussage eines urchristlichen Psalms,* WUNT 17 ($^2$1991). Hunzinger, C.-H., "Zu den Christus-Hymnen in Phil 2 und 1 Petr 3," in *Der Ruf Jesu und die Antwort der Gemeinde. Exegetische Untersuchungen, Festschrift J. Jeremias* (1970), 142-156. Jeremias, J., "Zur Gedankenführung in den paulinischen Briefen," (first published in 1953), now in his *Abba. Studien zur neutestamentlichen Theologie und Zeitgeschichte* (1966), 269-276 (274-276); "Zu Philipper 2,7: ἑαυτὸν ἐκένωσεν," (first published in 1963), in his *Abba,* 308-313. Käsemann, E., "Kritische Analyse von Phil 2,5-11," (first published in 1950) now in his *Exegetische Versuche und Besinnungen* I (1964): 51-95. Lohmeyer, E., *Kyrios Jesus. Eine Untersuchung zu Phil 2,5-11,* Sitzungsberichte der Heidelberg Akademie der Wissenschaft, Philosophisch-Historische Klasse 4 (1928, $^2$1961). Martin, R.P. "The Form-Analysis of Philippians 2,5-11," in *SE II/1* (= TU 87), ed. F.L. Cross (1984), 611-

620; *Carmen Christi. Philippians ii 5-11 in Recent Interpretation and in the Setting of Early Christian Worship* (²1983). Müller, U.B., "Der Christushumnus Phil 2,6-11," *ZNW* 79 (1988): 17-44. Strecker, G., "Redaktion und Tradition im Christushymnus Phil 2,6-11," (first published in 1964) now in his *Eschaton und Historie. Aufsätze* (1979), 142-157.

Out of many songs from early Christianity (cf. 1 Cor 14:26; Col 3:16[211]), the New Testament Letters pass on a few (1 Tim 3:16; 1 Pet 1:20, 2:22-24, 3:18-22; etc.). They describe the humiliation and exaltation of Jesus Christ (Phil 2:6-11), his role in creation (Col 1:15-20[212]), and his enthronement (Heb 1:3[213]). The Gospels also contain traditions of hymnic character (in the style of the Psalms: Luke 1:46-55, 68-79; John 1:1-18[214] and other passsages also have a hymnic character). Since E. Lohmeyer's work, Phil 2:6-11 has been the special object of research.[215]

I
[6] Who, though he was in the form of God,
did not count equality with God as something to be exploited,
[7] but emptied himself,
taking the form of a slave,
being born in human likeness,
and being found in human form.

---

[211] Cf. also W. Bauer, "Wortgottesdienst," 171ff.

[212] Against Käsemann, not a reworking of a pre-Christian hymn, although glosses of a redactor are probable. Cf. C. Burger, and for bibliography E. Schweizer, *Der Brief an die Kolosser*, EKKNT XII (²1981), 44.

[213] But Bornkamm characterizes this as a (hymnic) confession ("Bekenntnis," 197-199). On text, scope, and form cf. W.R.G. Loader, *Sohn und Hohepriester. Eine traditionsgeschichtliche Untersuchung zur Christologie des Hebräerbriefes*, WMANT 53 (1981), 64-71. Loader attributes the expressions on inthronization and forgiveness of sins to the author of Hebrews. Cf. also P. Vielhauer, *Geschichte der urchristlichen Literatur* (²1978), 44f.

[214] See below, pp. 178ff.

[215] E. Lohmeyer, *Kyrios Jesus.* Cf. also the history of exegesis in R.P. Martin *Carmen Christi.* H. Riesenfeld's critique, beginning with the hymn in Philippians ("Unpoetische Hymnen?" 157ff.), misses clear parallels from outside the New Testament to the early Christian hymns and is not persuasive. On the one hand, reference ought to be made to hymns in the Hebrew scriptures and also pagan hymnic poetry and hymn signing. On the other hand, certain formal differences are motivated by the content of the New Testament songs and hymns, i.e., by the hymnic expression of Christ's act and the resultant human participation in the coming eschatological salvation. On (pre-Hellenistic) Greek hymns cf. J.M. Bremer "Greek Hymns," in *Faith, Hope, and Worship: Aspects of Religious Mentality in the Ancient World,* ed. H.S. Vesnel, Studies in Greek and Roman Religion 2 (Leiden, 1981), 193-215 (with examples); G. Knebel, "Hymnus," in *Lexikon der Alten Welt* 1344f.; K. Ziegler, "Hymnos," in *Der kleine Pauly* 2 (1967): 1268-1271. On the numerous Hellenistic and Roman hymns, cf. P. Hommel, "Hellenistische Dichtung G [5]," in *Lexikon der Alten Welt* 1244; R. Wünsch, "Hymnos," in PW 6 (9196): 140-183 (164-181); cf. also E. Norden, *Agnostos Theos. Untersuchungen zur Formengeschichte religiöser Rede* (1913), 143-176.

[8] *He humbled himself and became obedient to the point of death–even death on a cross.*

II
[9] Therefore God also highly exalted him
and gave him the name that is above every name,
[10] so that at the name of Jesus every knee should bend
in heaven and on earth and under the earth,
[11] and every tongue should confess
that Jesus Christ is Lord to the glory of God the Father.[216]

Attempts to partition this traditional section bring up several problems. E. Lohmeyer attempts to divide the hymn into six strophes of three lines each.[217] But this will not work syntactically. Furthermore, this thesis neglects the *parallelismus membrorum* (especially 2:7c and 7d). J. Jeremias opposed this partitioning with his own:[218] three strophes of four lines each (I: 6-7a; II: 7b-8; III: 9-11). This attempt works if 2:8c, the genitive of 2:10b, and the concluding doxology of 2:11b are eliminated. But the grammatical construction in 2:10b-11 resists this tripartite division. Generally the division is based on two strophes or members.[219] U.B. Müller divided the first of these into two sections, διό at 9a marking the beginning of the second strophe.[220]

The bipartite division of the Christ hymn is corroborated by the redactional character of all of 2:8. The two parallel strophes, marked by two predicates joined by conjunctions, are each made up of about six lines. The hymn, which combines Hellenistic and Jewish traditions, arose in a Hellenistic-Jewish area (note the LXX type allusions in the second part). The renunciation of divine being by the same, even in humiliation, pre-existent Christ is the basis for exaltation (cf. 2:9 διό). Though a divine being, his incarnation, through which he is lowered to human form, is the high point in the drama of redemption. The exaltation is his installation to a position of authority, rule as κύριος over the the world, understood as breaking in. Only at the end of time will the authority, now present to faith, be visible to all humanity. The soteriological significance of this pre-Pauline hymn lies in the community following the redeemer on the way of withdrawal from the sphere of earthly corporeality (cf. μορφὴ δούλου . . . ὡς ἄνθρωπος) and thus freed worshipping Christ. It also concerns the apocalyptic future. Paul takes up this hymn with an ethical goal and adminishes the community to humility (ταπεινοφροσύνη, 2:3) and obedience (ὑπακοή, 2:12), cf. the connection with 2:8. Through his apostle, the pre-existent Lord establishes the norm to which the community is responsible.

Many questions remain about this passage in terms of its structure, traditional and religious origins, distinctions between tradition and redaction, and

---

[216] The italic text indicates an interpretive interpolation by Paul. For details, cf. G. Strecker, "Redaktion und Tradition im Christushymnus," 149f. A. Feuillet also regards this as a Pauline addition, but O. Hofius opposes this viewpoint in *Christushymnus,* 7ff.

[217] Lohmeyer, *Kyrios Jesus,* 5ff.

[218] J. Jeremias, "Zur Gedenkenführung," 274f. and "Philipper 2,7," 312. C.-H. Hunzinger, "Zu den Christus-Hymnen," 145ff., agrees.

[219] Already with E. Lohmeyer.

[220] Müller, "Chrystushymnus," 19f.

form-critical significance. The confessional traditions of 1 Pet 1:20 and 3:18-22 are also interpreted quite differently.[221] Furthermore there is seldom a consensus as to the *Sitz im Leben* of the songs.

Rather than traditional worship materials, the "worthy" (ἄξιος) acclamations[222] and hymns of the Apocalypse are literary creations of the author, permitting only indirect conclusions about liturgical texts.[223]

### 3.3.4 "Insertions" in Pauline Letters

*Literature*

Georgi, D., *Die Gegner des Paulus im 2. Korintherbrief. Studien zur religiösen Propaganda in der Spätantike*, WMANT 11 (1964). Käsemann, E., "1. Korinther 2,6-16," (first published in 1949) now in his *Exegetische Versuche und Besinnungen* I (1964): 267-276. von der Osten-Sacken, P., *Römer 8 als Beispiel paulinischer Soteriologie*, FRLANT 112 (1975). Schmithals, W., *Die theologische Anthropologie des Paulus. Auslegung von Röm 7,17-8,39*, Kohlhammer Taschenbücher 1021 (1980). Schulz, S., "Die Decke des Moses. Untersuchungen zu einer vorpaulinischen Überlieferung in II Cor 3,7-18," *ZNW* 49 (1958): 1-30. Widman, M., "1 Kor 2,6-16: Ein Einspruch gegen Paulus," *ZNW* 70 (1979): 44-53. Wilckens, U., *Weisheit und Torheit. Eine exegetisch-religionsgeschichtliche Untersuchung zu 1 Kor 1 und 2*, BHT 26 (1959).

"Insertions" are sections in the Letters "which break the structure of the correspondence, are only loosely anchored in the context, and betray a certain degree of isolation."[224] They are to be distinguished from later additions such as interpolations and glosses (cf. 3.1.2), since, partly in relation to the specific situation, they are used by Paul himself in his argumentation.

Since the apostle's relationship to his communities was sometimes contentious,[225] attempts have been made to isolate the traditions held by his opponents. These are based on the observation that Paul had to take issue with the views of dissidents who would influence his communities. Besides citations from his opponents (1 Cor 15:12; 2 Cor 10:10; Rom 6:1), longer sections have been attributed to alleged opponents. In their present context Paul cites them against his opponents: 2 Cor 3:7-18;[226] cf. also the supposition of the adoption of opponents'

---

[221] Cf. R. Bultmann, "Bekenntnis- und Liedfragmente," 285ff., L. Goppelt, *Der erste Petrusbrief*, ed. F. Hahn, MeyerK 12/1 (1978), 124; N. Brox, *Der erste Petrusbrief*, EKKNT 21 (1979, ³1989), 165. Order, scope, and structure of the texts taken as hymnic or confessional formulae remain largely undetermined.

[222] Cf. E. Käsemann, "Formeln II. Liturgische Formeln im NT," *RGG³* 2 (1958): 994.

[223] See below, pp. 216f.

[224] P. Vielhauer, *Geschichte der urchristlichen Literatur* (²1978), 69.

[225] Cf., e.g., G. Strecker in Strecker/Johann Maier, *Neues Testament—Antikes Judentum* (1989), 82f.

[226] D. Georgi, *Die Gegner*, 258; S. Schulz, *ZNW* 49 (1958).

expressions and viewpoints: 1 Cor 2:6-16.[227] Other passages from community tradition are also reconstructed and regarded as adapted by Paul and applied to their context, cf. Rom 8:31-39.[228] Alternatively, such sections might be attributed to the Pauline school,[229] whose school activity may be responsible for the preformulated passages of Paul's Letters.[230]

## 3.4 Paraenetic Texts

*Literature*

Dibelius, M., *Der Brief des Jakobus* ([1[7]]1921), revised by H. Greeven, MeyerK 15, ([5[11]]1964); *James,* Hermeneia (1976). Easton, B.S., "New Testament Ethical Lists," *JBL* 51 (1932): 1-12. Kamlah, E., *Die Form der katalogischen Paränese im Neuen Testament,* WUNT 7 (1964). Malherbe, A.J., *Moral Exhortation: A Creco-Roman Sourcebook,* Library of Early Christianity 4 (1986). Popkes, W., *Adressaten, Situation und Form des Jakobusbriefes,* SBS 125/126 (1986). Schroeder, D., "Lists, Ethical," *IDBSup* (1976), 546f. Schulz, S., *Neutestamentliche Ethik,* Zürcher Grundrisse zur Bibel (1987). Schweizer, E. "Gottesgerechtigkeit und Lasterkataloge bei Paulus (inkl. Kol und Eph)," in *Rechtfertigung. Festschrift E. Käsemann,* ed. J. Friedrich, *et al.* (1976), 461-477. Strecker, G., "Strukturen einer neutestamentlichen Ethik," *ZTK* 75 (1978): 117-146. Vögtle, A., *Die Tugend- und Lasterkataloge im Neuen Testament. Exegetisch, religions- und formgeschichtlich untersucht,* NTAbh XVI 4/5 (1936); "Lasterkataloge," *LTK²* 6 (1961): 806-808; "Tugendkataloge," *LTK²* 10 (1965): 399-401. Wibbing, S., *Die Tugend- und Lasterkataloge im Neuen Testament und ihre Traditionsgeschichte unter besonderer Berücksichtigung der Qumran-Texte,* BZNW 25 (1959). Wuellner, WlH., "Der Jakobusbrief im Licht der Thetorik und Textpragmatik," *LB* 43 (1978): 5-66.

---

[227] E. Käsemann, "1. Korinther 2,6-16," 267: "The apostle battles Christian enthusiasm with its own weapons." Cf. also U. Wilckens, *Weisheit und Torheit,* 52ff. But M. Widman disagrees. He sees this passage as the answer to a Pauline Letter, an answer later interpolated here. But despite some stylistic differences in the context, the train of thought in this passage can hardly be denied to Paul.

[228] P. von der Osten-Sacken, *Römer 8, 14-16,* sees this as the catechetical formula of a Jewish Christian community. W. Schmithals, *Anthropologie* 178, recognizes the Pauline character of this section and even calls it the "high point of the entire 'little theology,'" yet based on the assumption that there is in Romans 7:17-8:39 a "little theology," or a compendium of Pauline theology which comes from a rather early period of theological education within the Pauline school. But against this is the fact that Romans 7:17-8:39 does not go beyond the thought of Romans 5:1ff., of which the theme is the effectiveness of God's righteousness. Nor is the thesis of a new beginning at 7:17 persuasive.

[229] Cf. Vielhauer, *Geschichte,* 70.

[230] See below, pp. 82f.

*Literature on household codes and admonitions*

Balch, D.L., *Let Wives be Submissive. The Domestic Code in I Peter*, SBLMS 26 (1981); "Household Codes," in *Greco-Roman Literature and the New Testament*, ed. D.E. Aune, SBLSBS 21 (1988), 25-50. Crouch, J.E., *The Origin and Intention of the Colossian Haustafel*, FRLANT 109 (1972). Dassmann, E., and G. Schöllgen, "Haus II (Hausgemeinschaft)," *RAC* 13 (1986): 801-905. Dibelius, M., *An die Kolosser, Epheser. An Philemon*, HNT 3,2 ([1]1912), revised by H. Greeven, HNT 12 ([3]1953). Fiedler, "Haustafeln," *RAC* 13 (1986): 1063-1073. Gielen, M., *Tradition und Theologie neutestamentlicher Haustafelethik. Ein Beitrag zur Frage einer christlichen Auseinandersetzung mit gesellschaftlichen Normen*, BBB 75 (1990). Goppelt, L., "Jesus und die 'Haustafel'-Tradition," in *Orientierung an Jesus. Zur Theologie der Synoptiker. Festschrift J. Schmidt*, ed. P. Hoffmann, *et al.* (1973), 93-106. Lührmann, D., "Wo man nicht mehr Sklave oder Freier ist. Überlegungen zur Struktur frühchristlicher Gemeinden," *WD* 13 (1975): 53-83; "Neutestamentliche Haustafeln und antike Ökonomie," *NTS* 27 (1981): 83-97. Müller, K., "Die Haustafel des Kolosserbriefes und das antike Frauenthema. Eine kritische Rückschau auf alte Ergebnisse," in *Die Frau im Urchristentum*, ed. G. Dautzenberg *et al.* QD 95 (1983), 263-319. Nash, R.S., "Heuristic Haustafeln: Domestic Codes as Entrance to the Social World of Early Christianity. The Case of Colossians," in *Religious Writings and Religious Systems. Systematic Analysis of Holy Books in Christianity, Islam, Buddhism, Greco-Roman Religions, Ancient Israel, and Judaism, vol. 2, Christianity*, ed. J. Neusner *et al.* (1989), 25-50. Prostmeier, F.-R. *Handlungsmodelle im ersten Petrusbrief*, Forschungen zur Bibel 63 (1990). Schrage, W. "Zur Ethik der neutestamentlichen Haustafeln," *NTS* 21 (1975): 1-22. Schroeder, D., "Die Haustafeln des Neuen Testaments. Ihre Herkunft und ihr theologischer Sinn" diss. theol. Hamburg (1959). Strecker, G., "Die neutestamentlichen Haustafeln (Kol 3,18-4,1 und Eph 5,22-6,9)," in *Neues Testament und Ethik. Festschrift R. Schnackenburg*, ed H. Merklein (1989), 349-375; "Haustafeln," *EKL[3]* 2 (1989): 392f. Thraede, K. "Zum historischen Hintergrund der 'Haustafeln' des NT," in *Pietas. Festschrift B. Kötting*, ed. E. Dassmann *et al.*, JAC Ergänzungsband 8 (1980): 359-368. Weidinger, K. *Die Haustafeln. Eine Studie urchristlicher Paränese*, UNT 14 (1928). Weiser, A. "Titus als Gemeindeparänese," in *Neues Testament und Ethik. Festschrift R. Schnackenburg*, ed H. Merklein (1989), 397-414.

Early Christian literature has a strong paraenetic intention. Q[231] exemplifies a series of sayings with a paraenetic objective.[232] The New Testament Letters often have a paraenetic structure (1 Cor; cf. also the widely recognized sequence of a practical section after a theoretical, e.g., Gal 5:13-6:10; Rom 12:1-15:33).

---

[231] See below, pp. 124f.
[232] Cf. M. Dibelius, *Die Formgeschichte des Evangeliums*, ed. G. Bornkamm with supplement by G. Iber ([6]1971), 244ff.

James, considered paraenesis from beginning to end by Dibelius, is a relevant example.[233] Characteristic are its eclecticism (use of materials from very disparate origins), lack of a consistent train of thought (but instead a series of individual sayings), sudden changes of theme, repitition of similar motifs in separate contexts, and lack of a specific setting. Only a very narrow conception of "paraenesis" would permit one to see James as a publicity piece, the goal of which was not teaching or even admonishing (= paraenetic), but recruiting.[234]

If general ethical instructions predominate in James, the virtue- and vice catalogues (e.g. Rom 1:29-31, 13:13; 1 Cor 5:10f., 6:9f., Gal 5:19-23; Col 3:5-8, 12-14 and parallels, and cf. Mark 7:21f.[235]) are clear examples of customary admonitions. These catalogues are not a genre taken from the Hebrew Scriptures.[236] Rather the Christian community has adapted the catalogue tradition from Hellenistic Judaism, where it is found especially in wisdom literature (Wisd 14:25, etc.) and in Philo (*sacr* 32[237]). Hellenistic Jewish tradition was probably influenced by Cynic-Stoic popular philosophy.[238]

The New Testament household codes (in the true sense of the phrase only in Col 3:18-4:1 and Eph 5:22-6:9[239]), as paraenetic materials in parallel form specifying the duties of members of a Christian household,[240] have a broad background, not the least of which is secular Greek.[241]

---

[233] M. Dibelius, *Der Brief des Jakobus* (1921), 4; (1964), 16f.; *Geschichte der urchristlichen Literatur* ($^3$1990), 146ff. Cf. also W. Schrage, "Der Jakobusbrief," in H. Balz/W. Schrage, *Die Katholischen Briefe,* NTD 10, ($2^{[12]}$1980, $3^{[13]}$1985), 5-59; W.G. Kümmel, *Einleitung in das Neuen Testament* ($^{21}$1983), 360; *Introduction to the New Testament* (1975), 407: parenetic instruction. A.J. Malherbe calls James "a paraenetic work which has an epistolary opening," (*Moral Exhortation* 80). In RNT 13, F. Schnider raises the question of the specific situation and the acute problems of the community addressed. On this cf. the critical remarks of N. Walter in his review of Schnider's work in TLZ 114 (1989): 281.

[234] W.H. Wuellner, "Der Jakobusbrief," 65; K. Berger, *Formgeschichte des Neuen Testaments* (1984), 147, suggests an "symbuleutic [advisory] formulation."

[235] On the Apocalypse, cf. below, p. 218.

[236] Against D. Schroeder, *IDBSup*, 564f.

[237] Further evidence in H. Conzelmann, *Der erste Brief an die Korinther,* MeyerK 5 ($1^{(12)}$1981), 128, n. 66; *1 Corinthians,* Hermeneia (1975), 100, n. 66.

[238] Cf. Diogenes Laertius VII 110-111, etc. Cf. also H.D. Betz, *Lukian von Samosata und das Neue Testament. Religionsgeschichtliche und paränetische Parallelen. Ein Beitrag zum Corpus Hellenisticum Novi Testament,* TU 76 (1961), 183-194, 206-211 for materials from Lucian. See also Betz's *Der Galaterbrief. Ein Kommentar zum Brief des Apostels Paulus an die Gemeinden in Galatien* (1988), 480-482; A. Vögtle, *Tugend- und Lasterkataloge,* "Lasterkataloge," and "Tugendkataloge;" H. Conzelmann, *Erster Brief an die Korinther,* 128-130, *1 Corinthians,* 101f., with his critique of both S. Wibbing (who traces the catalogue form to Qumran) and E. Kamlah, *Die Form,* WUNT 7 (who traces it to Iran). K. Berger's suggestion (*ANRW* II 25.2, 1090ff.) that the dualistic form is derived from the tradition of Heracles' decision at the parting of the ways is very unpersuasive.

[239] Cf. G. Strecker, "Strukturen einer neutestamentlichen Ethik," ZTK 75 (1978):120; K. Müller, "Die Haustafeln," 267, n. 19, 317; A Weiser, "Titus 2," 398.

[240] G. Strecker, "Die neutestamentlichen Haustafeln," 349. Understanding a household code as a "model, or paradigm for the church" does not sufficiently take into

A. Seeberg's attempt to regard these household codes as part of an early Christian two-way teaching cannot be implemented. Others have emphasized the influence of Jewish tradition (E. Lohmeyer[242]), the significance of the household as specific Christian style (K.H. Rengstorf), connections with the Jesus tradition or the historical Jesus (D. Schroeder[243]), with the theology of Paul (L. Goppelt[244]) or associations with Hellenistic-Jewish propaganda literature (J.E. Crouch[245]).

D. Lührmann relates the codes to the "household management" (περὶ οἰκονομίας or ὁ οἰκονομικός[246]) tradition.[247] "Economy" in the ancient tradition dealt with the ethical conduct of a household, rather than its maximum financial profit. The decisive object of these texts is the master of the house.

P. Fiedler opposes a one-sided emphasis on the influence of the household management tradition, relating the household code tradition to "a popular ethic, also influenced by philosophy." He sees the wisdom paraenesis of Hellenistic Judaism as of only slight influence.[248]

If the household management tradition contains a latent political claim,[249] in Christian tradition the primary social background is the Christian community and not the city or polis. The codes are scarcely a matter of "a conscious middle position

---

account the code's parenetic character. "The Haustafel demonstrated what it meant to structure the ethos under the lordship of Christ." Cf. R.S. Nash, who seeks to interpret the household codes with respect to ancient Christian self-understanding. But ethical tradition does not produce Christology or ecclesiology; instead Christology motivates ethics. Moreover, the household code belongs to the general ethical context of the Letter.

[241] E.g. M. Dibelius's student K. Weidinger (*Die Haustafeln*) calls attention to the Stoic acceptance of 'unwritten laws' (νόμοι ἄγραφοι) of traditional Greek popular ethics in defining the καθῆκον (what is fitting or one's duty). Cf. also M. Dibelius, *An die Kolosser,* 91f. and Dibelius/H. Greeven, *An die Kolosser,* 48f.

[242] *Die Briefe an die Philipper, an die Kolosser und Philemon,* MeyerK 9 ([1(8)]1930), 154f.

[243] *Die Haustafeln,* 152.

[244] "Jesus und die 'Haustafel'-Tradition," 97f.; *Der erste Petrusbrief,* ed. F. Hahn, MeyerK 12/1 ([1(8)]1978)173f.

[245] W. Schrage, "Zur Ethik," 7f., also emphasizes Hellenistic-Jewish, without entirely excluding direct Hellenistic, influence.

[246] Cf. Xenophon, *Oikonomikos;* Aristotle, *Politics* I, etc. G. Schöllgen offers a survey of ancient economic literature in E.Dassmann/G. Schöllgen in *RAC* 13 (1986): 815-830. M. Gielen sketches the development of economics in *Tradition und Theologie,* 57-60. In ANRW II 25.2, 1079-1081, K. Berger sees both the household codes and the Stoic instruction on duties (responsible for the catalogue format and the connection with behavior toward the state) influenced by the genre "oikonomikos." But in *Formgeschichte des Neuen Testaments* (1984), 135-141 he regards gnomic collections with an "ancient social ethic" as the origin of the household codes.

[247] D. Lührmann, "Wo man nicht mehr," 76-80 and "Neutestamentliche Haustafeln." Cf. K. Thraede, "Zum historischen Hintergrund," 362ff.; K. Müller "Die Haustafel," 284-290; M. Gielen, *Tradition und Theologie,* 55ff.; F.-R. Prostmeier, *Handlungsmodelle.* For further bibliography, cf. A Weiser "Titus 2," 399, n. 10. For a survey of the philosophical discussion cf. D.L. Balch, *Let Wives be Submissive,* 21ff.

[248] "Haustafeln," in *RAC* 13: 1070.

[249] D. Lührmann, "Wo man nicht mehr," 80.

between patriarchalism and emancipation."[250] Rather, Christian social responsibility is seeking to realize an equality based in its Christology, in which social distinctions, while not annuled, are subordinated.

The formal characteristics of the household codes (tripartite character, pairings, reciprocity, apodictic form, and household setting)[251] were already present in pre-Christian Greek and Hellenistic Jewish traditions.[252] The secondary Christianization in the New Testament codes is recognizable by the addition of "in Christ" (Col 3:18, 20) and by their Christian motivation (Eph 5:23f.). A direct influence of Hellenistic Jewish tradition on the New Testament household codes is improbable. They were more likely taken over from earlier Christian tradition (cf. 1 Pet 2:13-3:7). Yet a Hellenistic Jewish intermediate stage should be presupposed, as is made probable in the play on "Lord–lords" (κύριος—κύριοι) at Col 3:22ff. and 4:1, and the expression "fear the Lord" at Col 3:22.

The *socio-ethical teaching* of 1 Pet 2:13-3:7 parallels but goes beyond the household codes, speaking of subordination to political authority and reflecting a non-Christian household setting. 1 John 2:12-14, an ecclesiological *community code* which, in the comprehensive perspective of an ethical challenge, expresses in the indicative the salvational status of the community,[253] goes even further. So do the *admonitions to various groups within the church* in the Pastorals (e.g., 1 Tim 5:1ff; 2 Tim 3:1ff; Tit 2:1-10).[254]

The tendency, by referring to the apostolic teaching, to give universally valid instructions fitting the church for its adjustment to the world as the present age continued is decisive for New Testament tradition.

# 3.5 Traces of the Pauline School and their Significance for Pauline and Deutero-Pauline Letters

*Literature*

Conzelmann, H., "Paulus und die Weisheit," in his *Theologie als Schriftauslesung. Aufsätze zum Neuen Testament,* BEvT 65 (1974), 177-190; "Die Schule des Paulus," in *Theologia crucis—Signum crucis, Festschrift E. Dinkler,* ed. C. Andresen et al. (1979), 85-96. Culpepper, R.A., *The Johannine School: An Evaluation of the Johannine-School Hypothesis Based on an Investigation of the Nature of Ancient Schools,* SBLDS 26 (1975). Dahl, N.A., "Formgeschichtliche Beobachtungen zur Christusverkündigung in der Gemeindepredigt," in *Neutestamentliche Studien für R. Bultmann,* BZNW 21 (²1957), 3-9. Ludwig, H., "Der Verfasser des Kolosserbriefes–Ein Schüler des Paulus," diss. theol., Göttingen (1974), esp. pp. 201-229. Merklein, H. "Paulinische Theologie in der Rezepation

---

[250] A. Weiser 399; cf. M. Gielen 60; K. Müller 304 and often; F.-R. Prostmeier 324, etc.

[251] Cf. Strecker, "Die neutestamentlichen Haustafeln," 356 with examples.

[252] Against M. Gielen 125-128, according to whom the form of the household code schema is of early Christian origin and was passed on through oral tradition.

[253] Cf. G. Strecker *Die Johannesbriefe,* 115-118; *The Johannine Letters,* 56-58.

[254] Cf. A. Weiser.

des Kolosser- und Epheserbriefes," in *Paulus in den neutestamentlichen Spätschriften. Zur Paulusrezeption im Neuen Testament,* ed. K. Kertelge, QD 89, 25-69. Müller, P., *Anfänge der Paulusschule. Dargestellt am zweiten Thessalonicherbrief und am Kolosserbrief,* ATANT 74 (1988).[255] Ollrog, W.-H., *Paulus und seine Mitarbeiter. Untersuchungen zu Theorie und Praxis der paulinischen Mission,* WMANT 50 (1979). Schnelle, U., "Paulus und Johannes," *EvT* 47 (1987): 212-228. Schüssler-Fiorenza, E., "The Quest for the Johannine School. The Apocalypse and the Fourth Gospel," *NTS* 23 (1977): 402-427.

Recent research has rightly concluded the existence of a Pauline school. It was a product of the teacher-pupil relationship between Paul and his co-workers, some of whom are listed as co-senders in his letter prescripts.[256] We may presuppose that Paul's person and theology played an authoritative role in this school.[257]

The so-called "revelation schema" may be regarded as a witness to discussions in the Pauline school (cf. 1 Cor 2:6-16).[258] Dahl used this expression for a preaching schema (with the key words, *"present from eternity – now revealed"*[259]), made known in two versions.

But the activity of the school is seen not only in the reception of such a schema, but also in private, esoteric passages of the Letters, which may be regarded as school discussions and as not to be explained exclusively on a literary-critical basis (e.g., private discourses which deal with texts or motifs from the Hebrew Scriptures or Judaism: cf. Rom 4; 5:12ff.; 1 Cor 10:1-10; 2 Cor 3:7-18, cf. also Rom 9-11; and according to P. Vielhauer Gal 4:21-31;[260] further cf. 1 Cor 1:18ff.; 2:6-16; 11:2-16;[261] Rom 1:18ff.; 7:7ff.; 12:3ff.; and the earliest forms of 1 Cor 13 and 15:35ff.).

Criteria for the recognition of such texts are their relatively private character, and the inner unity and Pauline content of a section which does not fit smoothly into its context. These show the text to be relevant tradition which source criticism cannot relegate to a source foreign to Paul. This is corroborated through the observation that several sections appear to presuppose familiar material. These then are units which come out of previous discussion or instruction. H. Conzelmann suggests a Pauline school in

---

[255] The phenomenon of the Pauline school was primarily located in the time after Paul's death. Cf. also the critical remarks of A. Lindemann against the concept of a Pauline school in TLZ 114 (1989):354-357 and in *Paulus im ältesten Christentum. Das Bild des Apostels und die Rezeption der paulinischen Theologie in der frühchristlichen Literatur bis Marcion,* BHT 58 (1979), 36-38.

[256] W.-H. Ollrog, *Paulus und seine Mitarbeiter,* 233, disagrees and understands the circle of Paul's co-workers as independent theologians only in the sense of their missionary function and the deutero-Pauline Letters as "products . . . of a community faithful to Paul." With regard to this one must recognize that the concept of a school does not imply slavish imitation of the teacher's outlook.

[257] Note the towering significance of the founder in ancient schools. Cf. R.A. Culpepper, *The Johannine School,* 259.

[258] Cf. H. Conzelmann, *Erster Brief an die Korinther,* 81, *1 Corinthians,* 58: in 1 Cor 2:6-16 the schema is *in statu nascendi.*

[259] N.A. Dahl, "Formgeschichtliche Beobachtungen," 4.

[260] P. Vielhauer, *Geschichte der urchristlichen Literatur,* 70.

[261] According to H. Conzelmann, *Erster Brief an die Korinther,* 231f, *1 Corinthians,* 182. School discussions show themselves in vss. 11f.

Ephesus, and connects it with Jewish wisdom tradition. This understanding provides a new orientation for the question of religious relationships to the Jewish-Hellenistic milieu.

The traditions produced by these school discussions between Paul and his co-workers gave rise to *imitations*. The authors of the *deutero-Pauline writings* also indicate by their particular theological articulation that they belonged to the circle of the Pauline school.[262]

The connections between the Johannine school and Pauline theology need to be investigated.[263] Yet transmission through a connection between the schools should not be presupposed. The geographical proximity of the two early Christian schools is responsible for Pauline thought being taken up in, and its outlook modified by, the Johannine school. The relationship is not one of literary dependence, but rather a matter of communication through the oral tradition. Thus the historical effects of Paul go beyond his own school to affect even the Johannine literature.

The relationship of Luke, whom Conzelmann regarded as a pupil of Paul,[264] is more distant. Luke subordinates Paul to the Jerusalem apostles (Acts 15:21[265]). Paul's own person is connected with, and subordinated to, Luke's conception of the history of salvation. The Pauline tradition which Luke takes up is apparently anonymous community tradition rather than being derived from the Pauline school. Given his distance from the person and theology of Paul, Luke could not have been his pupil.[266]

## 3.6 The Collection of the Pauline Letters

*Literature*

Aland, K. "Die Entstehung des Corpus Paulinum," in his *Neutestamentliche Entwürfe,* TBü 63 (1979), 302-350. Schmithals, W. "Zur Abfassung und ältesten Sammlung der paulinischen Hauptbriefe" (first published in 1960), now in *Paulus und die Gnostiker. Untersuchungen zu den kleinen Paulusbriefen, TF* 35 (1965): 175-200; "Die Sammlung der Paulusbriefe," *Theologia viatorum* 15 (1979/80): 111-122; "Die Briefe des Paulus in ihrer ursprünglichen Form," Zürcher Werkkommentare zur Bibel (1984). Strecker, G., "Kirchengeschichte, Textkritik

---

[262] See above, p. 38. In light of certain Pauline elements in its prescript, the naming of Paul's companions Silvanus and Mark (1 Pet 5:12, 14), possible correspondences in soteriology (1 Pet 2:14; 3:18; and often elsewhere), and the use of the "in Christ" formula (1 Pet 3:16, and often) 1 Peter is attributed to the Pauline school in a more remote sense. Cf. S. Schulz, Neutestamentliche Ethik (1987), 614f.; E. Schweizer, *Theologische Einleitung in das Neue Testament,* Grundrisse zum Neuen Testament 2 (1989), 106-108.

[263] For 1 John cf. G. Strecker, *Die Johannesbriefe,* 99, 142f.; *The Johannine Letters,* 43f., 79; on John's Gospel, cf. U. Schnelle, "Paulus und Johannes;" for the Apocalypse, cf. E. Schüssler-Fiorenza, "The Quest," 425.

[264] H. Conzelmann, "Die Schule des Paulus," 88.

[265] Note also the fact that on the basis of Luke's sketch the title of apostle would be withheld from Paul and restricted to witnesses of Jesus' earthly life, though Acts 4:4 and 14, where Paul and Barnabas are called apostles, are exceptions. But apostolicity is a basic factor in Paul's own self-understanding (cf. the letter prescripts, Rom 11:13, etc.).

[266] See below, pp. 196ff.

und Neues Testament," *TLZ* 106 (1981): 65-72. Trobisch, D. *Die Entstehung der Paulusbriefsammlung. Studien zu den Anfängen christlicher Publizistik,* NTOA 10 (1989).

Imitation of the letter formulas and various post-Pauline reminiscences from the Pauline Letters, though differently evaluated,[267] raise the question as to how Paul's Letters became literature and were assembled into a corpus. H.D. Betz sees the pseudepigraphical Letters presupposing the genuine Letters already as literature.[268]

W. Schmithals regards the earliest collection of seven Pauline Letters "condensed" by a collector out of 25 letters to six destinations. This basic collection of Pauline Letters, in the order 1 Corinthians, 2 Corinthians, Galatians, Philippians, 1 Thessalonians, 2 Thessalonians, Romans, provided the model for other early Christian collections of seven Letters (e.g. the seven "Catholic" Letters). This collection has an anti-Gnostic inclination, and was made in Corinth between 80 and 90 C.E. The collection was used in 1 Clement.[269]

But K. Aland questions the relevance of an original unified Corpus Paulinum in light of the varying order of the Letters in the manuscript tradition, so difficult to explain.[270] His solution begins with a collection (an "Ur-Corpora" made about 90 C.E.) consisting of 1 and 2 Corinthians, Hebrews, Romans, Galatians, Ephesians, and Philippians. To this pre-existing corpus other varied, extensive, and mutually overlapping collections ("Klein-Corpora") were added, along with Letters addressed to a community in question or to its neighbors.[271]

From the observation that "almost all letter collections of genuine letters... go back to an original collection from the lifetime of the author, published either by himself or due to his expressed wish," D. Trobisch reclaims for Paul the genre of the so-called authorial recension, which Paul prepared in light of the delay of the parousia and the threats of persecution and death.[272] The objective of this collection, which contained the individual letters to the various churches and arose during the apostle's own presence with them, was the preservation of his teaching for posterity. Trobisch identifies 1 Corinthians, 1 Thessalonians, Philippians, and 2 Corinthians as Pauline authorial recensions. An *original collection* consisted of the recensions of 1 and 2 Corinthians plus Galatians and Romans. Later, according to the manuscript tradition, other Pauline writings were added.

---

[267] On echoes outside the New Testament, cf. W. Schneemelcher, "Bible III. Die Entstehung des Kanons des Neuen Testaments und der christlichen Bibel," *TRE* 6 (1980): 34.

[268] H.D. Betz, "Hellenismus," *TRE* 15 (1986): 19-35.

[269] W. Schmithals, "Die Briefe des Paulus," 13-15, 17f., "Die Sammlung," 120ff.

[270] K. Aland, "Die Entstehung," 334: "The unified 'Ur-Corpus' of the first century, on which everything else depends, is a phantasy or an ideal. The development of the Pauline corpus is obviously much more complicated."

[271] "Die Entstehung," 335f.; 342f.; 349, cf. also K. Aland/B. Aland, *Der Text des Neuen Testaments. Einführung in die wissenschaftlichen Ausgaben sowie in Theorie und Praxis der modernen Textkritik* (²1989), 57f.

[272] D. Trobisch, *Die Entstehung,* 100.

It is difficult to harmonize this hypothesis, whose strongest but single argument is the analogy of ancient collections, with the observable changes in Pauline thought in the Letters.[273] The evident differences in the understanding of the law and justification in the early Letters would have had to be sacrificed in the rewriting assumed by Trobisch.

The varying order of the Pauline Letters in the manuscript tradition can with certainty prove only the variability of the Pauline corpus. Any hypothesis which goes beyond this cannot be substantiated. Behind this diverse order, displayed in Marcion, the Muratorian Canon, Tertullian and others since the middle of the second century, it is not possible to penetrate.[274]

## 3.7 Observations on the Development of the New Testament Letters

*Literature*

Grässer, E. "Kolosser 3,1-4 als Beispeil einer Interpretation secondum homines recipientes" (first published in 1967), in his *Text und Situation. Gesammelte Aufsätze zum Neuen Testament,* (1973), 123-151. Lohse, E., "Das apostolische Vermächtnis—Zum paulinischen Charakter der Pastoralbriefe," in *Studien zum Text und zur Ethik des Neuen Testaments.* Festschrift H. Greeven, ed. W. Schrage, BZNW 47 (1986), 266-281. Lüdemann, G., *Paulus, der Heidenapostel Bd. II. Antipaulinismus im frühen Christentum,* FRLANT 130 (²1990). Roloff, J., "Ansätze kirchlicher Rechtsbildungen im Neuen Testament" (first published in 1987), in his *Exegetische Verantwortung in der Kirche. Aufsätze,* ed. M. Karrer (1990), 279-336. Strecker, G., "Paulus in nachpaulinischer Zeit," in Strecker, *Eschaton und Historie. Aufsätze* (1979), 311-319. Trummer, P., *Die Paulustradition der Pastoralbriefe,* Beiträge zur biblische Exegese und Theologie

---

[273] Cf., e.g., U. Schnelle, *Wandlungen im paulinischen Denken,* SBS 137 (1989). H. Hübner (*Das Gesetz bei Paulus. Ein Beitrag zum Werden der paulinischen Theologie,* FRLANT 119 [²1980]) takes into account a development in Paul's thought in terms of his understanding of the law, and S. Schulz (*Neutestamentliche Ethik,* Zürcher Grundrisse zur Bibel [1987]) contrasts an early phase of Paul's ethical thinking with later Pauline statements. On the other hand, J.C. Beker (*Paul the Apostle* [²1982]) sees these distinctions as adjustments of the same basic outlook to different situations. The idea of development in Paul is not new. Patristic exegesis had already attributed to Paul an advance in his knowledge. Cf. Origen's judgment on Romans (*Com. in Ep. ad Rom.,* praef.), *"Praemittentes haec, quae ab studiosis observare solent, quod videtur apostolus in hac epistula perfectior fuisse quam in ceteris"* ["Let me state by way of preface the opinion which scholars tend to hold, namely that in this Epistle the apostle's thought is more thoroughly developed than in the other Epistles."] This is in comparison with 1 and 2 Corinthians and Philippians, admittedly on the basis of exegetical conclusions which would not be drawn today.

[274] Cf. G. Strecker, "Kirchengeschichte, Textkritik und Neues Testament," *TLZ* 106 (1981): 67; also A. Lindemann, *Paulus im ältesten Christentum. Das Bild des Apostels und die Rezeption der paulinischen Theologie in der frühchristlichen Literatur bis Marcion,* BHT 58 (1979), 29-33.

8 (1978).   Wrede, W., *Die Echtheit des zweiten Thessalonicherbriefes,* TU 24.2 (1903).

The oldest witnesses to Christian epistolography, i.e. the genuine Letters of Paul (cf. 3.1.1), shape this genre within early Christianity.[275]   This remains true not only in the immediate connection of those who write the deutero-Pauline Letters in the name of Paul (on the Pauline school, cf. 3.5[276]).   1 and 2 Peter and Jude display some formal parallels to the Pauline Letters.  This is especially recognizable in the prescripts (cf. the superscripts 1 Tim 1:1 and 2 Tim 1:1 as compared with 2 Cor 1:1; for a greeting compare 1 Cor 1:3 with 1 Pet 1:2, etc.).[277]   Hebrews is brought into the orbit of the Pauline school and Pauline Letters less through formal aspects (having no prescript, but a [secondary] letter conclusion[278]) than through naming a companion of Paul (13:23, Timothy).

M. Karrer would also include the Johannine Apocalypse among the early Christian letters initiated through the Pauline impetus.[279]   But it must be admitted that despite a slight epistolary framework, the writing belongs to the genre apocalypse.  The prescript of Apoc 1:4 clearly carries the signature of the seer, so that it cannot be explained solely through direct dependence on (deutero-)Pauline letter-writing;[280] more probable is a reversion to early Christian Asia Minor tradition, which may itself have been influenced by the Pauline Letters.

The reference to earlier Letters is made not only in matters of form, but also in content.  There are, above all, close literary relationships between Pauline and/or deutero-Pauline Letters (2 Thessalonians on 1 Thessalonians;[281] Ephesians on Colossians).  Some passages in James are probably also dependent on the Pauline Letters,[282] as well as 2 Peter on Jude.

---

[275] According to A. Dihle, *Die griechische und lateinische Literatur der Kaiserzeit* (1989), 217; *Greek and Latin Literature of the Roman Empire* (1994), 205: "But Paul's Epistles in turn established a specifically Christian tradition of epistolography during the following two or three generations."

[276] In contrast to section 3.5, which treats the theologico-historical and sociological relationships of the Letters from the Pauline school, this section deals with developments in form and theology and theological differences.

[277] Cf. also the list of J.M. Lieu, "'Grace to You and Peace:' The Apostolic Greeting," *BJRL* 68 (1985/86): 171.  Genuinely different relationships show themselves here, yet not in the sense that they can be interpreted geneologically.

[278] See above, p. 38.

[279] See below, pp. 210f.

[280] The two parts resemble Paul's prescripts.  After the naming of sender and recipients, there follows a salutation similar to Paul's χάρις ὑμῖν καὶ εἰρήνη (note however 2 John 3: ἔσται μεθ' ἡμῶν χάρις ἔλεος εἰρήνη παρὰ θεοῦ πατρὸς καὶ παρὰ Ἰησοῦ Χριστοῦ, τοῦ υἱοῦ τοῦ πατρός).  In distinction to the Pauline prescripts, the sender is here not further identified.  In addition, the characteristics of the giver of grace and peace are described in the terminology of the seer.

[281] Cf. the evidence in terms of thought and vocabulary already in W. Wrede, *Die Echtheit.*

[282] E.G., G. Lüdemann regards some literary contacts between James 2 and the Pauline Letters as probable (*Paulus,* 196-200).

Using the name of an apostle, the pseudepigraphical Letters place themselves under the authority of that apostle. Thus they betray a later stage of development.

The claim of apostolic authority in the *Pastorals,* in which the picture of Paul changes from an apostle to the nations to an organizer of churches, serves to communicate an obligatory church order for their times (i.e., church constitutions:[283] 1 Tim 2:1-3, 16; 5:1-6:2) and a defense against false teaching (4:1-16, etc.[284]). In this manner the pseudonymous author utilizes the apostle as a model with respect to commission and message, but also the apostolic way of life as an example of Christian life-style.[285] Occasionally it is suggested that the Pastorals look back on Pauline Letters already in the process of being collected (see above, section 3.6) with the intention of being added to that collection.[286]

Likewise the author of 2 Thessalonians utilizes the authority of the apostle to protect against opposing viewpoints. Against an enthusiastic expectation of the end he counts on the continuation of the world and accompanies this outlook with ethical admonitions (2:15ff).

Colossians and Ephesians stand closer to the picture of Paul in the genuine Epistles. Yet the authoritative example of Paul is heightened in these two Letters. A cosmological understanding of the function of Christ as πρωτότοκος πάσης κιτσεως, victorious over the cosmic powers, is emphasized (Col 1:15ff; 2:15). Corresponding to this conception of the cosmic Christ is an ecclesiastical universalism, subordinating the community as "body" to Christ as "head." Paul's proclamation and suffering is situated in this expanse between cosmic Christ and universal church, so that, as the times change, the Apostle to the Nations guarantees the unity of the church. The futuristic apocalyptic motifs of the Pauline Letters retire before a realized eschatology (Col 1:13; 2:12). Furthermore, under the influence of its baptismal theology, Colossians emphasizes the unification of Christ and the believers, in contrast to the Pauline tradition.[287]

Although most of the New Testament Letters which follow the genuine Letters of Paul are pseudonymous (cf. 3.2.1), this does not signal the end of the genre of genuine letters in early Christianity. In the New Testament there are genuine "presbyter-letters" (cf. 3.1.1) which have no formal relationship to the Pauline Letter form and stand close to the contemporary letter conventions of their milieu.[288] 1 Clement and the Epistles of Ignatius and Polycarp are genuine letters as well.[289]

---

[283] Cf. J. Roloff, "Ansätze," 320ff.

[284] A conflict within the Pauline school itself (cf. H. Conzelmann, "Die Schule des Paulus," in *Theologia crucis—Signum crucis, Festschrift E. Dinkler,* ed. C. Andresen et al. (1979), 90) seems improbable, since the position of the opponents as it is recognizable within the Pastorals is not clearly based on Pauline thought.

[285] Cf. E. Lohse, "Das apostolische Vermächtnis—Zum paulinischen Charakter der Pastoralbriefe," in *Studien zum Text und zur Ethik des Neuen Testaments. Festschrift H. Greeven,* ed. W. Schrage, BZNW 47 (1986), 277ff., who interprets the ethics of the Pastorals as describing "how Christian faith must preserve itself in its life and action within the world" (280).

[286] P.. Trummer, *Der Paulustradition,* 228; cf. W. Bauer, as early as BHT 10, 228.

[287] Cf. E. Grässer, "Kolosser 3,1-4."

[288] Cf., e.g., H.-J. Klauck, *Die Johannesbriefe,* ErFor 276 (1991), 78ff.

[289] Cf. P. Vielhauer, *Geschichte der urchristlichen Literatur* (²1978), 529ff.

# 3.8   Letters and the Writing of the Gospels

*Literature*

Allison, Jr., D.C., "The Pauline Epistles and the Synoptic Gospels: The Pattern of the Parallels," *NTS* 28 (1982): 1-32. Best, E., "1 Peter and the Gospel Tradition," *NTS* 16 (1969/70): 95-113. Brown, J.PP., "Synoptic Parallels in the Epistles and Form-History," *NTS* 10 (1962/63): 27-48. Koester, H. *Ancient Christian Gospels: Their History and Development* (1990). Schmithals, W., "Paulus und der historische Jesus," ZNW 53 (1962): 145-160. Wilckens, U., "Jesusüberlieferung und Christuskerygma—Zwei Wege urchristlicher Überlieferungsgeschichte," *Theologia viatorum* 10 (1966): 310-339.

A distinct knowledge of the Jesus tradition cannot be presupposed for the Pauline Letters. Paul knows something of a sayings tradition from Jesus (1 Cor 7:25), and has knowledge of his crucifixion (1 Cor 1:18ff, etc.) and of his passion (2 Cor 1:5; Phil 3:10); but authentic words of Jesus are seldom found in Paul.

The absolute prohibition of divorce apparently goes back to Jesus (cf. 1 Cor 7:10 with Mark 10:12; Matt 5:31f.).[290] Elsewhere it is a question of whether a genuine saying or community tradition underlies what Paul writes (e.g., 1 Thess 4:16f., which text Paul denotes as a λόγος κυρίου; it is also possible that this is Jewish tradition given a Christian modification). Seen as a whole however, the Pauline Letters scarcely ever refer to the Jesus-tradition.

It is nevertheless questionable whether the idea of two independent streams of tradition is justified for early Christianity, a Pauline-stream and a Jesus-stream, one finding its expression in the Epistles and the other in the Gospels.[291] Letters such as 1 Peter, which presupposes Matthew's Gospel (cf. 1 Pet 3:14 and Matt 5:10[292]), or 2 Peter, which refers to the transfiguration story (compare 2 Pet 1:17f. with Matt 17:5), show that even Letters acquainted with the gospel tradition do not

---

[290] Cf. the list in Koester, *Gospels,* 53. On the present state of research, cf. D.C. Allison Jr, "Pauline Epistles."

[291] U. Wilckens ("Jesusüberlieferung") suggests, without completely excluding contact and transference, a divided configuration in early Christianity: that the tradition of Palestinian Christianity was built on a "picture of the pre-Easter Jesus," and that of the Hellenistic Christian mission church on "the exalted Christ."

[292] For further allusions to gospel materials cf. H. Koester, *Gospels,* 64f. His suggestion to clarify the parallels in 1 Pet 3:15 and 2:12b that "1 Peter had access to a collection of sayings that was related to or identical with Matthew's special Jewish-Christian source" (66) remains hypothetical. The thesis of a pre-Matthean Jewish Christian special source for the Sermon on the Mount, which would support this suggestion (H.D. Betz, *Studien zur Bergpredigt* (1985), *Essays on the Sermon on the Mount* (1985), [cf. now *The Sermon on the Mount,* Hermeneia (1995), translator's note] receives detailed opposition from G.N.Stanton, "The Origin and Purpose of Matthew's Sermon of the Mount," in *Tradition and Interpretation in the New Testament. Festschrift for E.E. Ellis,* ed. G.F. Hawthorne *et al.,* 1987, 181-192. Questionable also is an extensive identification of materials from the Letters with (oral) Jesus tradition, as, e.g., in E. Best, "I Peter." This applies as well to the exposition of J.P. Brown in "Synoptic Parallels."

utilize it extensively. The letter form was not favorable to the utilization of gospel materials, so that the Letters give us no direct evidence as to the passing on of gospel tradition or the knowledge and utilization of such tradition in the contemporary communities.

# 4 Gospels

*Literature*

Becker, J., "Aus der Literatur zum Johannesevangelium (1978-1980)," *TRu* 47
(1982): 279-301, 304-347; *Das Evangelium nach Johannes,* Ökumenischer
Taschenbuch-kommentar zum Neuen Testament 4, Vol. 1 (1979, ²1985), Vol. 2
(1981, ²1984); "Das Johannesevangelium im Streit der Methoden (1980-1984),"
*TRu* 51 (1986): 1-78. Boring, M.E., *The Continuing Voice of Jesus. Christian
Prophecy and the Gospel Tradition* (1991). Bornkamm, G., "Evangelien,
formgeschichtlich," in *RGG³* 2 (1958): 749-753; "Evangelien, synoptische," in
*RGG³* 2 (1958): 753-756. Bultmann, R., "Evangelien, gattungsgeschichtlich
(formgeschichtlich)," in *RGG²* 2 (1928): 418-422; "Die Erforschung der
synoptischen Evangelien" (first published in 1961), in his *Glauben und Verstehen.
Gesammelte Aufsätze,* Vol. 4 (1965): 1-41. *Das Theologie des Neuen Testaments,*
rev. and enlarged by O. Merk, Uni-Taschenbücher 630 (⁹1984); *Theology of the
New Testament,* 2 vols. (1951, 1955); *Das Evangelium des Johannes,* MeyerK 2
(²¹1986); *The Gospel of John: a Commentary* (1971). Conzelmann, H.,
"Literaturbericht zu den synoptischen Evangelien," *TRu* 37 (1972): 220-272, 43
(1978): 3-51. Dodd, C.H., *The Interpretation of the Fourth Gospel* (1958, 1978);
*Historical Tradition in the Fourth Gospel* (1963, 1979). Dormeyer, D.,
*Evangelium als literarische und theologische Gattung,* Erträge der Forschung 263
(1989). *Der Erzähler des Evangeliums. Methodische Neuansätze in der
Markusforschung,* ed. F. Hahn, SBS 118/119 (1985). *Das Evangelium und die
Evangelien. Vorträge vom Tübinger Symposium 1982,* ed. P. Stuhlmacher, WUNT
28 (1983); *The Gospel and the Gospels* (1991); *L'Évangile de Jean. Sources,
Rédaction, théologie,* by M. de Jonge, BETL 44 (1977). Frankemölle, H.,
*Evangelium. Begriff und Gattung. Ein Forschungsbericht,* SBB 15 (1988).
Güttgemanns, E., *Offene Fragen zur Formgeschichte des Evangeliums, Eine
methodologische Skizze der Grundlagenproblematik der Form- und
Redaktionsgeschichte,* BEvT 54 (1970, ²1971). *The Interrelations of the Gospels,*
ed. D.L. Dungan, BETL 95 (1990). Koester, H., "Uberlieferung und Geschichte
der frühchristlichen Evangelienliteratur," in *ANRW* II 25.2 (1984): 1463-1542;
"Apocryphal and Canonical Gospels," *HTR* 73 (1980): 105-130; *Ancient Christian
Gospels: Their History and Development* (1990). Koester, H. and J.M. Robinson,
*Entwicklungslinien durch die Welt des frühen Christentums* (1971); *Trajectories
through Early Christianity* (1971). Lindemann, A., "Literaturbericht zu den
synoptischen Evangelien, 1978-1983," *TRu* 49 (1984): 223-276, 311-371. *Logia.
Les paroles de Jésus. The Sayings of Jesus,* ed. J. Delobel, BETL 59 (1982). *Das
Markus-Evangelium,* ed. R. Pesch, Wege der Forschung 411 (1979). *Markus-
Philologie. Historische, literargeschichtliche und stilistische Untersuchungen,* ed.
H. Cancik, WUNT 33 (1984). Marxsen, W., *Der Evangelist Markus. Studien zur
Redaktionsgeschichte des Evangeliums,* FRLANT 67 (²1959); *Mark the Evangelist:
Studies on the Redaction History of the Gospel* (1969); *Metaphorik und Mythos im
Neuen Testament,* ed K. Kertelge, QD 126 (1990). Perrin, N., "Towards an
Interpretation of the Gospel of Mark," in *Christology and a Modern Pilgrimage. A*

*Discussion with Norman Perrin,* ed. H.D. Betz (1971), 1-78. Robinson, J.M., "Die johanneische Entwicklungslinie," in H. Koester and J.M. Robinson, *Entwicklungslinien durch die Welt des frühen Christentums* (1971), 216-250; "The Johannine Trajectory," in Koester and Robinson, *Trajectories through Early Christianity* (1971), 232-268. Schmithals, W., *Das Evangelium nach Markus,* Ökumenischer Taschenbuchkommentar zum Neuen Testament 2, Vol. 1 (1979, ²1986), Vol. 2 (1979, ²1986); "Evangelien, Synoptische," in *TRE* 10 (1982): 570-626; *Einleitung in die drei ersten Evangelien* (1985). Schneemelcher, W., "Einleitung. A. Evangelien," in *Neutestamentliche Apokryphen in deutscher Übersetzung,* ed. W. Schneemelcher I (⁶1990): 65-75; "A. Gospels: Non-biblical Material about Jesus. Introduction" in *New Testament Apocrypha,* ed. W. Schneemelcher, rev. ed. I (1991): 77-87. Schnelle, U., *Antidoketische Christologie im Johannesevangelium. Eine Untersuchung zur Stellung des vierten Evangeliums in der johanneischen Schule,* FRLANT 144 (1987). Schniewind, J., "Zur Synoptiker-Exegese (Lit.-Bericht)," *TRu* 2 (1930): 129-189; *Euangelion. Ursprung und erste Gestalt des Begriffs Evangelium,* 2 vols., (1927, 1931, reprint 1970). Stanton, G.N., *The Gospels and Jesus.* The Oxford Bible Series (1989). Strecker, G., "Die historische und theologische Problematik der Jesusfrage" (first published in 1969), in his *Eschaton und Historie. Aufsätze* (1979), 159-182; "Redaktionsgeschichte als Aufgabe der Synoptikerexegese," in *Eschaton und Historie,* 9-32. Stuhlmacher, P., "Zum Thema: Das Evangelium und die Evangelien," in *Das Evangelium und die Evangelien. Vorträge vom Tübinger Symposium 1982,* ed. P. Stuhlmacher, WUNT 28 (1983), 1-26; "The Theme: The Gospel and the Gospels," in *The Gospel and the Gospels* (1991), 1-25; "Evangelium 1. Biblisch," in *EKL³* 1 (1986): 1217-1221. Taylor, V., *The Formation of the Gospel Tradition. Eight Lectures* (1957 = ²1935). Theissen, G. *Lokalkolorit und Zeitgeschichte in den Evangelien. Ein Beitrag zur Geschichte der synoptischen Tradition,* NTOA 8 (1989). Thyen, H., "Aus der Literatur zum Johannesevangelium," *TRu* 39 (1974): 222-252, 289-330; 43 (1978): 328-359; "Johannesevangelium," in *TRE* 17 (1988): 200-225. Vorster, W.S., "Der Ort der Gattung Evangelium in der Literaturgeschichte," *VF* 29 (1984): 2-25. Windisch, H., "Der Johanneische Erzählungsstil," in *EYXAPIΣTHPION. Studien zur Religion und Literatur des Alten und Neuen Testaments. Festschrift H. Gunkel.* Vol. 2 ed H. Schmidt, FRLANT 36/2 (1923), 174-213. Wrede, W., *Das Messiasgeheimnis in den Evangelien. Zugleich ein Beitrag zum Verständnis des Markusevangeliums* (1901 = ⁴1969); *The Messianic Secret* (1971).

# 4.1   The Gospel Form

### 4.1.1.   The Word "Gospel" ($\epsilon \dot{v} \alpha \gamma \gamma \acute{\epsilon} \lambda \iota o \nu$) and the Writing of the Gospels

*Literature*

Bovon, F., "The Synoptic Gospels and the Non-Canonical Acts of the Apostles," *HTR* 81 (1988): 19-32. Dautzenberg. G., "Die Zeit des Evangeliums. Mk 1,1-15 und die Konzeption des Markusevangeliums," *BZ* NF21 (1977): 219-234, 22 (1978): 76-91. Dormeyer, D., "Die Kompositionsmetapher 'Evangelium Jesu Christi, des Sohnes Gottes' Mk 1,1. Ihre theologische und literarische Aufgabe in der Jesus-Biographie des Markus," *NTS* 33 (1987): 452-468. Frankemölle, H., "Jesus als deuterojesajanischer Freudenbote? Zur Rezeption von Jes 52,7 und 61,1 im Neuen Testament, durch Jesus und in den Targumin," in *Vom Urchristentum zu Jesus. Festschrift J. Gnilka,* ed. H. Frankemölle, *et al.,* (1989), 34-67. von Harnack, A., *Marcion: Das Evangelium vom fremden Gott. Eine Monographie zur Geschichte der Grundlegung der katholischen Kirche,* TU 45 ($^2$1924). Hengel, M., *Die Evangelienüberschriften, Sitzungsbericht der Heidelberger Akademie der Wissenschaft, philosophisch-historische Klasse* 1984.3 (1984). Koester, H., "From the Kerygma-Gospel to Written Gospels," *NTS* 35 1989): 361-381. Strecker, G., "Literarkritische Überlegungen zum εὐαγγέλιον-Begriff im Markusevangelium" (first published in 1972), in his *Eschaton und Historie. Aufsätze* (1979), 76-89; "εὐαγγέλιον," in *EWNT* 2 (1981): 176-186. Stuhlmacher, P., *Das paulinische Evangelium. I. Vorgeschichte,* FRLANT 95 (1968); "Zum Thema: Das Evangelium und die Evangelien," in *Das Evangelium und die Evangelien. Vorträge vom Tübinger Symposium 1982,* ed. P. Stuhlmacher, WUNT 28 (1983), 1-26; "The Theme: The Gospel and the Gospels," in *The Gospel and the Gospels* (1991), 1-25.

In Christian usage, "gospel" has two meanings: the message that, in Jesus Christ, salvation has been manifested for the church and for the world; and a written work which tells the story of Jesus' life, work, suffering, death, and resurrection.[1]

Although no clear geneology of usage can be traced, New Testament usage of the root εὐαγγέλ- *(evangel-)* is based on both an Hebrew-Jewish and Greek-Hellenistic background. The use of the substantive "gospel" (εὐαγγέλιον) primarily goes back to Greek and Hellenistic precedents, especially from the milieu of the Hellenistic ruler worship or ruler cult.[2]

Instances in Mark,[3] where pre-Marcan language is recognizable, do not suggest that the proclamation of Jesus about the Kingdom of God as an eschatological interpretation of Isa 52:7 and 61:1 was described by the term "gospel" already in Jesus' lifetime. Rather, as a comparison with pre-Pauline Christian tradition indicates, such linguistic usage derives from the Hellenistic church.[4] The usage cannot be traced back to the Palestinian-Jewish church.[5] Early

---

[1] P. Vielhauer, *Geschichte der urchristlichen Literatur* ($^2$1978), 252.

[2] The calendar inscription from Priene is a significant example (*Orientis Graeci inscriptiones selectae* II, 458; translated in C.K. Barrett, *Texte zur Umwelt des Neuen Testaments,* ed. C.-J. Thornton, Uni-Taschenbücher 1591 ($^2$1991), 106f.). Cf. also Josephus, *War* IV 618, 656, and H. Koester, *Ancient Christian Gospels,* 3f.

[3] Except for Mark 16:15, which is post-Marcan, all instances are to be ascribed to the author's redaction; cf. G. Strecker, "Literarkritische Überlegungen," 76ff.

[4] Against P. Stuhlmacher, "Zum Thema," 21; "On the Theme," 20f. Cf. also Stuhlmacher's "Evangelium I. Biblisch," in *EKL³* 1 (1986): 1218.; and H. Merklein, "Zum Verständnis des paulinischen Begriffs 'Evangelium'" (first published in 1983), in his *Studien zu Jesus und Paulus,* WUNT 43 (1987), 279-295, esp. 283. In his Habilitationsschrift *Das paulinische Evangelium* (FRLANT 95, 243f.) Stuhlmacher was

Christian usage of "gospel" (εὐαγγέλιον) in the singular is of Hellenistic derivation, but distinguishes between the unique eschatological event in Christ and the various "gospels" (εὐαγγέλια) of the surrounding world.

"Gospel" (εὐαγγέλιον) has a double meaning in Paul. It describes a) the *proclamation* as *nomen actionis* (e.g., 1 Thess 1:5) and b) the *Christ-event* as the contents of the Pauline missionary proclamation (1 Thess 1:9f.[6]). The gospel is effective through the Spirit, and produces pneumatic actions (1 Thess 1:5; 1 Cor 2:4). Paul probably found the word associated with confessional formulas (cf. 1 Thess 1:9; 1 Cor 15:1ff.; Rom 1:1-4).

In contrast to the pre-Marcan usage of "gospel" (εὐαγγέλιον) with the genitive, primarily in the objective sense (i.e., the gospel about God or Jesus), the description of Jesus as originator and announcer of the gospel[7] is the work and achievement of the Evangelist Mark. The genitive expression "gospel of God" (εὐαγγέλιον θεοῦ) cannot be juxtaposed to this as an alternative expression wherein Mark is following an earlier pre-Pauline usage which joined together the "gospel of God" and the Kingdom proclamation of Jesus,[8] for the expression occurs not only in Mark 1:14f. but also in Rom 1:1. But it should be considered an original usage in both places.[9]

In comparison with Mark, Matthew displays greater influence of Greek and Hellenistic usage. Rather than using "gospel" by itself, he generally explicates it with genitives or demonstratives (εὐαγγέλιον τῆς βασιλείας 4:23; 9:35; 24:14; or εὐαγγέλιον τοῦτο 24:14; 26:13). For Matthew, as for Mark, "gospel" denotes the proclamation of the coming Kingdom of God.[10] As Jesus' proclamation and teaching it is both ethical and eschatological, and directed both to the church and the world (cf. Matt 28:16-20).

Despite the differences in their usage of the term, the gospels agree on its eschatological signification. This is true also for Luke, who, while avoiding the term in his gospel, uses it in Acts 15:7 and 20:24 as a *terminus technicus* for the apostolic preaching.

---

more reserved about the possibility that the concept "gospel" in the sense of the proclamation of Isaiah 40-55 went back to Jesus himself.

[5] Cf. also H. Frankemölle, "Jesus als deuterojesanischer Freudenbote?" throughout.

[6] An apocalyptic context which does not yet presuppose Paul's message of justification must be considered for 1 Thessalonians. The concept of justification first appears in Galatians and affirms that Christ's act, the content of Paul's gospel, replaces the way to human righteousness through the law and constitutes life on the basis of the "grace of God" (χάρις θεοῦ), cf. Gal 2:19-21.

[7] Mark 1:14f.; taking 'Ιησοῦ as a subjective genitive in 1:1. But for an example of a different viewpoint, cf. D. Dormeyer, "Die Kompositionsmetapher," 464, who understands εὐαγγελίου 'Ιησοῦ Χριστοῦ υἱοῦ θεοῦ in both the subjective and objective senses, taking it as a "compositional metaphor." It includes both "God's revelatory actions," and "the interactions between Jesus and his compatriots."

[8] As does G. Dautzenberg, "Der Wandel der Reich-Gottes-Verkündigung in der urchristlichen Mission," in Dautzenberg, H. Merklein, and K. Müller, *Zur Geschichte des Urchristentums,* QD 87 (1979), 11-32, esp. 23f. and 30f.

[9] Cf. P. Vielhauer, *Geschichte,* 252.

[10] Not individual speech-complexes; cf. W. Marxsen, *Der Evangelist Markus²,* 82, 92-94; *Mark the Evangelist,* 138-141.

In the New Testament, neither the substantive nor the verb have a literary significance.[11] "Gospel" denoting a literary genre is clearly demonstrable only towards the end of the second century (Irenaeus, *adv. haer.* V 26,6; Clement of Alexandria, Stromateis I 136,1; Epistle of Diognetus 11:6). In Mark 1:1 "The beginning of the gospel of Jesus Christ" is probably a subjective genitive indicating the beginning of the proclamation of Jesus, dated by the career of John the Baptist.[12] Ancient parallels indicate that it is not a book title. On this basis Martin Hengel's early dating of the gospel headings is questionable. According to Hengel, copyists of the Synoptics, concerned "for dissemination of the first editions of the Gospels to the churches of the Roman world," added these headings to the Synoptics already in the first century. The heading and conclusion of John were added later.[13]

Justin refers to plurality of the Gospels as "memoirs" (ἀπομνημονεύματα = εὐαγγέλια).[14] Reference to the individual authors occurs first in Papias,[15] yet it remains questionable exactly what literary entities are meant.[16] When the Didache alludes to the gospel, apparently this is primarily the written Gospel (of Matthew)[17] rather than the oral, preached, gospel;[18] even though liturgy may have influenced the tradition.[19] Yet the reference in Didache 11:3 to "the ordinance of the gospel" is most likely to oral preaching.[20] But the citation formula in 2 Clement 8,5, "The Lord says in the Gospel," followed by a quotation with a close parallel in

---

[11] Cf., among others, H. Koester "From the Kerygma-Gospel to Written Gospels." Understanding Mark 1:1 as a "rhetorical proclamation of a theological declamation (= genos epideiktikon)" as with D. Dormeyer, *Gattung,* 456-458.

[12] But for another viewpoint, cf. W. Schmithals, *Das Evangelium nach Markus,* 73f and *Einleitung,* 31. For Schmithals it is a "copyist's note."

[13] Hengel, *Die Evangelienüberschriften,* passim, but esp. 47-51, cf. the citation on 47. F. Bovon opposes the argument for constancy in the tradition of the inscriptions *(inscriptio)* and subscriptions *(subscriptio).* He suggests they are "the result of an effort of stabilisation" in light of the aprocryphal gospel tradition (23).

[14] *Apol* I 66,3; cf. also above, pp. 2f.

[15] Eusebius, E.H. III 39, 15f., without using the term "evangelium" (εὐαγγέλιον).

[16] On Papias, cf. H. Koester, "From the Kerygma-Gospel to Written Gospels," 374. That the rhetorical terms which Papias may have used (cf. above, p. 1) speak against Papias possessing a written Gospel of Mark, as Schmithals thinks ("Evangelien, Synoptische," *TRE* 10:574), is not persuasive.

[17] As in Didache 8:2; 11:3; 15:3f. Cf. *Didache (Apostellehre), Barnabasbrief, Zweiter Klemensbrief, Schrift an Diognet,* ed. K. Wengst. Schriften des Urchristentums 2 (1984): 24-30; W. Schmithals, "Evangelien, Synoptische," *TRE* 10:573; W.-D. Köhler, *Die Rezeption des Matthäusevangeliums in der Zeit vor Irenäus,* WUNT II 24 (1987), 30ff. (on *Didache* 8:1f) and 39 (on 15:3f.).

[18] H. Koester, *ANRW* II 25.2, 1464ff and *Ancient Christian Gospels,* 16 sees *Didache* 8:2 as "a reference to the preaching of Jesus during his earthly ministry." He ascribes the citation formula in *Didache* 11:3 and 15:3f to a later redactor; cf. *Ancient Christian Gospels,*17 and "From the Kerygma-Gospel to Written Gospels,"371f.

[19] Cf. K. Niederwimmer, *Die Didache,* Kommentar zu den apostolischen Vätern 1 (1989), 170.

[20] P. Vielhauer, *Geschichte der urchristlishen Literatur,* 254.

Luke 16:10f. is a different matter. It is too complex to see this citation as based on "a sayings collection based on a harmony of Matthew and Luke."[21] This postulated document is never evident elsewhere in the tradition, and, as observed in other ancient Christian authors, a certain permissiveness in citing the Hebrew Scriptures and New Testament must be taken into account.[22] Martyrdom of Polycarp 4:1, Ignatius to the Philadelphians 8:2 and to the Smyrnaeans 7:2 are other early examples for the transition to later Christian usage whereby "gospel" denotes a book.[23]

Though the word "gospel" had been used for a long time to designate a book,[24] the decisive change in meaning of the traditional Christian concept "gospel" comes with Marcion. He identified the Pauline gospel (cf. Gal 1:11; Rom 2:16, etc.) with the Gospel of Luke, and, in the form of his own edition, may have designated it a "gospel."[25] Yet our indirect and late witnesses to Marcion do not permit us to come to a definite conclusion on that issue.

---

[21] H. Koester, "From the Kerygma-Gospel to Written Gospels," 372 and *Ancient Christian Gospels*, 18; cf. also K. Wengst, *Didache*, 221, who refers to a "post-synoptic gospel."

[22] Cf. G. Strecker, "Eine Evangelienharmonie bei Justin und Pseudoklemens?" *NTS* 24 (1978): 297-316.

[23] W. Bauer, *Griechisch-deutsches Wörterbuch zu des Schriften des Neuen Testaments und der frühchristlichen Literatur*, ed. K. Aland and B. Aland (⁶1988), 644; *A Greek-English Lexicon of the New Testament and Other Early Christian Literature* [BAGD](²1979), 318.

[24] P. Vielhauer, *Geschichte*, 255.

[25] Cf. A. von Harnack, *Marcion*, 184; Koester, "From the Kerygma-Gospel to Written Gospels," 376f., 381; *Ancient Christian Gospels*, 35f.; H. von Campenhausen, *Die Entstehung der christlichen Bibel*, BHT 39 (1968), 174ff., *The Formation of the Christian Bible* (1972), 148ff.; with whom W. Schneemelcher agrees, cf. "Bibel. III. Die Entstehung des Kanons des Neuen Testaments und der christlichen Bible," *TRE* 6 (1980): 36.

## 4.1.2    The Gospel Genre as a Literary-historical Problem

### 4.1.2.1    Origin and Criteria of the Gospel Genre[26]

*Literature*

Bauernfeind, O., "Die literarische Form des Evangeliums," Diss. theol. Greifswald (1915). Breytenbach, C., "Das Markusevangelium als episodische Erzählung. Mit Überlegungen zum 'Aufbau' des zweiten Evangeliums," in *Der Erzähler des Evangeliums. Methodische Neuansätze in der Markusforschung,* ed. F. Hahn, SBS 118/119 (1985), 137-169. Dodd, C.H., "The Framework of the Gospel Narrative,"

---

[26] That which is included in the genre "gospel" corresponds in structure to the canonical and apocryphal Gospels as defined here (cf. section 4.1.2.2). It is a misunderstanding to use this title also "for writings which contain traditions that at least partially became components of Mark and other similar gospels." Cf. H. Koester, "One Jesus and Four Primitive Gospels" (first published in 1968), now in Koester and J.M. Robinson, *Trajectories through Early Christianity* (1971), 162, n. 12; "Ein Jesus und vier ursprüngliche Evangeliengattungen" in Koester and J.M. Robinson, *Entwicklungslinien durch die Welt des frühen Christentums* (1971), 150, n. 12; "Apocryphal and Canonical Gospels," *HTR* 73 (1980): 111; *Einfuhrung in das Neue Testament im Rahmen der Religionsgeschichte und Kulturgeschichte der hellenistischen und römischen Zeit,* (1980), 431; *Introduction to the New Testament, Vol 2: History and Literature of Early Christianity* (1982), 4. Cf. also H. Cancik's comprehensive use of the concept in "Die Gattung Evangelium. Das Evangelium des Markus im Rahmen der antiken Historiographie," in *Markus-Philologie. Historische, literargeschichtliche und stilistische Untersuchungen,* ed. H. Cancik, WUNT 33 (1984), 91f.

Despite the occasional (self-) determination of apocryphal writings as gospels, formal distinctions demand a differentiating terminology. (Cf., e.g., the *inscriptio* or the *incipit* and the *subscriptio* of the gnostic writings from Nag Hammadi such as the Gospels of Thomas, of Philip, of the Egyptians and of Truth, generally raise the suspicion of being secondary. On these cf. J.M. Robinson, "LOGOI SOPHON. Zur Gattung der Spruchquelle" (first published in 1964), in *Entwicklungslinien durch die Welt des frühen Christentums* (1971), 71ff.; "LOGOI SOPHON: On the Gattung of Q, in *Trajectories through Early Christianity* (1971), 71ff..; on the Gospel of Thomas, cf. H. Koester, "From the Kerygma-Gospel to Written Gospels," *NTS* 35 1989): 372f.; on the Gospel of Philip, cf. H.-G. Gaffron, "Studien zum koptischen Philippusevangelium unter besonderer Berücksichtigung der Sakramente," Diss. theol. Bonn (1969), 10-13; on the canonical Gospels, cf. above pp. 94f. P. Vielhauer, *Geschichte der urchristlichen Literatur,* 257, accepts "Gospel" in the title of the Gospel of Truth as genuine.) This self-description therefore poses no objection to the use of "gospel" in the first place for that genre which we encounter in the canonical Gospels.

The so-called apocryphal gospels, which are very diverse in both form and content, may be described as gospels whenever their structural proximity to the Gospels of the New Testament, which they often literarily presuppose, becomes apparent, provided that the fragmentary tradition permits such a description at all. (On this whole issue, cf. P. Vielhauer, *Geschichte,* 256-258, W. Schneemelcher, in *Neutestamentliche Apokryphen in deutscher Übersetzung* 1 [⁶1990]: 65-75; *New Testament Apocrypha* 1 [²1991]: 77-87.)

in his *New Testament Studies* ([2]1954), 1-11; *The Apostolic Preaching and its Developments,* ([11]1966). Kähler, M. *Der sogennante historische Jesus und der geschichtliche, biblische Christus,* new ed. E. Wolf, TBü 2 ([2]1956); *The So-called Historical Jesus and the Historic Biblical Christ* (1964. 1988). Koester, H., "Ein Jesus und vier ursprüngliche Evangeliengattungen" (first published in 1968), in H. Koester and J.M. Robinson, *Entwicklungslinien durch die Welt des frühen Christentums* (1971), 147-190; "One Jesus and Four Primitive Gospels," in H. Koester and J.M. Robinson, *Trajectories through Early Christianity* (1971), 158-204. Du Plessis, I., "Die genre van Lukas se evangelie," *Theologia Evangelica* 15 (1982): 19-28. Pokorny, P., "Zur Entstehung der Evangelien," *NTS* 32 (1986): 393-403. Robinson, J.M., "On the *Gattung* of Mark (and John)," in *Jesus and Man's Hope,* ed. D.G. Buttrick and J.M. Bald (1970), 1:99-129; "Zur Gattung des Markus-Evangeliums," in his *Messiasgeheimnis und Geschichtsverständnis. Zur Gattungsbestimmung des Markus-Evangeliums,* TBü 81 (1989), 126-148. Roloff, J., *Das Kerygma und der irdische Jesus. Historische Motive in den Jesus-Erzählungen der Evangelien* ([2]1973). Vorster, W.S., "Kerygma/History and the Gospel Genre," *NTS* 29 (1983): 87-95.

"Gospel" as a literary genre first occurs with Mark's book, and is a genuine Christian creation.[27] But this recognition[28] should not lead us to restrict the significance of analogies or to give up the search for antecedents.

In that the authors of the Gospels historicize the Christ-event, and at the same time treat it as an eschatological occurence, their presentations are structurally and formally influenced by a salvation-historical (*heilsgeschichtlich)* concept, by the alignment of history to God's will for salvation in the earthly Christ-event. The general form of the Gospels[29] mirrors the common concern of the Evangelists to join kerygma and history (cf. 4.1.2.3), despite occasional specific theological emphases. This combining of kerygma and history uniquely characterizes the gospel genre.[30] Because of this synthesis the genre points beyond itself and raises the issue of literary analogies. Since a historicizing tendency characterizes the Gospels, as is evident from their general form as well as the numerous geographical and chronological references, the question of formal analogies to the gospel genre, in

---

[27] So, e.g., R. Bultmann, "Evangelien, gattungsgeschichtlich (formgeschichtlich)," in *RGG*[2] 2 (1928): 419; M. Dibelius, *Geschichte der urchristlichen Literatur. Neudruck der Erstausgabe von 1926 unter Berücksichtigung der Änderung der englischen Übersetzung von 1936,* ed. F. Hahn, TBü 58 (1975), 41f.; *A Fresh Approach to the New Testament and Early Christian Literature* (1936), 56f.; K.L. Schmidt, "Die Stellung der Evangelien in der allgemeinen Literaturgeschichte" (first published in 1923), in his *Neues Testament–Judentum–Kirche. Kleine Schriften,* ed. G. Sauter, TBü 69 (1981), 37-130; W. Schmithals, *Einleitung in die drei ersten Evangelien* (1985), 416f.

[28] With J.M. Robinson, "On the Gattung," 101, "Zur Gattung," 129.

[29] On the basic structure shared by the Gospels, cf. below, section 4.1.2.2.

[30] But Bultmann sees the "Christ-myth" giving Mark's gospel its "non-biographical unity" (*Die Geschichte der synoptischen Tradition* [[9]1979], 397, 399f.; *The History of the Synoptic Tradition* (1963), 346-350. In this he is correctly opposed by D. Dormeyer, *Evangelium als literarische und theologische Gattung,* Erträge der Forschung 263 (1989), 91.

which the originally isolated bits of the Jesus tradition are now joined, is unavoidable. Nor can it be solved apart from an examination of the concept of biography as it was known in Hellenism.[31]

As to origin, despite occasional chronological and geographical presentations in the pre-synoptic traditions and collections,[32] no gospel structure is evident before the New Testament.[33] O. Bauernfeind sought in vain for such a derivation in his 1915 licentiate dissertation.

He regarded early Christian preaching, the unwritten gospel, as the point of departure for the written Gospels. This unwritten gospel, which he sought to demonstate as a unified message through an undifferentiated portrayal of the New Testament,[34] formed the root of the written Gospels and the basis on which the gospel genre could be explained. "The understanding of the 'gospel' form can only be recovered from the soil of primitive Christianity."[35]

The gospel genre is likewise not plausibly derived from the speeches of Acts (10:36-43; 13:23-31; etc.)[36] or the kerygma tradition. In the latter, historical data occur only infrequently (e.g. 1 Cor 11:23-25; 15:3-7).[37]

---

[31] G. Strecker, *Der Weg der Gerechtigkeit. Untersuchung zur Theologie des Matthäus*, FRLANT 82 ([3]1971), 45f. Cf. D.E. Aune, *The New Testament in its Literary Environment* (1987), 64: "The view proposed here, that the Gospels are a subtype of Greco-Roman biography, assumes that the Evangelists wrote with historical intentions," Cf. also below, section 4.1.2.3.

[32] Cf. J. Roloff, *Das Kerygma*, 270f.

[33] Cf. also D.E. Aune, *Literary Environment*, 24f.

[34] Bauernfeind, "Literarische Form," 15ff.

[35] Bauernfeind, 89.

[36] E.g., R. Guelich, "The Gospel Genre," in *Das Evangelium und die Evangelien. Vorträge vom Tübinger Symposium 1982*, ed. P. Stuhlmacher, WUNT 28 (1983), 183-219, 209-213; and in *The Gospel and the Gospels* 1991), 173-208, 198-202; H. Riesenfeld, "Tradition und Redaktion im Markusevangelium" (first published in 1954), in *Das Markus-Evangelium*, ed. R. Pesch, Wege der Forschung 411 (1979), 103-112, 104-106; P. Stuhlmacher, "Evangelium 1. Biblisch," in *EKL[3]* 1 (1986): 1217-1221, 1220. For further bibliography cf. the sruvey in H. Frankemölle, *Evangelium. Begriff und Gattung. Ein Forschungsbericht*, SBB 15 (1988)177-192. Cf. also the analysis of the viewpoints of R. Guelich and others in A. Weiser, "Tradition und lukanische Komposition in Apg 10,36-43," in *A cause de l'évangile. Études sur les Synoptiques et les Actes*, Festschrift J. Dupont, LD 123 (1985), 757-767. Weiser correctly emphasizes the significance of redaction for the speeches and therefore rejects any underlying pre-gospel structure for them. For further criticism, cf. G. Schneider, "Die Petrusrede vor Kornelius. Das Verhältnis von Tradition und Redaktion in Apg 10,34-43," in his *Lukas, Theologe der Heilsgeschichte. Aufsätze zum lukanischen Doppelwerk*, BBB 59 (1985), 253-279; H. Frankemölle, *Evangelium*, 191.

[37] Against C.H. Dodd, *Framework*, cf. also his *Preaching*, 46-55; J. Schniewind, "Synoptiker-Exegese," 183. H. Koester, "Ein Jesus und vier ursprüngliche Evangeliengattungen," 150: "This [canonical Gospel, ed.] genre is a creation of the kerygma of the primitive church. Confessional statements such as that which Paul quotes as 'gospel' in 1 Cor 15:1ff. his have given the genre its structure." But for a different viewpoint cf. his *Einführung* 432, etc., *Introduction* 2:169, etc., where biography has a role in the origin of the genre. Cf. also his "Formgeschichte/Formenkritik. II. Neues Testament," *TRE* 11 (1983): 296 and the

It is a stimulating suggestion to see in the liturgically-shaped Easter formula (I Cor 15:3b-5) a tendency to further literary development. But is it possible to presume a relationship between the (oral) "gospel" (εὐαγγέλιον, cf. 1 Cor 15:1-11) and the Gospel of Mark?[38] It is also questionable that we are on a dependable "path from the gospel to the Gospels" when, with P. Pokorny we see stages of gospel development in the transmission of the passion narrative within the framework of the last supper tradition and in a complex of reminiscences passed on with the proclamation of the gospel.[39]

The Evangelists did not attempt to write "passion narratives with long introductions."[40] Instead they have arranged disparate traditional units in chronological and geographical frameworks: from the beginning to the end of Jesus' ministry, including the resurrection; and from Galilee and Jerusalem. The passion of Jesus occupies an important, but not central place. Broadening the "tension between a miracle and the intended response of the hearer found within all miracle the narratives" to interpret Mark's Gospel as an "aretalogical composition"[41] fails to grasp that the second Evangelist delivers his presentation in a discontinuous form, in the medium of history. It is also a problem to grant to a single category the power to give birth to the different forms and traditions included in the gospel genre.[42]

Consequently, the "evolutionary model"[43] cannot satisfactorily account for the structure and form of the gospel genre. This conclusion leads to the thesis that the gospel genre must be understood as as original creation of Mark, without denying the question of analogies.

Not only is derivation from the kerygma set aside but the problem of analogies is also reduced by an analysis of the Gospels according to "text types," regarding them as narratives.[44] However, the proposed terminology with respect to the "narrative

---

development in *IDBSup* 555. For further bibliography, cf. Frankemölle, *Evangelium,* 163ff.

[38] As does P. Pokorny, "Zur Entstehung," 394: "The Gospel of Mark culminates therefore in the confessional formula adapted to narrative."

[39] Pokorny, 396f.

[40] As in M. Kähler, *Christus,* 59f., n. 1. Often quoted subsequently with varying intent, e.g., by D. Dormeyer, *Evangelium als literarische und theologische Gattung,* Erträge der Forschung 263 (1989), 185; Koester, "Ein Jesus und vier ursprüngliche Evangeliengattungen," 150; "One Jesus and Four Primitive Gospels," 161f.; P. Vielhauer, *Geschichte der urchristlichen Literatur,* 354; W. Schmithals, *Das Evangelium nach Markus,* Ökumenischer Taschenbuchkommentar zum Neuen Testament 2, Vol. 1 (1979, ²1986), 47.

[41] G. Theissen, *Urchristliche Wundergeschichten. Ein Beitrag zur formgeschichtlichen Erforschung der synoptischen Evangelien,* SNT 8 (1974, ⁶1990), 214; *The Miracle Stories of the Early Christian Tradition* (1983), 214.

[42] For more on "framework theories" as the basis for the development of the gospel genre, cf. R. Bultmann, *Geschichte der synoptischen Tradition, Ergänzungsheft⁵,* 124.

[43] W.S. Vorster, "Der Ort der Gattung Evangelium in der Literaturgeschichte," *VF* 29 (1984): 6.

[44] W.S. Vorster, "Kerygma/History," 91ff.; "Der Ort," 24f. Cf. also I du Plessis, "Die genre van Lukas," 26: "A biography with a dramatic impact and a pastoral-theological outline, but with the claim of historical thoroughness." According to C. Breytenbach, an episodic narrative.

model"[45] must be questioned.   This characterization[46] also leaves the Gospels too abstract and too general[47] and lacks the specificity of a particular genre.[48]

## 4.1.2.2  The Relationship of the Gospels to the Gospel Genre; Reflections on their Development

*Literature*

Gundry, R.H., "Recent Investigations Into the Literary Genre 'Gospel,'" in *New Dimensions in New Testament Study,* ed. R.N. Longenecker *et al.* (1974), 97-114. Marxsen, W., "Bemerkungen zur 'Form' der sogenannten Evangelien," *TLZ* 81 (1956): 345-348.   Pilgaard, A., "The Gospel of John as Gospel Writing," in *Aspects on the Johannine Literature,* ed. L. Hartman et al. ConBNT Series 18 (1987), 44-55.    Schulz, S., "Die Bedeutung des Markus für die Theologiegeschichte des Urchristentums" (first published in 1964), now in *Das Markus-Evangelium,* ed. R. Pesch, Wege der Forschung 411 (1979), 151-162.

A similar basic structure is perceptible for the Synoptic Gospels (and with certain restrictions also for the Fourth Gospel, though viewed in terms of form it is partially incomplete).   They are introduced by either the infancy of Jesus or the account of John the Baptist.   This is followed by the public career of Jesus, beginning with his preaching in Galilee and ending in Jerusalem.   There the course of his life is finished, as portrayed in the passion narratives and resurrection accounts which conclude the Gospels.

This is not to suggest a formal distinction between Mark and the other Evangelists, as if, in contrast to the others, the second Evangelist does not show a tendency to "historical development."[49]   Similarly, N. Perrin distinguished Mark's Gospel, which, like the Apocalypse, involves the church or the reader in the narrative and stresses the necessity of discipleship in awaiting the parousia,[50] from the Gospels of Luke and Matthew, whose Evangelists separate between the sacred era and the era of the church.[51]   According to W. Marxsen, in this case only Mark's Gospel would would be labeled a gospel (= a proclamation), with the other Gospels, which are other types of

---

[45] Vorster, "Der Ort," 24.

[46] D. Dormeyer, *Evangelium als literarische und theologische Gattung,* 151, shows that these categories describe not types of texts but "basic forms of literature" which are "inherent in every type of text."

[47] Cf. on this in general, Dormeyer, 151f.

[48] Thus Vorster does not differentiate between "evangelium" and "apocalypse;" both are identified as narratives. Cf. below, p. 209.

[49] W. Marxsen, *Der Evangelist Markus. Studien zur Redaktionsgeschichte des Evangeliums,* FRLANT 67 ([2]1959), 141-147 *Mark the Evangelist* (1969), 207-216; cf. also his "Bemerkungen," 347, and his "Literaturgeschichte II. Das NT," *EKL[2]* 2 (1962): 1127.

[50] N. Perrin, *The New Testament: An Introduction* (1974), 165.

[51] N. Perrin, "Towards an Interpretation of the Gospel of Mark," in *Christology and a Modern Pilgrimmage. A Discussion with Norman Perrin,* ed. H.D. Betz (1971), 60f.

texts, being constructed on the basis of Mark.[52]  But these distinctions cannot be supported on the basis of the genre's history.

Likewise false, based on the history of this genre, are the differentiations between the Synoptics and the Fourth Gospel,[53] and between Luke's Gospel complemented through Acts and the other Gospels.[54]

Differences between the individual Gospels to which redaction criticism directed its attention are worth observing, but do not necessarily imply distinctions in genre.[55] Despite their different literary formation and theological interests, the formal approach of Mark's Gospel was adopted and adapted by the other Evangelists without losing the genre. The objection that the literary form "gospel" should not be considered a category of text from the point of view of the history of genre[56] proves itself invalid since the genre "gospel" is also found outside the New Testament.[57]

### 4.1.2.3  The Motifs and Central Theological Ideas of the Gospels

*Literature*

Bultmann, R., "Das Verhältnis der urchristlichen Christusbotschaft zum historischen Jesus" (first published in 1960), now in *Exegetica. Aufsätze zur Erforschung des Neuen Testaments,* ed. E. Dinkler (1967), 445-469. Conzelmann, H., *Die Mitte der Zeit. Studien zur Theologie des Lukas,* BHT 17 ([5]1964, [6]1977), *The Theology of St. Luke* (1960). Crossan, J.D., "A Form for Absence: The Markan Creation of Gospel," *Semeia* 12 (1978): 41-55. Ebeling, G. *Theologie und*

---

[52] W. Marxsen, *Der Evangelist Markus,* [2]77ff., *Mark the Evangelist* (1969), 117ff.; S. Schulz, "Die Bedeutung," 151; G. Petzke, *Die Traditionen über Apollonius von Tyana und das Neue Testament,* SCHNT 1 (1970), 62. Cf. also the diffrentiation in G. Theissen, *Urchristliche Wundergeschichten. Ein Beitrag zur formgeschichtlichen Erforschung der synoptischen Evangelien,* SNT 8 (1974, [6]1990), 226; *The Miracle Stories of the Early Christian Tradition* (1983), 227.

[53] On this cf. the extensive discussion in the first volume of R Schnackenburg's *Das Johannesevangelium,* HTKNT 4/1 ([2]1967, [6]1986), 2-9: which speaks of a common "literary genus." Cf. also K. Wengst, *Bedrängte Gemeinde und verherrlichter Christus. Der historische Ort des Johannesevangeliums als Schlüssel zu seiner Interpretation,* Biblisch-theologische Studien 5 ([2]1983), 119, and A. Pilgaard, "The Gospel of John," who, among others, tie the form of the Fourth Gospel closely to that of the Synoptics. For a different viewpoint, cf., e.g., G. Richter's review of R. Schnackenburg's *Das Johannesevangelium. I. Teil* in *MTZ* 18 (1967): 247-250, according to whom it is not a gospel but "Christological instruction." Cf. also W. Heitmüller, *Das Johannes-Evangelium,* SNT[3] 4 (1920), 9-184, 14 and often.

[54] So, e.g., P. Vielhauer, Geschichte der urchristlichen Literatur, 7, 408; C.H. Talbert, *What is a Gospel? The Genre of the Canonical Gospels* (1977), 107f.

[55] This applies also to the attempt of C.H. Talbert, What is a Gospel? 134f., who divides the gospel form into four biographical sub-classifications.

[56] Cf. R.H. Gundry, "Recent Investigations," 114.

[57] Thus the Gospel of the Ebionites or of the Nazarenes ought not be excluded from the history of the gospel genre to the extent that either corresponds formally to the canonical Gospels.

*Verkündigung. Ein Gespräch mit Rudolf Bultmann,* HUT 1 ($^2$1963). Käsemann, E., "Das Problem des historischen Jesus" (first published in 1954), now in his *Exegetische Versuche und Besinnungen,* 1 (1964): 187-214; "The Problem of the Historical Jesus," in his *Essays on New Tesament Themes,* SBT 41 (1964), 15-47; "Sackgassen im Streit um den historischen Jesus," in *Exegetische Versuche und Besinnungen,* 2 (1964): 31-68; "Blind Alleys in the 'Jesus of History' Controversy," in his *New Testament Questions of Today* (1969), 23-65; Weeden, T.J., "The Heresy That Necessitated Mark's Gospel," Ph.D. diss., Claremont (1964); "The Heresy that Necessitated Mark's Gospel," *ZNW* 59 (1968): 145-158; "Die Häresie, die Markus zur Abfassung seines Evangeliums veranlasst hat," in *Das Markus-Evangelium,* ed. R. Pesch, Wege der Forschung 411 (1979), 238-258.

In a negative sense, Martin Dibelius described the Gospels as "substitutes" for, and an "ossification" of, the oral tradition.[58] But on the positive side, the writing of the Gospels has been regarded as directed against enthusiastic, docetic, or gnostic tendencies.[59]

On the other hand, it should not be overlooked that the Gospels as a group are closely connected with ancient historical or biographical literature (as the Lucan prologue displays with special clarity). As products of the second or third Christian generation, the Gospels display the transition from Jewish Christian to gentile Christian tradition. As a consequence of the hellenization of Christian thought, they correspond to the self-orientation of gentile Christian throught. Though Jewish Christian influences are certainly present, they recede in the course of the tradition, and were least determinative for the form of the Gospels.

The theological interests of the redactors with respect to the history of salvation are most decisive. That history, filled with saving acts and centered on the person of Jesus, speaks to the present and future of the Christian community. It is not to be identified with the "kerygma" (originally "the herald's proclamation"). The address is indirect, mediated through the historical recitation which is intended to be primary.[60] Though seemingly abstract from the contemporary situation, the picture is addressed to the hearer, for the authors intend not simply to recite a

---

[58] M. Dibelius, *Die Formgeschichte des Evangeliums,* with a supplement by G. Iber, ed. G. Bornkamm ($^6$1971), 264f.; From Tradition to Gospel (1934), 264f.; *Geschichte der urchristlichen Literatur* ($^3$1975, $^3$1990), 48; *A Fresh Approach to the New Testament and Early Christian Literature* (1936), 66.

[59] E.g., E. Käsemann, "Sackgassen," 47, "Blind Alleys, 40f.: "a reaction already in process against primitive Christian enthusiasm which thought itself, at least in part, able to do without the earthly Jesus." Cf. also "Sackgassen," 55, "Blind Alleys," 49f., and often elsewhere. On the Fourth Gospel cf. "Sackgassen" 54, "Blind Alleys," 49, which refer to the "polemical intention" of the author. Cf. also his "Das Problem," 196, "The Problem," 25: "contends actually, on the one hand, against an enthusiastic docetism and, on the other, against a doctrine of historical kenosis;" cf. also 201 and often elsewhere. J.D. Crossan also argues, sometimes forcedly, for a polemical intention for Mark. Cf. also T.J. Weeden "Heresy" [Diss], 234ff. and "Heresy" [ZNW], "Häresie," according to whom the gospel genre corrects a "divine man" (θεῖος ἀνήρ) Christology.

[60] On the historicizing of the tradition, cf. G. Ebeling, Theologie und Verkündigung, 125-127. For a different outlook, cf. R. Bultmann, "Das Verhältnis," 453.

certain narrative, but to express clearly that what they have composed, the history of Jesus Christ from the past, is really an eschatological event whose essential significance evades the categories of time and space. Since the Christological kerygma proclaims that within time something without temporal qualification has happened, historical and eschatological interests are combined. The result is "salvation history" *(Heilsgeschichte), since* eschatological salvation has become something which can be expressed in historical language. In making concrete the "what" and the "how" of the kerygma through history, the authors are affirming:

1. that the Christ-event is once for all (ἐφ' ἅπαξ), and within the framework the history of salvation is more than just one point along the chronological line. Rather, Jesus is the "middle of time" (H. Conzelmann). God's saving will toward humanity has oriented history to the Christ-event. The time after Jesus is also determined and interpreted through this event. Since the Christ-event has been introduced into time, it has its place in the continuity of history and yet, as an eschatological occurence, it is a criterion which is not continuous with history.
2. that the Christian faith is *extra nos,* not subjective, but grounded in the Christ-event. The Evangelists write a specialized history affirming that the event which they describe, while historical, is not immanent within time, but has an eschatological quality and therefore transcends time. Such a convergence of history and the eschaton can only be expressed dialectically and is comprehensible only to faith.
3. that the Christ-event is a paradoxical occurence resulting from the incursion of the eschaton into history. The Evangelists signify this paradox when they present Jesus not as a human among humans, but as the Christ in whom they believe. Thus they say basically nothing different than what has been affirmed all along in the kerygma (cf. John 1:14, 1 Corinthians 13:3b-5a). In this they draw out from the faith expressed in the kerygma essential implications from the past which precede the community and on which its faith is based. When they affirm that the Christ in whom they believe is a historical reality, they express their own paradoxical understanding of faith. This faith is dialectically oriented to the world, without intending to be of the world and therefore worldly.[61]

In Mark's Gospel this paradox of faith finds its expression in the "messianic secret."[62] This motif allows Mark to express the dialectic of hiddenness and revelation in a biography of Jesus without dissolving the dialectic of eschaton and history in a life of Jesus.

Although Albert Schweitzer's pupil Martin Werner explained the origin of Christian theology as a result of the postponement of the parousia,[63] no acute

---

[61] On this generally, cf. G. Strecker, "Die historische und theologische Problematik der Jesusfrage" (first published in 1969), in his *Eschaton und Historie. Aufsätze* (1979), 178-181.

[62] See below on the so-called parable theory (p. 147) and on the command to silence in the Marcan miracle narratives (p. 152f.).

[63] M. Werner, *Die Entstehung des christlichen Dogmas problemgeschichtlich dargestellt* (²1954), *Die Entstehung des christlichen Dogmas. Problemgeschichtlich*

problem of the this postponement is reflected in the redaction of the Gospels. This delay is a presupposition of their writing rather than a topic about which they are written. The temporal indeterminateness of the eschaton supplants the question of sooner or later. Attention is focused on the world, on time and place. This parallels the effort to make Christian existence at home in the world, without shutting out its eschatological components.[64] Luke has been accused of "de-eschatologizing" through historicizing, i.e., arranging the eschatological events at the end of the history of salvation.[65] Yet for Luke, the Spirit is not a "substitute" for the realities of eschatological salvation.[66] According to Acts 2:17 the Spirit informs the community that it is standing in the last days, since the event of Pentecost fulfills the prophecy of Joel 3:1-5. While in Luke the Spirit remains the free gift of God, it is a significant entity of the last times. This gift gives the age of the church an eschatological determination. The eschatological motivation of Christian paraenesis (Luke 17:20ff. and elsewhere) reveals that the present is eschatologically determined.[67] Thus Luke does not intend to remove the eschatological but to restructure it. The dialectic between eschaton and history is preserved, as in the other Gospels. It is, regardless of the genuine effects of the individual gospel redactors, an expression of the Synoptic authors' unity. Despite the transformation of parousia expectation, the relationship to the eschaton remains constitutive for Christian existence (cf. Paul).

#### 4.1.2.4  The Genre of the Gospels and Contemporary Ancient Literature

*Literature*

Aune, D.E., "The Problem of the Genre of the Gospels: A Critique of C.H. Talbert's What is a Gospel?" in *Gospel Perspectives: Studies of History and Tradition in the Four Gospels,* vol. II, ed. R.T. France *et al.* (1981), 9-60; "Greco-Roman Biography," in Greco-Roman Literature and the New Testament: Selected Forms and Genres, ed. D.E. Aune, SBLSBS 21 (1988), 107-126. Bahr, D.L. and J.L. Wentling, "The Conventions of Classical Biography and the Genre of Luke-Acts: A Preliminary Study," in *Luke-Acts. New Perspectives from the Society of Biblical Literature Seminar,* ed. C.H. Talbert (1984), 63-88. Baltzer, K., *Die Biographie der Propheten* (1975). Bilezikian, G.G., *The Liberated Gospel. A Comparison of the Gospel of Mark and Greek Tragedy* (1977). Boring, M.E., *Sayings of the Risen Jesus. Christian Prophecy in the Synoptic Tradition,*

---

*dargestellt,* Urban-Bücher 38 (1959); *The Formation of Christian Dogma* (1957, [2]1965).

[64] Cf. G. Strecker, *Der Weg der Gerechtigkeit. Untersuchung zur Theologie des Matthäus,* FRLANT 82 ([3]1971), 46f.

[65] H. Conzelmann, *Die Mitte der Zeit* ([5]1964), 6, 14 n. 3, *The Theology of St. Luke* (1960), 13f., 20, n. 3. Cf. also E. Käsemann, "Das Problem," 199; "The Problem," 29: "in Luke, eschatology has become a special form of the problem of history."

[66] H. Conzelmann disagrees, cf. *Mitte,* 87, 108 n. 3, 127, 216.

[67] For further evidence cf. G. Strecker, *Der Weg,* 47f. n. 4; on the appearance of John the Baptist, *Der Weg,* 91 n. 1.

SNTSMS 46 (1982). Bowman, J., *The Gospel of Mark. The New Christian Jewish Passover Haggadah,* SPB 8 (1965). Brown, R.E., "Jesus and Elijah," *Perspective* 12 (1971): 85-104. Cancik, H., "Die Gattung Evangelium. Das Evangelium des Markus im Rahmen der antiken Historiographie," in *Markus-Philologie. Historische, literargeschichtliche und stilistische Untersuchungen,* ed. H. Cancik, WUNT 33 (1984), 85-113. Dihle, A. "Die Evangelien und die biographische Tradition der Antike," *ZTK* 80 (1983): 33-49; "Die Evangelien und die griechische Biographie," in *Das Evangelium und die Evangelien. Vorträge vom Tübinger Symposium 1982,* ed. P. Stuhlmacher, WUNT 28 (1983), 383-411; "The Gospels and Greek Biography," in *The Gospel and the Gospels* (1991), 361-386. Dormeyer, D. and H. Frankemölle, "Evangelium als literarische Gattung und als theologischer Begriff. Tendenzen und Aufgaben der Evangelienforschung im 20. Jahrhundert, mit einer Untersuchung des Markusevangeliums in seinem Verhältnis zur antiken Biographie," *ANRW* II 25.2 (1984): 1543-1704. Esser, D., "Formgeschichtliche Studien zur hellenistischen und zur frühchristlichen Literatur unter besonderer Berücksichtigung der vita Apollonii des Philostrat und der Evangelien," Diss. theol. Bonn (1969). Goulder, M.D., *Midrash and Lection in Matthew* (1974); *The Evangelist's Calendar. A Lectionary Explanation of the Development of Scripture* (1978). Guelich, R., "The Gospel Genre," in *Das Evangelium und die Evangelien,* 183-219; and in *The Gospel and the Gospels* (1991) 173-208. Hadas, M. and H. Smith, *Heroes and Gods. Spiritual Biographies in Antiquity* (1965). Hengel, M., "Probleme des Markusevangeliums," in *Das Evangelium und die Evangelien,* 221-265; "Literary, Theological, and Historical Problems in the Gospel of Mark, in *The Gospel and the Gospels* (1991), 209-251. Kany, R., "Der lukanische Bericht von Tod und Auferstehung Jesu aus der Sicht eines hellenistischen Romanlesers," *NovT* 28 (1986): 75-90. Kee, H.C., "Aretalogy and Gospel," *JBL* 92 (1973): 403-422. Kline, M.G., "The Old Testament Origins of the Gospel Genre," *WTJ* 38 (1976): 1-27. Lührmann, D., "Biographie des Gerechten als Evangelium. Vorstellungen zu einem Markus-Kommentar," *WD* 14 (1977): 25-50; *Das Markusevangelium,* HNT 3 (1987). Perrin, N., "The Literary *Gattung* 'Gospel' — Some Observations," *ExpTim* 82 (1970/71): 4-7. Radl, W., *Das Lukas-Evangelium,* ErFor 261 (1988). Reiser, M., "Der Alexanderroman und das Markusevangelium," in *Markus-Philologie. Historische, literargeschichtliche und stilistische Untersuchungen,* ed. H. Cancik, WUNT 33 (1984), 131-163. Robbins, V.K., *Jesus the Teacher. A Socio-Rhetorical Interpretation of Mark* (1984). Schenk, W., *Evangelium — Evangelien — Evangeliologie. Ein "hermeneutisches" Manifest,* Theologische Existenz heute 216 (1983). Shuler, P.L. *A Genre for the Gospels. The Biographical Character of Matthew,* (1982); "The Genre of the Gospels and the Two Gospel Hypothesis," in *Jesus, the Gospels and the Church,* Festschrift W.R. Farmer, ed. E.P. Sanders (1987), 69-88. Suggs, M.J., "Gospel, Genre," *IDBSup* (1976), 370-372. Talbert, C.H., *What is a Gospel? The Genre of the Canonical Gospels* (1977); "Biographies of Philosophers and Rulers as Instruments of religious Propaganda in Mediterranean Antiquity," in *ANRW* II 16.2 (1978): 1619-1651; "The Gospel and the Gospels," *Int* 33 (1979): 350-362; *Reading Luke. A Literary and Theological Commentary on the Third Gospel* (1982); "Once Again: Gospel Genre," *Semeia* 43 (1988): 53-73. Via, D.O., Kerygma and Comedy in the

New Testament. A Structuralist Approach to Hermeneutic (1975). Votaw, C.W., *The Gospels and Contemporal Biographies in the Greco-Roman World* (first published in 1915), FBBS 27 (1970). Zahn, T., "Der Geschichtsschreiber und sein Stoff im Neuen Testament," *Zeitschrift für kirchliche Wissenschaft und kirchliches Leben* 9 (1888): 581-596; *Geschichte des neutestamentlichen Kanons.* 2 vols. (1888-1892).

Numerous contributions of admittedly differing value indicate the growing interest in literary models or parallels for the genre "gospel."[68] Different analogies are often cited at the same time in explaining the origin of this genre, so that the overall picture appears complex and disparate.

Attempts to explain the Gospels on the basis of *parallels from the Hebrew Scriptures,*[69] such as their historiography (T. Zahn[70]), the Jonah narrative (E. Schweizer[71]), the genre of the prophetic books as "ideal biography" (K. Baltzer[72]), the "biographies of the righteous," understood as a inclusive genre in contrast to the prophetic biographies (D. Lührmann[73]), or the Book of Exodus derived questionably from the "treaty genre" (M. E. Kline[74]), are not very persuasive. The interpretation of the title "Son of God" as a term for a righteous person, implicit in Lührmann's thesis,[75] is hard to maintain. It is much more credible that the title refers to the eschatological king, with whom Mark expressly identifies Jesus in 1:11, 9:7, and 15:39. This makes the thesis of a typology questionable.[76] Rather,

---

[68] Further information in W.S. Vorster, "Der Ort der Gattung Evangelium in der Literaturgeschichte," *VF* 29 (1984): 2-25; D. Dormeyer, *Evangelium als literarische und theologische Gattung,* Erträge der Forschung 263 (1989); Dormeyer and H. Frankemölle, "Evangelium als literarische Gattung," *ANRW* II 25.2 (1984): 1543-1704.

[69] For the model of Semitic analogies, cf. Vorster, "Der Ort," 17-21.

[70] T. Zahn, "Der Geschichtsschreiber," 585-589.

[71] E. Schweizer, *Das Evangelium nach Markus,* NTD 1 ([15(5)]1978, [16(6)]1986), 8.

[72] K. Baltzer, *Die Biographie,* 184-189. H. Koester, *Ancient Christian Gospels: Their History and Development* (1990), 27-29, finds the connection between "life" and "office," which is mirrored in the biographies of the prophets, also reflected in the Gospels. Koester seeks to strengthen this thesis by references to "Greco-Roman instances of office biography."

Cf. the characterization as "prophetic book" by H. Cancik, "Die Gattung,"96-98. Likewise M. Hengel refers to the identity of the Evangelist Mark as determined equally by his historical reliability and high cultural level ("Probleme," 231f., 233). Along with these he lists further analogies which he sees as influential for the formation of Mark's Gospel: Hellenistic biography and a disposition along the lines of ancient tragedy ("Probleme," 223 n. 8, 226). R.E. Brown considers the Elisha cycle of traditions as a pattern for the pre-Marcan collection of miracle narratives. Brown describes the prophetic histories as models for the new literary form gospel, referring to Jeremiah and the Elisha cycle ("Jesus and Elijah," 98f.).

[73] D. Lührmann, *Biographie,* 14; *Markusevangelium.*

[74] M.G. Kline, "Old Testament Origins," esp. 3-8.

[75] Lührmann, *Biographie,* 31, 35; *Markusevangelium,* 38.

[76] Lührmann, Biographie, 43f., and often elsewhere. Lührmann characterizes the "appeal to identify with Jesus, and specifically with Jesus whom the Evangelist pictures as the exemplary suffering righteous one," as the pervasive motif of Mark's Gospel (43).

since Mark works the community's confession of Jesus into history, he is attempting to show that this event expresses a comprehensive history of God's saving activity, of which Jesus is the midpoint. If it is doubtful that the motif of the "suffering righteous" can support a separate genre, it is further questionable that the Hebrew scriptural forms called upon as analogies actually contain the same suspense as the biographical presentations of the Gospels. That materials from the Hebrew Scriptures are utilized in individual gospel traditions does not support the derivation of the gospel genre from them. This material is disparate and simply cannot be reduced to a single determining motif.[77]

Likewise unpersuasive are attempts to understand the Gospels on the basis of *Jewish genres* such as midrash (M.D. Goulder), apocalyptic drama (Norman Perrin's interpretation of Mark[78]), or as Passover haggadah.[79]

*Analogies from the realm of Hellenistic literature* are (among others) aretalogies[80] or aretalogical biographies, i.e., genres which picture their heroes as miracle workers and therefore betray a close relationship with the concept of the "divine man" (θεῖος ἀνήρ, as proferred by M. Hadas, M. Smith, M. J. Suggs).[81] Others suggest as models the memoir-literature (T. Zahn),[82] tragedy (G.G. Bilezikian; H. Windisch previously compared the Gospel of John with drama and tragedy, yet without analyzing the parallels in terms the history of genres[83]) or

---

[77] As, e.g., with M.E. Kline's motif of the covenant.

[78] N. Perrin, "Towards an Interpretation of the Gospel of Mark," in *Christology and a Modern Pilgrimage. A Discussion with Norman Perrin,* ed. H.D. Betz (1971), 61; *The New Testament: An Introduction* (1974), 143ff.; 162. H. von Soden, in his *Geschichte der christlichen Kirche I: Die Entstehung der Kirche. Voraussetzungen und Anfänge der kirchlichen Entwicklung des Christentums,* Aus Kultur und Geisteswelt 690 (1919), 66, had already derived the gospel genre from that of apocalypse.

[79] J.W. Bowman, *The Gospel of Mark,* and N. Perrin, "Literary *Gattung,*" 7, refer to parallels.

[80] For critical remarks on the genre "aretalogy," cf. D. Esser, "Formgeschichtliche Studien," 100-102; H.C. Kee, "Aretalogy and Gospel;" P. Vielhauer, *Geschichte der urchristlichen Literatur,* 310. While literature assembled under the category "aretalogy" may include miracle narratives, as the Asclepius stele of Epidaurus indicate, what is common to this literature is primarily not its form but its content: praise for benefits from the gods and extraordinary human beings. This content may be expressed in various genres.

[81] M.J. Suggs, "Gospel, Genre," 371, speaks of "biography with aretalogical traits," Cf. also G. Theissen, *Urchristliche Wundergeschichten. Ein Beitrag zur formgeschichtlichen Erforschung der synoptischen Evangelien,* SNT 8 (1974, ⁶1990), 214; *The Miracle Stories of the Early Christian Tradition* (1983), 214: "a composition based on the aretalogical acclamation." Cf. also Theissen, 132.

[82] T. Zahn, Geschichte des neutestamentlichen Kanons 1 (1888): 471-476, where Zahn agrees with Justin's characterization of the gospel genre.

[83] H. Windisch, "Der Johanneische Erzählungsstil," in *EYXAPIΣTHPION. Studien zur Religion und Literatur des Alten und Neuen Testaments. Festschrift H. Gunkel.* Vol. 2 ed H. Schmidt, FRLANT 36/2 (1923), 210. D. Dormeyer, *Evangelium als literarische und theologische Gattung,* Erträge der Forschung 263 (1989), 158, contains further bibliography.

tragicomedy (D. O. Via[84]), the novel (M. Reiser[85]), etc. M.E. Boring interprets the Gospel of Mark as a work of Christian prophecy.[86]

Since, with the exception of Luke (Luke 1:1-4 and Acts 1:1), the New Testament Evangelists make no literary claims, genre analysis begins with the description of the Gospels as popular cult books.[87] As such, the Gospels mirror the tradition of (anonymous) communities rather than the activity of literary personalities. This is not to denigrate the individual redactional activity of the Evangelists[88] — which is rather to be preserved as a supplement to form criticism — but only to exclude any identification of the Evangelists with literary authors in either the ancient or modern sense.[89] As spokespersons of and for their communities, they collected originally isolated traditions or groups of pericopes about Jesus or of his sayings,[90] joined them with kerygmatic materials, and gave them a common form, as this best corresponded to the popular conception of biography in the Hellenistic world *and* to the theological needs of the gentile Christian communities from the second half of the first into the early second century.

Form critical objections to this viewpoint focus on the distinction between *biography in antiquity* and the Gospels. Biography is a literary form of high standing written by literary personalities; gospels are lowly popular literature.[91] This interpretation, based partially on the thinking of J.G. Herder and Franz Overbeck (cf. 1.1.5), sees the Gospels at most as continuations of the oral kerygma

---

[84] D.O.Via, *Kerygma and Comedy,* 99-101: "Mark is primarily tragicomedy because of the global and detailed presence of the death and *resurrection* or *life*-through-death motif" (101).

[85] M. Reiser, "Der Alexanderroman," 159: "novelistic biography." R. Kany affirms novelistic themes in the Gospel of Luke.

[86] M.E. Boring, Sayings, 196-203: *"Mark has so few sayings of Jesus because he is suspicious of Christian prophecy as it is present in his community and expressed in the sayings tradition. He creates a new prophetic form intended as an alternative"* (198). In a reworking of his theory Boring no longer considers this new Marcan form as questionable, but defines it as *"a new narrative form to mediate the continuing voice of Jesus intended as an alternative" (The Continuing Voice of Jesus. Christian Prophecy and the Gospel Tradition* [1991], 244; cf. 242-246, 271).

[87] With K.L. Schmidt, "Die Stellung der Evangelien in der allgemeinen Literaturgeschichte" (first published in 1923), now in his *Neues Testament— Judentum—Kirche. Kleine Schriften,* ed. G. Sauter, Theologische Bücherei 69 (1981), 37-130, 118; cf. also 34.

[88] Cf. the survey on the redactional activity of the evangelists in H. Zimmermann, *Neutestamentliche Methodenlehre. Darstellung der historisch-kritischen Methode.* Neubearbeitet von K. Kleisch ([7]1982), 226-234.

[89] So, e.g., D.E. Aune, "The Problem of the Genre of the Gospels: A Critique of C.H. Talbert's What is a Gospel?" in *Gospel Perpsectives: Studies of History and Tradition in the Four Gospels,* vol. II, ed. R.T. France *et al.* (1981), 38. Cf. below, p. 123.

[90] G. Strecker, "Redaktionsgeschichte als Aufgabe der Synoptikerexegese," in *Eschaton und Historie. Aufsätze* (1979), 23.

[91] So P. Wendland, *Die urchristlichen Literaturformen,* HNT 1/3 ([2]1912), 270 and K.L. Schmidt, "Die Stellung der Evangelien in der allgemeinen Literaturgeschichte," *passim.*

(cf. 4.1.2.1). In this light, form critical research also disputes any "historical or biographical" interests on the part of the synoptic Evangelists.[92] Against this we should observe that alongside "proclamation" the Evangelists also offer "report,"[93] more accurately "proclamation *as* report."[94] Nor is the distinction between cultivated *(Hochliteratur)* and popular *(Kleinliteratur)* literature a persuasive argument against reference to ancient biography as an analogy. Literary and rhetorical conventions of so-called cultivated literature were imitated in popular literature. Thus equating biography with cultivated literature and the Gospels as popular literature does not necessarily negate the signficance of the genre "biography" for the Gospels. On the contrary, ancient biography influenced popular literature. Although only a few examples of such popular biographies are extant (e.g., the *Life of Aesop,* and the anonymous[95] and abridged *Lives of the Poets,* e.g., the Life of Homer[96]), the parallels between gospel and biography should not be overlooked. Here as there a "hero" stands in the foreground. Each pictures a life, with chronological and geographical details. Of course it can be presupposed that the New Testament Evangelists did not make it their concern to compete with Greek literature. Rather, they intended to write in a manner understandable to their communities, i.e., in a popular style. But this excludes neither contacts with early Christian literary tradition (proof from Scripture) nor occasional use of techniques and rhetorical possibilities of cultivated literature. (Luke 1:1-4 betrays more an acquaintance with contemporary literary and rhetorical conventions[97] and a

---

[92] Cf. R. Bultmann, *Die Geschichte der synoptischen Tradition* ([9]1979), 397; *History of the Synoptic Tradition* (1963), 372; M. Dibelius, *Die Formgeschichte des Evangeliums,* with a supplement by G. Iber, ed. G. Bornkamm ([6]1971), 300; *From Tradition to Gospel* (1934), 300f. Yet Bultmann indicates in *Geschichte* 370, *History* 345f., and in *Die Theologie des Neuen Testaments,* rev. and enlarged by O. Merk, Uni-Taschenbücher 630 ([9]1984) 478; *Theology of the New Testament* (1951, 1955), 2:125f., that he does not dispute all historical or biographical data in the Gospels. Cf. similarly H. Zimmermann, *Neutestamentliche Methodenlehre. Darstellung der historisch-kritischen Methode.* Neubearbeitet von K. Kliesch ([7]1982), 134f.

[93] G. Bornkamm, "Evangelien, formgeschichtlich," in *RGG[3]* 2 (1958): 750.

[94] G. Strecker, *Der Weg der Gerechtigkeit* ([3]1982), 46 n. 1; "Zur Messiasgeheimnis-theorie im Markusevangelium," in his *Eschaton und Historie. Aufsätze* (1979), 33-51, 51.

[95] On the anonymity of the Evangelists, cf. D.E. Aune, "The Problem of the Genre of the Gospels: A Critique of C.H. Talbert's What is a Gospel?" in *Gospel Perpsectives: Studies of History and Tradition in the Four Gospels,* vol. II, ed. R.T. France *et al.* (1981), 44f.

[96] Cf. D.E. Aune, *The New Testament in its Literary Environment* (1987), 63f.; D. Dormeyer, *Evangelium als literarische und theologische Gattung,* Erträge der Forschung 263 (1989), 159; C.W. Votaw, *The Gospels and Contemporary Biographies.* On Votaw's classifications, cf. Dormeyer 71f. Votaw distinguishes between biography in the "historical sense" and in the "popular sense." The former report data and facts; the latter sketch character. Votaw subdivides the latter caregory into biography of political ("warriors and statesmen") and intellectual leaders ("philosophers and teachers").

[97] E. Klostermann, *Das Lukasevangelium,* HNT 5 ([2]1929), 1f., contains examples of such proems or prologues.

commitment to "historical" writing, than Luke's attempt to include his work with literary, biographical, or historical Greek literature.)

The same is true of the *language (and style)* of the Gospels, which for the most part may be regarded as the language of the literarily uneducated lower classes, and with a strong Semitic influence. While the thesis that Mark's Gospel is written in "Jewish Greek" has not been satisfactory proven,[98] still a defined and not too modest linguistic level is indisputable. The Gospels may be said to be written in a "popular literary style."[99]

Elements of *myth* can be demonstrated as present in (popular) Hellenistic biography. Against Rudolf Bultmann's denial of any analogy between the gospel genre and ancient biography,[100] C. H. Talbert affirms myth as a structural characteristic of both genres when he refers to the taking up of human beings after death into heaven with consequent divine status as a special case of the "divine man" (θεῖος ἀνήρ) motif.[101] Although the question of mythical themes or motifs needs further consideration,[102] it is clear that the reference to such mythical markings in the Gospels cannot separate them in any basic way from contemporary biography.[103]

Nor can their *world-denying character* serve as a point of distinction. The Gospels express more the orientation of faith within the world than a flight out of the world.[104]

But utilizing genres found in the milieu of the Gospels does not mean taking them over unmodified. Theological intention and content are also influential, so that in the case of the Gospels we are only dealing with analogous forms (cf. 4.1.2.1). Both the specific parallels and differences of genre are important for the interpretation of the Gospels and of their authorship.[105]

Accordingly it is to be concluded that ancient biography[106] provides the closest contemporary analogies to the genre of the Gospels.

---

[98] See above, p. 33, and note there also comments on Luke's style.

[99] Cf. D.E. Aune, *The New Testament in its Literary Environment* (1987), 47.

[100] C.H. Talbert sees Bultmann making three distinctions between the biographical genre and the Gospels: (α) the Gospels have a mythic structure; (β) they are cult legends; and (γ) the Gospels are produced by communities with an eschatologically motivated world-denying perspective. Cf. *What is a Gospel?* 2, 115.

[101] Talbert, *What is a Gospel?* 25-89, with whom W. Schenk, *Evangelium*, 18f., agrees.

[102] D.E. Aune, "The Problem of the Genre of the Gospels," 18. In contrast to Talbert, Aune refers the motif of assumtion of divine status to Greco-Roman folklore. As "folklore elements" they invade biographical conventions. Cf. Aune, "The Problem of the Genre of the Gospels," 18-34 and the citation on 34.

[103] C.H. Talbert, "Once Again: Gospel Genre," 57. 60.

[104] See above p. 103.

[105] On the basis of this analogy, even the aspect of historicizing should be preserved.

[106] On the genre "biography," cf. D.E. Aune's definition in *The New Testament in its Literary Environment*, 29: "a discrete prose narrative devoted exclusively to the portrayal of the whole life of a particular individual perceived as historical." Cf. also his comments on the history, function, form and content of the genre in *Literary*

With different nuances David E. Aune,[107] Gerd Theissen,[108] and V. K. Robbins[109] share this position. Similarly, Detlev Dormeyer[110] and H. Cancik[111] refer to the significance of prophetic biographies. Others seek a more specific arrangement of the Gospels within the genre of hellenistic biography. C. H. Talbert attempts to insert the Gospels precisely within ancient biography, as he develops the classification.[112] P. L.

---

*Environment,* 29-36, 43f. (bibliography). Cf. also A. Dihle, *Studien zur griechischen Biographie,* Abhandlungen der Akademie der Wissenschaften in Göttingen, Philosophisch-historische Klasse III/37 (²1970); Die Entstehung der historischen Biographie, Sitzungsberichte der Heidelberger Akademie der Wissenschaften, Philosophisch-Historische Klasse 1986.3 (1987); "Die Evangelien und die biographische Tradition der Antike," *ZTK* 80 (1983): 36-43 (for careful distinction between biography and other texts with some biographical content); M. Fuhrman, "Biographie," in *Der kleine Pauly* 1 (1964): 902-904; H. Koester, *Einführung in das Neue Testament,* 136-140, *Introduction to the New Testament,* 1:132-136 (which emphasize a connection with so-called aretalogy); A. Momigliano, *The Development of Greek Biography* (1971). Cf. also the classical presentation by A. Leo, *Die griechisch-römische Biographie nach ihrer litterarischen Form,* (reprint, 1965). (Leo identifies three types of biography: peripatetic, Alexandrian, and encomium. W. Schenk, *Evangelium — Evangelien — Evangeliologie. Ein "hermeneutisches" Manifest,* Theologische Existenz heute 216 (1983), 86, n. 33, names a fourth type, popular biography [e.g., the Life of Aesop].)

[107] A joining of Hellenistic form and function with Jewish content, *Literary Environment,* 22 and often elsewhere.

[108] *Lokalkolorit und Zeitgeschichte in den Evangelien. Ein Beitrag zur Geschichte der synoptischen Tradition,* NTOA 8 (1989), 246: "early Christian variants of ancient 'biography'."

[109] *Jesus the Teacher. A Socio-Rhetorical Interpretation of Mark* (1984), 4, 10, 60-68 (suggests a close relationship to Xenophon's *Memorabilia,* a connection alreay put forward by Justin, cf. above, p. 2). For others who hold to a generic connection between ancient biography and gospels, cf. D. Dormeyer, *Evangelium als literarische und theologische Gattung,* Erträge der Forschung 263 (1989), 58-64.

[110] Dormeyer and H. Frankemölle, "Evangelium als literarische Gattung," *ANRW* II 25.2 (1984): 1596-1601. Cf. also H. Koester, "Formgeschichte/Formenkritik. II. Neues Testament," in *TRE* 11 (1983): 296, where he even more strongly aims at a connection with the prophetic biographies (cf. above, n. 72).

[111] "Die Gattung Evangelium. Das Evangelium des Markus im Rahmen der antiken Historiographie," in *Markus-Philologie. Historische, literargeschichtliche und stilistische Untersuchungen,* ed. H. Cancik, WUNT 33 (1984), 94-96, 98. Yet historical monographs and the genre biography (βίος), despite many connections, must be differentiated more than does Cancik. Cf. D.E. Aune, *Literary Environment,* 29-31; A Dihle, "Die Evangelien und die biographische Tradition der Antike," *ZTK* 80 (1983): 36-38; F. Leo, Die griechisch-römische Biographie, 317. On Cancik's derivation of the passion narrative, cf. also the comments of D. Dormeyer, *Evangelium als literarische und theologische Gattung,* 173f.

[112] On the classification of biographies, cf. C.H. Talbert, *What is a Gospel?* 92-98; on Gospels, cf. 108f., 134f. Cf. also his *Reading Luke,* 2-5. In this commentary Talbert interprets Luke on the basis of this postulated genre. For a critical response, cf. D.E. Aune, "The Problem of the Genre of the Gospels," 39f.

Shuler identifies Matthew as "laudatory biography" (=encomium).[113] Influenced by his foundation in the two gospel hypothesis,[114] Shuler extends this formulation also to the Gospels of Luke and Mark.[115]   Acording to W. Radl, the Gospels "generally most resemble in type the Hellenistic biographies of the philosophers."[116] Emphasizing the distinction between biographical and historical literature, A. Dihle regards the Gospels as biographies and in proximity to the more strictly historical lives of the Roman Caesars.[117]   Against this D. Esser underlines the formal resemblance of the Gospels, especially Luke, to contemporary biography,[118] yet his decisive criterion is the postulate that the Gospels have no close analogies.[119]

That the structure of the Gospels is replicated most closely in Hellenistic biography corresponds to the historicizing tendency of the gospel authors.[120] But the uniqueness of the gospel genre, as discovered in the motivation and theological emphasis of the authors, must also be taken into account (cf. 4.1.2.3). The orientation to the history of salvation is especially significant (cf. 4.1.2.1), and must be preserved as a central factor distinguishing between the genres "gospel" and "biography."

---

[113] P.L. Shuler, *A Genre for the Gospels.*

[114] See below, pp. 117f.

[115] P.L. Shuler, "The Genre of the Gospels and the Two Gospel Hypothesis."

[116] W. Radl, Das Lukas-Evangelium, 261. Cf. also K. Berger, "Hellenistische Gattungen im Neuen Testament," *ANRW* II 25.2 (1984): 1231-1245, where Berger refers to the lives of the philosophers.

[117] A. Dihle, "Die Evangelien und die biographische Tradition der Antike," *ZTK* 80 (1983): 48f.; "Die Evangelien und die griechische Biographie," in *Das Evangelium und die Evangelien. Vorträge vom Tübinger Symposium 1982,* ed. P. Stuhlmacher, WUNT 28 (1983), 383-411; "The Gospels and Greek Biography," in *The Gospel and the Gospels* (1991), 361-386.

[118] D. Esser, "Formgeschichtliche Studien," 169: "A genre so widely disseminated and so little specialized as biography ought to be . . . of special significance." Cf. also 156f., 260, n. 35 on Luke's Gospel.

[119] Esser, 146, 150f., 185, n. 196; similarly, G.N. Stanton, *The Gospels and Jesus. The Oxford Bible Series* (1989), 18.

[120] Not to be understood in the sense of liberal research on the life of Jesus. On that research and its perplexities, cf. the classic work of Albert Schweitzer, *Geschichte der Leben-Jesu-Forschung,* Uni-Taschenbücher 1302 ([9]1984); *The Quest of the Historical Jesus* ([3]1954).

# 4.2 Literary Antecedents to the Synoptic Gospels

## 4.2.1 The Two-document Theory and its Modifications

*Literature*

Aichinger, H., "Quellenkritische Untersuchung der Perikope vom Ährenraufen am Sabbat. Mk 2,23-28 par Mt 12,1-8 par Lk 6,1-5," in Studien zum Neuen Testament und seiner Umwelt, Series A, 1 (1976): 110-153; "Zur Traditionsgeschichte der Epileptiker-Perikope Mk 9,14-29 par Mt 17,14-21 par Lk 9,37-43a," in Studien zum Neuen Testament und seiner Umwelt, Series A, 3 (1978): 114-143. Dungan, D.L., "Mark—The Abridgement of Matthew and Luke," in *Jesus and Man's Hope*, ed. D.G. Buttrick, A Perspective Book XI (1970), 51-97. Ennulat, A., *Die "Minor Agreements." Untersuchungen zu einer offenen Frage des synoptischen Problems*, WUNT (1994). Farmer, W.R. *The Synoptic Problem: A Critical Analysis* (1964); *Jesus and the Gospel: Tradition, Scripture, and Canon* (1982). Fuchs, A., *Sprachliche Untersuchungen zu Matthäus und Lukas. Ein Beitrag zur Quellenkritik*, AnBib 49 (1971); "Die Behandlung der mt/lk Übereinstimmungen gegen Markus durch S. McLoughlin und ihre Bedeutung für die Synoptische Frage," in Studien zum Neuen Testament und seiner Umwelt, Series A, 3 (1978): 24-57; "Die Überschneidungen von Mk und 'Q' nach B.H. Streeter und E.P. Sanders und ihre wahre Bedeutung (Mr 1,1-8 par.)," in *Wort in der Zeit. Neutestamentliche Studien.* Festgabe K.H. Rengstorf, ed. W. Haubeck *et al.* (1980), 28-81; *Die Entwicklung der Beelzebulkontroverse bei den Synoptikern. Traditionsgeschichtliche und redaktionsgeschichtliche Untersuchung von Mk 3,22-27 und Parallelen, verbunden mit der Rückfrage nach Jesus*, Studien zum Neuen Testament und seiner Umwelt, Series B 5 (1980); "Durchbruch in der synoptischen Frage. Bemerkungen zu einer 'neuen' These und ihren Konsequenzen," in Studien zum Neuen Testament und seiner Umwelt, Series A, 8 (1983): 1-17. Gaboury, A., *La structure des évangiles synoptiques. La structure-type à l'origine des synoptiques*, NovTSup 22 (1970). Griesbach, J.J., *Commentatio qua Marci Evangelium totum e Matthaei et Lucae commentariis decerptum esse monstratur* (2 vols , 1789/90, expanded in J.C. Velthusen *et al*, eds., *Commentationes theologicae* 1 [1794], 360-434), now in *J.J. Griesbach. Synoptic and Text-Critical Studies 1776-1976*, ed. B. Orchard *et al.*, SNTSMS 34 (1978), 74-102 (with an English translation by B. Orchard, 103-135).Grobel, K., *Formgeschichte und synoptische Quellenanalyse*, FRLANT 53 (1937). Herder, J.G., "Von Gottes Sohn, der Welt Heiland. Nach Johannes Evangelium. Nebst einer Regel der Zusammenstimmung unsrer Evangelien aus ihrer Entstehung und Ordnung" (first in 1797), in *Herder SW* 19, ed. B. Suphan (1880): 253-424. Holtzmann, H.J., Die synoptischen Evqangelien, ihr Ursprung und geschichtlicher Charakter (1863). Jeremias, J., "Perikopen-Umstellung bie Lukas?" (first published in 1957/58), now in his *Abba. Studien zur neutestamentlichen Theologie und Zeitgeschichte* (1966), 93-97. Kogler, F., *Das Doppelgleichnis vom Senfkorn und vom Sauerteig in seiner traditionsgeschichtlichen Entwicklung. Zur Reich-Gottes-Vorstellung Jesu und ihren Aktualisierungen in der Urkirche*, FB 59 (1988). Kosch, D., *Die eschatologische Tora des Menschensohnes. Untersuchungen zur Rezeption der Stellung Jesu zur Tora in Q,* NTOA 12 (1989); "Q: Rekonstruktion und Interpretation. Eine methodenkritische Hinführung mit einem Exkurs zur Q-Vorlage des Lk," *Freiburger Zeitschrift für Philosophie und Theologie* 36 (1989): 409-425. Lachmann, C., "De ordinare narrationum in evangeliis synopticis," *TSK* 8 (1835): 570-590 [with an English translation of the greater part, 573-584, in N.H. Palmer, "Lachmann's Argument," *NTS* 13 (1966/67): 368-378, 370-376]. Longstaff, T.R.W., *Evidence of Conflation in Mark? A Study in the Synoptic Problem,* SBLDS 28 (1973). Luz, U., *Das Evangelium nach Matthäus. Mt 1-7. 8-17,* MeyerK I/1-2 (1985, ²1989; 1990). Morgenthaler, R., *Statische Synopse* (1971). Neirynck, F., in collaboration with T. Hansen and F. van Segbroeck, *The Minor Agreements of Matthew and Luke against Mark with a Cumulative List,* BETL 37 (1974); Neirynck, F., "Deuteromarcus et les accords Matthieu-Luc," *ETL* 56 (1980): 397-408. Niemand, C., *Studien zu den Minor Agreements der synoptischen Verklärungsperikopen. Eine Untersuchung der literarkritischen Relevanz der gemeinsamen Abweichungen der Matthäus und Lukas von Mk 9,2-10 für die synoptische Frage,* Einleitung in die Heilige Schrift XXIII/352 (1989); "Bermerkungen zur literarkritischen Relevanz der minor agreements. Überlegungen zu einigen Aufgaben und Problemen der agreement-Forschung, " in Studien zum Neuen Testament und seiner Umwelt, Series A, 14 (1989): 25-38. Orchard, J.B., ed., *A Synopsis of the Four Gospels in Greek. Arranged According to the Two-Gospel Hypothesis* (1983). Orchard, J.B. and H. Riley, The Order of the Synoptics. Why Three Synoptic Gospels? (²1988). Rehkopf, F., *Die lukanische Sonderquelle. Ihr Umfang und Sprachgebrauch,* WUNT 5 (1959). Reicke, B., "From Strauss to Holtzmann and Meijboom. Synoptic Theories Advanced During the Consolidation of Germany, 1830-1870," *NovT* 29 (1987): 1-21. Sanders, E.P., *The Tendencies of the Synoptic Tradition,* SNTSMS 9 (1969); "The Argument from Order and the Relationship between Matthew and Luke," *NTS* 15 (1968/69): 249-261. Schmid, J., *Matthäus und Lukas. Eine Untersuchung des Verhältnisses ihrer Evangelien,* Biblische Studien [Freiburg, Br.], XXIII, 2-4 (1930). Schürmann, H., "Protolukanische Spracheigentümlichkeiten" (first published in 1961), now in his *Traditionsgeschichtliche Untersuchungen zu den synoptischen Evangelien. Beiträge,* Kommentare und Beiträge zum Alten und Neuen Testament (1968), 209-227. Stoldt, H.-H., *Geschichte und Kritik der Markushypothese* (1977). Streeter, B.H., *The Four Gospels. A Study of Origins* (⁵1936). Weisse, C.H., *Die evangelische Geschichte kritisch und philosophisch bearbeitet.* 2 vols (1938). Wendlung, E., *Ur-Markus. Versuch einer Wiederherstellung der ältesten Mitteilungen über das Leben Jesu* (1905); *Die Entstehung des Marcus-Evangeliums. Philologische Untersuchungen* (1908). Wernle, P. *Die synoptische Frage* (1899). Wilke, C.G., *Der Urevangelist oder exegetisch kritische Untersuchung über das Verwandtschaftsverhältnis der drei ersten Evangelien* (1838).

The so-called "synoptic problem" is one of the most important source-critical issues of New Testament literary criticism. It addresses the problem of the commonness (common basic outline, common order of pericopes, and linguistic similarity) and distinctiveness (in selection of materials and composition) of the first three Gospels. Since a simple literary dependence (e.g., in the order of Matthew, Mark, Luke[121]) cannot solve the problem, a number of literary hypotheses have been suggested.[122] According to a widely shared scholarly opinion, a solution is to be found in the "two-source theory," a specific form of the utilization hypothesis. The foundations of this theory were already laid in the first thirty years of the nineteenth century with the work of Karl Lachmann, Christian Gottlob Wilke (on the priority of Mark),[123] and Christian Hermann Weisse (on the Sayings Source).[124] The theory was brought to widely shared recognition within the community of New Testament research by Heinrich Julius Holtzmann.[125]

In his *Die synoptischen Evangelien, ihr Ursprung und geschichtlicher Charakter*, H. J. Holtzmann summarized the work on synoptic issues up to his time. In contrast to the Tübingen school (F. C. Baur), Holtzmann accepted the priority of Mark on the basis of Mark's more primitive narrative style and vocabulary as compared with Matthew and Luke. Moreover, he demonstrated the necessity of a further source common to Matthew and Luke (= Λ) alongside A, regarded as the document underlying Mark. Λ is a collection of sayings and speeches of Jesus, present in a comparatively early form in Luke. Given Holtzmann's meticulous analysis of the linguistic attributes and literary relationships of the sources, the two-source theory has subsequently stood on a firm foundation. Beginning with the A-source, the assumption of which he later abandoned,[126] Holtzmann sketched a picture of the historical Jesus in "liberal-psychological application."[127]

---

[121] As Augustine would have it in his *de consensu evangelistarum* I,2.

[122] The four most important viewpoints characterizing research on the Synoptic Gospels since the eighteenth century are:

a. The Urgospel hypothesis: that all three Synoptics developed out of one original gospel or recensions of that original gospel. It was written in Hebrew or Aramaic and comprised the entire life of Jesus.

b. The fragment (or diegesis, cf. Luke 1:1: διήγησις) hypothesis: the Gospels are the final stage of a process of gathering individual notes.

c. The tradition hypothesis: like the Urgospel hypothesis, it predicates one original gospel, but in oral rather than written form.

d. The utilization hypothesis: Unlike all the preceding hypotheses, this one postulates literary dependence among the Gospels (cf. Augustine). Various arguments have been advanced to support the priority of each one of the three. In the general course of synoptic research, the conclusion of Marcan priority has prevailed (cf. below).

[123] Already in J.G. Herder, "Von Gottes Sohn, der Welt Heiland," 419, 428.

[124] C.H. Weisse, *Die evangelische Geschichte, passim*.

[125] On H.J. Holtzmann, cf. O. Merk, "Holtzmann, Heinrich Julius (1832-1910)," in *TRE* 15 (1986): 519-522.

[126] Cf. H.J. Holtzmann, *Lehrbuch der historisch-kritischen Einleitung in das Neue Testament*, ($^3$1892), 3440ff., 382ff.; his review of L. Naumann, *Die neutestamentliche Lehre vom Lohn und ihre Bedeutung für die evangelische Kirche* (1881), *TLZ* 6 (1881): 183f.; and also his *Die Synoptiker*, Hand-Commentar zum Neuen Testament I$^3$, iv-v.

[127] A. Schweitzer, *Leben-Jesu-Forschung*, 229; *Quest of the Historical Jesus* ($^3$1954).

*Paul Wernle* gave the theory its classical presentation in 1899. It penetrated Roman Catholic exegesis in 1930 through Josef Schmid's postdoctoral qualifying dissertation *Matthäus und Lukas*.[128]

According to the two-source theory, the Evangelists Matthew and Luke, independent of one another, used as sources Mark and a second underlying source, the so-called "Sayings Source" (Q) composed largely of sayings. It is reconstructed primarily out of material shared by Matthew and Luke but not found in Mark.[129] Deviations between Matthew and Luke in the sayings make it probable that each Evangelist utilized a different version of Q (Q Mt or Q Lk, cf. below, section 4.2.3.1). But oral (community-) tradition may also have been of influence.[130]

The formula quotations of Matthew (introduced by the formula [ἵνα] πληρωθῇ τὸ ῥηθὲν . . . διὰ τοῦ προφήτου λέγοντος, etc.. cf. Matt 1:23; 2:6, 15, 17f., 23) allow the conclusion of a further written source for the first Evangelist, presupposing a "prophecy-fulfillment" exegetical schema.[131] This conclusion is not set aside by the assertion that Matthew is responsible for the formula quotations himself. The text type displayed in these quotations differs from that in Matthew's own redaction (= LXX).[132] Beyond this we must reckon with further materials special to Matthew or Luke (pericopes which each are found *only* in the first or third Gospel). As to their origin, certain information is not available (though some of this material may come from Q, cf. below, section 4.2.3.1).

The "minor agreements" (small verbal parallels) between Matthew and Luke against Mark, found in Marcan materials shared by Matthew and Luke,[133] lead us to presume that it is not our Mark, but a revised exemplar (a Deuteromarkus[134]) which they used.

---

[128] For the history of research on the synoptic problem, cf. W. Schmithals, "Evangelien, Synoptische," in *TRE* 10 (1982): 575-599; and his *Einleitung in die drei ersten Evangelien* (1985), 44-233; G. Strecker and U. Schnelle, Einführung in die neutestamentliche Exegese, Uni-Taschenbücher 1253 (³1989), 48-51; and B. Reicke, "From Strauss to Holtzmann," with his critical approach to the two source hypothesis.

[129] On particulars, cf. below, section 4.2.3.

[130] W. Schmithals minimizing the role of "oral tradition" and attendant avoidance of form critical data should be opposed. Cf. also below pp. 119f. and 132f.

[131] Cf. G. Strecker, *Der Weg der Gerechtigkeit. Untersuchung zur Theologie des Matthäus,* FRLANT 82 (³1971), 49-85.

[132] For a different viewpoint cf. E. Schweizer, *Matthäus und seine Gemeinde,* SBS 71 (1974), 145f. For yet a different viewpoint, cf. U. Luz, *Das Evangelium nach Matthäus,* 137-139, according to whom the scriptural citations were already bound to their contexts in the pre-Matthaen tradition. But this viewpoint undervalues Matthew's redactional activity.

[133] See the list in F. Neirynck, *The Minor Agreements of Matthew and Luke against Mark with a Cumulative List,* BETL 37 (1974), 55-195.

[134] A. Fuchs, above all others, supports this view on the basis of stylistic analysis. (Cf. *Sprachliche Untersuchungen;* "Die Behandlung;" "Die Überschneidungen;" *Die Entwicklung;* "Durchbruch.") Cf. also H. Aichinger, "Quellenkritische Untersuchung;" F. Kogler, *Das Doppelgleichnis;* C. Niemand, *Studien.* A. Lindemann ("Literaturbericht zu den synoptischen Evangelien, 1978-1983," *TRu* 49 [1984]: 256) and F. Neyrinck ("Deuteromarcus," 400-408, and "Q^Mt and Q^Lk and the Reconstruction of Q," *ETL* 66 [1990]: 385-390, 390) are examples of scholars who oppose the idea of a Deutero-Mark.

The extent to which the "three-step- or three-stage theory," maintaining the order Mark–Deutero-Mark–Matthew or Luke, restricts the significance of the Sayings Source[135] remains hypothetical, since the compass of the Deutero-Marcan editing ought to be seen as limited. So it remains an open question whether Lucan materials with parallels in Mark (except Q passages and particuarly special-Luke) but found in contexts not parallel to Mark's should be attributed to Deutero-Mark.[136] The doublets preserved in the double-tradition[137] at least show us that there was overlapping between Mark and Q.

The somewhat parallel thesis of a earlier version of Mark (an *Urmarkus*), later worked into our canonical Mark, is less probable, but cannot be entirely ruled out.[138] W. Schmithals has spelled out such a thesis, according to which our Mark is based on an earlier version (Grundschift = GS[139]) and a collection of sayings (cf. below, section 4.2.2).

B. H. Streeter enlarged the two-source theory in his attempt to support four sources. Luke's Gospel is based on "Proto-Luke" (itself built up out of Lucan special material plus Q) and Mark. Joachim Jeremias[140] and Friedrich Rehkopf[141] also accept a special source like Proto-Luke.[142] Streeter's fourth source was "M," which Matthew used along with Mark and Q.

W. R. Farmer revived the hypothesis of J. J. Griesbach, whereby Luke used Matthew and Mark used Matthew and Luke as sources.[143] This "neo-Griesbach

---

[135] Cf. F. Kogler, *Das Doppelgleichnis,* 219f., and notes 7 and 10: "that Matthew and Luke simply took from Q all the non-Marcan material which they share in common can no longer be maintained without qualification." Cf. also A Fuchs, "Die Behandlung," 55-57 and "Durchbruch," 16f. On the parallel tradition of Mark and Q, cf. C. Niemand, "Bemerkungen," 36f. (and section 4.2.3.1 below).

[136] Thus F. Kogler attempts to identify the Parable of the Mustard Seed in Luke 13:18-19 and its parallel in Matt 13:31-32 with considerable evidence as deuteromarcan (*Das Doppelgleichnis,* 207); although in Luke it occurs in a Q context, which could argue for its derivation from the sayings source.

[137] E.g. the logion about the power of faith in Mark 11:22 and its parallel in Matt 21:21, or that in Luke 17:6 with its parallel in Matt 17:20. Likewise the word about taking up the cross in Mark 8:34 with parallels in Matt 16:24 and Luke 9:23 with the similar saying in Luke 14:27 and its parallel in Matt 10:38.

[138] E. Wendling, *Ur-Markus;* cf. also W. Schmithals, "Evangelien, Synoptische," in *TRE* 10 (1982): 594f. As a parallel to the hypothesis of an Ur-Markus, H.-M. Schenke and K.M. Fischer, in association with H. G. Bethge and G. Schenke, *Einleitung in die Schriften des Neuen Testaments,* 20-23, describe the synoptic source Mark as a "fluctuating quantity," so that at least three different versions must be taken into account: the canonical Mark as well as the source for each Matthew and Luke.

[139] Cf. W. Schmithals, *Einleitung in die drei ersten Evangelien* (1985), 410ff.; and his "Kritik der Formkritik," *ZTK* 77 (1980): 149-185.

[140] J. Jeremias, "Perikopen-Umstellungen," 93ff.; *Die Abendmahlsworte Jesu* ([4]1967), 91-94; *The Eucharistic Words of Jesus* (1966), 97-100.

[141] On this cf. H. Schürmann, "Protolukanische Spracheigentümlichkeiten."

[142] K. Grobel, *Formgeschichte,* 85-95, had already opposed this viewpoint.

[143] W.R. Farmer, *The Synoptic Problem,* 199ff; and *Jesus and the Gospel,* 93-176. Cf. also C.M. Tuckett, *The Revival of the Griesbach hypothesis: And Analysis and Appraisal,* SNTSMS 44 (1983).

hypothesis"[144] has recently received emphasis, especially in English-speaking areas, with the publication of J. B. Orchard's synopsis.[145]

In the French-speaking realm A. Gaboury's solution based on structural history (i.e., Mark 1:1-13 and 6:14-16:8 are the common synoptic source) is influential.

But these hypotheses have led to great perplexity, as they admittedly imply that the two-course theory cannot answer all the literary questions. Yet the priority of Mark is indisputable. In the alternative case, the relationship of Mark and his sources would be full of contradictions and not understandable. The order of the synoptic pericopes is also significant. Matthew and Luke follow the order of Mark, with only occasional minor redactional rearrangements.[146] The comparative length of the Gospels and the development of their language and content all point in the same direction. Redaction-critical analysis shows that there are no traces of specific Matthean or Lucan redactional elements in Mark.[147] Hence, the two-source theory, although applied less mechanically in specific instances, should remain the starting point for studying the synoptic problem.[148]

## 4.2.2.  The Sources of Mark

*Literature*

Achtemeier, P.J., "Toward the Isolation of Pre-Markan Miracle Catenae," *JBL* 89 (1970): 265-291.  Best, E., "Mark's Preservation of the Tradition" (first published

---

[144] Generally called the "Two Gospel Hypothesis," in distinction to the "Two Document Hypothesis" (= the two source theory).

[145] Similarly, E.P. Sanders, *The Tendencies* and "The Argument;" D.L. Dungan, "The Abridgement;" J.B. Orchard and H. Riley, *The Order.*  When H.-H. Stoldt affirms that "there can be no doubt of the temporal posteriority of Mark's Gospel," he also leans toward this hypothesis.  Thus he emphasizes the independence of Mark's Gospel when he describes it as a "new spiritual creation of independent character" (*Geschichte und Kritik,* 234).  Cf. also T.R.W. Longstaff, *Evidence of Conflation in Mark?*

[146] Cf. G. Strecker and U. Schnelle, *Einführung in die neutestamentliche Exegese,* Uni-Taschenbücher 1253 ($^3$1989), 51-54.  According to R. Morgenthaler, *Statistische Synopse* (1971), 231, only 12 of the approximately 128 pericopes do not stand in the Marcan order.

[147] Cf. W. Schmithals, "Evangelien, Synoptische," in *TRE* 10 (1982): 587.

[148] In his dissertation *(Die eschatologische Tora)* D. Kosch, for example, modifies the two source theory (with a Deutero-Mark and different recensions of Q).  As an additional variant, he assumes the "pre-Lucan blending of Q materials and those from so-called $S^{Lk}$."  He supports his viewpoint with the evidence that in Luke 14-17, a section especially full of special material, there are scattered data from Q.  In light of Luke's otherwise observed use of his material in blocks, this is best accounted for by a blending of $Q^{Lk}$ and $S^{Lk}$ before the time of the Lucan redaction.  Cf. also his "Rekonstruktion und Interpretation," 414f.  To support the idea of different rescensions of Q, Kosch ("Rekonstruktion und Interpretation," 416-420) seeks to establish his own theological "profile of $Q^{Lk}$," which he sees characterized by socio-ethical interests.  Of course it might be asked to what extent the development of these recensions is due to conscious redaction, and whether $Q^{Lk}$ is satisfactorily charaterized by the term "socio-ethical."

in 1971), now in *Disciples and Discipleship: Studies in the Gospel According to Mark* (1986), 31-48; "Markus als Bewahrer der Überlieferung," in *Das Markus-Evangelium,* ed. R. Pesch, Wege der Forschung 411 (1979), 390-409. Brown, J.P., "Mark as Witness to an Edited Form of Q," *JBL* 80 (1961): 29-44. Hahn, F., Einige Überlegungen zu gegenwärtigen Aufgaben der Markusinterpretation," in *Der Erzähler des Evangeliums. Methodische Neuansätze in der Markusforschung,* ed. F. Hahn, SBS 118/119 (1985), 171-197. Keck, L.E., "Mark 3: 7-12 and Mark's Christology," *JBL* 84 (1965): 341-358. Kuhn, H.-W., *Ältere Sammlungen im Markusevangelium,* SUNT 8 (1971). Lambrecht, J., "Die Logia-Quellen von Markus 13," *Bib* 47 (1966): 321-360; "Q-Influence on Mark 8,34-9,1," *Logia. Les paroles de Jésus. The Sayings of Jesus,* ed. J. Delobel, BETL 59 (1982), 277-304. Larfeld, W., *Die neutestamentlichen Evangelien nach ihrer Eigenart und Abhängigkeit untersucht* (1925). Lindemann, A. "Die Erzählung der Machttaten Jesus in Markus 4,35-6,6a. Erwägungen zum formgeschichtlichen und zum hermeneutischen Problem," in *Anfänge der Christologie,* Festschrift F. Hahn, ed. C. Breytenbach *et al.* (1991), 185-207. Luz, U., "Markusforschung in der Sackgasse?" *TLZ* 105 (1980): 641-655. Neirynck, F., "Recent Developments in the Study of Q," in *Logia. Les paroles de Jésus. The Sayings of Jesus,* ed. J. Delobel, BETL 59 (1982), 29-75. Pesch, R., *Das Evangelium nach Markus,* HTKNT 2, I (1976, ⁵1989); II (1977, ³1984). Petersen, N.R., "Die 'Perspektive' in der Erzählung des Markusevangeliums," in *Der Erzähler des Evangeliums. Methodische Neuansätze in der Markusforschung,* ed. F. Hahn, SBS 118/119 (1985), 67-91. Schenk, W., "Der Einfluss der Logienquelle auf das Markusevangelium," ZNW 70 (1979): 141-165. Vielhauer, P. and G. Strecker, "Einleitung zu XIX, 'Apokalyptik des Urchristentums,'" in *Neutestamentliche Apokryphen in deutscher Übersetzung,* ed. Wilhelm Schneemelcher, II (⁵1989); "Introduction to XIX 'Apocalyptic in Early Christianity,'" in *New Testament Apocrypha,* ed. W. Schneemelcher, rev. ed. II (1992): 569-602. Vorster, W.S., "Markus – Sammler, Redaktor, Autor oder Erzähler?" in *Der Erzähler des Evangeliums. Methodische Neuansätze in der Markusforschung,* ed. F. Hahn, SBS 118/119 (1985), 11-36.

Since Marcan priority may be accepted as certain (cf. above, section 4.2.1), the question of Mark's written sources becomes a significant problem. Unlike Matthew's and Luke's, none of Mark's sources are known or can be reconstructed by comparison, as in the case of Q.

Form-critical research has made it evident that Mark utilized pre-existing oral tradition and for the most part did not independently reword his materials.[149]

W. Schmithals disagrees. Beginning with the observations of E. Wendling and on the grounds of stylistic resemblances in four narratives, Schmithals concludes that there was an earlier document (a *"Grundschrift"* = GS) behind Mark. It began with the appearance of John the Baptist and ended with the passion and resurrection narratives. It

---

[149] On the partially written passion narrative probably used by Mark, cf. below, section 4.3.2.c.

contained miracle narratives, apophthegms, and some sayings material.[150] It was not merely a collection, but the *"literary work"* of a theologian who deserves to be named alongside Paul and John.[151] The author presented pre-existing materials "in a unified style and in a form customary to the Synagogue."[152] Recognition of this thesis depends on whether or not one accepts as satisfactorily proven Schmithals' "objections to the form critical premise with regard to the pre-Marcan tradition and the Mark's collection of traditional material."[153] If one judges more reservedly and grants form criticism a priority, since it may be more capable of clarifying the emergence of the different pre-Marcan traditional units than a literary criticism which deals with specific differences, one must also oppose the theological presupposition that, according to the viewpoint of the *Grundschrift's* author, "Jesus is not publicly presented as Messiah."[154] This viewpoint was improbable as found in William Wrede's explanation of the (pre-Marcan) messianic secret, and the same is true for the postulated *Grundschrift,* written shortly after 70 CE.[155] Further questions are raised by Schmithals' theory. Redactional-critical research is able to bring out the the particular editorial work of the second Evangelist through linguistic analysis, etc., and Schmithals' theory disregards this analysis.[156]

More promising is the question of pre-Marcan collections. H.-W. Kuhn joins the form-critical formulation of the question with literary-critical argumentation in referring Mark 2:1-3:6; 4:1-34; 10:1-45 and perhaps 4:35-6:52 to such pre-Marcan collections.[157] Comparison with other similar attempts[158] indicates that there is no consensus on this question. In some instances it may be questioned whether the Evangelist himself gathered together materials of similar

---

[150] W.Schmithals, *Einleitung in die drei ersten Evangelien* (1985), 410. Based on the discovery of a manuscript, Morton Smith regards a "secret gospel," later given a churchly revision, as the earliest form of our canonical Mark. Cf. his *Clement of Alexandria and a Secret Gospel of Mark* (1973). H. Merkel denies the validity of this hypothesis in his "Auf den Spuren des Urmarkus? Ein neuer Fund und seine Beurteilung," *ZTK* 71 (1974): 123-144, 130 and 144.

[151] W. Schmithals, "Evangelien, Synoptische," in *TRE* 10 (1982): 623; and *Das Evangelium nach Markus,* Ökumenischer Taschenbuchkommentar zum Neuen Testament 2, Vol. 1 (1979, ²1986), 44f.

[152] Schmithals, "Evangelien," 623f.; *Evangelium nach Markus,* 44f.

[153] Schmithals, *Einleitung,* 409.

[154] Schmithals, *Evangelium nach Markus,* 47 and "Evangelien," 624.

[155] Schmithals, *Evangelium nach Markus,* 46.

[156] For a critique, cf. U. Luz, "Markusforschung," 651-653 and A. Lindemann, "Literaturbericht zu den synoptischen Evangelien, 1978-1983," *TRu* 49 (1984): 323-327.

[157] H.-W. Kuhn, *Ältere Sammlungen,* 8. For a different viewpoint cf., among others, A. Lindemann, "Literaturbericht," 205, according to whom in Mark 4:35-41; 5:1-20; 5:21-23 and 35-43; and 5:25-34 there are "four miracle narratives originally independent of one another, which Mark consciously joined together as miracle narratives."

[158] E.g., J. Gnilka, *Das Evangelium nach Markus,* EKKNT 2/1 (1978, ²1986): 2, 15-28; 10. Cf. also the surveys in H.-W. Kuhn, *Ältere Sammlungen,* 14-45 and R. Bultmann, *Die Geschichte der synoptischen Tradition,* Supplement ⁵113.

form. It is especially difficult to make an intentional distinction between earlier collections and that of the redactor in Mark 10.[159]

The situation is different with regard to the collection of parables in Mark 4 (as well as the Passion Narrative of Mark 14-15[160]). Mark 4:3-(9), 10*, (13)-20, 26-29, 30-32, 33 are evident as a pre-Marcan collection, from gaps and jumps in the text, as well as from comparison with the redactional tendency characterized by the so-called "parable theory."[161] Mark contributed the setting (4:1-2), the interpolations at 4:11-12 and 4:21-25, and the conclusion (4:34). 4:10 and 13 have been expanded or reworked.

Mark 13 is based on a pre-Marcan source.[162] The process probably began with a Jewish leaflet[163] picturing the present distress and referring to an imminent end (13:7-8, 12, 14-20, 24-27). Next followed a Christian level (13:5b-6, 9, 11, [13], 21-22, 28-32, 34-36) centering on false teaching, persecution, and the time of the parousia. Finally, Mark's redaction (13:10, [13], 23, 33, 37) adapted the previous discourse to the setting and outlook of his Gospel.

Rudolf Pesch's assertion that Mark 8:27-16:8 is based on an ancient and extensive passion report from before 37 CE in Jerusalem is not persuasive.[164]

In this relatively unified section interpolations occur only to a very limited extent; there is scarcely any distinction to be made between tradition and redaction. Even the verses connecting pericopes, which before were justifiably relegated to redaction, are here regarded as pre-Marcan. Hans Conzelmann characterized Pesch's first volume on Mark as "a significant advance in the form critical discussion."[165] But the discontinuity between the first and second volumes as well as the attenuation of form-, redaction-, and tradition criticism in the latter through its attempt to deny the presence of breaks and repititions in the text has led to rejection of its approach.[166]

Parallel to the sign-source hypothesis of Johannine research (cf. below, section 4.4.1.1) is the assumption that a collection of miracle narratives underlies Mark, as in the work of P. J. Achtemeier.[167] Helmut Koester claims a close relationship between the collection of miracle narratives in Mark and the sign-source

---

[159] For a critique, cf. H. Conzelmann, "Literaturbericht zu den synoptischen Evangelien," *TRu* 37 (1972): 246f. and W. Schmithals, *Einleitung,* 280.

[160] Cf. below, section 4.3.2.c.

[161] Cf. below, pages 146ff.

[162] Cf. Vielhauer, P. and G. Strecker, "Einleitung zu XIX, 'Apokalyptik des Urchristentums,'" 525-528 or "Introduction to XIX 'Apocalyptic in Early Christianity,'" 579-582, both with bibliography.

[163] But E. Brandenburger, among others, interprets the history differently. He derives the earliest version from a "Christian group with strong ties to Jewish tradition, as probable for the Christian community of Jerusalem." Cf. his *Markus 13 und die Apokalyptik,* FRLANT 134 (1984), 69.

[164] R. Pesch, *Das Evangelium nach Markus,* 1-27.

[165] Conzelmann, "Literaturbericht zu den synoptischen Evangelien," *TRu* 43 (1978): 34.

[166] E.g., cf. E. Luz, "Markusforschung," 644-646.

[167] I: 4:35-5:43; 6:34-44. II: 6:45-51; 8:22-26; 7:24b-30 and 32-37; 8:1-10. L.E. Keck assumes a "divine man" (θεῖος ἀνήρ) source in Mark 3:7-12; 4:35-5:43; 6:31-52 and 53-56. Cf. his "Mark 3: 7-12 and Mark's Christology," 348-351.

of John, which he sees as the use of common source materials.[168]   But the (pre-Marcan) miracle narratives do not stand out as a comprehensive unity with its own intention over against that of Mark.   Not only is the existence of such a pre-Marcan collection problematical, the sign-source hypothesis itself has been called into question on good grounds by U. Schnelle.[169]   Thus the far-reaching implications drawn, e.g., by J. Becker[170] and J.M. Robinson,[171] whereby the collections of miracle narratives (regarded as aretalogies) in connection with the passion narratives of Mark and John are considered responsible for the independent origin of the genre "gospel," lack support.[172]   The intention to narrate the story of Jesus from the beginning through the death and resurrection, which despite some distinctions and omissions is common to our four Gospels, does not characterize these smaller collections.[173]

A topic of contemporary discussion is the *relationship of Mark to Q* in light of literary material common to both (cf. esp. Mark 3:22-26 and parallels; Mark 4:21-25, 30-32 and parallels; 6:6b-13 and parallels; 8:11-12 and parallels; 12:38-40 and parallels; 13:14-16 and parallels).   Mark is generally considered independent of the Sayings Source.[174]   Yet on the basis of an accumulation of problematical hypotheses W. Schmithals attempts to prove mutual influence between the two. Mark used Q[1] (cf. below, section 4.2.3.1), but also influenced the christological redaction of Q.[175]   But presupposing a dependence on or even knowledge of Q by Mark raises the question as to why he omitted most of Q's material.   No persuasive explanations can be advanced either for Mark's supposed methods of dealing with or his criteria for selecting Q materials.   Affirming that Mark wrote his Gospel as a

---

[168] H. Koester, *Einführung in das Neue Testament* (1980), 481; *Introduction to the New Testament* 2 (1982): 47; cf. also his "Ein Jesus und vier ursprüngliche Evangeliengattungen" (first published in 1968), in Koester and J.M. Robinson, *Entwicklungslinien durch die Welt des frühen Christentums* (1971), 174.

[169] See below, pp. 163f.

[170] J. Becker, *Das Evangelium nach Johannes*, Ökumenischer Taschenbuchkommentar zum Neuen Testament 4, Vol. 1 (1979, ²1985), 39f.

[171] J.M. Robinson, "The Johannine Trajectory," in *Trajectories through Early Christianity* (1971), 266-268; *Entwicklungslinien durch die Welt des frühen Christentums* (1971), 248-250.

[172] Cf. also p. 167.

[173] See above, pp. 99f.

[174] E.g., D. Lührmann, *Das Markusevangelium*, HNT 3 (1987), 12; J. Gnilka, *Das Evangelium nach Markus*, EKKNT 2/1 (1978, ²1986): 20; R. Laufen, *Die Doppelüberlieferung der Logienquelle und das Markusevangelium*, BBB 54 (1980), 59-77, esp. 73-75 (a survey of research with bibliography; beyond this cf. F. Neirynck, "Recent Developments," 41-53).

[175] W. Schmithals, "Evangelien," 612f., 625; and *Einleitung*, 427f., 403. Here Q is considered to be a "supplement" redacted by the same author or in the same school. Dependence of Mark on Q is likewise accepted by J.P. Brown, "Mark as Witness;" W. Schenk, "Der Einfluss;" and J. Lambrecht, "Die Logia-Quellen" and in *Logia. Les paroles de Jésus. The Sayings of Jesus*, ed. J. Delobel, BETL 59 (1982), among others.

complement to the Sayings Source[176] implies what it would prove. W. Schenk's idea[177] that Mark's use of only certain sections of the Sayings Source is due to his critical reaction to the "Sophia Christology" of Q, presupposes for Q a Christology which has not been satisfactorily demonstrated.[178] It is more probable that each Mark and the Sayings Source independently used similar traditions about Jesus.

Despite all, there are no certain answers to the question about Mark's use of written sources. Against the description of the second Evangelist as a "conservative" guardian of his traditional material,[179] the redactional achievement of Mark should be recognized without going to the other extreme of emphasizing his literary creativity[180] in a one-sided manner.[181] This applies also to attempts prompted by a "narrative theology" to place the synchronic context of the Evangelist in the foreground.[182] Alongside emphasis on the influence of the author's milieu, consideration of the history of tradition remains essential for reconstructing and understanding the redaction of Mark.

### 4.2.3 The Sayings Source Q in the Gospels

*Literature*

(von) Harnack, A., Sprüche und Reden Jesu. *Die zweite Quelle des Matthäus und Lukas,* Beiträge zur Einleitung in das Neue Testament 2 (1907). Hoffmann, P., *Studien zur Theologie der Logienquelle,* Neutestamentliche Abhandlungen new series 8 (1972). Kloppenborg, J.S., *The Formation of Q. Trajectories in Ancient Wisdom Collections,* Studies in Antiquity & Christianity (1987); *Q Parallels: Synopsis, Critical Notes, and Concordance,* Foundations and Facets Reference Series (1988). Polag, A., *Die Christologie der Logienquelle,* WMANT 45 (1977).

---

[176] W. Larfield, *Die neutestamentlichen Evangelien,* 251; see also J. Lambrecht in *Logia,* 304.

[177] W. Schenk, "Der Einfluss," 162.

[178] For a critique, cf. P. Vielhauer, *Geschichte der urchristlichen Literatur,* 325.

[179] E. Best, "Mark's Preservation of the Tradition" (first published in 1971), now in *Disciples and Discipleship: Studies in the Gospel According to Mark* (1986), 31-48; "Markus als Bewahrer der Überlieferung" in *Das Markus-Evangelium,* ed. R. Pesch, Wege der Forschung 411 (1979), 390-409; R. Pesch, *Das Evangelium nach Markus,*16 and 53.

[180] C.G. Wilke, B. Bauer, and F.C. Baur in their time regarded Mark as an author (cf. W. Schmithals, "Evangelien," 590f, 589). For the direction of contemporary research which de-emphasizes the results of form criticism, cf. Schmithals. On the earliest version of Mark (the *Grundschrift*), cf. above. Cf. also A. Dihle, *Die griechische und lateinische Literatur der Kaiserzeit* (1989), 221f.; *Greek and Latin Literature of the Roman Empire* (1994), 208f., who sees Mark's Gospel as an "account deliberately styled by one single author." W.S. Vorster, *Markus,* sees Mark as a narrator. A. Lindemann's remarks "Die Erzählung," 185, also tend in this direction: "the narrative (Mark 4:35-6:6a) as a whole appears to be a product of the literary activity of Mark."

[181] Cf. G. Strecker, "Redaktionsgeschichte als Aufgabe der Synoptikerexegese," in his *Eschaton und Historie* (1979), 9-32.

[182] Cf. W.S. Vorster, *Markus,* 31-35 and N.R. Petersen, "Die 'Perspektive,'" 90f.

Scholer, D.M., "Q Bibliography: 1981-1989," in SBLSP 28 (1989): 23-37. Schulz, S., *Q – Die Spruchquelle der Evangelisten* (1972); *Griechisch-deutsche Synopse der Q-Überlieferungen* (1972).

#### 4.2.3.1  The Origin, Form, and Scope of the Q-source[183]

*Literature*

Jeremias, J. "Zur Hypothese einer schriftlichen Logienquelle Q" (first published in 1930), in his *Abba. Studien zur neutestamentlichen Theologie und Zeitgeschichte* (1966), 90-92. Kloppenborg, J.S., "Tradition and Redaction in the Synoptic Sayings Source," *CBQ* 46 (1984): 34-62. Laufen, R., *Die Doppelüberlieferungen der Logienquelle und das Markusevangelium,* BBB 54 (1980). Lührmann, D., *Die Redaktion der Logienquelle,* WMANT 33 (1969). Neirynck, F., "The Symbol Q (=Quelle)," *ETL* 54 (1978): 119-125; "Once more: The Symbol Q," *ETL* 55 (1979): 382-383. Petrie, S., "'Q' is Only What You Make It," *NovT* 3 (9159): 28-33. Schulz, S., "'Die Gottesherrschaft ist nahe herbeigekommen' (Mt 10,7/Lk 10,9. Der kerygmatische Entwurf der Q-Gemeinde Syriens," in *Das Wort und die Wörter,* Festschrift G. Friedrich, ed. H. Balz *et al.* (1973), 57-67. Taylor, V., "The Order of Q," JTS n.s. 4 (1953): 27-31; "The Original Order of Q," in *New Testament Essays. Studies in Memory of T.W. Manson 1893-1958,* ed. A.J.B. Higgins (1959), 246-269. Tödt, H.E., *Der Menschensohn in der synoptischen Überlieferung* (²1963, ⁵1984); *The Son of Man in the Synoptic Tradition* (1965). Vassiliadis, P., Η ΠΕΡΙ ΤΗΣ ΠΗΓΗΣ ΤΩΝ ΛΟΓΙΩΝ ΘΕΩΡΙΑ. (The Q-Document Hypothesis. A Critical Examination of Today's Literary and Theological Problems concerning the Q-Document), Diss. Athens 1977; "The Nature and Extent of the Q-Document," *NovT* 20 (1978): 49-73 (= his Η ΠΕΡΙ ΤΗΣ ΠΗΓΗΣ ΤΩΝ ΛΟΓΙΩΝ ΘΕΩΡΙΑ, 86-118). Wrege, H.-T. *Die Überlieferungsgeschichte der Bergpredigt,* WUNT 9 (1968).

Frequent agreements between Matthew and Luke as well as doublets (i.e., texts which in both Matthew and Luke transmit once in a Marcan context and another time against Mark[184]) make it very probable that when they wrote these two Evangelists had the Q-source before them in written form[185] and in the Greek language.[186] A Greek-speaking redactor somewhere in Palestine joined together traditional collections, creating a work with a paraenetical objective which could be

---

[183] On the abbreviation Q, cf. F. Neirynck, "The Symbol Q (=Quelle)," *ETL* 54 (1978): 119-125; "Once more: The Symbol Q," *ETL* 55 (1979): 382-383.

[184] On this cf. R. Laufen, *Die Doppelüberlieferung,* who seeks to identify the earliest stratum of the tradition on this basis.

[185] But it is the hypothesis of J. Jeremias that most of Q material comes from oral tradition. H.T. Wrege, *Die Überlieferungsgeschichte,* S. Petrie, "'Q' is Only What You Make It," and others agree.

[186] P. Vielhauer, *Geschichte der urchristlichen Literatur,* 312f., assumes an early written Aramaic Q text, which, did not comprise the whole of later Q but was written expansions on the oral tradition.

used by early Christians, perhaps in catechesis.[187] Aramaic traditional material, yet without chronological organization, apparently stood at the beginning of this process. The most ancient materials are rooted in sayings of the historical Jesus, though it remains uncertain in what manner and to what extent these sayings can be reconstructed. The principle of development must be taken into account. Elements of the historical Jesus' proclamation were adapted through later additions to the needs and circumstances of the early Christian communities until the process found its provisional conclusion in the redaction of the Gospels.[188]

With respect to the order of pericopes in the Sayings Source, Luke has preserved the order of his sources better than Matthew, where we can observe this in his treatment of Mark. Thus, in the reconstruction of Q, the Lucan order is usually accepted as closer to the original sequence than the Matthean.[189] Along with occasional discrepancies in the order of Q materials there are a great number of sections in which individual Q sayings occur in the same order in both Gospels, making reconstruction of Q to a large degree possible. On this basis it can be concluded that Q was constructed with a chronological outline beginning with John the Baptist (his preaching: Luke 3:7-9, 16f., and parallels) and finishing with instructions about the eschaton.

Despite the sometimes verbatim agreement between the texts of Matthew and Luke, there are difficulties in exactly reconstructing the wording of Q. Some differences in wording can be explained as redactional, ascertained from the vocabulary or theological outlook of the two Evangelists. But extraordinary distinctions in the wording of material common to Matthew and Luke,[190] and further secondary developments in this material which are not attributable to redaction, e.g., the beatitudes of the Sermon on the Mount, make it probable that each Evangelist used a different version of the Sayings Source.

Into these two recensions of Q (QMt and QLk), without question written in Greek, the gospel redactors must also have introduced other fragments of tradition. Yet many elements of their special materials must derive from Q (e.g., Luke 15:8-10, 11-32; Matt 5:21ff., 33ff.).[191]

---

[187] Cf. M. Dibelius, *Die Formgeschichte des Evangeliums* ([6]1971), 244ff.: ". . . the sayings of Jesus were at first collected with a parenetic objective, to give the Christian communities counsel, answers and commands" (247) *From Tradition to Gospel* (1934), 243ff. (246). Against this cf. H.E. Tödt, *Der Menschensohn,* 224f.; *The Son of Man,* 246f.

[188] Cf. G. Strecker, *Die Bergpredigt. Ein exegetischer Kommentar* ([2]1985), 11; *The Sermon on the Mount: An Exegetical Commentary,* (1988), 13f.

[189] Cf. V. Taylor, "The Order of Q," F.W. Horn, *Glaube und Handeln in der Theologie des Lukas,* GTA 26 ([2]1986), 22.

[190] On the probable scope of the sayings source, cf. G. Strecker and U. Schnelle, *Einführung in die neutestamentliche Exegese* ([3]1989), 53-55. F. Neirynck gives a survey of attempts at reconstructing Q up through 1981 as well as an overview in *Logia. Les paroles de Jésus. The Sayings of Jesus,* ed. J. Delobel, BETL 59 (1982), 35-41.

[191] Cf. W. Schmithals, *Einleitung in die drei ersten Evangelien* (1985), 222 (for bibliography). Cf. also C.S. Patton, *Sources of the Synoptic Gospels,* University of Michigan Studies, Humanistic Series V (1915), 126f. Building on his own understanding of Q as originally an Aramaic document, Patton thought that Matthew

While the redactors of the Gospels also introduced further segments on tradition into these recensions ($Q^{Mt}$ and $Q^{Lk}$), undoubtedly written in Greek, yet many elements found only in either Matthew or Luke must also derive from Q (e.g., Luke 15:8-10 and 11-32; Matt 5:21ff. and 33ff.[192])

The development of the Sayings Source does not appear as only an anonymous traditional process, but also as a composition of successive redactions.[193]

The Sayings Source includes various forms, primarily sayings materials (e.g., apophthegms,[194] I-sayings,[195] legal sayings[196]). Only a few narratives were transmitted (the temptation of Jesus: Matt 4:1-11, Luke 4:1-13; the centurion from Capernaum: Matt 8:5-10, 13, Luke 7:1-10;[197] the discourse on John the Baptist in Matt 11:2-19, Luke 7:18-35 includes narratives themes[198]). The Sayings Source

---

and Luke presupposed different Greek recensions of Q. each with its onw history. W. Schmithals demurs, refusing "to make distinctions beyond the usual variations due to copying by hand." P. Vassiliadis is also critical of Patton's hypothesis in "Η ΠΕΡΙ ΤΗΣ ΠΗΓΗΣ," 116 and in "The Nature and Extent," 71. Cf. F. Neirynck, "$Q^{Mt}$ and $Q^{Lk}$ and the Reconstruction of Q," *ETL* 66 (1990): 389f., who refers to the redactional activity of the Evangelists.

[192] Cf. G. Strecker, *Die Bergpredigt,* 65f.; *The Sermon on the Mount,* 63f.

[193] So D. Lührmann, *Die Redaktion.* Critical reaction and further bibliography in J.S. Kloppenborg, *The Formation of Q,* 47-54.

[194] Luke 11:29-32 par, and often, cf. below, section 4.3.3.

[195] Luke 11:26, 27 par and often, cf. below, section 4.3.1.

[196] Luke 11:42 par and often, cf. below, section 4.3.1.

[197] This narrative, with its very diverse form, is probably a miracle narrative (cf. below, section 4.3.2a). Cf. G. Theissen, *Urchristliche Wundergeschichten. Ein Beitrag zur formgeschichtlichen Erforschung der synoptischen Evangelien,* SNT 8 (1974, ⁶1990), 183; *The Miracle Stories of the Early Christian Tradition* (1983), 182f.; and the indices under "Therapien" or "Healings." Cf. also W. Schmithals, *Das Evangelium nach Lukas,* Zürcher Bibelkommentar NT 3.1 (1980), 91 and D.E. Aune, *The New Testament in Its Literary Environment* (1987), 52. R. Bultmann disagrees, *Die Geschichte der synoptischen Tradition* (⁹1979), 39 and 223; *The History of the Synoptic Tradition* (1963), 38f.., 225: the miracle serves the apophthegmatic point. Similarly J.A. Fitzmyer, The Gospel According to Luke, AB 28 (1981), 649. U. Wegner, *Der Hauptmann von Kafarnaum (Mt 7,28a; 8,5-10.13 par Lk 7,1-10). Ein Beitrag zur Q-Forschung,* WUNT II 14 (1985), 343 calls it an "apophthegmatic miracle narrative." Cf. also R. Bultmann, *Geschichte der synoptischen Tradition,* Erg.-H. ⁵31: "formally the narrative stands between miracle narrative and apophthegm." For yet another viewpoint, cf. J.S. Kloppenborg, *The Formation of Q,* 118 and 120, who sees the narrative originating as a miracle narrative and then conformed to an apophthegm. U. Busse sees the development in the opposite direction in *Die Wunder des Propheten Jesu. Die Rezeption, Komposition und Interpretation der Wundertradition im Evangelium des Lukas,* Forschungen zur Bibel 24 (²1979), 150f. Luke attempted to form a genuine narrative out of Q material of which the formal emphasis was on (a revised) dialogue.

[198] R. Bultmann, *Geschichte der synoptische Tradition* (⁹1979), 56f., *The History of the Synoptic Tradition* (1963), 54f., classifies these sayings as school dialogues and therefore as apophthegms. But classifying apophthegms simply as sayings material does not satisfactorily define their genre. Cf. below, section 4.3.3.

lacks passion and resurrection narratives,[199] so that A. Jülicher could refer to it as a "half-gospel."[200]

Q is no unified work in terms of the history of its tradition. Distinguishing the kerygma of a Palestinian Q community from that of later Q communities in Syria is questionable,[201] since the existence of such Q communities is only theoretical.[202] In terms of the history of religions Q also presents a complex picture, in which wisdom (cf. Luke 7:35; 10:21; 11:31, 49), apocalyptic (cf. Matt 7:24-27; 19:28; 25:14-30; Luke 13:26-27; 17:22-37), Palestinian Jewish Christian, and Hellenistic gentile Christian elements are bound into a tense unity.

### 4.2.3.2 The Genre of the Q-source

*Literature*

Bammel, E., "Das Ende von Q," in Verborum veritas. Festschrift G. Stählin, ed. O. Böcher et al. (1970), 39-50. Boring, M.E., *Sayings of the Risen Jesus. Christian Prophecy in the Synoptic Tradition,* SNTSMS 46 (1982). Downing, F.G., "Quite Like Q. A Genre for 'Q:' The 'Lives' of the Cynic Philosophers," *Bib* 69 (12988): 196-225. Hirsch, E. *Die Frühgeschichte des Evangeliums,* 2 vols., I (²1951), II (1941). Hodgson, R., "On the Gattung of Q: A Dialogue with James M. Robinson," *Bib* 66 (1985): 73-95. Kelber, W.H., *The Oral and Written Gospel. The Hermeneutics of Speaking and Writing in the Synoptic Tradition, Mark, Paul, and Q* (1983). von Lips, H., *Weisheitliche Traditionen im Neuen Testament,* WMANT 64 (1990). Robinson, J.M., "LOGOI SOPHON. Zur

---

[199] This does not imply that the passion and resurrection of Jesus were insignificant for the church's traditon, as, e.g., for H.E. Tödt, *Der Menschensohn,* 225-231, *The Son of Man,* 247-253. For Tödt, the community centered on continuing Jesus' proclamation of the nearness of the Kingdom of God. The resurrection was restricted to a proof of the authority of Jesus, whom these groups awaited as the coming Son of Man. Cf. also W. Schmithals, *Einleitung in die drei ersten Evangelien* (1985), 402 for his earliest, non-christological version of Q (Q¹). But for neither the Palestinian nor the Greek area can a community be demonstrated to which the *kerygma* of the cross and resurrection was without significance. Even for the sayings source, discipleship is following the crucified, and this confession presupposes the salvational significance of his death (cf. Matt 10:38; Luke 14:27 and below, page 129). Despite the objections of Tödt and others, the lack of a passion and resurrection account in the sayings source is best explained as due to its parenetic function (cf. above, n. 187). A further reason is that a nucleus of Q goes back to a pre-Easter time and contains authentic Jesus-tradition. This nucleus could not speak of passion and resurrection. Thus it is also doubtful that explaining the death of Jesus on the basis of the model "rejected wisdom" accounts for the lack of a passion narrative, as in H. von Lips, "Christus als Sophia? Weisheitliche Traditionen in der urchristlichen Christologie," in *Anfänge der Christologie.* Festschrift F. Hahn, ed. C. Breytenbach *et al.* (1991), 75-95, 87.

[200] A. Jülicher, *Einleitung in das Neue Testament* (⁵,⁶1906), 322, rev. E. Fascher (⁷1931), 347f.

[201] Cf. S. Schulz, "Q–Die Spruchquelle," and "Der kerygmatische Entwurf."

[202] Cf. A. Lindemann, "Literaturbericht zu den synoptischen Evangelien, 1978-1983," *TRu* 49 (1984): 223-276, 311-371, 262.

Gattung der Spruchquelle Q" (first published in 1964); in H. Koester and J.M. Robinson, *Entwicklungslinien durch die Welt des frühen Christentums* (1971), 67-106; "LOGOI SOPHON: On the Gattung of Q," in H. Koester and J.M. Robinson, *Trajectories through Early Christianity* (1971), 71-113; "Early Collections of Jesus' Sayings," in *Logia. Les paroles de Jésus. The Sayings of Jesus,* ed. J. Delobel, BETL 59 (1982), 389-394.   Sato, M., *Q und Prophetie. Studien zur Gattungs- und Traditionsgeschichte der Quelle Q,* WUNT II 29 (1988). Schürmann, H., "Das Zeugnis der Redenquelle für die Basileia-Verkündigung Jesu. Eine traditionsgeschichtliche Untersuchung," in *Logia. Les paroles de Jésus. The Sayings of Jesus,* ed. J. Delobel, BETL 59 (1982), 121-200.   Steck, O.H., *Israel und das gewaltsame Geschick der Propheten. Untersuchungen zur Überlieferung des deuteronomistischen Geschichtsbildes im Alten Testament, Spätjudentum und Urchristentum,* WMANT 23 (1967).

Q is often regarded as a collection of wisdom materials (ΛΟΓΟΙ ΣΟΦΩΝ) corresponding to a type of sayings collection such as that found in gnostic literature in the Gospel of Thomas.[203] Jewish analogies (e.g., Proverbs 30, 31, 22:17-24:22) are instructive for understanding the history of the genre.[204] But this description of the genre fails to take account of the biographical aspect of Q. Thus it makes sense that Heinz Schürmann regarded the "Sayings Source" Q or the "collection of sayings and (often dialogically or scenically separated) instructions" as a unique genre.[205]

Other attempts at describing the genre draw parallels to the form of the "wisdom book" (H. Koester)[206] or the testament (Ernst Bammel),[207] or assert the influence of the testimony collection (R. Hodgson). O. H. Steck understands Q as a sayings collection for the instruction of Jewish Christian preachers, from which they can derive "their proclamation to Israel, words to their congregations, words for themselves, as well as woes and judgment sayings for the obstinate."[208]    Others

---

[203] J.M. Robinson, "LOGOI SOPHON;" H. Koester calls it a "wisdom book," "Apocryphal and Canonical Gospels," *HTR* 73 (1980): 105-130; note also the attempt to reconstruct other early Christian sayings collections as in J.M. Robinson's "Early Collections."

[204] Cf. M. Küchler, *Frühjüdische Weisheitstraditionen. Zum Fortgang weisheitlichen Denkens im Bereich des frühjüdischen Jahweglaubens,* OBO 26 (1979), 173. According to Küchler, "there existed in early Judaism . . . until the classical rabbinic era an unbroken tradition of collections of wisdom sayings in which such Christian collections would first find their place."

[205] H. Schürmann, "Das Zeugnis," 130f., 121, n. 2. For a critical reaction to Schürmann's genre definition, cf. M. Sato, *Q und Prophetie,* 2.

[206] H. Koester, "Apocryphal and Canonical Gospels," *HTR* 73 (1980): 113 and *IDBSup* 553f. "Wisdom book" implies no drastic difference from "ΛΟΓΟΙ ΣΟΦΩΝ," cf. Koester, Einführung in das Neue Testament (1980), 480, *Introduction to the New Testament* (1982), 2:47.

[207] E. Bammel, "Das Ende von Q." 48, who cites Luke 22:28-30 as the ending of Q.

[208] O.H. Steck, *Israel und das gewaltsame Geschick der Propheten,* 286-288. Likewise, P. Hoffmann, *Studien zur Theologie der Logienquelle,* Neutestamentliche

refer to analogies from Hellenistic forms: the Cynic-Stoic philosophical biography (F. W. Downing) and the sentences of Epicurus, named κύριαι δόξαι (Philipp Vielhauer).[209] The prophetic book or rather prophetic sayings may have influenced the form of Q (M.E. Boring;[210] cf. also the Bern dissertation of M. Sato, with its extensive reference to comparative materials from the Hebrew Scriptures[211]). Undoubtedly there are parallels between Q and the prophetic books, both in terms of genre and of specific forms. One might also inquire as to the similarity of social milieu.[212] But against such an evaluation of Q theology are the facts that Jesus is hardly presented in any emphatic manner as a prophet[213] and that Q lacks a prophetic call, since Luke 3:21-2 and Matt 3:13, 16-17 do not verify a call narrative for Q. That the Sayings Source does not picture the passion and death of Jesus is likewise not due to the genre of the prophetic books.[214] Rather, his death is mentioned in the service of admonition (Luke 14:27 and Matt 10:38 refer not to the bearing of a cross of ashes, for σταυρός cannot be considered apart from the death of Jesus[215]). In determining the genre of the Sayings Source we must observe that the

---

Abhandlungen new series 8 (1972), 332f., who sees Q as a collection for the mission of a "charismatic-prophetic missionary movement."

[209] P. Vielhauer, *Geschichte der urchristlichen Literatur* (²1978), 316f. The κύριαι δόξαι may be numbered with the "gnomologia" which Kloppenborg seees as analogous to Q. (See the discussion below.)

[210] M.E. Boring, *Sayings of the Risen Jesus,* 179-182, "Q is ... related more to traditional prophetic forms than to wisdom" (181); cf. also his *The Continuing Voice of Jesus. Christian Prophecy and the Gospel Tradition* (1991), 232, "... it is often wisdom in the prophetic mode." Cf. also W.H. Kelber, *The Oral and Written Gospel,* 201-203, "It ... functions in an oral, prophetic manner of speech" (202).

[211] The "exclusive exaltation of the prophets' status" in light of which Jesus is given "divine status as decisive for eschatological salvation" establishes the genuine character of Q as compared with the books of the Hebrew prophets (M. Sato, *Q und Prophetie,* 95).

[212] Cf. M Sato, *Q und Prophetie,* 407f., who refers to a "prophetic circle oriented toward the end of time" with and double structure: "wandering preachers of Jesus and sedentary communities of followers."

[213] So also D. Lührmann, "The Gospel of Mark and the Sayings Collection Q," *JBL* 108 (1989): 51-71, 64f. Cf. also J.S. Kloppenborg, *The Formation of Q,* 36, who refers to the lack of the prophetic formula τάδε λέγει ὁ κύριος, "Thus says the Lord."

[214] Cf. M. Sato, *Q und Prophetie,* 383.

[215] As with E. Dinkler, who interprets the expression "cross" (σταυρός) in the sense of a tattooed χ- or +-sign, a living custom before and after the first century CE. Cf. his "Das Wort Jesu vom Kreuztragen" (first published in 1954), now in his *Signum Crucis. Aufsätze zum Neuen Testament und zur Christlichen Archäologie* (1967), 77-98 (on this point 85ff. and 91ff.). Cf. also his "Kreuzzeichen und Kreuz. Tav, Chi und Stauros" (first published in 1962), now in his *Signum Crucis,* 26-54 (on this 27-35). Similarly, R. Eisler, Ο ΙΗΣΟΥΣ ΒΑΣΙΛΕΥΣ ΟΥ ΒΑΣΙΛΕΥΣΑΣ. *Die messianische Unabhängigkeitsbewegung vom Auftreten Johannes des Täufers bis zum Untergang Jakobs des Gerechten nach der neuerschlossenen Eroberung von Jerusalem des Flavius Josephus und den christlichen Quellen* II, Religionswissenschaftliche Bibliothek 9 (1930), 238f. This saying which Dinkler attributes to Jesus is interpreted

prior tradition was disparate in terms of its religious, traditonal, and formal history;[216] and not primarily wisdom or prophetic (a fact which we also encounter in respect to the writing of the Gospels).

The narrative aspirations of the Sayings Source, recognizable in a certain historical interest (e.g., geographical frameworks[217]) and the (admittedly minor) use of narrative material, must be considered in determining its genre. The designation "half-gospel" befits these phenomena.[218] This narrative claim receives appropriate emphasis if we start from the temptation narrative and grant it a function specific to the genre: here Jesus exemplifies of what he proclaims, as he also exemplifies the church's proclamation. The use of narrative, biographical introductions in a collection of sayings parallels showing the trustworthiness of the collected words by means of an authoritative guarantee, as found in the genres *instruction, gnomologium,* and *chreia collections.*[219]  On the basis of such analysis John S. Kloppenborg justifies various stages in the development of the Q-source.[220]  Six wisdom sayings comprise the earliest stage. The next stratum of Q is expanded through groups of sayings (mainly chreias[221] which take a critical and polemical stance toward, and pronounce judgment on, Israel: a *chreia collection*).  However,

---

as an expression of his demand for eschatological repentance (Dinkler, "Das Wort," 96). R. Bultmann also takes it in a figurative sense in his *Geschichte der synoptischen Tradition* ([9]1979), 173, "a traditional figure for suffering and sacrifice;" W. Grundmann, *Das Evangelium nach Lukas,* THKNT 3 ([10]1984), 303, as meaning "full surrender to God," For criticism cf. the interpretations of Mark 8:35 in E. Haenchen, *Der Weg Jesu. Eine Erklärung des Markusevangeliums und der kanonischen Parallelen* (1966, [2]1968), 298 and in D. Lührmann, *Das Markusevangelium,* HNT 3 (1987), 152.

[216] H. von Lips, *Weisheitliche Traditionen,* 225f., speaks of the high proportion of diverse traditional elements as a problem in determining the basic genre of Q.

[217] Cf. M.E. Boring, *Sayings of the Risen Jesus,* 232.

[218] Cf. S. Schulz, *Q – Die Spruchquelle der Evangelisten* (1972), 24, who notes, "The category 'half-gospel' may actually be the only satisfactory description of the genre of the Q source as a whole ...." Yet as a generic description it has problems since it defines the genre of the sayings source not on the basis of other texts which are form-critically analogous, but in relation to another genre which is at a more advanced stage of generic history. Yet in earlier exegesis Q was actually perceived as a gospel, but on the basis of additions, especially of narrative and passion materials. Cf. E. Hirsch, *Die Frühgeschichte,* 340ff.; and for earlier literature J.S. Kloppenborg, *Formation,* 9-12.

[219] J.S. Kloppenborg, Formation, 325-327. "Thus, the temptation sequence in a sayings collection serves to demonstrate the trustworthiness of the sage, and hence, to undergird and buttress his teachings" (327). The temptation narrative tells of no specific messianic miracle to be christologically interpreted, but has parenetic intention. Jesus' behavior becomes a pattern for the correct miracle activity of the community.

[220] J.S. Kloppenborg understands definition of genre as an important criterion in proving redactional strata in Q. Cf. his "Tradition and Redaction in the Synoptic Sayings Source," *CBQ* 46 (1984): 34-62, 57ff., and for what follows his *Formation, passim.*

[221] For a definition and discussion of the concept *chria,* cf. below, section 4.3.3.

the temptation narrative, as the latest framework, points in the direction of a biographical genre.[222]

## 4.3    Traditions in the Synoptic Gospels[223]

*Literature*

Blank, R., *Analyse und Kritik der formgeschichtlichen Arbeiten von Martin Dibelius und Rudolf Bultmann,* Theologische Dissertationen 16 (1981). Breytenbach, C., "Das Problem des Übergangs von mündlicher zu schriftlicher Überlieferung," *Neot* 20 (1986): 47-58. Dibelius, M., "Zur Formgeschichte der Evangelien," *TRu* 1 (1929): 185-216. Ellis, E.E., "New Directions in Form Criticism," in *Jesus Christus in Historie und Theologie. Festschrift H. Conzelmann,* ed. G. Strecker (1975), 299-315. Gerhardsson, B., *Memory and Manuscript: Oral Tradition and Written Transmission in Rabbinic Judaism and Early Christianity,* ASNU 22 (1961); *The Gospel Tradition,* Coniectanea biblica, New Testament Series 15 (1986). Haacker, K., "Leistung und Grenze der Formkritik," *TBei* 12 (1981): 53-71. Kelber, W.H., "Markus und die mündliche Tradition," *Linguistica biblica. Interdisziplinäre Zeitschrift für Theologie und Linguistik* 45 (1979): 5-58. Lightfoot, R.H., *History and Interpretation in the Gospels* (1935). Redlich, E.B., *Form Criticism, its Value and Limitations* (1939). Riesenfeld, H. "The Gospel Tradition and its Beginnings" (first published in 1959), now in his *The Gospel Tradition* (1970), 1-29. Riesner, R., *Jesus als Lehrer. Eine Untersuchung zum Ursprung der Evangelienüberlieferung,* WUNT II 7 ([3]1988). Schmithals, W. "Kritik der Formkritik," *ZTK* 77 (1980): 149-185. Sellin, G., "'Gattung' und 'Sitz im Leben' auf dem Hintergrund der Problematik von Mündlichkeit und Schriftlichkeit synoptischer Erzählungen," *EvT* 50 (1990): 311-331. Stanton, G.N., *Jesus of Nazareth in New Testament Preaching,* SNTSMS 27 (1974). Teeple, H.C., "The Oral Tradition That Never Existed," *JBL* 89 (1970): 56-68. Thyen, H., "Positivismus in der Theologie und ein Weg zu seiner Überwindung?" *EvT* 31 (1971): 472-495.

The stratum of the oral transmission of independent "sayings of Jesus" and narratives was very significant for the process which led to the composition of the Gospels. The oral tradition stratum is recognizable in isolated units which, sociologically speaking, are oriented not primarily to individuals, but to the earliest Christian communities. With respect to form, the sayings and narrative materials may be divided into several types. Separate units [individual units, larger units] (e.g., the passion narrative of Mark 14-16, on which cf. 4.3.2.c) came to the

---

[222] Cf. D. Dormeyer, *Evangelium als literarische und theologische Gattung,* Erträge der Forschung 263 (1989), 189, who speaks of "Q as half-way between the collection of a generically similar, thematically connected series and a 'gospel' formulated from the start as a biography." Note also J.S. Kloppenborg, *Formation,* 326.

[223] For traditional materials which share forms with NT letters, cf. below, section 3.3.1-3.

Evangelists in written form and partly in larger collections (cf. the parable source in Mark 4 and the synoptic apocalypse in Mark 13; on these collections cf. 4.2.2).

This data was shown to be basic to New Testament research by Martin Dibelius and Rudolf Bultmann.[224] Each used a different methodological approach. On the basis of a *constructive [synthetic] method* Dibelius sought to account for the development of the tradition with his "preaching theory."[225] Yet regarding the sermon [preaching] as the original setting of traditional forms did not do justice to the complexity of the synoptic tradition. Instead, various settings are required. Only so is concrete historical and sociological categorizing possible. Bultmann, committed to an analytical methodology, began with the traditional material itself and sought to ascertain the original form of each unit.

Recently criticism has been directed against the insights of form criticism from other approaches. First, and mainly in English-speaking countries, an esthetic understanding of form criticism confronted above all Bultmann's historical scepticism and subordinated form critical method to affirmations of the tradition's authenticity.[226] Harald Riesenfeld[227] and Bertil Gerhardsson have the same objective when they attempt to explain the synoptic tradition on the basis of rabbinic transmission and to prove an unbroken continuity between Jesus and community tradition.[228]

Very different is the reference to discontinuity connected with the writing of the Gospels;[229] a discontinuity to the point of denying a significant oral tradition underlying the synoptic narrative materials.[230] For G. Sellin, who postulates "that–at least for the narrative materials of Mark–every new story is not a

---

[224] H. Koester gives a short survey of the rise of form criticism in his "Formgeschichte/Formenkritik. II. Neues Testament," in *TRE* 11 (1983), 287-289. Cf. also above, section 1.1.5.

[225] On this theory, see below, page 158

[226] Cf. V. Taylor, *The Formation of the Gospel Tradition* ([2]1935); R.H. Lightfoot, *History and Interpretation;* E.B. Redlich, *Form Criticism;* G.N. Stanton, *Jesus of Nazareth,* 27. For a similar example from Germany, cf. P. Fiebig, whom Dibelius opposed in "Zur Formgeschichte," 187.

[227] H. Riesenfeld, "The Gospel Tradition."

[228] Cf. also E.E. Ellis, "New Directions;" R. Riesner, *Jesus als Lehrer;* P. Stuhlmacher, "Warum musste Jesus sterben?" *TBei* 16 (1985): 273-285, 274: "the synoptic tradition is transmitted by means of a carefully controlled continuum."

[229] E. Güttgemanns expresses scepticism with respect to reconstructing the oral pre-history of the tradition and considers the text itself synchronously as a unity behind which we cannot go. Thus, for Güttmanns, the gospel is "an autosemantic form of speech," cf. his *Offene Fragen zur Formgeschichte des Evangeliums,* BEvT 54 (1970, [2]1971), 197, also 183, 187, 257, and often. Cf. also W.H. Kelber, "Markus," *passim,* but esp., 15f, 40-44. For a critique, cf. P. Vielhauer, *Geschichte der urchristlichen Literatur* ([2]1978), 351f.; H. Thyen, "Positivismus," esp. 480-482 and 490-492.

[230] W. Schmithals, *Einleitung in die drei ersten Evangelien* (1985), 313 and often; cf. also his "Kritik." Cf. also H.M. Teeple, "The Oral Tradition That Never Existed." Against calling into question the oral tradition, cf. G. Theissen, *Lokalkolorit und Zeitgeschichte in den Evangelien. Ein Beitrag zur Geschichte der synoptischen Tradition,* NTOA 8 ((1989), 2-4; G. Strecker, "Schriftlichkeit oder Mündlichkeit der synoptischen Tradition?" in *The Four Gospels,* Festschrift F. Neirynck, ed. F. Segbroeck *et al.,* BETL 100 (1922).

reproduction, but a new creation shaped through a unique social kerygmatic filter," neither the existence nor endurance of an earlier oral form can be deduced from the written text.[231]

K. Haacker criticizes the form critical designs of Bultmann and Dibelius at a fundamental level;[232] on the one hand for the historical scepticism of form critical work (cf. above), and on the other for the axiom of *pure form*.[233] Postulating an ideal type is a questionable procedure. We must also assume that sometimes a mixed form was the earliest form of a specific tradition.[234]

### 4.3.1    Forms of the Sayings Material

*Literature (for sections a through d, below)*

Bauer, U., "'Rechtssätze' im Neuen Testament? Eine form- und gattungsgeschichtliche Untersuchung zu den Synoptikern," theological dissertation, Bamberg (1988). Berger, K., *Die Amen-Worte Jesu. Eine Untersuchung zum Problem der Legitimation in apokalyptischer Rede*, BZNW 39 (1970); "Zu den sogennanten Sätzen heiligen Rechts," *NTS* 17 (1970/71): 10-40; "Die sog. 'Sätze heiligen Rechts' im Neuen Testament. Ihre Funktion und ihr Sitz im Leben," *TZ* 28 (1972): 305-330. Boring, M.E., "Christian Prophecy and the Sayings of Jesus: The State of the Question," *NTS* 29 (1983): 104-112. Edwards, R.A., "The Eschatological Correlative as a *Gattung* in the New Testament," *ZNW* 60 (1969): 9-20. Käsemann, E., "Sätze heiligen Rechtes im Neuen Testament" (first published in 1954/55), now in his *Exegetische Versuche und Besinnungen*, II (1964), 69-82; "Sentences of Holy Law in the New Testament," in his *New Testament Questions of Today* (1969), 66-81; "Die Anfänge christlicher Theologie" (first published in 1960), now in *Exegetische Versuche*, 2:82-104; "The Beginnings of Christian

---

[231] G. Sellin, "'Gattung' und 'Sitz im Leben'," 318. Cf. also 313: "the medium of writing (gives) the oral-literary productions a new form ..., which completely destroys the older oral form." Similar is A. Lindemann's thesis in "Die Erzählung der Machttaten Jesu in Markus 4,35-6,6a. Erwägungen zum formgeschichtlichen und zum hermeneutischen Problem," in *Anfänge der Christologie*. Festschrift F. Hahn, ed C. Breytenbach *et al* (1991), 185-207, that Mark's reworking of the tradition makes reconstructing it impossible. C. Breytenbach also refers to the discontinuity of oral and written tradition, but describes the Evangelists as transmitters of immediate pre-Marcan tradition, who, as collectors, gathered together materials for their educational purposes. Thus putting the materials into writing did not always change them into other genres, and a certain amount of reconstruction is possible (but not for the apophthegms or miracle narratives).

[232] Cf. also R. Blank, *Analyse und Kritik.*

[233] R. Bultmann, *Die Geschichte der synoptischen Tradition* ([9]1979), 7, *The History of the Synoptic Tradition* (1963), 4f.; M. Dibelius, *Die Formgeschichte des Evangeliums* ([6]1971), 57, *From Tradition to Gospel* (1934), 60.

[234] Cf. G. Strecker and U. Schnelle, *Einführung in die neutestamentliche Exegese*, Uni-Taschenbücher 1253 ([3]1989), 97. For a critique of the new approach of K. Berger, which adopts the form within the framework of its current textual setting as the object of form-critical research, cf. above, 22f.

Theology," in his *New Testament Questions of Today* (1969), 82-107. Maahs, C.H., "The Makarisms in the New Testament. A Comparative Religious and Form Critical Investigation," theological dissertation, Tübingen (1965). Strecker, G., "Die Makarismen der Bergpredigt" (first published in 1971), now in his *Eschaton und Historie, Aufsätze* (1979), 108-131. Tuck, S.A., "The Form and Function of Sayings-Material in Hellenistic Biographies of Philosophers," Ph.D. dissertation, Harvard (1985). On this, cf. *Dissertation Abstracts* 46/7 (1985/86): 1975: "The form of the tradition of transmission of the sayings-material [rather than the content] was influenced by Hellenism."

*Literature on the parables*

Bassland, "Zum Beispiel der Beispielerzählungen. Zur Formenlehre der Gleichnisse und zur Methodik der Gleichnisauslegung," *NovT* 28 (1986): 193-219. Berger, K., "Materialien zu Form und Überlieferungsgeschichte neutestamentlicher Gleichnisse," NovT 15 (9173): 1-37. Black, M. "The Parables as Allegory," *BJRL* 42 (1960): 273-287; "Die Gleichnisse als Allegorien," in *Gleichnisse Jesu. Positionen der Auslegung von Adolf Jülicher bis zur Formgeschichte,* ed. W. Harnisch, Wege der Forschung 366 (1982), 262-280. Boucher, M., *The Mysterious Parable. A Literary Study,* CBQMS 6 (1977). Crossan, J.D., *In Parables. The Challenge of the Historical Jesus* (1973); "Parables as Religious and Poetic Experience," *JR* 53 (1973): 330-358. Dahl, N.A., "Gleichnis und Parabel II. In der Bibel 3. Im NT," in *RGG³* 2 (1958), 1617-1619. Dodd, C.H., "Die Gleichnisse der Evangelien" (first published in English in 1932), now in *Gleichnisse Jesu. Positionen der Auslegung von Adolf Jülicher bis zur Formgeschichte,* ed. W. Harnisch, Wege der Forschung 366 (1982), 116-136; *The Parables of the Kingdom,* rev. ed. (1961). Dschulnigg, P., "Positionen des Gleichnisverständnisses im 20. Jahrhundert. Kurze Darstellung von fünf wichtigen Positionen der Gleishnistheorie (Jülicher, Jeremias, Weder, Arens, Harnisch)," *TZ* 45 (1989): 335-351. Eichholz, G., *Einführung in die Gleichnisse,* BibS(N) 37 (1963); "Das Gleichnis als Spiel" (first published in 1961), now in his *Tradition und Interpretation. Studien zum Neuen Testament und zur Hermeneutik,* Theologische Bücherei 29 (1965), 57-77; *Gleichnisse der Evangelien. Form, Überlieferung, Auslegung* (⁴1984). Engdahl, E., "Jesu liknelser som språkhändelser," in *SEÅ* 39 (1974): 90-108. Fuchs, E. "Bermerkungen zur Gleichnisauslegung" (first published in 1954), now in his *Zur Frage nach dem historischen Jesus* (1960), 136-142. Funk, R.W., *Language, Hermeneutik, and Word of God. The Problem of Language in the New Testament and Contemporary Theology* (1966); "The Good Samaritan as Metaphor," in his *Parables and Presence: Forms of the New Testament Tradition* (1982), 29-34. Fusco, V., *Oltre la parabola. Introduzione alle parabole di Gesù* (1983). *Gleichnisse Jesu. Positionen der Auslegung von Adolf Jülicher bis zur Formgeschichte,* ed. W. Harnisch, Wege der Forschung 366 (1982). *Die neutestamentliche Gleichnisforschung im Horizont von Hermeneutik und Literaturwissenschaft,* ed W. Harnisch, Wege der Forschung 575 (1982). Harnisch, W., *Die Gleichniserzählungen Jesu. Eine hermeneutische Einführung,* Uni-Taschenbücher 1343 (1985, ²1990); "Gleichnis," in *EKL³* 2 (1989): 213-215. Heininger, B.,

*Metaphorik, Erzählstruktur und szenisch-dramatische Gestaltung in den Sondergutgleichnissen bei Lukas,* NTAbh, NF 24 (1991). Jeremias, J., *Die Gleichnisse Jesu* ([9]1979, [10]1984), *The Parables of Jesus* (revised edition, 1963, second revised edition, 1972). Jüngel, E., *Paulus und Jesus. Eine Untersuchung zur Präzisierung der Frage nach dem Ursprung der Christologie,* HUT 2 ([6]1986), 87ff. Jülicher, A., "Parables," in *Encyclopaedia Biblica,* ed T.K Cheyne and J.S. Black III (1902): 3563-3567; "Gleichnisse" now in *Gleichnisse Jesu. Positionen der Auslegung von Adolf Jülicher bis zur Formgeschichte,* ed. W. Harnisch, Wege der Forschung 366 (1982), 1-10; *Die Gleichnisreden Jesu* (reprint, 1976 = [2]1910). Klauck, H.-J., *Allegorie und Allegorese in synoptischen Gleichnisse,* NTAbh, NF 13 ([2]1986). Kümmel, W.G., "Jesusforschung seit 1981. IV. Gleichnisse," TRu 56 (1991): 27-53. Linnemann, E., *Gleichnisse Jesu. Einführung und Auslegung* ([4]1966, [7]1978). Marxsen, W., "Redaktionsgeschichtliche Erklärung der sogennanten Parabeltheorie des Markus" (first published in 1955), now in his *Der Exeget als Theologe. Vorträge zum Neuen Testament* (1968), 13-28. Olrik, A., "Epische Gesetze der Volksdichtung" (first published in 1909), now in *Gleichnisse Jesu. Positionen der Auslegung von Adolf Jülicher bis zur Formgeschichte,* ed. W. Harnisch, Wege der Forschung 366 (1982), 58-69. Rau, E., *Reden in Vollmacht. Hintergrund, Form und Anliegen der Gleichnisse Jesu,* FRLANT 149 (1990). Ricoeur, P., "Stellung und Funktion der Metapher in der biblischen Sprache," in Ricoeur, P. and E. Jüngel, *Metapher. Zur Hermeneutik religiöser Sprache,* EvT Sonderheft (1974), 45-70. Scholz, G., *Gleichnisaussage und Existenzstruktur. Das Gleichnis in der neueren Hermeneutik unter besonderer Berücksichtigung der christlichen Existenzstruktur in den Gleichnisses des lukanischen Sonderguts,* Einleitung in die Heilige Schrift XXIII/214 (1983). Sellin, G., "Studien zu den grossen Gleichniserzählungen des Lukas-Sonderguts. Die ἄνθρωπος-τις-Erzählungen des lukanischen Sonderguts–besonders am Beispiel von Lk 10,25-37 und Lk 16,14-31 untersucht," theological dissertation Münster (1973); "Lukas als Gleichniserzähler: die Erzählung vom bermherzigen Samariter (Lk 10,15-37)," *ZNW* 65 (1974): 166-189, 66 (1975): 19-60. Via, D.O., *The Parables: Their Literary and Existential Dimension,* (1967); *Die Gleichnisse Jesu. Ihre literarische und existentiale Dimension,* BEvT 57 (1970). Weder, H., *Die Gleichnisse Jesu als Metaphern. Traditions- und redaktionsgeschichtliche Analysen und Interpretationen,* FRLANT 120 ([3]1984, [4]1990). Westermann, C., *Vergleiche und Gleichnisse im Alten und Neuen Testament,* Calwer Theologische Monographien A. 14 (1984).

*a) Logia*[235] *or wisdom sayings*[236]

Rudolf Bultmann divided the logia into three sub-categories. First are *maxims* (factually or personally formulated sayings): factual, e.g., Matt 6:34b:

*Today's trouble is enough for today.*

---

[235] R. Bultmann, *Geschichte,* 73ff., *History,* 69ff.: the term "logia" refers not to words or sayings in general, but specifically to wisdom sayings.
[236] M. Dibelius, *Formgeschichte,* 247, *From Tradition to Gospel,* 247.

Cf. also Matt 12:34b and 24:28; and personal, Luke 10:7b:

> *For the laborer deserves to be paid.*

Cf. also Matt 22:14, etc.

The second sub-category of logia is *admonitions* (in the imperative, e.g., Luke 4:23:

> *Doctor, cure yourself!*

Cf. also Matt 8:22/Luke 9:60).

Finally, there are *questions* (e.g., Luke 6:39[/Matt 15:14]:

> *Can a blind person guide a blind person?    Will not both fall into a pit?*

Cf. also Mark 2:19/Mathew 9:15/Luke 5:34 and Matt 6:27/Luke 12:25).

Because he used these wisdom sayings borrowed from the Hebrew Scriptures and Hellenistic-Jewish wisdom literature, Jesus appears in the tradition as a wisdom teacher. Logia may be formulated with ornamental motifs, such as synonyms or antithetical parallelism. According to Bultmann, for these sayings there is only the slightest guarantee "that they are genuine words of Jesus; but they are least characteristic for the historical significance of Jesus."[237]  In the history of tradition, individual logia were often combined with others similar to them to form larger compositions (e.g., Mark 8:34-37, Matt 5:39b-42/Luke 6:29-30).

*b) Prophetic and apocalyptic sayings*

As in the case of the wisdom sayings, here also Jewish and Christian individual traditions have been secondarily attributed to Jesus (as, e.g., in the "apocalypse" of Mark 13:5-27[238]). Yet with some legitimacy, among these words which proclaim the breaking in of the Kingdom of God, genuine sayings of Jesus may be suspected. Here again we may identify sub-categories.

*Proclamations of salvation,* e.g., in the form of beatitudes, form a first group (e.g., Matt 11:6/Luke 7:23:

> *And blessed is anyone who takes no offense at me.*

Cf. also Luke 6:20-22 and the Matthean parallel in 5:3-12, etc.[239]

*Threats* (such as the woes against the unbelieving cities in Matt 11:21-24/Luke 10:13-15) are a second class:

---

[237] R. Bultmann, "Die Erforschung der synoptischen Evangelien" (first published in 1961), in *Glauben und Verstehen. Gesammelte Aufsätze* 4 (1965): 1-41, 27. For a different viewpoint, cf. P. Vielhauer, *Geschichte der urchristlichen Literatur* ($^2$1978), 292.

[238] On distinguishing tradition and redaction in Mark 13, cf. above, p. 121.

[239] Cf. C.H. Maahs.  On the beatitudes of the Sermon on the Mount and their parenetic inclination, cf. G. Strecker, "Die Makarismen," (with its bibliography).

*Woe to you, Chorazin! Woe to you, Bethsaida! For if the deeds of power done in you had been done in Tyre and Sidon, they would have repented long ago in sackcloth and ashes. But I tell you, on the day of judgment it will be more tolerable for Tyre and Sidon than for you. And you, Capernaum, will you be exalted to heaven? No, you will be brought down to Hades. For if the deeds of power done in you had been done in Sodom, it would have remained until this day. But I tell you that on the day of judgment it will be more tolerable for the land of Sodom than for you.*[240]

Cf. also Matt 12:41-42/Luke 11:31-32.

*Warnings* (e.g., Mark 13:33-37) are a third group:

*Beware, keep alert; for you do not know when the time will come. It is like a man going on a journey, when he leaves home and puts his slaves in charge, each with his work, and commands the doorkeeper to be on the watch. Therefore, keep awake—for you do not know when the master of the house will come, in the evening, or at midnight, or at cockcrow, or at dawn, or else he may find you asleep when he comes suddenly. And what I say to you I say to all: Keep awake.*

*Apocalyptic prophecies* ( as in Mark 13:2) comprise a fourth sub-category:

*Do you see these great buildings? Not one stone will be left here upon another; all will be thrown down.*

Cf. also Mark 14:58 and parallels, etc.

Other genres of prophetic words are also used. Ernst Käsemann's reference to the *sentences of holy law* deserves special attention.[241] These are artistic sayings in legal style,[242] based on the schema of an eschatological *jus talionis,*[243] and delivered through early Christian charismatic prophets. Beginning with a

---

[240] It is uncertain whether Luke abbreviated the tradition or Matthew, corresponding to his manner throughout, expanded it, bringing in material also found in Matt 10:15. R. Bultmann, *Geschichte* 118 and *History* 112, considers Matthean priority "probable."

[241] For the discussion of Käsemann's thesis in contemporary research, cf. U. Bauer, "'Rechtssätze'," 43-55.

[242] E. Käsemann, "Sätze," 70f., 80; "Sentences," 67, 79; and "Anfänge," 90f..; "Beginnings," 90-93. Reference to early Christian charismatic prophets is especially common in sociologically-oriented research.. E.g, cf. G. Theissen, *Soziologie der Jesusbewegung. Ein Beitrag zur Entstehungsgeschichte des Urchristentums.* Kaiser Taschenbücher 35 (⁵1988), 14ff.; *The First Followers of Jesus* [=*Sociology of Early Palestinian Christianity*] (1978), 8ff. Theissen interprets early Christian history from the viewpoint of the influence of wandering charismatics. While there is evidence of early Christian prophets who were not tied to specific locations (cf. the reference to Agabus in Acts 11:27f., which must presuppose earlier references; cf. also Did 11:7-12), we must nonetheless assume that it was mainly the class of prophets connected with specific communities who were responsible for not only "prophetic and apocalyptic" sayings, but also for many "legal sayings and community rules." Cf. below, n. 256.

[243] E. Käsemann, "Anfänge," 91; "Beginnings,," 92.

juridically formulated description of present circumstances, the sayings conclude with a promise for the eschatological future.[244]   Cf. Mark 8:38:

> *Whoever* (ὅς γὰρ ἐάν) *is ashamed of me and of my words in this adulterous and sinful generation, of that one the Son of Man will also be ashamed when he comes in the glory of his Father with the holy angels.*

(Cf. also Mark 4:24-25; Matt 5:19, 6:14-15; in Paul, 1 Corinthians 3:17, 14:38, etc.[245])

Other types of prophetic and apocalyptic sayings are *aphorisms about the eschatological future* (e.g., Matt 5:12, 6:4, etc.[246]); ἤλθον-*sayings* (e.g., Matt 9:13, 10:34, etc.[247]); *curses* (e.g., Matt 8:11ff.[248]); *eschatological correlations* (e.g., Luke 11:30, etc.[249]); and *Amen-sayings.*[250]

In connection with his proclamation of the imminent Kingdom of God, Jesus appears as a(n) (eschatological) prophet.

### c) I-sayings[251]

These sayings mark Jesus as one sent by God and portray his mission. In some of them Jesus speaks of his coming, e.g., Luke 12:49:

> *I came to bring fire to the earth, and how I wish it were already kindled!*[252]

---

[244] E. Käsemann, "Anfänge," 92; "Beginnings," 93.

[245] E. Käsemann ("Sätze" and "Sentences," *passim,* and for the synoptic texts, "Sätze," 78-80 and "Sentences," 77-80) relates these sentences to the "community rules" (cf. below), yet distinguishes them on the basis of their apocalyptic outlook and "prophetically inspired enthusiasm" Cf. also Käsemann, "Anfänge," 92; "Beginnings," 92f. E. Lohse classifies them differently in *Die Entstehung des Neuen Testaments,* Theologische Wissenschaft 4 (⁴1983), 69.  So does K. Berger, who applies a thoroughgoing critique to the *sentences of holy law* and derives these sayings from wisdom paraenesis.  Thus the *lex talionis* is regarded as a wisdom phenomenon (K. Berger, "Die sog. 'Sätze.'" and "Zu den sogenannten").  While there is an affinity between "do this--and this will result" collections and wisdom, there is also a difference between wisdom paraenesis and these sentences. E.g., the "uncommon radicality" of the New Testament sentences and the "absence of any validation" are striking. (U. Bauer, "'Rechtsätze'," distinguishes the "legal sentences" with respect to form and function: 396f., apodictic and 397f. casuistic legal sentences.)

[246] E. Käsemann, "Anfänge," 93; "Beginnings," 94.

[247] E. Käsemann, "Anfänge," 96; "Beginnings," 97f.  Yet these sayings could be more satisfactorily classified as "I sayings" (cf. below, section 4.3.1.c).

[248] E. Käsemann, "Anfänge," 98; "Beginnings," 100.

[249] R.A. Edwards, "The Eschatological Correlative."

[250] K. Berger, *Die Amen-Worte Jesu;* on this topic cf. also R. Bultmann, *Die Geschichte der synoptischen Tradition, Ergänzungsheft⁵,* 51f.

[251] Cf. G. Bornkamm, "Formen und Gattungen II. Im NT," in *RGG³* 2 (1958), 1001; and E. Lohse, *Die Entstehung des Neuen Testaments,* Theologische Wissenschaft 4 (⁴1983), 70, which calls them "Christ-words."

[252] For reconstruction of the underlying tradition, cf. Bultmann, *Die Geschichte der synoptischen Tradition,* 172f.; *History of the Synoptic Tradition,* 160f.

(Cf. also Mark 2:17; Matt 12:30, etc.)  In others he speaks about his person, e.g., Luke 14:26:

> *Whoever comes to me and does not hate father and mother, wife and children, brothers and sisters, yes, and even life itself, cannot be my disciple.*

(Cf. also Luke 14:27/Matt 10:38, etc.)

"I sayings" may be attributed principally to the Hellenistic communities.

*d) Legal sayings and community rules*

Legal sayings comment on Old Testament law, e.g., Mark 3:4 on the Sabbath commandment.  Mark 7:15 states a position with respect to the purity regulations of Leviticus 11-15:

> *...there is nothing outside a person that by going in can defile, but the things that come out are what defile.*

Often, as legal regulations, they have an imperative character, e.g., among others, Mark 10:11ff., and 11:25:

> *Whenever you stand praying, forgive, if you have anything against anyone; so that your Father in heaven may also forgive you your trespasses.*

To this category belong also the antitheses of the Sermon on the Mount, e.g., Matt 5:21-22a:

> *You have heard that it was said to those of ancient times, "You shall not murder"; and "whoever murders shall be liable to judgment."  But I say to you that if you are angry with a brother or sister, you will be liable to judgment.*

Cf. also 5:27-28, 31-32, 33-34, 38-39, 43-44.   The first, second, and fourth of these probably go back to Jesus himself.   Here Jesus at first criticizes the contemporary interpretation of the Torah; but his criticism also touches the Torah itself.   Since repentence and decision are "here and there" necessary, Jesus thus articulates his authority even against the law in the categorical claim of the will of God made present in him.[253]

According to Rudolf Bultmann, to the legal sayings also belong such materials as "by means of a proverb, or by an appeal to scripture, justify or establish a new outlook over against the old."[254]   E.g. Mark 2:25-26/Matt 12:3-4/Luke 6:3-4:

---

[253] Cf. G. Strecker, "Das Gesetz in der Bergpredigt–Die Bergpredigt als Gesetz," in *The Law in the Bible and in its Environment,* ed T. Veijola, Suomen Esegeettisen Seuran Julkaisuja. Schriften der Finnischen Exegetischen Gesellschaft 51 (1990), 109-125, esp. 111-114.

[254] R. Bultmann, *Die Geschichte der synoptischen Tradition,* 144; *History of the Synoptic Tradition,* 136.

> *Have you never read what David did when he and his companions were*
> *hungry and in need of food? He entered the house of God, when Abiathar*
> *was high priest, and ate the bread of the Presence, which it is not lawful*
> *for any but the priests to eat, and he gave some to his companions.*[255]

Cf. also Mark 7:6-8, etc.

For the formation of community rules, the words of the Lord were collected in the early churches, reinterpreted for the circumstances and needs of religious fellowship, or newly created by Christian prophets appealing to the authority of the ascended one.[256] E.g., Matt 23:8-10:

> *But you are not to be called rabbi, for you have one teacher, and you are all*
> *students. And call no one your father on earth, for you have one Father–the*
> *one in heaven. Nor are you to be called instructors, for you have one*
> *instructor, the Messiah.*

(Cf. also Mark 6:8-11, etc.)

Collections of these sayings developed through various traditional stages. The sayings were shaped and changed in the process to offer the communities concrete instructions for their situations (e.g., Mark 9:33-50, and the communal regulations of Matt 18:1-35).

No sufficient basis exists for a unique category of so-called "succesion-sayings" as suggested by H. Zimmermann and K. Kliesch.[257] Since the emphasis of these units falls "clearly on the concluding saying of Jesus,"[258] which is introduced through the previous narrative, these sayings can satisfactorily be characterized as apophthegms (cf. 4.3.3).[259]

*e) Parables*[260]

The parable tradition can be enlisted as evidence for the proclamation of Jesus as well as for the situation and self-understanding of the early Christian

---

[255] An inexact allusion to 1 Sam 21:1-7; e.g., it is not Abiathar, but his father Abimelech, who is named there as the priest.

[256] On early Christian prophecy and its significance for words attributed to Jesus in the synoptic tradition, cf., e.g., M.E. Boring, "Christian Prophecy and the Sayings of Jesus," for the situation of current research and methodological considerations. Early Christian prophets repeatedly influenced the traditions used in the Synoptics, which could mean directly or indirectly renovating or creating new words of Jesus. Cf. also Boring's *The Continuing Voice of Jesus. Christian Prophecy and the Gospel Tradition* (1991), *passim*.

[257] Cf. H. Zimmermann, *Neutestamentliche Methodenlehre. Darstellung der historisch-kritischen Methode*. Neubearbeitet von K. Kliesch (⁷1982), 148f. As examples they cite Matt 8:18-22; Luke 9:57-62.

[258] Zimmermann/Kliesch, 149.

[259] As with R. Bultmann, *Die Geschichte der synoptischen Tradition*, 27f.; *History of the Synoptic Tradition*, 28f.

[260] Cf. Bultmann, *Geschichte*, 179-222; *History*, 166-205.

communities.[261]   Attempts to reconstruct in detail a historical kernel or the "original setting in the life of Jesus"[262] for the parables remain hypothetical. Joachim Jeremias' influential work made such an attempt, following C.H. Dodd and T.A. Cadoux.[263] For Jeremias the reconstruction of the earliest level of the tradition was primarily the issue, recovering the *ipsissima vox Jesu,* spoken in a specific situation.[264] As Jeremias emphasized,[265] the parables reflect not an already realized eschatology,[266] but one in the process of being realized.

Whether we can derive the original meaning of the parables of Jesus from the introductory reference to the Kingdom of God is doubtful, given that the formula is frequently used in a stereotypical manner.[267] On the contrary, the relationship of the parables of Jesus–insofar as that is what they are–to the proclamation of Jesus can more likely offer information as to its original meaning.

Adolf Jülicher's work, *Die Gleichnisreden Jesu,* worked out in a definitive sense the conceptualizations for interpreting parables (*Gleichnis, Parabel, Beispielerzählung, Bildhälfte, Sachhälfte, tertium comparationis*). In encountering the allegorical interpretation of the parables, Jülicher showed that allegorical features were secondary on the grounds of the developed Christology or ecclesiology of such passages. Attempts to rescind this judgment are at the expense of theological interpretation compatible with a historical understanding.

Within the parable genre are to be distinguished:

a. The *simple figurative expression, or figure,* wherein the figurative and the literal are set alongside one another without a comparative particle. The figurative portion is often passed on by itself as a proverb (e.g., Mark 2:19; Matt 5:14). Figurative sayings are sometimes bipartite; the second member of synonymous parallelism perhaps joined with καί, οὐδέ, or ἤ; e.g., Mark 2:21-22:

> No one sews a piece of unshrunk cloth on an old cloak; otherwise, the patch pulls away from it, the new from the old, and a worse tear is made. And no one puts new wine into old wineskins; otherwise, the wine will burst the skins, and the wine is lost, and so are the skins; but one puts new wine into fresh wineskins.

---

[261] For the limits to reconstructing the proclamation and conduct of Jesus on the basis of the parables, cf. G. Strecker, "Die historische und theologische Problematik der Jesusfrage" (first published in 1969), in his *Eschaton und Historie. Aufsätze* (1979), 159-182, 168f.

[262] As J. Jeremias puts it in *Die Gleichnisse Jesu,* 19 or *The Parables of Jesus,* 22.

[263] A.T. Cadoux, *The Parable of Jesus. Their Art and Use* (1931).

[264] J. Jeremias, *Die Gleichnisse Jesu,* 17f., 19; *The Parables of Jesus,* 22.

[265] J. Jeremias, *Die Gleichnisse Jesu,* 227; *The Parables of Jesus,* 230.

[266] Against C.H. Dodd, *The Parables of the Kingdom,* 159.

[267] E.g., J. Weiss, *Die Predigt Jesu vom Reiche Gottes,* ed. F. Hahn (³1964), 45ff. Cf. also F. Vouga, "Jesus als Erzähler," 70, whose literary-critical theses need questioning in specifics, along with his isolation of parables, "stories whose meaning must be sought in themselves," from the proclamation of Jesus.

(Cf. also Luke 6:44b, etc.) The figure may be provided with an "application in a corresponding style;"[268] cf. Mark 2:17a:

> *Those who are well have no need of a physician, but those who are sick; I have come to call not the righteous but sinners.*

The originality of the application is appropriate to the style of such figures, but cannot in every case be regarded as certain. Often figures are associated on a catch-word basis; then the application is almost always a secondary addition to the context.

b. Related to the figure is the *metaphor,* an abbreviated comparison. It also utilizes no comparative particle; cf. Matt 5:13:

> *You are the salt of the earth; but if salt has lost its taste, how can its saltiness be restored?*

(Cf. also Matt 7:13-14.) Since the figurative dynamically serves a purpose, metaphor can be understood as a sort of speech.

c. Actual *comparisons* occurs relatively seldom. Here the figurative and the literal are related to one another by "as-(so)." Cf. Matt 24:27:

> *For as the lightning comes from the east and flashes as far as the west, so will be the coming of the Son of Man.*

(Cf. also Matt 10:16.)

d. *Hyperbole* is an intensification of figurative words. Cf. Matt 10:30:

> *And even the hairs of your head are all counted.*

(Cf. also Matt 5:29-30, 6:3.) *Paradox* also displays instensification, as in Mark 10:44:

> *...and whoever wishes to be first among you must be slave of all.*

(Cf. also Mark 4:25; Matt 10:39.)

e. The *similitude* [*"Gleichnis im engeren Sinne"*] is laid out in more detail than the simple figure or the comparison, but understood as its further development. It challenges hearers to their own decisions by describing frequently observable conditions out of everyday life. Luke 12:39-40, e.g., is developed out of a figure and given an application:

---

[268] Cf. R. Bultmann, *Geschichte,* 182, *History,* 168f.

*...if the owner of the house had known at what hour the thief was coming, he would not have let his house be broken into. You also must be ready, for the Son of Man is coming at an unexpected hour.*

Mark 4:26-29 and Matt 11:16-19, e.g., are developed out of comparisons.

f. While the parable in the narrower sense depicts the typical, the *parable narrative* [*"Parabel* oder *Gleichniserzählung"*] describes "an interesting individual event;"[269] e.g., Luke 13:6-9:

*A man had a fig tree planted in his vineyard; and he came looking for fruit on it and found none. So he said to the gardener, "See here! For three years I have come looking for fruit on this fig tree, and still I find none. Cut it down! Why should it be wasting the soil?" He replied, "Sir, let it alone for one more year, until I dig around it and put manure on it. If it bears fruit next year, well and good; but if not, you can cut it down."*

(Cf. also the Parable of the Prodigal Son in Luke 15:11-32, of the Sower in Mark 4:3-9/Matt 13:3-9/Luke 8:5-8, etc.) The parable narrative is further distinguished from the parable in the narrower sense in that the former is narrated in a past tense. Yet, despite these fundamental differences, the transition between the two is fluid in particulars. Narrative tendencies are not restricted to narrative parables, and the decision between the individual (the narrative parable) and the typical (the narrower parable) is occasionally not clear.

The assumption, widely shared since Jülicher, that there is only <u>one</u> *tertium comparationis* in similitudes and parables is questionable.[270] On the contrary, as a rule they are built on several points of comparison.

g. *Example stories*[271] depict model behavior directly on the literal level, apart from figurative dressing. Some representatives of the type are the Good Samaritan (Luke 10:30-37), the Rich Farmer (Luke 12:16-21), the Rich Man and Lazarus (Luke 16:19-31), and the Pharisee and the Publican (Luke 18:9-14).[272] They have a formal affinity to the parables.

---

[269] Cf. R. Bultmann, *Geschichte*, 188, *History*, 174.

[270] Cf. A. Jülicher, *Die Gleishnisreden Jesu*, 1:70. For a fundamental critique on the *"tertium comparationis,"* cf. C. Westermann, who, in his enlightening *Vergleiche und Gleichnisse*, with reference to D.O. Via and P. Ricoeur, roots the comparative phenomenon from the New Testament Gospels in the Hebrew Scriptures (though not exclusively so). The *tertium conparationis* "does not correspond to the narrative form of the parable. The narrative itself must speak ... the narrative as a whole, the structure of which should always be the focus of our questions" (122).

[271] Questioned, e.g., by W. Harnisch, *Die Gleichniserzählungen Jesu*, 84-97 and E. Bassland, "Zum Beispiel der Beispielerzählungen," 28.

[272] To these instances of example stories listed by A. Jülicher, *Die Gleichnisreden Jesu*, 2:585ff., Bultmann adds Luke 14:7-11 (on the seating priority of guests at a meal) and Luke 14:12-14 (on the proper guests to invite).

h. *Allegories*, of which metaphors represent a less developed form, contain several points of contact between the figurative and the literal. Characteristically, the literal bursts open the figurative, since the latter is developed out of the former, so that figurative element has splits and joins. In the synoptic parables allegorical elements display an entirely secondary character, as can usually be demonstrated from parallel traditions. (Cf. Mark 4:13-20; Matt 13:36-43; etc. In Matt 22:2ff. a [history of salvation] allegorizing is carried out by the Evangelist, though not in all details.)

It is customary to distinguish allegory as a literary form, allegorical interpretation as a hermeneutical method, and allegorizing as a secondary interpretation of a passage rich in imagery.[273]

We cannot here address in detail the stylistic elements of parables; a few short comments must suffice. While figures and parables can very well begin without an introduction, usually there is one, either a question (e.g., τί ὑμῖν δοκεῖ in Matt 18:12 and 21:28) or a double question. With respect to the beginning of the narrative parables Joachim Jeremias[274] distinguishes between a dative introduction utilizing a comparative particle (ὡς, ὥσπερ, ὅμοιός ἐστιν or ὁμοία ἐστιν) or a corresponding verb (ὁμοιωθήσεται or ὡμοιώθη as in Matt 7:24, 26, etc.)[275] and the nominative introduction, where the narrative begins without an introductory formula. The dative introduction or "comparative formula"[276] corresponds to the introductory ‎ל of the rabbinic parables. The narrative parables may be concluded with an application, but not necessarily. That the introduction, the parable itself, and the application may be posed in the form of a question allowed Rudolf Bultmann to emphasize the "argumentative character" of the parable.[277] In parables, narrative technique is characterized by conciseness and reserve (Einsträngigkeit). Seldom are attributes of the characters portrayed. Emotions and motives are only pictured insofar as they are significant to the action. The same goes for subsidiary characters. Other characteristics are concrete expression, direct address, soliloquy, the law of twos or threes, and the emphasis on the end of the narrative.[278]

Although distinctions between the individual categories of parables are disputed in contemporary research, Bultmann's comments remain foundational in terms of both data and terminology. The distinction between parable and

---

[273] Cf. H.-J. Klauck, *Allegorie und Allegorese*, 354ff . (and his index III under Allegorese, Allegorie, and Allegorisierung). Klauck understands allegory not as a unique genre, but as a "rhetorical and poetical approach."

[274] *Die Gleichnisse Jesu*, 99-102; *The Parables of Jesus*, 100-103.

[275] A redactional formulation.

[276] R. Bultmann, *Die Geschichte der synoptischen Tradition*, 194; *History of the Synoptic Tradition*, 180.

[277] *Geschichte*, 194, 197, 208; *History*, 179, 182, 192., and earlier, A. Jülicher, *Gleichnisreden*. Cf. also V. Fusco, *Oltre la parabola* (on whom cf. W.G. Kümmel, "Jesusforschung seit 1981. IV. Gleichnisse," 39f.). On the basis of his thesis, Fusco sees the category "example story" as inadequate.

[278] Cf. R. Bultmann, *Geschichte*, 203-208; *History*, 187-192, with reference to A. Olrik, *Epische Gesetze*.

similitude on the one hand, and allegory on the other, should be maintained.[279] For Bultmann this distinction is based on the fact that parables "support the transfer of a thought (acquired in neutral material) to another realm under discussion. In allegory it is not a matter of transferring a thought, but of an arcane or bizarre disguising something in the service of prophecy or another goal."[280]

Recent parable interpretation[281] is concerned with providing the perceptions of secular literary scholarship and of (philosophical) hermeneutics admission to New Testament research and connecting them with theological viewpoints.

Thus the parables are not interpreted as the description of actual fact, but as a (speech-)*event* relevant to the hearer.[282] If the parable is conceived as play, in which the history of the hearer is played out, so is the hearer questioned with respect to his or her own existence.[283] This approach is carried further in the analysis of Dan O. Via, where the parable is understood as an "aesthetic object, an actual work of art,"[284] the structure of which should be interpreted through comparison with drama (comedy and tragedy).[285] Historical questions about the setting and the intention of the narrator recede in consideration of the question bound up with the synchronic structure of the parable, the question about the possibilities of human existence.[286]

American research, in addition to structural analysis, is especially concerned with metaphorical interpretation of the parables, i.e. the attempt to grasp them on the basis of a new understanding of metaphor.[287] Robert W. Funk distinguishes between an

---

[279] For a different viewpoint, cf. M Boucher, "The Mysterious Parable," and M. Black, "Die Gleichnisse als Allegorien;" "The Parables as Allegory."

[280] *Geschichte,* 214, *History,* 197f.

[281] On this cf. the collection in *Die neutestamentliche Gleichnisforschung im Horizont von Hermeneutik und Literaturwissenschaft,* ed W. Harnisch, Wege der Forschung 575 (1982). In an extremely varied manner and partly with a historical-critical approach, it reflects methodologically questionable new approaches to the parable tradition.

[282] E. Linnemann, *Gleichnisse Jesu,* 38, calls it a "speech event." Cf. also E. Jüngel, *Paulus und Jesus,* 135. For Jüngel the guiding principle for interpreting the parable is that "The Kingdom comes to expression *in* parable *as* parable. The parables of Jesus bring the Reign of God to expression *as* parable." Cf. Engdahl's survey in *Jesu liknelser som språkhändelser.* Cf. also G. Eichholz, *Gleichnisse der Evangelien,* 20: The "event" revealed in the parables is the call to human beings to conduct themselves on the basis of God's prior activity.

[283] Eichholz, "Das Gleichnis als Spiel," 73 and *Einführung in die Gleichnisse,* 31f. Cf. also W. Harnisch, *Gleichniserzählungen,* 26, who suggests the parallel with "drama."

[284] *The Parables: Their Literary and Existential Dimension* (1967), 70f.; *Die Gleichnisse Jesu. Ihre literarische und existentiale Dimension* (1970), 72. Cf. also W. Harnisch, *Gleichniserzählungen,* 12f., who sees the parables as works of poetic artistry.

[285] Thus in his interpretation Via distinguishes between tragic and comic parables.

[286] G. Scholz, *Gleichnisaussage und Existenzstruktur,* emphasizes the structure of human existence as the theme of his work on Luke's special parables.

[287] Whether this approach can be considered an "opinio communis" (B. Heininger, *Metaphorik,* 3) is questionable. Even where New Testament exegesis makes this

illustrative (comparative) and a creative (metaphorical) function of parables and emphasizes their openness. The hearer is incorporated as a participant in the parable in that the metaphor both conceals and reveals the hiddenness of God.[288]   Likewise W. Harnisch, who in describing metaphor as "essential speech"[289] expresses a new conception of metaphor in contradistinction to the classical,[290] promotes a "metaphorical essense to the parables of Jesus" whose potential for meaning is only revealed from case to case. This occurs "in a open hermeneutical discourse which attempts to paraphrase what a narrative which involves the hearer would communicate."[291]   While the "metaphorical interpretation of the parables"[292] rightly calls attention to that element of the parabolic teaching which goes beyond literary form, differentiation between literal and metaphorical approaches to interpreting the parables remains an open problem.[293]

Given the argumentative character of the parables, rhetorical analysis is also concerned with their interpretation.[294] But we should hold back from the hypothesis that rhetorical conventions, as these are described in the literary handbooks, have influenced the parables. Rather it belongs to the form of the parables that they make their content accessible to the audience, and thus have a certain affinity for a rhetorical outlook and methodology, without reflecting theoretical rhetoric or that of the schools.

---

deduction, there is seldom a consensus about details.    Too stark a divergence exists in the understanding of "metaphor" itself.

[288] R.W. Funk, *Language,* 133-162; cf. also his "The Good Samartian as Metaphor."

[289] *Die Gleichniserzählungen Jesu,* 140.

[290] Classical understanding sees metaphor more as a "figurative manner of speaking" (A. Jülicher, *Die Gleichnisreden Jesu,* 52), which replaces a concept with a figurative analogy. According to Jülicher, metaphor understood in this way is "the basic element of authentic speech." On the classical concept of metaphor, cf. Aristotle, Rhetoric 1404b-1405b; Poetics 1457b: "μεταφορὰ δέ ἐστιν ὀνόματος ἀλλοτρίου ἐπιφορὰ ἢ ἀπὸ τοῦ γένους ἐπὶ εἶδος ἢ ἀπὸ τοῦ εἴδους ἐπὶ τὸ γένος ἢ ἀπὸ τοῦ εἴδους ἐπὶ εἶδος ἢ κατὰ τὸ ἀνάλογον [Metaphor is the application of *another* (or a *foreign*) expression either from the genus to the species or from the species to the genus, or from one species to another, or by analogy]" (emphasis added by author). Cf. also Poetics 1459a. This shows the illustrative character of metaphor as it was understood in antiquity. H.J. Klauck, *Allegorie und Allegorese,* 7, n. 14, emphasizes this against Jülicher. But this cannot be played off against the figurative character, the "foreignness," of analogy.

[291] W. Harnisch, *Die Gleichniserzählungen Jesu,* 158.

[292] Cf. also J.D. Crossan, *In Parables;* H.J. Klauck, *Allegorie und Allegorese;* H. Weder, *Die Gleichnisse Jesu,* 120; and *Metaphorik und Mythos im Neuen Testament,* ed K. Kertelge, QD 126 (1990).

[293] For a critique, cf. G. Strecker in G. Strecker and Johann Maier, *Neues Testament—Antikes Judentum,* Grundkurs Theologie 2 (1989), 52-54.

[294] Although the parables of Jesus are rooted in their Palestinian milieu, E. Rau (*Reden in Vollmacht,* 405f.) affirms that they may still be understood with the help of Hellenistic rhetorical categories. In fact these provide a background for Jesus' parabolic speech. B. Heininger condenses the acquaintance of Luke with Hellenistic practice to the thesis that Luke was an "educated author" (*Metaphorik,* 226) who sought "a conversation with those he addressed" (227).    So through special accents and compositional insertions Luke sympathetically narrates the parables he utilizes from oral tradition.

While accepting the stimulus of the newer parable interpretation, G. Sellin seeks to promote the compositional activity of the Evangelists by means of structural analysis.[295] This is in reference to a redaction-critical aspect, also significant for the parable tradition.[296] It is expressed in the secondary supplements of introductions and applications, in interpretive additions, but also in orientating the parables to their context or combining several parables, etc.

In light of fissures and discontinuities, a source document should be affirmed for the parable tradition in Mark 4. [297] Decisive for understanding the Marcan redaction is the difference between 4:33 and 4:34. According to 4:33, the parables are understandable. According to 4:34, the people can listen, but they will not understand. The meaning remains reserved for the disciples. The most extreme expression of this outlook is in the so-called "Parable theory" of 4:11-12.[298] In this brusque saying based on Isaiah 6:9-10 a distinction is made between a circumscribed group which will grasp the meaning, and those outside to whom the stubborn outlook mentioned in Isaiah 6:9-10 is attributed. Here again it is clear that Mark's Gospel must be understood in light of the overarching motif of the messianic secret.[299] Mark 4:11-12 emphasize the stubbornness, here in the framework of the parable theory. The revelatory activity of Jesus takes as its goal to restrict itself from those who are "outside." This involves a dialectical relationship: on the one hand revelation does not occur without concealment, and on the other hand the concealing of Christ is not without revelation.

## 4.3.2   Forms of the Narrative Material

*Literature on the Miracle Narratives*

Busse, U., *Die Wunder der Propheten Jesus. Die Rezeption, Komposition und Interpretation der Wundertradition im Evangelium des Lukas,* FB 12 (²1979); "Metaphorik in neutestamentlichen Wundergeschichten? Mk 1,21-28; Joh 9,1-41," in *Metaphorik und Mythos im Neuen Testament,* ed K. Kertelge, QD 126 (1990), 110-134. Held, H.J., "Matthäus als Interpret der Wundergeschichten," in G. Bornkamm, G. Barth, and H.J. Held, *Überlieferung und Auslegung im Matthäus-Evangelium,* WMANT 1 (²1961, ⁷1975), 155-287, "Matthew as Interpreter of the Miracle Stories," in *Tradition and Interpretation in Matthew* (1963), 165-299. Herzog, R., *Die Wunderheilungen von Epidauros. Ein Beitrag zur Geschichte der Medizin und Religion,* Philologus Supplement 22.3 (1931). Kertelge, K., *Die Wunder Jesu im Markusevangelium. Eine redaktionsgeschichtliche Untersuchung,* SANT 23 (1970); "Die Wunder Jesu in der neueren Exegese," in Theol. Berichte 5, ed J. Pfammater (1976), 71-105. Koch, D.A., *Die Bedeutung der Wundererzählungen für die Christologie des Markusevangeliums,* BZNW 42 (1975). Kratz, R., *Rettungswunder. Motiv-, traditions- und formkritische Aufarbeitung einer biblischen Gattung,* Einleitung in die Heilige Schrift XXIII.123 (1979). Legasse, S., "L'historien en quête de l'événement," in *Les miracles de*

---

[295] Cf. "Lukas als Gleichniserzähler," and *Studien.*
[296] On the Lucan redaction, cf. B. Heininger, *Metaphorik.*
[297] Cf. above, page 121.
[298] Cf. W. Marxsen, "Redaktionsgeschichtliche Erklärung."
[299] Cf. above, p. 103.

*Jésus selon le Nouveau Testament,* par J.N. Aletti *et al.,* ed X. Léon-Dufour, Parole de Dieu 16 (1977), 109-145. Petzke, G., *Die Traditionen über Apollonius von Tyana und das Neue Testament,* SCHNT 1 (1970); "Historizität und Bedeutsamkeit von Wunderberichten. Möglichkeiten und Grenzen des religionsgeschichtlichen Vergleiches," in *Neues Testament und christliche Existenz,* Festschrift H. Braun, ed. H.D. Betz *et al.* (1973), 367-385. Schenke, L., Die Wundererzählungen des Markusevangeliums, SBB 5 (1974). Schille, G., "Die Topographie des Markusevangeliums, ihre Hintergründe und ihre Einordnung," *ZDPV* 73 (1957): 133-166; *Anfänge der Kirche. Erwägerungen zur apostolischen Frühgeschichte,* BEvT 43 (1966); *Die urchristliche Wundertradition. Ein Beitrag zur Frage nach dem irdischen Jesus,* Arbeiten zur Theologie I/29 (1967). Schmidt, K.L., *Der Rahmen der Geschichte Jesu. Literarkritische Untersuchung zur ältesten Jesusüberlieferung,* (1919, new editions 1964 and subsequently). Schmithals, W., *Wunder und Glaube. Eine Auslegung von Markus 4,35–6:6a,* Biblische Studien (Neukirchen) 59 (1970); "Die Heilung des Epileptischen (Mk 9, 14-29). Ein Beitrag zur notwendigen Revision der Formgeschichte," *Theologia viatorum* (Berlin) 13 (1975/76): 211-233. Tagawa, K., *Miracles et Évangile. La pensée personnelle de l'évangéliste Marc,* Études d'histoire et de philosophie religieuses 62 (1966). Theissen, G., *Urchristliche Wundergeschichten. Ein Beitrag zur formgeschichtlichen erforschung der synoptischen Evangelien,* SNT 8 (1974, [6]1990); *The Miracle Stories of the Early Christian Tradition* (1983). Thraede, K., "Exorzismus," in *RAC* 7 (1969), 44-117. Weder, H., "Wunder Jesu und Wundergeschichten," *VF* 29/1 (1984): 25-49. Weinreich, O., *Antike Heilungswunder. Untersuchungen zum Wunderglauben der Griechen und Römer,* Religionsgeschichtliche Versuche und Vorarbeiten 8.1 (1909). *Antike Wundertexte,* ed. G. Delling, KlT 79 ([2]1960).

*Literature on the Passion Narrative*

Conzelmann, H., "Historie und Theologie in den synoptischen Passionsgeschichten," in his *Theologie als Schriftauslesung. Aufsätze zum Neuen Testament,* BEvT 65 (1974), 74-90. Dormeyer, D., *Die Passion Jesu als Verhaltensmodell. Literarische und theologische Analyse der Traditions- und Redaktionsteschichte der Markuspassion,* NTAbh, N.F. 11 (1974). Ernst, J., "Die Passionserzählung des Markus und die Aporien der Forschung," *TGl* 70 (1980): 160-180. Fendler, F., *Studien zum Markusevangelium. Zur Gattung, Chronologie, Messiasgeheimnistheorie und Überlieferung des Zweiten Evangeliums,* GTA 49 (1991). Finegan, J. *Die Überlieferung der Leidens- und Auferstehungsgeschichte Jesu,* BZNW 15 (1934). Gese, H., "Psalm 22 und das Neue Testament. Der älteste Bericht vom Tode Jesu und die Entstehung des Herrenmahles" (first published in 1968), in his *Vom Sinai zum Zion. Alttestamentliche Beiträge zur biblischen Theologie,* BEvT 64 ([2]1984, [3]1990), 180-201. Kelber, W.H., "Conclusion: From Passion Narrative to Gospel," in *The Passion in Mark. Studies on Mark 14-16,* ed. W.H. Kelber (1976), 153-180. Linnemann, E., *Studien zur Passionsgeschichte,* FRLANT 102 (1970). Maurer, C., "Knecht Gottes und Sohn Gottes im Passionsbericht des Markusevangeliums" (first published in 1953), in *Redaktion und Theologie des Passionsberichtes nach den Synoptikern,* ed. M.

Limbeck, Wege der Forschung 481 (1981), 112-153. Pesch, R., "Die Überlieferung der Passion Jesu" (first published in 1974), in *Redaktion und Theologie des Passionsberichtes nach den Synoptikern,* ed. M. Limbeck, Wege der Forschung 481 (1981), 339-365. *Redaktion und Theologie des Passionsberichtes nach den Synoptikern,* ed. M. Limbeck, Wege der Forschung 481 (1981). Schenk, W., *Der Passionsbericht nach Markus. Untersuchungen zur Überlieferungsgeschichte der Passionstraditionen* (1974); "Leidensgeschichte Jesu," in *TRE* 20 (1990): 714-721. Schenke, L., *Studien zur Passionsgeschichte des Markus. Tradition und Redaktion in Markus 14,1-42,* Forschungen zur Bibel 4 (1971); *Der gekreuzigte Christus. Versuch einer literarkritischen und traditionsgeschichtlichen Bestimmung der vormarkinischen Passionsgeschichte,* SBS 69 (1974). Schneider, G., *Verleugnung, Verspottung und Verhör Jesus nach Lukas 22,54-71,* SANT 22 (1969); *Die Passion Jesu nach den drei älteren Evangelien,* Biblische Handbibliothek 11 (1973). Schreiber, J., *Die Markuspassion. Wege zur Erforschung der Leidensgeschichte Jesu* (1969); *Der Kreuzigungsbericht des Markusevangeliums Mk 15, 20b-41. Eine traditionsgeschichtliche Untersuchung nach William Wrede (1859-1906),* BZNW 48 (1986). Taylor, V., *The Passion Narrative of St. Luke. A Critical and Historical Investigation,* ed O.E. Evans SNTSMS 19 (1972).

*a) Miracle narratives.*[300]

An account whose content centers on an extraordinary, supernatural event (= a miracle) is described as a miracle narrative.

It is unconvincing to argue that the genre "miracle narrative is a "modern portrayal of an ancient understanding of reality;" that it is not a form-critical description but belongs in the realm of the phenomonology of religion as a "marvelous proof of charismatic power in narrated history."[301] In the first place, despite the variety within the New Testament miracle narratives, several characteristics of the genre are obvious. And second, the Gospels' arrangement of the miracle narratives both in terms of terminology and content is also evident: cf. δυνάμεις (Matt 11:20, 23; Mark 6:2, 14), θαυμάσια (Matt 21:15), σημεῖα (John 2:11, etc.).[302] This corresponds to the juxtaposition of miracles and non-miraculous events in antiquity.[303]

While according to Rudolf Bultmann healing miracles were to be distinguished from the less frequent nature miracles (e.g., Mark 4:37-41 and 6:45-52), Martin Dibelius defined miracle narratives partly as paradigms and partly as novellas.[304]

---

[300] For a survey of research, cf. K. Kertelge, "Die Wunder Jesu in der neueren Exegese," in Theol. Berichte 5, ed J. Pfammater (1976), 71-105; H. Weder, "Wunder Jesu und Wundergeschichten," *VF* 29/1 (1984): 25-49.

[301] K. Berger, *Formgeschichte des Neuen Testaments* (1984), 305.

[302] Cf. G.Theissen, *Lokalkolorit und Zeitgeschichte in den Evangelien. Ein Beitrag zur Geschichte der synoptischen Tradition,* NTOA 8 (1989), 102f., n. 92.

[303] Cf. H. Conzelmann and A. Lindemann, *Arbeitsbuch zum Neuen Testament,* Uni-Taschenbücher 52 (⁹1988), 89.

[304] Cf. M. Dibelius, *Die Formgeschichte des Evangeliums* (⁶1971), 55f.; *From Tradition to Gospel* (1934), 58f. E.g., paradigmatic healings: healing of the lame (Mark 2:1ff.); healing in the synagogue (Mark 1:23-27); healing of the withered hand (Mark

Miracle narratives may be further classified as: *exorcisms* (Matt 9:32-34):

> *And after thay had gone away, a demoniac who was mute was brought to him. And when the demon had been cast out, the one who had been mute spoke; and the crowds were amazed and said, "Never has anything like this been seen in Israel." But the Pharisees said, "By the ruler of the demons he casts out the demons.*

(cf. also Mark 1:21-28[305]); *therapeutic miracles* (Mark 1:29-31, Matt 8:5-13, Luke 7:11-17) in which the boundaries between the forms are fluid; *epiphanies* (Mark 6:45-52, 9:2-10); *miraculous rescues* (Mark 4:35-41);[306] *miraculous gifts* (Luke 5:1-11, Mark 6:32-44); and *miracles which define norms* (or *rule miracles,* Mark 3:1-6, 2:1-12, Luke 13:10-17).[307]

In terms of structure, the *exposition* of the miracle narrative depicts (occasionally in great detail, cf. Mark 5:3-5) the seriousness of the malady, demonstrating the difficulty of the cure and thus the greatness and power of the healer. The exposition is followed by the *healing* itself, in the New Testament described more reticently than in contemporary Greek or Hellenistic parallels. With the occasional non-public miracle (e.g., Mark 5:40, 7:33, etc.), a miraculous action (such as touching with a hand, as in Mark 1:41, 8:22, etc.) or a word of Jesus (as in Mark 2:11, 10:52, and in a foreign language, Mark 5:41 ταλιθὰ κοῦμ, and 7:34 ἐφφαθά)[308] may play a role. In exorcisms the demon(s) recognize the power of their exorciser in the encounter following the exposition. In response to a command the demon leaves the possessed, often after a final display of its might. The conclusion of the miracle narrative expresses the effects of the healing through the testimony of witnesses (the acclamation of the miracle worker as by a chorus,[309] e.g., Luke 5:26, 7:16: "Fear seized all of them; and they glorified God, saying, 'A great prophet has risen among us!' and 'God has looked favorably on his people!'") or through a demonstration by the one healed (e.g., Mark 1:31, etc.).[310]

---

3:1-6); healing of the dropsy (Luke 14:1-6). Examples of novellas: healing of the leper (Mark 1:40-45); stilling the storm (Mark 4:35-41); (p. 68) the demons and the swine (Mark 5:1-20). This analysis is based on Dibelius's theory about the significance of preaching. On this see pp. 132 and 158.

[305] On this form, cf. K. Thraede, "Exorzismus," in *RAC* 7 (1969), 44-117, esp. 58-63. Assigning all the miracle narrative of Mark to the genre of exorcisms [with R. Pesch, *Das Evangelium nach Markus,* HTKNT 2,1 (1976, [5]1989); II (1977, [3]1984), 117f.] must be viewed as erroneous.

[306] Cf. the monograph by R. Kratz, *Rettungswunder. Motiv-, traditions- und formkritische Aufarbeitung einer biblischen Gattung,* Einleitung in die Heilige Schrift XXIII.123 (1979).

[307] Cf. G. Theissen, *Lokalkolorit und Zeitgeschichte in den Evangelien. Ein Beitrag zur Geschichte der synoptischen Tradition,* NTOA 8 (1989), 8.

[308] Exorcism occurs only through a command, never physical contact.

[309] M. Dibelius, *Die Formgeschichte des Evangeliums* ([6]1971), 67; cf. also 55; *From Tradition to Gospel* (1934), 67, cf. also 57.

[310] On this construction, cf. R. Bultmann, *Geschichte,* 224, 236ff., *History,* 210, 220ff.; P. Vielhauer, *Geschichte der urchristlichen Literatur* ([2]1978), 302f.

The intention of the miracle narrative is to prove the power of God's Son. This must be taken into account if the relationship of the miracle narratives to the historical Jesus is viewed positively. Thus S. Légasse attempts to develop a methodology to validate apparently historical miracles.[311] Primarily healings and exorcisms are accepted as authentic. Apart from healing miracles (especially exorcisms) there is little possibility of making a historical place for miracle narratives in the life of Jesus,[312] given the general fondness for them in the ancient world.[313]

That the miracles of Jesus were transmitted outside the Christian communities as folk tradition without specific Christian content, then harmonized with the communal tradition by means of the Marcan command to silence, remains hypothetical.[314] But to reject on principle searching for an original *Sitz im Leben* should also be questioned. Such an approach regards the miracle reports as "products of theological artistry"[315] with the role merely to warn against "basing faith in Christ on miracle instead of expecting miracles through faith in Christ."[316] Here there is little place for a discriminating differentiation of the motifs in New Testament miracle narratives or for questions about the history of the miracle traditon.[317]

Pre-Marcan collections of miracle narratives are variously regarded, although these viewpoints clearly cannot stand in contrast to the conception of Mark's Gospel (cf. 4.2.2). The existence of a sign-source for John's Gospel is also

---

[311] S. Légasse, "L'historien en quête de l'événement," in *Les miracles de Jésus selon le Nouveau Testament,* par J.N. Aletti *et al.,* ed X. Léon-Dufour, Parole de Dieu 16 (1977), 121-129: ". . . in presenting Jesus with traits of an exorcist or healer, the early church, far from inventing, has only preserved the memory of some essential aspects of its founder" (128). Cf. also H Weder, "Wunder Jesu und Wundergeschichten," *VF* 29/1 (1984): 26-32,

[312] Cf. G. Petzke, *Die Traditionen über Apollonius von Tyana und das Neue Testament,* SCHNT 1 (1970), as well as his "Historizität und Bedeutsamkeit von Wunderberichten. Möglichkeiten und Grenzen des religionsgeschichtlichen Vergleiches," in *Neues Testament und christliche Existenz,* Festschrift H. Braun, ed. H.D. Betz *et al.* (1973), 367-385. Yet H. Weder emphasizes the special character of New Testament miracles and belief in miracles in "Wunder Jesu und Wundergeschichten," 33-39. [Note 313 in the German text.]

[313] Comparative material in *Antike Wundertexte,* ed. G. Delling, KIT 79 (²1960), O. Weinreich, *Antike Heilungswunder. Untersuchungen zum Wunderglauben der Griechen und Römer,* Religionsgeschichtliche Versuche und Vorarbeiten 8.1 (1909), R. Herzog, *Die Wunderheilungen von Epidauros. Ein Beitrag zur Geschichte der Medizin und Religion,* Philologus Supplement 22.3 (1931), R. Bultmann, *Geschichte,* 236-241, *History,* 220-226 (on style) and *Geschichte,* 247-253, *History,* 231-239. On belief in miracles in antiquity, cf. "Wunderglaube, -täter," in *Der kleine Pauly* 5 (1975): 1395-1398 (with bibliography). [Note 312 in the German text]

[314] Cf. G. Theissen, *Lokalkolorit und Zeitgeschichte,* 102-111 and 119.

[315] W. Schmithals, "Die Heilung des Epileptischen," 232.

[316] W. Schmithals, *Wunder und Glaube,* 96, on Mark 6:1-6a.

[317] For a critique, cf. also W.G. Kümmel, *Dreissig Jahre Jesusforschung (1950-1980),* ed. H. Merklein, BBB 60 (1985), 291-293.

questionable (cf. 4.4.1.1), so that it cannot serve as an analogy for pre-Marcan miracle narrative collections.[318]

In more recent research the form critical approach has taken second place to the literary critical, especially inquiry into the oral stage of tradition and its significance for the development of the tradition's history.

An exception to this is the attempt to derive the miracle tradition from missionary genres and especially mission legends, which are separable into the so-called community foundation legends and the sphere legends (or sphere programmes). Here, on the grounds of their place designations, miracle narratives are regarded as aetiological reports of community foundations carried back to Jesus himself.[319] Yet the relevant narratives betray no aetiological interest. And few place names belong to the primary stratum of the synoptic tradition. Furthermore, common form critical elements and structures which they draw from other forms do not lend themselves to the traditions of communal foundations.

The redaction-critical aspect, i.e., the question of the Evangelists own understanding of miracle, is absolutely indispensible.[320]

D.-A. Koch assumes two mutually-conflicting tendencies in Mark's interpretation of the miracles: a "critical-restrictive" and a "positive" outlook.[321] Thus he challenges alternative Christologies of miracle and cross in Mark. Rather the dignity of the miracle-working Son of God is placed under the proviso of the cross and resurrection and is only to this degree a sign for faith.[322] This raises the question as to what degree the Gospel of Mark should be understood as centered on the theology of the cross.

The command to silence is conspicuously associated with the miracle narratives in Mark (e.g., Mark 1:33, 44, 3:12). Jesus' proclamation and his miracle-working word occur in private and imply an intention to remain hidden. Jesus' hearers and even his disciples encounter the announcement of his claim without understanding it. The revelation of Jesus occurs in such hiddenness.[323] This should not be seen, however, as the Evangelist's attempt to correct a conception of Jesus as a miracle worker,[324] nor as an attempt to deal with the historical distinction between a non-

---

[318] In response to P. Vielhauer, *Geschichte,* 304.

[319] G. Schille, *Anfänge der Kirche,* 64-71; "Die Topographie des Markusevangeliums;" and *Die Urchristliche Wundertradition,* 26f.

[320] On Mark, cf. K. Kertelge, "Die Wunder Jesu;" D.-A. Koch, *Die Bedeutung der Wundererzählungen;* L. Schenke, *Die Wundererzählungen;* K. Tagawa, *Miracles et Évangile.* On Matthew, cf. H.J. Held, "Matthäus als Interpret der Wundergeschichten." On Luke, cf. U Busse, *Die Wunder der Propheten Jesus.*

[321] *Die Bedeutung der Wundererzählungen,* 182.

[322] Koch, *Die Bedeutung der Wundererzählungen, 191-193.*

[323] As early as the baptism of Jesus in Mark 1:11 (the voice from heaven) and carried forward in the preaching of Jesus in 1:14. Cf. also the confession of Peter in 8:29 and 9:2ff. But here also Mark is depending almost totally on tradition. This observation led Dibelius to describe Mark as "a book of secret epiphanies" [*Die Formgeschichte des Evangeliums* (⁶1971), 232; *From Tradition to Gospel* (1934), 230].

[324] J.D. Crossan sees this as motivation for the writing of Mark (see above, pp. 99f.). Yet Mark is not an apologetic work but a positive testimony to faith (cf. section 4.1.2.3). It is not defense against the attacks of opponents which motivates the confrontation with the world. This intention is rooted in faith itself. The primary factor is the self-orientation of faith to the world in which it lives.

messianic tradition about Jesus and the post-Easter messianic faith of the church (William Wrede[325]). The two structural elements of the messianic secret, revelation motif and secrecy motif, have the same objective as the Marcan theory of the parables.[326] Revelation is not without hiddenness and *vice versa.* Mark 9:9 marks the historical end of secrecy: the resurrection is the transition point between two epochs. Hiddenness lasts till the resurrection. But this involves no epistemological claim that Jesus' way is understandable only after Easter. On the contrary, the messianic secret identifies the paradox of faith. God's promise becomes human in Jesus. An eschatological event which transcends time and space occurs in history, in the here and now. The heavenly is accessible only in the person of Jesus. That which is not at human disposal has, in Jesus, made itself open and available: a dialectical event characterized by a becoming evident and by a self-veiling.

U. Busse pursues the issue of "the metaphorical in New Testament miracle narratives" in order to reconstruct its function at the level of the gospel text. As it is implicit in the extensive inventory of the miracle narratives, metaphorical speech serves to characterize "the true opinion or interpretation of the Evangelist to the narrated reality."[327]

*b) Legends.*

As religious stories (as, e.g., legends of the saints)[328] these are distinguished by their edifying character from secular novellas. Constituted with an aetiological or biographical interest, legends include aetiological cult legends (such as the institution of the Lord's Supper) and personal legends (e.g. the infancy narratives of Luke 1-2 and Matt 1:18-2:23; finding the colt in Mark 11:1ff., or the upper room in Mark 14:12ff.; the call of the disciples in Mark 1:16-20, Matt 4:18-22, and Luke 5:1-11).

Their form-critical placement is controversial. While Rudolf Bultmann regards "story-narratives and legends" as a unity, for Martin Dibelius traditions considered as legends are a parallel category to pericopes designated as "myth" (e.g., the transfiguration of Mark 9:2ff., which Bultmann classifies as a legend). Yet Dibelius does not assess story-narratives and myths as comparable entities. The latter applies more to stories "which in some manner narrate significant activity of the gods."[329]

Günther Bornkamm refers to these materials as "Christ-stories."[330] Their specific characteristic is that they are "from the beginning and throughout stamped with this faith."[331] But this differentiation is not convincing, since miracle stories and the passion narrative are also permeated by the faith of the community. Moreover, Bornkamm

---

[325] W. Wrede, *Das Messiasgeheimnis in den Evangelien. Zugleich ein Beitrag zum Verständnis des Markusevangeliums* (1901 = [4]1969); *The Messianic Secret* (1971). (An unmessianic tradition of Jesus is, however, unknown to early Christianity.)

[326] See above p. 147.

[327] U. Busse, "Metaphorik in neutestamentlichen Wundergeschichten?" 133.

[328] Cf. M. Dibelius, *Die Formgeschichte des Evangeliums* ([6]1971), 101ff.; *From Tradition to Gospel* (1934), 104ff.

[329] Dibelius, *Formgeschichte,* 265; *Tradition,* 266.

[330] "Formen und Gattungen II. Im NT," in *RGG[3]* 2 (1958):1001.

[331] "Formen und Gattungen II. Im NT," in *RGG[3]* 2 (1958):1001; similarly E. Lohse in *Die Entstehung des Neuen Testaments,* Theologische Wissenschaft 4 ([4]1983), 71f.

attributes very different materials to this genre: "baptism, temptation, Peter's confession, transfiguration, triumphal entry, eucharist, infancy narratives of Matthew and Luke, and the resurrection narratives."[332]  A more differentiated terminolgy is more suitable for these traditions.

### c) The passion narrative.[333]

Because of the special significance of the suffering and death of Jesus for early Christian faith (cf. 3.3.1), the passion narrative was from early times transmitted as a self-contained unity, although containing numerous differentiable and originally separate traditions[334] (e.g, the institution of the Lord's Supper in Mark 14:22-25,[335] and the anointing of Jesus at Bethany in Mark 14:3-8.[336]) The oldest passion narrative, underlying the present Mark, shows itself to have contained materials which were not passed on independently of the whole report, even though determining what is due to Marcan redaction remains an open question. E.g., the place of Mark 14:1f. and 14:10f. in the history of tradition is debatable. The enumeration of days in 14:1 may be presupposed as Marcan; thus the passage may be a redactional transition. On good grounds F. Fendler attributes the schema of a passion week to the Evangelist Mark himself, and so determines that Mark was following a Greek enumerative schema, even though this involved him in inconsistencies.[337]  On the other hand, there is evident in the passion narrative a series of individual pericopes in non-interchangeable order, indicating that before the redaction of the Gospel this narrative was transmitted as a fragment of tradition, that "already in a very early time incidents were presented in wider association."[338]

It may be questioned whether the passion narrative resulting from Marcan redaction is the product of a process of growth[339] or whether it resulted from the combination of two distinct passion traditions: an older tradition marked by the use

---

[332] G. Bornkamm, "Formen und Gattungen II. Im NT," in *RGG³* 2 (1958):1001.

[333] R. Bultmann arranges these traditions as narratives and legends (*Geschichte,* 282-308; *History,* 275-291).  Dibelius treats them separately (*Formgeschichte,* 178-218; *Tradition,* 178-217).

[334] Cf. R. Bultmann, *Geschichte,* 298, *Ergänzungsheft⁵,* 101; *History,* 276; M. Dibelius, *Formgeschichte,* 180; *Tradition,* 179f.

[335] For a different understanding cf. H. Gese, "Psalm 22 und das Neue Testament," who refers to Psalm 22. On this approach, cf. below, p. 157.

[336] P. Vielhauer, *Geschichte der urchristlichen Literatur,* 308, understands this as a Marcan passage. Yet perhaps only the concluding verse, 14:9, should be attributed to Marcan redaction. Cf. also D. Lührmann, Das Markusevangelium, HNT 3 (1987), 232f. and G. Strecker, "Literarkritische Überlegungen zum εὐαγγέλιον-Begriff im Markusevangelium," in *Eschaton und Historie. Aufsätze* (1979), 76-89, esp. 86-89.

[337] *Studien,* 102f.

[338] M. Dibelius, *Formgeschichte,* 180; *Tradition,* 179f.

[339] E.g, R. Bultmann, *Geschichte,* 301f.; *History,* 278-280; D. Dormeyer, *Die Passion Jesu,* 11; J. Finegan, *Die Überlieferung,* 82; L. Schenke, *Studien, Der gekreuzigte Christus;* G. Schneider, *Die Passion Jesu.*

of the historical present tense, and another, apocalyptically oriented, stratum.[340] But the passion narrative is also intepreted as a Marcan composition *in toto.*[341]

Corresponding to the approach of a structural analysis (as advocated by H. Güttgemanns among others[342]) are attempts to interpret the passion narrative an an integral component of Mark's Gospel. The Marcan permeation of the passion narrative materials is taken to indicate that no great weight should be attached to individual traditions as such.[343] W. Schenk's interpretation of the passion narrative's structure through the schemata of "prediction and fulfillment" and "rejection and rehabilitation" also support Marcan composition.[344] If the attempt to understand the passion narrative on the level of Marcan narration is justified, it still must be remembered that these materials, as the obvious gaps in the Marcan corpus show, have their own prehistory and meaning to be set off from that of the redaction.

In his analysis of the Marcan passion narrative, Schenk correctly refuses to regard Jesus' expiatory death as its theme. The tradition of the Lord's Supper (Mark 14:24) shows that this convention was known in the Marcan community. But it is not in itself the theme of the passion narrative. The death of Jesus is primarily a historical fact, a moment in time, a necessary transition from the time of the messiah's hiddenness to that of revelation. It is the plan of God, which here comes to its realization (Mark 8:31). Jesus accepts his destiny (Mark 14:32ff.). Through his supernatural prescience he knows of this event and affirms it (Mark 14:8, 18, 27). It is a saving event wherein the eschaton penetrates time, expecting a human response of faith.[345] Faith expects from it freedom from sin and guilt, though without the development of an expiatory theology.

There is also no consensus among comtemporary researchers on the origin or the extent of the pre-Marcan passion narrative.[346] The question cannot be answered on the basis of the third Marcan passion-resurrection prediction (Mark 10:32-34),[347] since this itself has been influenced by the Marcan passion narrative.[348]

---

[340] W. Schenk, *Der Passionsbericht,* passim; for an overview of the materials from each of these layers, cf. 272f. Note also the hypothesis of to traditions of the crucifixion combined by Mark in J. Schreiber, *Der Kreuzigungsbericht,* 48f.

[341] J. Schreiber, *Die Markuspassion;* E. Linnemann, *Studien,* 102.

[342] See above, p. 132.

[343] W.H. Kelber, "Conclusion: From Passion Narrative to Gospel," in *The Passion in Mark. Studies on Mark 14-16,* ed. W.H. Kelber (1976), 153-180, 156-158: *"The understanding of Mk 14-16 as a theologically integral part of the Mkan Gospel calls into question the classic form critical thesis concerning an independent and coherent Passion Narrative prior to Mk"* (157).

[344] W. Schenk, "Leidensgeschichte."

[345] This course of events can hardly be evaluated as the "expression of a philosophical historicism which considers the relevant events of the future as determined by their past according to a pattern of historical necessity" (W. Schenk, "Leidensgeschichte," 715f.).

[346] J. Ernst, "Die Passionerzählung," 163-167, provides a survey of research.

[347] As in, e.g., E. Lohse, *Die Geschichte des Leidens und Sterbens Jesu Christ,* Van Gorcum's theologische bibliothek 316 ($^4$1984), 18-21, 23.

[348] G. Strecker, "Die Leidens- und Auferstehungsvoraussagen im Markusevangelium (Mk 8,31; 9,31; 10, 32-34)" (first published in 1967), now in *Eschaton und Historie. Aufsätze* (1979), 52-75, 67.

The question has also been posed as to whether, alongside the pre-Marcan report of the passion, there circulated other passion narratives which were utilized by Luke and/or John. In conjunction with his Proto-Luke hypothesis[349] Vincent Taylor attempted to reconstruct a connected report of the passion special to Luke.[350] But since the dependence of Luke on the Marcan passion report cannot be questioned, the heuristic implication is that the substance of the Lucan report should be explained on the basis of the Marcan. While traditions special to Luke are present, Lucan expansions must also be recognized. Reordering of pericopes can also be understood as a mark of Lucan redaction.[351]

No certain answer to the question about an independent Johannine passion narrative tradition is possible, dependent as it is on the author's knowledge of the Synoptics. In various ways and with some persuasive arguments researchers have attempted to prove connections between stages of synoptic and Johannine redaction (cf. 3.4.1.2).[352] Thus both the postulate of a comprehensive pre-synoptic passion tradition and that of a pre-Johannine are questionable. Superfluous also are all attempts to evaluate alleged traditions by means of research on the basis of historically ancient and authentic material.

The different versions of the passion narrative in the New Testament Gospels show the high degree to which historical tradition and faith-based interpretation permeate one another. Accordingly, confidence in historical trustworthiness as assumed, for example, in R. Pesch's postulating and early dating of a comprehensive passion report,[353] is revealed as illusory.[354] The obvious insertions and expansions rule out the possibility of regarding the [a] pre-Marcan passion report as an early and unaltered text.

The Hebrew Scriptures are often referred to as the decisive backdrop to the passion narrative. Yet no single tradition, e.g. that of the suffering righteous one,[355] has a determinative significance. Actually various Hebrew-Jewish traditions have been utilized in the presentation. Thus other suggestions proceeding from the same assumption are likewise unpersuasive.[356]

---

[349] See above, p. 117

[350] *The Passion Narrative of St. Luke.* In *Verleugnung,* G. Schneider accepts a pre-Lucan source for the portrayal of Jesus' interrogation and derision.

[351] Cf. G. Strecker's review of V. Taylor, *The Passion Narrative of St. Luke* in *TLZ* 101 (1976): 33-35, 34f.

[352] W. Schenk (*Der Passionsbericht,* 123-129 and "Leidensgeschichte," 715) decides for the dependence of the Johannine Gospel on the Synoptics, as does P. Borgen, "John and the Synoptics in the Passion Narrative," *NTS* 5 (1958/59): 246-259.

[353] R. Pesch, *Das Evangelium nach Markus,* HTKNT 2, II (1977, ³1984), 1-27. On the problem of tradition and redaction, cf. above, p. 121.

[354] H. Conzelmann ("Historie und Theologie," 74f.) concisely sums up the essence of the passion narrative: "the volume of that which we can know as certain is minimal. The kernel of fact is that Jesus was crucified. From this we may deduce that he was arrested and that a judicial process followed–a Roman process." All further reconstruction is characterized to varying degrees by uncertainty.

[355] Cf. D. Lührmann, *Das Markusevangelium* HNT 3 (1987), 230f.

[356] Cf. H. Gese, "Psalm 22," 193-196, on the influence of Psalm 22; C. Maurer "Knecht Gottes," on the motive of the servant of God, and esp. Isa 53.

## 4.3.3. Apophthegms, Paradigms, and Chreias

*Literature*

Albertz, M., *Die synoptischen Streitsprädche. Ein Beitrag zur Formengeschichte des Urchristentums* (1921). Buchanan, G.W., "Chreias in the New Testament," in *Logia. Les paroles de Jésus. The Sayings of Jesus,* ed. J. Delobel, BETL 59 (1982), 501-505. Fascher, E., "Apophthegma," in *BHH* 1 (1962): 111. Gärtner, H., "Chreia," in *Der kleine Pauly* 1 (1964): 1161. Gigon, O., and K. Rupprecht, "Apophthegma," in *Lexikon der Alten Welt* (1965), 222f. Hock, R.F., and E.N. O'Neill, *The Chreia in Ancient Rhetoric. Vol. 1. The Progymnasmata. Translation and Commentary.* Texts and Translations 27. Graeco-Roman Religion Series 9 (1986). Horna, K., and K. von Fritz, "Gnome, Gnomendichtung, Gnomologien," PWSup 6 (1935): 74-90. Hultgren, A.J., *Jesus and His Adversaries. The Form and Function of the Conflict Stories in the Synoptic Tradition* (1979). Klauser, T., and P. de Labriolle, "Apophthegma," in *RAC* 1 (1950): 545-550. Porton, G.G., "The Pronouncement Story in Tannaitic Literature: A Review of Bultmann's Theory," *Semeia* 20 (1981): 81-99. Robbins, V.K., "A Rhetorical Typology for Classifying and Analyzing Pronouncement Stories," SBLSP 23 (1984): 93-122. Schneider, G., "Jesu überraschende Antworten. Beobachtungen zu den Apophthegmen des dritten Evangeliums" (first published in 1983), in his *Lukas. Theologe der Heilsgeschichte. Aufsätze zum lukanischen Doppelwerk,* BBB 59 (1985), 130-155. Tannehill, R.C., ed, "Pronouncement Stories," *Semeia* 20 (1981); "Introduction: The Pronouncement Story and its Types," *Semeia* 20 (1981): 1-13; "Varieties of Synoptic Pronouncement Stories," *Semeia* 20 (1981): 101-119; "Types and Functions of Apophthegms in the Synoptic Gospels," in *ANRW* II 25.2 (1984): 1792-1829. Vouga, F., "Die Entwicklungsgeschichte der jesuanischen Chrien und didaktischen Dialoge des Markusevangeliums," in *Jesu Rede von Gott und ihre Nachgeschichte im frühen Christentum. Beiträge zur Verkündigung Jesus und zum Kerygma der Kirche.* Festschrift W. Marxsen, ed D.-A. Koch *et al.* (1989), 45-56.

The English category "pronouncement story"[357] corresponds to Rudolf Bultmann's designation of this genre as *apophthegma.*[358]   Martin Dibelius introduced the concept of *paradigma,*[359] determined by his "constructive method" whereby early Christian preaching[360] was the starting point for form criticism.[361]

---

[357] E.g., V. Taylor, *The Formation of the Gospel Tradition* (1957 = ²1935), 30; R.C. Tannehill, "The Pronouncement Story," 1; "Types and Functions," 1793, n. 3. [Note 358 in the German edition.]

[358] Bultmann, *Geschichte,* 8ff.; *History,* 11ff. [Note 357 in the German edition.]

[359] *Formgeschichte,* 34ff.; *Tradition,* 37ff.

[360] Dibelius's concept of preaching is very comprehensive, including all possibilities of Christian proclamation: "missionary preaching,   preaching during worship, and catechumen instruction." Cf. his *Formgeschichte,* 13; *Tradition,* 15; and

The genre *paradigma,* i.e., illustration used in preaching, represented accordingly the "oldest Christian narrative style."[362] This genre was also named *chreia.*[363]

Yet demarcation of the concepts chreia and apophthegma, both drawn from ancient rhetoric, is not to be carried through rigorously.[364] The terms emphasize two aspects of the same genre or of two closely related genres.[365] Generally the apophthegma is related more strongly to the person (cf. Diogenes Laertes IV, 47f.), and the chreia to the situation, since in the latter a generalizing sentence is applied ($\chi\rho\epsilon\iota\alpha$) to a specific case.[366] If those literary units in which a saying's reference to the situation is de-emphasized may be described as apophthegmata, the description chreia is appropriate where the point is connected with, or the product of, a striking action.[367]

In the rhetorical schools of antiquity, apophthegmata or chreias and fables belonged to "progymnasmata," i.e., "to practice in paraphrasing or explicating assigned themes with the objective of improving a student's expressive capacity."[368] It can be demonstrated that in antiquity apophthegmata or chreias circulated in a rich variety, as displayed in New Testament apophthegmata and chreias. Their critical character, challenging weak points, convictions, and general conventions,[369] made them a preferred traditional form of the Cynic diatribe.

---

"Evangelienkritik und Christologie," in *Zur Formgeschichte des Evangeliums,* ed F. Hahn, Wege der Forschung 81 (1985), 52-117, 66.

[361] M. Dibelius, *Formgeschichte,* 12; *Tradition,* 13: "missionary purpose was the cause and preaching was the means of spreading abroad that which the disciples of Jesus possessed as recollections." Cf. also *Formgeschichte,* 23-25, esp. 24, n. 1; *Tradition,* 24-26, 26, n. 1. On Dibelius's theory of the centrality of preaching cf. his "Die alttestamentlichen Motive in der Leidensgeschichte des Petrus- und des Johannes-Evangeliums" (first published in 1918), in his *Botschaft und Geschichte. Gesammelte Schriften* I, with H. Kraft ed G. Bornkamm (1953), 221-247, 242f. Cf. also P. Vielhauer, *Geschichte der urchristlichen Literatur,* 288-290.

[362] Dibelius, *Formgeschichte,* 24; *Tradition,* 26.

[363] K. Berger, Formgeschichte des Neuen Testaments (1984), 80ff; "Hellenistische Gattungen im Neuen Testament," *ANRW* II 25.2 (1984): 1092ff.; G.W. Buchanan, "Chreias;" and F. Vouga, "Die Entwicklungsgeschichte."

[364] The varying definitions in the literature can appeal to distinctions in ancient praxis. Cf. O. Gigon and K. Rupprecht, "Apophthegma," 222; T. Klauser in Klauser and P. de Labriolle, "Apophthegma," 546; R.C. Tannehill, "Types and Functions," 1793, n. 3.

[365] Cf. R.C. Tannehill, "The Pronouncement Story and its Types," *Semeia* 20 (1981):1.

[366] K. Berger, "Hellenistische Gattungen im Neuen Testament," 1093: "... a stronger connection to a specific case...."

[367] H. Lausberg, *Handbuch der Literarischen Rhetorik. Eine Grundlegung der Literaturwissenschaft* ($^2$1973), § 1118, distinguishes sayings-chreias, action-chreias, and mixed chreias; in the latter case the saying accompanies the action. Cf. also K. von Fritz in K. Horna and von Fritz, "Gnome, Gnomendichtung, Gnomologien," 87-89, and G. Schneider, "Jesu überraschende Antworten," 142, n. 13.

[368] H. Gärtner, "Progymnasma," 1156; cf. also Quintilian, *inst* I,9; X,5,11f.

[369] G. Theissen, *Lokalkolorit und Zeitgeschichte in den Evangelien. Ein Beitrag zur Geschichte der synoptischen Tradition,* NTOA 8 (1989), 123. According to R.C. Tannehil, the apophthegmata of the synoptic tradition express "value conflicts" ("Types

The orientation of this genre within the history of literature is disputed. Martin Dibelius arranged it within the narrative material in accordance with his theory of early Christian preaching. Rudolf Bultmann, on the contrary, placed it within the sayings material, since many of the apophthegmata have a secondary framework.[370] This corresponds to the fact that the emphasis of the apophthegma is on the saying of Jesus.[371] It seems most advisable therefore to specify this genre as an intermediate form between narrative and sayings material.[372]

Where the narratives of the apophthegms are short, sayings of Jesus are embedded in them as the point of emphasis. Or sometimes the narratives are created to introduce or clarify a dominical saying. Thus they may be described as framed dominical sayings.

Bultmann distinguishes three classes of apophthegmata. Mark 2:15-17 exemplifies the *controversy saying:*[373]

> *And as he sat at dinner in Levi's house, many tax collectors and sinners were also sitting with Jesus and his disciples—for there were many who followed him. When the scribes of the Pharisees saw that he was eating with sinners and tax collectors, they said to his disciples, "Why does he eat with tax collectors and sinners?" When Jesus heard this, he said to them, "Those who are well have no need of a physician, but those who are sick: I have come to call not the righteous but sinners.*[374]

See also Mark 3:1-6, Luke 14:1-6, etc. *Scholastic sayings* are exemplified by Luke 12:13-14:

> *Someone in the crowd said to him, "Teacher, tell my brother to divide the family inheritance with me." But he said to him, "Friend, who set me to be a judge or arbitrator over you?"*

See also Luke 13:1-5, etc. Luke 9:57-62 and parallels and Mark 6:1-6 are *biographical apophthegmata.*

A *dominical saying* may be occasioned by what someone else says (mainly scholastic sayings; whether by a statement, e.g., Mark 9:38; a request, e.g., Mark 10:35; or a question, e.g., Luke 12:13-14), by an action (e.g., Mark 1:16-20), or by

---

and Functions," 1826, cf. also 1795). Note also G. Schneider, "Jesu überraschende Antworten," 130, and often.

[370] *Geschichte,* 48f., 51; *History,* 47f., 49. Cf. for example, his analysis of Luke 14:1-6 and Mark 2:15-17.

[371] *Geschichte,* 66f.; *History,* 62f.; cf. also his "Die Erforschung der synoptischen Evangelien" (first published in 1961), in his *Glauben und Verstehen. Gesammelte Aufsätze,* Vol. 4 (1965): 1-41, 17f.

[372] Cf. P. Vielhauer, *Geschichte der urchristlichen Literatur,* 298ff.

[373] On controversy sayings cf. the works by M. Albertz and A..J. Hultgren listed in the bibliography to this section (and the critique of A. Lindemann, "Literaturbericht zu den synoptischen Evangelien, 1978-1983," *TRu* 49 (1984): 243f.).

[374] The saying of Jesus which forms the conclusion to this pericope may have originally circulated independently; cf. R. Bultmann, *Geschichte,* 16; *History,* 18.

mixture of both forms. It is mainly the controversy sayings which are introduced in this manner. Specific action or behavior (e.g., plucking grain on the Sabbath, Mark 2:23-28 and parallels) leads to a reproach or a question, prompting a word from Jesus.

R.C. Tannehill offers a new attempt at classification, understanding the apophthegma as an act of communication between a speaker and a listener.[375] Corresponding to the interaction between situation and answer,[376] he differentiates five types of apophthegmata: *corrections, commendations, quests, objections, and inquiries* (and, in addition, outside the Synoptics the *description story*). Nor are combinations of motifs excluded. With this classification he intends to take the sociological context into account. In contrast to Bultmann, Tannehill is not interested in the pre-history of the apophthegmata, but in the final redaction of the present text.[377] But it is exactly scrutiny of the pre-history which would be heuristic for sociological examination as well as for the issue of redactional intention.

F. Vouga's approach from the point of view of argumentation theory and Vernon K. Robbins attempt at rhetorical analysis for the interpretation of the apophthegmata raise the question of whether alien categories are being applied to this genre. Expecially with respect to Vouga's formulation it must be asked to what degree categories and methodologies developed in contemporary literary study may be applied to ancient texts.

With respect to the origin and derivation of this genre in the New Testament, Rudolf Bultmann sought its setting mainly in the early Palestinian Christian community, suggested by its formal resemblance to rabbinic controversy sayings and anecdotes.[378] G. G. Porton objects, affirming that closer parallels are found among Greek philosophers and political figures.[379] But the use of scriptural citations is evident in rabbinic parallels.[380] Furthermore, both in the rabbinic and the Jesus tradition answers are frequently in the form of counter-questions or parables.[381] Accordingly both Jewish and Hellenistic influence must be taken into account in the development of the synoptic apophthegmata. F. Vouga emphasizes the uniqueness of the New Testament genre,[382] paradoxically asserting a "discontinuous continuity" with the genres of the surrounding world. But this is

---

[375] "Types and Functions," 1794.

[376] "Types and Functions," 1794. Cf. 1795: "Study of the relation between stimulating occasion and response... leads to the recognition of five types...."

[377] "Types and Functions," 1794; "The Pronouncement Story," 4.

[378] *Geschichte*, 41, 42ff., 49, 57f., 60ff.; *History*, 40, 41ff., 48, 55, 57ff. Cf. H. Koester, "Formgeschichte/Formenkritik. II. Neues Testament," in *TRE* 11 (9183): 291. For a Hellenistic setting Bultmann cites only a few examples, e.g., Luke 6:5D; 17:20f; and 2 Clem 12:2. Cf. also his "Die Erforschung der synoptischen Evangelien" (first published in 1961), in his *Glauben und Verstehen. Gesammelte Aufsätze*, Vol. 4 (1965): 19.

[379] "The Pronouncement Story in Tannaitic Literature," 83, 96f. Compare K. Berger, *Formgeschichte des Neuen Testaments* (1984), 83.

[380] G. Theissen, *Lokalkolorit und Zeitgeschichte*, 128-130, with n. 143. Note the evidence adduced there.

[381] R. Bultmann, "Die Erforschung der synoptischen Evangelien" (first published in 1961), in his *Glauben und Verstehen. Gesammelte Aufsätze*, Vol. 4 (1965): 18. Cf. Mark 2:19; 3:4; 3:24-26; and often elsewhere.

[382] "Die Entwicklungsgeschichte," 46.

not, as G. W. Buchanan thinks, to be derived from the instruction of the disciples by Jesus.[383] The question of whether traditional materials go back to Jesus himself is most likely to be answered positively about logia which stand at the beginning of the developmental process.[384]

# 4.4   The Gospel of John

## 4.4.1   The Sources of John's Gospel

### 4.4.1.1   Source Theories on John's Gospel

*Literature*

Becker, H., *Die Reden des Johannesevangeliums und der Stil der gnostischen Offenbarungsrede,* ed. R. Bultmann, FRLANT 68 (1956). Boismard, M.-É and A. Lamouille, *Synopse des quatre évangiles en français III. L'évangile de Jean* (1977). Bousset, W., "Ist das vierte Evangelium eine literarische Einheit?" *TRu* 12 (9109): 1-12, 39-64. Brown, R.E., *The Gospel According to John,* 2 vols. AB 29 (1966), 29A (1970). Bultmann, R., "Analyse des ersten Johannesbriefes" (first published in 1927), in *Exegetica. Aufsätze zur Erforschung des Neuen Testaments,* ed. E. Dinkler (1967), 105-123; "Die kirchliche Redaktion des ersten Johannesbriefes" (first published in 1951), in *Exegetica,* 381-393; "Johannesbriefe," in *RGG³* 3 (1959): 836-839; "Johannes-evangelium," in *RGG³* 3 (1959): 840-850. Eckermann, J.C.R., Theologische Beyträge V.2 (1796). Fortna, R.T., *The Gospel of Signs: A Reconstruction of the Narrative Source Underlying the Fourth Gospel,* SNTSMS 11 (1970). Haenchen, E., *Das Johannesevangelium. Ein Kommentar, aus den nachgelassenen Manuskripten* ed. U. Busse (1980); *A Commentary on the Gospel of John,* 2 vols. (1984). Heitmüller, W., "Zur Johannes-Tradition," *ZNW* 15 (1914): 189-209. Hirsch, E., *Das vierte Evangelium in seiner ursprünglichen Gestalt verdeutscht und erklärt* (1936); *Studien zum vierten Evangelium (Text/Literarkritik/Entstehungsgeschichte),* BHT 11 (1936). Kennedy, G.A., "An Introduction to the Rhetoric of the Gospels," *Rhetoric* 1 (1983): 17-31. Langbrandtner, W., *Weltferner Gott oder Gott der Liebe. Der Ketzerstreit in der johanneischen Kirche. Eine exegetische Untersuchung mit Berücksichtigung der koptisch-gnostischen Texte aus Nag Hammadi,* Beiträge zur biblischen Exegese und Theologie 6 (1977). Noack, B., *Zur johanneischen Tradition. Beiträge zur Kritik an der literarkritischen Analyse des vierten Evangeliums* (1954). Richter, G., *Studien zum Johannesevangelium,* ed. J. Hainz, Biblische Untersuchungen 13 (1977). Ruckstuhl, E., *Die literarische Einheit des Johannesevangeliums. Der*

---

[383] "Chreias," 505. Cf. also V. Taylor, *The Formation of the Gospel Tradition* (1957 = ²1935), 87; and earlier, M. Albertz, *Die synoptischen Streitgespräche,* 57-80, had accepted the so-called original dialogue ("Urgespräche") of Jesus as underlying the tradition. Cf. Bultmann's critique of his position in *Geschichte,* 41, n. 1, and *History,* 40, n. 2.

[384] Cf. R. Bultmann, *Geschichte,* 50f. and often; *History,* 49 and often.

*gegenwärtige Stand der einschlägigen Forschungen,* NTOA 5 (1988).  Schwartz, E., "Aporien im vierten Evangelium," in Nachrichten der Gesellschaft der Wissenschaften in Göttingen, Philologisch-Historische Klasse (1907) 342-372, (1908) 115-148, 149-188, 497-560.  Schweizer, A., *Das Evangelium Johannes nach seinem inneren Werth und seiner Bedeutung für das Leben Jesu kritisch untersucht* (1841).  Schweizer, E., *EGO EIMI. Die religionsgeschichtliche Herkunft und theologische Bedeutung der johanneischen Bildreden, zugleich ein Beitrag zur Quellenfrage des vierten Evangeliums,* FRLANT 56 (²1965).  Smith, D.M., *The Composition and Order of the Fourth Gospel. Bultmann's Literary Theory,* Yale Publications in Religion 10 (1965).  Thyen, H., "Entwicklungen innerhalb der johanneischen Theologie und Kirche im Spiegel von Joh 21 und der Lieblingsjüngertexte des Evangeliums," in *L'Évangile de Jean. Sources, Rédaction, Théologie,* by M. de Jonge, BETL 44 (1977).  Weisse, C.H., *Die evangelische Geschichte kritisch und philosophisch bearbeitet.* 2 vols (1938); *Die Evangelienfrage in ihrem gegenwärtigen Stadium* (1856).  Wellhausen, J., *Erweiterungen und Änderungen im vierten Evangelium* (1907); *Das Evangelium Johannis* (1908).  Wilkens, W., *Die Entstehungsgeschichte des vierten Evangeliums* (1958).

Literary criticism remains up to the present a central concern of Johannine research.

The first attempt to discover a re-editing of the Gospel of John was presented by J.C.R. Eckermann in 1796.  In the nineteenth century C.H. Weisse,[385] A. Schweizer, and others expressed doubts about the unity of the Fourth Gospel; these approaches remained without much effect until the end of the century.[386]  But about the turn of the century literary-critical issues became the focus of attention.  The works of Julius Wellhausen and E. Schwartz are significant.  To them New Testament research owes the indication of fundamental problems which are still determinative today;[387] e.g., fissures and discontinuities in the text.  Cf. the continuation of John 13:31-14:31 at 18:1ff., noting especially 14:31.  But the intervening chapters 15 through 17 take up Jesus' farewell address again.  Contradictory geographical data offer other problems (e.g., in 5:1 Jesus is in Jerusalem, but in 6:1f. on the other side of the Sea of Galilee, without mention of any transition).

Rudolf Bultmann sought to deal with these questions through textual rearrangements and considerations of source criticism.  As the pre-existing elements of the Fourth Gospel he identified a collection of miracle narratives (the Semeia Source),[388] a collection of revelatory statements,[389] and the passion and Easter

---

[385] At first in his *Die evangelische Geschichte,* 183ff., and then in a critical continuation of his own earlier work in *Die Evangelienfrage,* 56-58 and 111-118.

[386] Older bibliography in W. Bousset, "Literarische Einheit;" and B. Weiss, *Das Johannesevangelium,* MeyerK 2 (⁹1902), 26, n*.

[387] Cf. the survey in H. Thyen, "Johannesevangelium," in *TRE* 17 (1988): 203-205.

[388] A Faure, "Die alttestamentlichen Zitate im 4. Evangelium und die Quellenscheidungshypothese," *ZNW* 21 (1922): 99-121, had already suggested the existence of a book of miracles on the basis of the enumeration of signs in John 2:11 and 4:54 in connection with John 20:30.  R.T. Fortna sees a passion and resurrection narrative as part of the semeia source, which he characterizes as a (foundation) gospel.  For a report on

narratives.[390] These were reworked by an ecclesiastical redactor (who appended chapter 21 and inserted further elements, especially of sacramental or futuristic eschatological character[391]) thus seeking both to correct the existing disorder[392] and to give the work an "ecclesiastical" sense. In its pure source critical approach this theory is as outdated as the attempt to account for inconsistencies through the rearrangement of manuscript pages.[393] The postulate of a revelatory Sayings Source is unprovable for lack of parallels, particularly since a linguistic contrast between these passages and the style of the Evangelist has never been demonstrated. This hypothesis has been largely abandoned in New Testament research.[394] The supposition of a semeia source also has recently encountered well-founded opposition. U. Schnelle has verified the unity of saying and miracle, including the signs of Jesus, in the theology of the Fourth Evangelist.[395]

Another attempt to solve the riddles of the Gospel is based on the hypothesis of an earlier version *(Grundschrift)*.

Julius Wellhausen sought to prove that the *Grundschrift* was an original creation of an outspoken personality, a true author, and re-edited by several successors.[396] After Wellhausen and E. Schwartz, E. Hirsch identified the *Grundschrift* with the original Johannine Gospel.[397] It was enlarged and changed in an ecclesiastical, anti-Gnostic redaction. W. Wilkens subscribed the *Grundschrift* (= the basic Gospel,

---

the history of research and its present situation, cf. U. Schnelle, *Antidoketische Christologie im Johannesevangelium. Eine Untersuchung zur Stellung des vierten Evangeliums in der johanneischen Schule*, FRLANT 144 (1987), 105f., with n. 105.

[389] Cf. H. Becker, *Die Reden.* R. Bultmann postulates a similar source for 1 John, cf. his "Analyse des ersten Johannesbriefes."

[390] Cf. the reconstruction of the Greek text of this source in D.M. Smith, *Composition and Order*, 23-34, 38-44, and 48-51.

[391] R. Bultmann has also suggested an ecclesiastical redaction of 1 John (cf. "Die kirchliche Redaktion des ersten Johannesbriefes"). For a critique of this position, cf. G. Strecker, *Die Johannesbriefe*, MeyerK 14 (1989), 54.

[392] R. Bultmann, *Das Evangelium des Johannes*, MeyerK 2 ([21]1986), 162; *The Gospel of John: a Commentary* (1971), 219f.

[393] Still represented by P. Vielhauer, *Geschichte der urchristlichen Literatur*, 422f. Cf. also the data in S. Schulz, *Untersuchungen zur Menschensohn-Christologie im Johannesevangelium. Zugleich ein Beitrag zur Methodengeschichte der Auslegung des vierten Evangeliums* (1957), 41ff. For critiques, cf. K. Aland, "Glosse, Interpolation, Redaktion und Komposition in der Sicht der neutestamentlichen Textkritik," in his *Studien zur Überlieferung des Neuen Testaments und seines Textes*, ANTF 2 (1967), 50ff.; E. Haenchen, *Johannesevangelium* 48-57, *A Commentary on the Gospel of John* 1:44-51, with further bibliography.

[394] Cf. the critiques of E. Käsemann in *VF* (1942/46), 187f.; R. Schnackenburg, *Das Johannesevangelium*, HTKNT 4/1 ([2]1967, [6]1986), 39f, 54f; *The Gospel According to St. John* (1990), 1:51f., 67f.; H. Thyen, "Johannesevangelium," in *TRE* 17 (1988): 206f. But in support of such a source, cf. Vielhauer, *Geschichte der urchristlichen Literatur*, 425-427.

[395] *Antidoketische Christologie im Johannesevangelium*, 168ff., 182ff.; cf. H. Thyen, "Johannesevangelium," in *TRE* 17 (1988): 207.

[396] *Evangelium Johannis*, 6f., 100-102.

[397] E. Hirsch, *Das vierte Evangelium; Studien zum vierten Evangelium.*

largely narrative[398]) and its re-editing to the same author.   Wilcken makes it clear that literary-critical observations based on linguistic and material differences should have an extraordinarily limited role in this reconstruction.   Further recent attempts to determine a Grundschrift have been undertaken by Raymond E. Brown,[399] W. Langbrandtner, G. Richter,[400] H. Thyen,[401] etc.

The development of John's Gospel as pictured by M.-É Boismard and A. Lamouille is more complex;   and in view of the state of the tradition too complicated. They assume a protracted series of redactions to a *Grundschrift,* document C. Supplementing and restructuring of material occured in *John IIA, John IIB* (both from the same author,[402] who in *IIB* was influenced by the three Synoptics and especially Luke-Acts[403]), and *John III,* editions dating from about 50 C.E. through the end of the first century.

Lest literary-critical theses be regarded out of proportion, E. Schweizer[404] and E. Ruckstuhl stress the extensive linguistic and stylistic unity of the Gospel. In addition, Ruckstuhl refuses to exclude the influence of oral tradition.[405] According to B. Noack, the materials of the Fourth Evangelist come not from a revelatory or sign source, but from the oral tradition of the author's community.[406] Although Ernst Haenchen begins with the thesis of a source (= "Vorlage"[407]), in the commentary edited by U. Busse from Haenchen's papers[408] Haenchen attempts to determine the Evangelist's own method.[409]

If the Fourth Evangelist has utilized traditions which are to be investigated by literary-critical methods, most worthy of recognition as the core of the *Grundschrift* hypothesis is the fact that the Johannine Gospel presupposes the

---

[398] W. Wilkens, *Die Entstehungsgeschichte,* 32-93.

[399] *The Gospel According to John* (1966), 1:xxxiv-xl.

[400] *Studien zum Johannesevangelium,* passim.   For a description and evaluation of Richter's source hypothesis cf. A. Dauer, "Schichten im Johannesevangelium als Anzeichen von Entwicklungen in der (den) johanneischen Gemeinde(n) nach G. Richter. Darstellung und Kritik," in *Die Kraft der Hoffnung. Gemeinde und Evangelium. Festschrift J. Schneider,* ed. by the Catholic Faculty of the University of Bamberg (1986), 62-83.

[401] "Entwicklungen."

[402] *Synopse,* 69.

[403] *Synopse,* 47: "He has... drawn numerous details from the three evangelists in their present form."

[404] *EGO EIMI,* 82-112.

[405] *Die literarische Einheit,* 219.

[406] *Zur johanneischen Tradition,* 124: "We propose, therefore, for the narrative materials of John's Gospel the same origin as for the sayings material: the evangelist created out of the oral tradition of his church."

[407] E. Hanechen, *Johannesevangelium,* 83; *A Commentary on the Gospel of John,* 77f.

[408] On the biographical details of the origin of this commentary, cf. U. Busse, "Ernst Haenchen und sein Johanneskommentar. Biographische Notizen und Skizzen zu seiner johanneischen Theologie," *ETL* 57 (1981): 125-143, 131-135 and the forward of the editor in Haenchen's *Johannesevangelium,* xiff.., *A Commentary on the Gospel of John,* 1: xvff.

[409] *Johannesevangelium,* 103, *A Commentary on the Gospel of John,* 1:90.

Synoptics (cf. 4.4.1.2). In all this, the distinction between various forms of oral and written traditions in the preliminary stage of the composition of the Fourth Gospel has heretofore had only an insufficiently realized role in matters of tradition and redaction history. This does not imply that the Johannine Gospel should be interpreted only in its final form, which would be to overlook the meaning of earlier traditions for the work of the redactor. The differentiation between tradition and redaction is a necessary presupposition for proper access to the present text. In this connection, the subsequent history of the Gospel remains a problem (cf. 7:53-8:11 and 21:1-25). The degree to which various representatives of the Johannine school (cf. 4.4.2) have influenced both the traditions underlying the Fourth Gospel and traditions after it, and with what effects, must be more carefully researched. Undoubtedly the tensions in the Fourth Gospel reflect discussions of this school and events in its history.[410]

#### 4.4.1.2 The Relationship of John to the Synoptics

*Literature*[411]

Barrett, C.K., *The Gospel According to St. John,* 2nd ed. (1978); *Das Evangelium nach Johannes,* MeyerK Sonderband (1990). Blinzler, J., *Johannes und die Synoptiker. Ein Forschungbericht,* SBS 5 (1965). DAUER, A., Die Passionsgeschichte im Johannesevangelium. Eine traditionsgeschichtliche und theologische Untersuchungen zu Joh 18,1-19,30, SANT 30 (1972); *Johannes und Lukas. Untersuchungen zu den johanneischen Parallelperikopen Joh 4,46-54/Lk 7,1-10 – Joh 12,1-8/Lk 7,36-50; 10,38-42 – Joh 20,19-29/Lk 24,36-49,* FB 50 (1984). Klein, H., "Die lukanisch-johanneische Passionstradition" (first published in 1976), in *Redaktion und Theologie des Passionsberichtes nach den Synoptikern,* ed M. Limbeck, Wege der Forschung 481 (1981), 366-403. Kleinknecht, K.T., "Johannes 13, die Synoptiker und die 'Methode' der johanneischen Evangelienüberlieferung," *ZTK* 82 (1985): 361-388. Mohr, T.A., *Markus- und Johannespassion. Redaktionsgeschichtliche Untersuchungen der Markinischen und Johanneischen Passionstraditionen,* ATANT 70 (1982). Myllykoski, M., "The Material Common to Luke and John, A Sketch," in *Luke-Acts. Scandinavian Perspectives,* ed. P. Luomanen, Suomen Eksegeettisen Seuran julkaisuja 54 (1991), 115-156. Neirynck, F., "John and the Synoptics," in *L'Évangile de Jean. Sources, Rédaction, Théologie,* by M. de Jonge, BETL 44 (1977), 73-106; with the collaboration of J. Delobel, T. Snoy, G. van Belle, and F. van Segbroeck, *Jean et les synoptiques. Examen critique de l'exégèse de M.-É. Boismard,* BETL 49 (1979); "John and the Synoptics. The Empty Tomb Stories," *NTS* 30 (1984): 161-

---

[410] On Docetic and anti-Docetic school tradition in John's Gospel, cf. G. Strecker, "Chiliasm and Docetism in the Johannine School," Australian Biblical Review 38 (1990): 45-61, 59-61. W. Bousset, "Literarische Einheit?" 64 and W. Heitmüller in *ZNW* 15:207 long ago suggested that the mental leaps and contradictions in the Johannine Gospel might be explained through its origin in a circle or school.

[411] For bibliography, cf. also E. Haenchen, *Johannesevangelium,* 74-76, *A Commentary on the Gospel of John,* 1: 67-74.

187.   Sabbe, M., "The Arrest of Jesus in Joh 18,1-11 and its Relation to the Synoptic Gospels. A Critical Evaluation of A. Dauer's Hypothesis," in *L'Évangile de Jean. Sources, Rédaction, théologie,* by M. de Jonge, BETL 44 (1977), 203-234; "Can Mt 11,27 and Lk 10,22 Be Called a Johannine Logion?" in *Logia. Les paroles de Jésus. The Sayings of Jesus,* ed. J. Delobel, BETL 59 (1982), 363-371; "The Footwashing in Jn 13 and its Relation to the Synoptic Gospels," *ETL* 58 (1982): 279-308.   Schnider, F. and W. Stenger, *Johannes und die Synoptiker. Vergleich ihrer Parallelen,* Biblische Handbibliothek 9 (1971).   Windisch, H., *Johannes und die Synoptiker. Wollte der vierte Evangelist die älteren Evangelien ergänzen oder ersetzen?* UNT 12 (1926).

In place of attempting to determine separate sources for the Johannine Gospel, newer research is giving new emphasis to the relationship of the Fourth Gospel to the Synoptics.   Yet C.H. Dodd presupposed that only pre-synoptic tradition was used in John,[412] and Rudolf Bultmann doubted that the Fourth Gospel had knowledge of the Synoptics.[413]

Parallels between the synoptic and Johannine presentations of Jesus' passion were generally attributed to a pre-Johannine and pre-synoptic passion account.[414]   But the influence of the Synoptic Gospels on the pre-Johannine tradition was also accepted,[415] along with a knowledge of the Synoptics through which the Fourth Evangelist "in not a few places supplemented, deepened, and corrected" his work.[416]

K.T. Kleinknecht affirms "a direct literary relationship" between John 13 and the synoptic passion account, based on examination of the text's structure.[417] M. Sabbe (who would also note "sayings and speeches"[418]), F. Neirynck, and others find evidence for the literary dependence of the Fourth Gospel on the redacted

---

[412] *The Interpretation of the Fourth Gospel* (1958), 444-453.

[413] *Johannesevangelium, Gospel of John;* cf. the references in Index II ("Literary and Historico-critical Questions") on "Relation to the Synoptics."   Cf. also his "Johannesevangelium," in *RGG³* 3 (1959): 841.  Note also J. Becker, *Das Evangelium nach Johannes,* Ökumenischer Taschenbuchkommentar zum Neuen Testament 4, Vol. 1 (1979, ²1985), 36-38; "Aus der Literatur zum Johannesevangelium (1978-1980)," *TRu* 47 (1982): 289-292;"Das Johannesevangelium im Streit der Methoden (1980-1984)," *TRu* 51 (1986): 26-28; M. Myllykoski, "Material Common."   For older bibliography which questions Johannine knowledge of synoptic materials, cf. W.G. Kümmel, *Einleitung in das Neue Testament* (²¹1983), 167, n. 21; *Introduction to the New Testament,* rev. ed. (1975), 202, n. 21; F. Neirynck, "John and the Synoptics," in *L'Évangile de Jean,* 79, n. 28.

[414] H. Klein, "Die lukanisch-johanneische Passionstradition," presupposes a pre-Lucan passion account; as does T.A. Mohr, *Markus- und Johannespassion,* 406f.

[415] According to A. Dauer, *Johannes und Lukas,* the pre-Johannine source presupposes the Synoptics in their canonical form.   Cf. also his *Die Passionsgeschichte.* For a critique, cf. H. Thyen, "Johannesevangelium," in *TRE* 17 (1988): 208.

[416] T.A. Mohr, *Markus- und Johannespassion,* 409.

[417] "Johannes 13," 364, 382.

[418] "The Arrest of Jesus in Joh 18,1-11," 371, n. 20.

Synoptics.[419] Given the supplementary questions on specific points which this might raise, it still follows that there is a dependent relationship between the Synoptics and John, which should be assigned to the broad field of living, oral efforts at interpreting the gospel tradition.

John's Gospel probably knew the Synoptics, since it is hardly likely that Mark and John independenly created the gospel genre.[420] Though William Wrede took account of pre-Marcan and pre-Johannine elements in his classical work of 1901 on the Messianic secret,[421] Mark's redactional work is much more evident,[422] so that elements of the Messianic secret in John imply the influence of redacted Mark on John.

Divergences in the material common to John and the Synoptics may be referred to school discussions of the Johannine circle,[423] which influenced the form of the material and resulted in productive formulations of peculiar Johannine interpretations and Johannine language. Criteria decisive for the development and formulation of this material, used first not by the Fourth Evangelist but by the Johannine school, are the juxtaposition with the sect of John the Baptist, with the

---

[419] Cf. also P. Dschulnigg, "Sprache, Redaktion und Intention des Markus-Evangeliums und ihre Bedeutung für die Redaktionskritik," SBB 11 ([2]1986), who calls attention to Marcan speech in John. C.K. Barrett, *St. John,* 43-46 and 70ff.; *Das Evangelium nach Johannes,* 33-35 and 59ff., accepts a knowledge of Mark and some small acquaintance with Luke. For older bibliography, cf. W.G. Kümmel, *Einleitung in das Neue Testament* ([21]1983), 168-170, 572; *Introduction to the New Testament,* rev. ed. (1975), 202-204; 556. J. Blinzler works through the research up to 1964 in *Johannes und die Synoptiker.* On the current state of research, cf. H. Thyen, "Johannesevangelium," in *TRE* 17 (1988): 208: "a new consensus is developing, that in any case those to whom we owe the Gospel in its transmitted form knew and used the Synoptics." For an analysis of the relevant texts from the perspective of redaction criticism, cf. F. Schnider and W. Stenger, *Johannes und die Synoptiker,* 9.

[420] J.M. Robinson's objection, in *Entwicklungslinien durch die Welt des frühen Christentums* (1971), 248-250, *Trajectories in Early Christianity* (1971), 266-268, that since Matthew and Luke independently used Q and Mark, an independent creation of the gospel genre by Mark and John is thinkable, fails to differentiate between usage and creation of a literary genre through the interpretative adaptation of ancient popular biography (cf. above, section 4.1.2.4).

[421] W.Wrede, Wrede, W., *Das Messiasgeheimnis in den Evangelien. Zugleich ein Beitrag zum Verständnis des Markusevangeliums* (1901 = [4]1969); *The Messianic Secret* (1971).

[422] Cf. G. Strecker, "Zur Messiasgeheimnistheorie im Markusevangelium" (first published in 1964), in his *Eschaton und Historie. Aufsätze* (1979), 33-51, 34f., 35-39. For a different viewpoint, cf. H. Räisänen, *Das "Messiasgeheimnis" im Markusevangelium. Ein redaktionsgeschichtlicher Versuch,* Suomen Eksegeettisen Seuran julkaisuja 28 (1976).

[423] Yet it is doubtful that priestly tradition-practices of schools such as Qumran, tied to the Hebrew Scriptures, or the relationship of Jubilees to its tradition should be cited, as does K.T. Kleinknecht, "Johannes 13," 388.

"Jews," and above all with Docetic teachers, who were already opposed in 1 John.[424]

This is justified so long as a relatively late date for the Fourth Gospel is acceptable (not before the second quarter of the second century).[425] Such a dating is not really contradicted by Papyrus Egerton 2 or P[52], since their dating by "common consensus" to "about 125 C.E."[426] is questionable.[427]

Regarding the Fourth Gospel as a supplement or substitute for the Synoptics is not a satisfactory explanation for its origin.[428] It is rather a consistent product of the theology of the Johannine school; it is the Gospel of the Johannine circle.

The Fourth Gospel represents no unique genre as compared with the Synoptics and extracanonical gospels. Most of the literary forms found in John are also found in these other gospels (cf. below, section 4.4.3).

## 4.4.2    Johannine Literature and the Johannine School

*Literature*

Becker, J. *Das Evangelium nach Johannes,* Ökumenischer Taschenbuch-kommentar zum Neuen Testament 4, Vol. 1 (1979, [2]1985), 40-43. Cullmann, O., "Von Jesus zum Stephanuskreis und zum Johannesevangelium," in *Jesus und Paulus,* Festschrift W.G. Kümmel, ed E.E. Ellis *et al.* (1975), 44-56; *Der johanneischen Kreis. Zum Ursprung des Johannesevangeliums* (1975). Culpepper, R.A., *The Johannine School: An Evaluation of the Johannine-School Hypothesis Based on an*

---

[424] Cf. G. Strecker, "Die Anfänge der johanneischen Schule," *NTS* 32 (1986): 31-47, 42.

[425] K. Wengst's hypothesis of an active confrontation with Syrian Judaism [*Bedrängte Gemeinde und verherrlichter Christus. Der historische Ort des Johannesevangeliums als Schlüssel zu seiner Interpretation,* Biblisch-theologische Studien 5 ([2]1983), 94-96; cf. also J.L. Martyn, History and Theology in the Fourth Gospel ([2]1979)] is not persuasive, given the impossibility of precisely locating the relationship between church and synagogue geographically.

[426] K. Aland, "Der Text des Johannesevangeliums im 2. Jahrhundert," in *Studien zum Text und zur Ethik des Neuen Testaments.* Festschrift H. Greeven, ed. W. Schrage, BZNW 47 (1986), 1-10; cf. also his "Glosse, Interpolation, Redaktion und Komposition in der Sicht der neutestamentlichen Textkritik," in his *Studien zur Überlieferung des Neuen Testaments und seines Textes,* ANTF 2 (1967), 35-57.

[427] On the dating of these papyri, cf. G. Strecker, *Die Johannesbriefe,* MeyerK 14 (1989) 27f., n. 27. Cf. also A. Schmidt, "Zwei Anmerkungen zu P. Ryl III 457," Archiv für Papyrusforschung 35 (1989): 11f. W. Schneemelcher is also hesitant about an early date of the Egerton Papyrus; cf. Joachim Jeremias and Wilhelm Schneemelcher, "Fragments of Unknown Gospels, 2. Papyrus Egerton 2," in *Neutestamentliche Apokryphen in deutscher Übersetzung,* ed. W. Schneemelcher I ([6]1990), 82-85, 82f.; and in *New Testament Apocrypha,* rev. ed. edited by W. Schneemelcher I (1991), 96-100, 96.

[428] For older bibliography, cf. H. Windisch, *Johannes und die Synoptiker,* 1-40. Windisch himself preferred a displacement theory, according to which the Fourth Gospel tolerated no other witness alongside itself (134).

*Investigation of the Nature of Ancient Schools,* SBLDS 26 (1975). Heitmüller, W., "Zur Johannes-Tradition," *ZNW* 15 (1914): 189-209. Hengel, M., *The Johannine Question* (1990). Klauck, H.-J. *Die Johannesbriefe,* ErFor 276 (1991), 101-105. Schnelle, U., *Antidoketische Christologie im Johannesevangelium. Eine Untersuchung zur Stellung des vierten Evangeliums in der johanneischen Schule,* FRLANT 144 (1987). Strecker, G., *Die Johannesbriefe,* MeyerK 14 (1989), 19-28; "Die Anfänge der johanneischen Schule," *NTS* 32 (9186): 31-47; "Chiliasm and Docetism in the Johannine School," *Australian Biblical Review* 38 (1990): 45-61 [German in *KD* 38 (1992): 30-46]. Vouga, F., "The Johannine School: A Gnostic Tradition in Primitive Christianity," *Bib* 69 (1988): 371-385.

The close relationship in language and conceptual world between the Letters and Gospel of John has led researchers to speak of a "Johannine circle."[429] The connection between these writings is more precisely indicated by the phrase "Johannine school." School traditions and the relationship between teacher and pupils, basic to the definition of an ancient school, explain the resemblances and differences within this group of writings.[430] School activity has contributed to the creation and transmission of literary and pre-literary sayings and speeches, as is apparent through comparison with schools in the Jewish and Hellenistic environment of early Christianity,[431] and as is evident in other New Testament traditions.[432]

---

[429] E.g., O. Cullmann, *Der johanneischen Kreis.* Cullmann seeks to draw a theological-historical line in which the Johannine school stands, through "a Hellenistic splinter group of the earliest Jerusalem church," the Johannine disciples of Jesus (the disciple who Jesus loved), the historical Jesus, to the disciples of the Baptist, back to a "marginal heterodox Judaism." These groups are identified by their common communal structure, interest in missions, polemic against heresy, and efforts toward their own legitimation. Cf. also Cullmann's "Von Jesus zum Stephanuskreis." Much earlier W. Heitmüller, "Zur Johannes-Tradition," *ZNW* 15 (1914): 189-209, sought to prove the existence, on the grounds of the data in Papias, of a circle or school in Asia Minor which used the title "presbyster" and whose thought was related to that of the Gospel and Apocalypse of John. As the leading authority Heitmüller referred to the Presbyter John, whose real or ideal figure appears in 2 and 3 John and in Rev 1-3 (201-204). Yet the differences between the various Johannine writings ought not to be so smoothed out that the old thesis of common authorship of Letters and Gospel can rightly be resuscitated. M. Hengel, *The Johannine Question,* passim, holds this viewpoint. He identifies the Johannine letters as written by the Presbyter John, who also wrote the Gospel over a long period of time, completing it shortly before his death. Section 6.4, below, goes more fully into the relationship between the Apocalypse and the Johannine school.

[430] U. Schnelle, *Antidoketische Christologie im Johannesevangelium. Eine Untersuchung zur Stellung des vierten Evangeliums in der johanneischen Schule,* FRLANT 144 (1987), 53ff. lists a series of such main thoughts common to the literature.

[431] Cf. W. Bousset, *Jüdisch-Christlicher Schulbetrieb in Alexandria und Rom. Literarische Untersuchungen zu Philo und Clemens von Alexandria,* FRLANT 23 (1915). R.A. Culpepper, The Johannine School (258f.), lists a series of criteria of varying significance: 1. emphasis on "friendship" (φιλία) and "community" (κοινωνία); 2. assembly around a founder honored as exemplary and wise; 3. attention to the teaching of the founder; 4. the members of the school are pupils of the founder; 5. teaching and

The criterion for a school is derivation from a founder who certifies its independence over against other groups. Since the "beloved disciple" of John's Gospel is less a historical person than an ideal entity, reflecting on the Johannine school founder as a part of the life of Jesus, the specification of "the elder" (ὁ πρεσβύτερος) as the sender (2 John 1 and 3 John 1) is the only direct description of an author in the Johannine writings. This is the most productive place to begin a search for the founder of the school, since the absolute form of expression presupposes that the sender was well known and an accepted authority to the recipients.

The "presbyter tradition" attributed by Eusebius to Bishop Papias of Hierapolis also suggests that the presbyter was the founder of the Johannine school.

> *And I shall not hesitate to append to the interpretations all that I ever learned well from the presbyters (παρὰ τῶν πρεσβυτέρων) and remember well, for of their truth (ἀλήθεια) I am confident. For unlike most I did not rejoice in them who say much, but in them who teach the truth, nor in them who recount the commandments (ἐντολάς) of other, but in them who repeated those given to the faith by the Lord and derived from truth itself; but if ever anyone came who had followed the presbyters (τοῖς πρεσβυτέροις), I inquired into the words of the presbyters, what Andrew or Peter or Philip or Thomas or James or John or Matthew, or any other of the Lord's disciples (τις ἕτερος τῶν τοῦ κυρίου μαθητῶν), had said, and what Aristion and the presbyter John, the Lord's disciples, were saying (οἱ τοῦ κυρίου μαθηταὶ λέγουσιν).*[433]

This tradition displays a verbal relationship with the Johannine world. Moreover, there are resemblances in the inclination to apocalyptic expression. Papias' tradition distinguishes Aristion and the presbyter John, as disciples of the Lord, from the presbyters (πρεσβύτεροι) who are equated with Jesus' twelve disciples and who,

---

learning are communal activities; 6. communal meals are often celebrated in memory of the founder; 7. the lives of the members are determined by rules; 8. a distance is preserved toward common human society; 9. organizational structures are developed to insure the continuity of the school.

[432] It is to be expected that already in the relation between John the Baptist and his disciples and even more between Jesus and his the basic elements of school practice developed. But that Jesus intended to found a genuine and continuing school operation may be rejected, given the immediateness of his call to repentence. Besides the unclear relationship between Jesus and his disciples, the literary traditions used by Matthew were shaped by Christian scribes and have been designated as school traditions. Cf. K. Stendahl, *The School of St. Matthew and its Use of the Old Testament,* ASNU 20 (1954). On the substantial problems of this approach, cf. G. Strecker, *Der Weg der Gerechtigkeit. Untersuchungen zur Theologie des Matthäus,* FRLANT 82 ([3]1971), esp. 15ff and 49ff. In the traditions in Acts, C.K. Barrett most recently attempted to make evident traces of early Christian school activity ["School, Conventicle, and Church in the New Testament," in *Wissenschaft und Kirche.* Festschrift E. Lohse, ed K. Aland *et al.* Texte und Arbeiten 4 (1989), 96-110, on this 102-108]. On the Pauline school, cf. above, section 3.5.

[433] Eusebius, *h.e.,* III 39,3f.,; translation, Loeb CL.

due to the passage of time, Papias himself could not have known. It is striking that the title of presbyter is not applied to Aristion, but restricted to John. Both Aristion and John were still living in the time of Papias, as the present tense (λέγουσιν) suggests and as Eusebius himself testifies.[434] This implies that the presbyter of 2 and 3 John is the same person as Papias' presbyter.

The letters of the presbyter represent an earlier stage in the history of tradition than the other Johannine writings.[435] They may be regarded as the earliest extant writings of the Johannine school, and owe their transmission and preservation as a part of the New Testament canon to regard for the presbyter as the founding authority of the Johannine school. The triple repetition of the aorist "I have written" (ἔγραψα) in 1 John 2:14 suggests that the succession is from the presbyterial letters 2 and 3 John to 1 John. The objection that there is no express parallel to 2 and 3 John[436] is too general. The author of 1 John does not intend to cite earlier writings, but to stand in the tradition of these writings. Note also that 1 John has actual reminiscences of 2 and 3 John. The author of 1 John consciously takes up the tradition of the Johannine school, and equates his own authority with that of the presbyter or connects it with his.

Hans Conzelmann regards 1 John as a "Johannine pastoral letter"[437] assuming the literary order of Gospel, then Letter. The linguistic resemblance between them–especially the Johannine key words ἀλήθεια, ἀγάπη, etc.–suggest not literary dependence but a basic school tradition underlying both. There are various differences between them. The formal distinction between Letter and Gospel is striking. Alongside this, 1 John shows no knowledge of tradition about the life of Jesus and the Gospel offers a "Life of Jesus."[438]  1 John possesses an ecclesiological inclination; the Gospel is more Christologically-oriented. Furthermore, there are differences in their terminologies. In 1 John the "Advocate" (παράκλητος) refers to Jesus Christ (1 John 2:1), whereas in the Gospel it refers to the Spirit. Their are also distinctions in eschatology. In contrast to 1 John, futuristic eschatological elements recede in the Gospel. While the atoning character of the death of Jesus is presupposed in John 1:29 and 36, it is expressly spelled out in 1 John 1:7, 9; 2:2, and 4:10.[439] The independence of the two writings assumes different authors. The Gospel is probably later than the Letter, since the acute confrontation underlying the writing of 1 John seems to lie further in the past for John.

According to ancient church tradition the Johannine literary activity was located in Asia Minor. This agrees with the authorship of the Johannine apocalypse on the island of Patmos off the coast of Asia Minor (Rev. 1:9). It also fits with the evidence

---

[434] Eusebius, *h.e.,* III 39,7.

[435] G. Strecker, "Chiliasm and Docetism," 47ff.

[436] R. Schnackenburg, *Die Johannesbriefe,* HTKNT 13/3 (⁷1984), 125.

[437] H. Conzelmann, "Was von Anfang war," in his *Theologie als Schriftauslesung. Aufsätze zum Neuen Testament,* BEvT 65 (1974), 207-214, on this point 214.  A. Neander, in his *Geschichte der Pflanzung und Leitung der christlichen Kirche durch die Apostel* (⁵1862), 590, had already described 1 John as a " pastoral circular writing."

[438] Cf. above, p. 100.

[439] For further differentiation between the writings, cf. G. Strecker, *Die Johannesbriefe,* MeyerK 14 (1989), 52f.

that 1 John was known in the mid-second century by Polycarp of Smyrna.  Papias' tradition points also to Asia Minor.   Irenaeus also betrays knowledge of Asia Minor as home to the Johannine tradition, regarding the Fourth Gospel as having been written by John, the son of Zebedee, in Ephesus.[440]

## 4.4.3   Tradition and Literary Genre in the Fourth Gospel

*Literature*

Beutler, J., "Literarische Gattungen im Johannesevangelium. Ein Forschungsbericht 1919-1980," in *ANRW* II 25.3 (1985): 2506-2568.   Kysar, R., The Fourth Evangelist and his Gospel. An Examination of Contemporary Scholarship (1975); "The Fourth Gospel. A Report on Recent Research," in *ANRW* II 25.3 (1985): 2389-2480.

Relatively little form-critical analysis has been dedicated to the Fourth Gospel.[441]

Rudolf Bultmann's *History of the Synoptic* (sic!) *Tradition* shows that classical form criticism has hardly been interested in the Fourth Gospel.   But the disinterest has not been total.[442]   A growing interest in form-critical aspects of the Fourth Gospel is evident in mention of the Fourth Gospel in Helmut Koester's *TRE* article "Formgeschichte/Formkritik II," in J. Beutler's report Literarische Gattungen im Johannesevangelium, and in Klaus Berger's *Formgeschichte.*

Studies on the context of the Johannine school in the history of Christian tradition (cf. above, section 4.4.2) should be consulted in this connection.

Classification of forms follows essentially from the distinction found in the Synoptics between sayings and narrative materials (cf. above on apophthegms, section 4.3.3). E. Haenchen calls attention to the limits of this differentiation (e.g., the description of the Baptist in John 1 and the prologue of John 1:1-18 resist such classifying[443]); yet it retains its value when it is conceived not as a rigidly set pattern but rather as an aid to orientation.

### 4.4.3.1  Forms of the Sayings Material

*Literature*

Becker, H., *Die Reden des Johannesevangeliums und der Stil der gnostischen Offenbarungsrede,* ed R. Bultmann, FRLANT 68 (1956).  Becker, J., "Aufbau,

---

[440] Irenaeus, *adv. haer.* III 11; Eusebius, E.H. V 8,4.  With this also agrees the connection of Cerinthus of Asia Minor with the Johannine tradition as well as the confrontation between Montanists and Alogoi over the Fourth Gospel and the Johannine Apocalypse, which was localized in Asia Minor.

[441] Cf. the all too pessimistic judgment of R. Kysars in "The Fourth Evangelist," 66, "What is needed... is a more highly developed method of johannine form criticism; and until such methodology can be developed, our efforts in this regards may satisfy little more than the fancy."

[442] Cf. the evidence in J. Beutler, "Literarische Gattungen," 2510ff., and R. Schnackenburg, *Das Johannesevangelium,* HTKNT 4/1 (²1967, ⁶1986), 46ff.

[443] E. Haenchen, *Johannesevangelium,* 102; *Gospel of John,* 1: 90.

Schichtung und theologiegeschichtliche Stellung des Gebetes in Johannes 17," *ZNW* 60 (9169): 56-83. Beutler, J., *Habt keine Angst. Die erste johanneische Abschiedsrede (Joh 14)*, SBS 116 (1984). Borgen, P., *Bread from Heaven. An Exegetical Study of the Concept of Manna in the Gospel of John and the Writings of Philo*, NovTSup 10 (²1981). Guilding, A., *The Fourth Gospel and Jewish Worship. A Study of the Relation of St. John's Gospel to the Ancient Jewish Lectionary System* (1960). Koester, H., "Dialog und Spruchüberlieferung in den gnostischen Texten von Nag Hammadi," *EvT* 39 (1979): 532-556. Leroy, H., Rätsel und Missverständnisse. Ein Beitrag zur Formgeschichte des Johannesevangeliums, BBB 30 (1968); "Das johanneische Missverständnis als literarische Form," *Bibel und Leben* 9 (1968): 196-207. Müller, U.B., "Die Parakletenvorstellung im Johannesevangelium," *ZTK* 71 (1974): 31-77. Schnelle, U., "Die Abschiedsreden im Johannesevangleium," *ZNW* 80 (1989): 64-79. Schulz, S., *Komposition und Herkunft der Johanneischen Reden*, BWANT 81 (1960).

Alongside the synoptic forms of the sayings material (cf. 4.3.1), additional forms characterize the structure of the Fourth Gospel.

*a) "I am" sayings* (e.g., John 6:35, 8:12).[444]
These self-expressions of the Logos-revealer may be differentiated as follows. There are *figurative sayings which are spelled out*, e.g., John 6:35:

> *I am the bread of life. Whoever comes to me will never be hungry, and whoever believes in me will never be thirsty.*

(See also 8:12; 10:11, 14; 14:6; 15:1, 5). Other sayings are *indirect* (with reference to what has preceded), such as 6:41:

> *I am the bread that came down from heaven* (with reference to 6:35).

Some "ego eimi" (ἐγώ εἰμι) sayings are *absolute* (8:24 and 28 are elliptical) or in the sense of a recognition formula (originally from the secular world), as at 6:20. Explicated "ego eimi" sayings contain both a self-predication and a soteriological conclusion. The former are revelatory sayings which utilize figurative language, which is carried through to a greater degree in the figurative speeches such as the shepherd speech of John 10 and the vine and branches allegory of 15:1-8 and 15:17. The latter are promises with an invitation and an added final promise.[445]
The derivation of these sayings in terms of the history of religion is debatable. (There are parallels to them in the Mandaean and gnostic literature, in the magical papyri, in the Hebrew Scriptures, where, however, no figurative sayings are associated with "I

---

[444] Cf. also E. Schweizer, *EGO EIMI. Die religionsgeschichtliche Herkunft und theologische Bedeutung der johanneischen Bildreden, zugleich ein Beitrag zur Quellenfrage des vierten Evangeliums*, FRLANT 56 (²1965).
[445] Cf. S. Schulz, *Komposition und Herkunft*, 86f.

am" the Lord, and in Ancient Near Eastern tradition.[446]) But their meaning in John is clear. The "ego eimi" sayings express Jesus Christ's claim to be the Logos-revealer. The figurative sayings are not intended to be taken literally, but utilize symbolic language portraying the revealer's claim to be the true life. The sayings thus have a Christological and soteriological point. They demand a response of faith; faith which does not demand a legitimizing "sign" (cf. 6:35).

*b) Amen amen sayings.*

These sayings, found only in the Fourth Gospel, are expansions of the synoptic "amen formula" in ceremonial language. They are found fifteen times in John 1-21, and are restricted to Jesus himself (e.g., 1:51; 3:3, 5; etc.).

Double amen appears also in the Hebrew Scriptures and in texts from New Testament era Judaism.[447] But there is no certain proof of the expanded non-responsive amen in Judaism or the mouth of Jesus.[448]

*c) Speeches of the Revealer, Jesus Christ.*

Jesus' speeches in John provided Rudolf Bultmann with the starting point for reconstructing a source consisting of revelational speeches and derived from a gnostic milieu, with parallels in Mandaean and Manichaean texts, as well as in the Odes of Solomon and the Hermetic literature.[449] While Bultmann's source hypothesis has been opposed on good grounds (cf. 4.4.1.1), his derivation of these speeches in terms of the history of religions remains determinative. It is correct that parallels to the Johannine speeches are found in these texts. Yet it must be asked to what extent these parallels or their later developments reflect the Johannine forms.

Helmut Koester has sought to understand the Johannine speeches and dialogues as further developments of the sayings tradition. Sayings of Jesus which may have different origins from a form-critical perspective, with the use of other materials, were built up into speeches or dialogues. Parallels to such processes are found in gnostic texts. Koester sees the *Sitz im Leben* in the "self reflections of Christian groups with an orientation toward wisdom."[450]

In this connection, the *Sitz im Leben* within the Johannine school also needs to be examined more precisely.

---

[446] Cf. A. Deissmann, *Licht vom Osten. Das Neue Testament und die neuentdeckten Texte der hellenistisch-römischen Welt* (⁴1923), 108-114; *Light From the Ancient East* (1927), 136-143.

[447] Cf. the evidence in J. Jeremias' review of E.R. Goodenough, *Jewish Symbols in the Greco-Roman Period* I-VI (1953-1956) in *TLZ* 83 (1958): 502-505, 504.

[448] As rightly stated by H.-W. Kuhn, "ἀμήν," in *EWNT* 1 (1980): 166-168, 166.

[449] Cf. R. Bultmann, "Die Bedeutung der neuerschlossenen mandäischen und manichäischen Quellen für das Verständnis des Johannesevangeliums" (first published in 1925), in *Exegetica. Aufsätze zur Erforschung des Neuen Testaments,* ed E. Dinkler (1967), 55-104.

[450] Koester, "Formgeschichte/Formenkritik. II. Neues Testament," in *TRE* 11 (1983): 286-299, 292f.; "Dialog und Spruchüberlieferung in den gnostischen Texten von Nag Hammadi," *EvT* 39 (1979): 532-556.

The farewell addresses of John 14-16 should be included with the revelational speeches.[451] In terms of the history of religion, their derivation is debatable.[452] They contains materials which are formally very diverse.

*d) Dialogues*[453] *and controversy speeches* (e.g., John 3:1ff; cf. also 7:50ff; 19:38ff).
Narative as well as sayings elements are found in the Johannine controversy speeches just as in the synoptic. Yet especially the dialogues show a close resemblance to the revelational speeches, so that it is possible to speak of "revelatory speeches interrupted by questions."[454] Correspondly, answers in the controversy accounts are also presented in the form of longer speeches. Thus both dialogues and controversy speeches may be understood as having a school connection. Whether the instructional dialogue "chiding human incapacity" (John 21:20-23) should be distinguished from the general revelatory discourses (John 3:1-13, 4:7-15, 4:31-38, 6:25-59, 11:11-16, etc.,)[455] is questionable. As in the case of the synoptic controversy accounts, "debates within the community,"[456] and here specifically the Johannine community, may be behind it.

*e) Riddles and misunderstandings.*
Hans Windisch regarded expressions of misunderstanding in the Fourth Gospel as a mark of Johannine style.[457] H. Leroy interpreted this technique as the genre riddle, related to oracle and joke.[458] Real and unreal riddles should be distinguished: the unreal riddles of John are given abstract answers which could not be understood without the accompanying clarification. Perhaps these are the speeches of a special group. Johannine misunderstandings have their *Sitz im Leben* in the preaching and catechesis of the early Christian community.[459] But it must

---

[451] For interpretation of John 13:31-17:26 in connection with the Johannine school, cf. U. Schnelle, "Die Abschiedsreden," esp. 78: the farewell addresses are directed to the community and seek "fully to reveal the significance of Jesus' glorification."

[452] U.B. Müller, "Die Parakletenvorstellung," refers to the Jewish genre of the farewell address. J. Becker, *Das Evangelium nach Johannes,* Ökumenischer Taschenbuch-kommentar zum Neuen Testament 4, Vol. 2 (1981, [2]1984): 439ff., calls them a "very individualistic type of literary testament." K. Berger, *Formgeschichte des Neuen Testaments* (1984), 75, emphasizes the significance of pagan "last words" *(ultima verba)* alongside the even stronger influence of the Hebrew-Jewish genre of literary testament.

[453] Cf. C.H. Dodd, *The Interpretation of the Fourth Gospel* (1958, 1978), *passim.*

[454] J. Beutler, "Literarische Gattungen," in *ANRW* II 25.3 (1985), 2554.

[455] K. Berger, *Formgeschichte,* 252.

[456] R. Bultmann, *Geschichte der synoptischen Tradition,* 56; *History of the Synoptic Tradition,* 53; cf. also the synoptic school discussions, *Geschichte,* 56ff.; *History,* 54ff.

[457] H. Windisch, "Der Johanneische Erzählungsstil," in *EYXAPIΣTHPION. Studien zur Religion und Literatur des Alten und Neuen Testaments. Festschrift H. Gunkel.* Vol. 2 ed. H. Schmidt, FRLANT 36/2 (1923), 174-213, 199.

[458] "Rätsel," 200.

[459] H. Leroy, "Rätsel;" and *Missverständnis.*

be questioned whether these misunderstandings are a genre, as are riddles, or whether they should be regarded as stylistic devices[460] and thus be more properly interpreted in connection with the dialogues. The reaction to misunderstandings is certainly a typical element of the revelatory dialogues.[461]

*f) Prayers.*

Special attention has been given to the "high priestly prayer of Jesus" in John 17, generally with reference to the forms of gnostic literature. H. Becker discerns in it (or rather in its *Vorlage*) the "farewell prayer of the revealer."[462] Against the background of the hermetic corpus, C.H. Dodd interpreted John 17 by analogy to the hermetic hymns, in which those who receive instruction, at the end of a dialogue join together in praise of the revealer.[463] J. Becker and H. Ritt agree in describing John 17 as a "farewell prayer," although they differ in details. J. Becker's outline of the prayer is: report, introduction to the request, the request and its support.

*g) Preaching.*

Less promising are attempts to explain Johannine texts on the basis of preaching (B. Lindars)[464] or midrash (A. Guilding). Despite some general agreement in classification, specific genres (e.g., the speeches of the revealer, etc.) differentiate them. It is contestable whether the "homiletic pattern" postulated by P. Borgen for John 6 can be utilized for its interpretation.[465]

### 4.4.3.2 Forms of the Narrative Material

*Literature*

Formesyn, R., "Le Sèmeion johannique el le sèmeion hellénistique," *ETL* 38 (1962): 856-894. Hahn, F., "Die Jüngerberufung Joh 1,35-51," in *Neues Testament und Kirche.* Festschrift R. Schnackenburg, ed J. Gnilka (1974), 172-190. Nicol, W., *The Semeia in the Fourth Gospel. Tradition and Redaction,* NovTSup 32 (1972).

*a) Miracles ("Semeia").*

Because the first two miracles are numbered (John 2:11 and 4:54), this form has been untilized as a starting point for source-critical analysis (cf. 4.4.1.1). Even if form-critical parallels do not provide evidence for the reconstruction of a

---

[460] As H. Windisch did already in "Der Johanneische Erzählungsstil."

[461] Cf. K. Berger, *Formgeschichte,* 252.

[462] *Die Reden des Johannesevangeliums,* 119f.

[463] *The Interpretation of the Fourth Gospel* (1958, 1978), 420-423.

[464] B. Lindars, *The Gospel of John,* NCB (1972), 51-54. Cf. also P. Borgen, *Bread from Heaven.*

[465] For a critique, cf. H. Thyen, Thyen, H., "Aus der Literatur zum Johannesevangelium," *TRu* 43 (1978): 338-351.

"sign source,"[466] divergences in terms of both religious background and the history of their traditions distinguish the miraculous elements of these narratives. The history of particular traditions from the Johannine school must be taken into account along with synoptic-type traditions. In some cases (indirect) literary dependence on the Synoptics is possible (cf. John 6:1-25 on Mark 6:32-56[467]).

Religious-historical examination as to the origins of the Johannine miracle narratives should not be reduced to the alternatives of Hellenistic[468] vs. Jewish/Old Testament parallels.[469] Old Testament, Hellenistic Jewish, and pagan Hellenistic influences are all perceptible.

In general, compared with the synoptic miracle narratives, those in John show a more advanced interpretation which regards the miracles as revealing "signs" of the Logos/Son of God (e.g., John 2:1ff.).

*b) Legends.*

John 1:35-51 draws on the genre of the *call narrative.* F. Hahn finds there two sorts of call-narratives,[470] distinguished by the type of person called. The first form is analogous to the synoptic call narratives, describing the situation, presenting the call, and describing its effect. Here Jesus himself is the agent (John 1:43; 1:45f. take the place of a report on the effects of the call[471]). The second and further developed form relates more closely to the needs of the community. Here emphasis is on a disciple, once called by Jesus, now himself doing the calling. The structure consists of "situation, messianic confession, and leading the called to Jesus" (cf. John 1:41, 42a, 45f.[472]). John 1:35-37 offers a mixed form, where John the Baptist points disciples to Jesus.[473] Here the structural elements are a description of the situation, witness to Christ, and the effects of the call.

*Appearance narratives*[474] are found in 20:14-18, 19-23, 24-29, and in the epilogue at 21:1-14 and 15-17. Rudolf Bultmann explained the miraculous draught of fish (John 1:1-14) as originally an Easter narrative, which Luke 5:1-11 read back into the public life of Jesus. He considered both the motivation for the catch and

---

[466] Cf. U. Schnelle, *Antidoketische Christologie im Johannesevangelium. Eine Untersuchung zur Stellung des vierten Evangeliums in der johanneischen Schule,* FRLANT 144 (1987), 177-179.

[467] Cf. Schnelle, *Christologie,* 170.

[468] E.g., R. Bultmann; for further examples, cf. J. Beutler, "Literarische Gattungen im Johannesevangelium. Ein Forschungsbericht 1919-1980," in *ANRW* II 25.3 (1985): 2546, n. 270.

[469] E.g., W. Nicol. In "Le Sèmeion," 894, R. Formesyn writes, "... the close semantic connections existing between the Johannine 'sign' (σημεῖον) and the demonstrative and symbolic 'signs' (σημεῖα) of the Septuagint must be noted."

[470] F. Hahn, "Die Jüngerberufung," *passim.*

[471] F. Hahn, "Die Jüngerberufung," 177.

[472] F. Hahn, "Die Jüngerberufung," 178.

[473] F. Hahn, "Die Jüngerberufung," 178f.

[474] Cf., H. Koester, "Formgeschichte/Formenkritik. II. Neues Testament," in *TRE* 11 (1983): 294. According to Koester, these are not legends, but epiphanies with elements of data on place and situation, a miracluous appearance, a reaction, the self-presentation of the one who appears, and a commission.

the concluding meal to be "fictional decoration."[475]  R. Pesch disagrees.  He regards 21:1-14 as two narratives,[476] a fish miracle (classified with the miracle narrative by genre [cf. 4.3.2.a]) and an epiphany, combined with one another and reworked by a redactor.[477]  Traits of a personel legend are also worked in through the naming of Peter and the Beloved Disciple (cf. also the comments on the Beloved Disciple in the epilogue, 21:15ff.).

In John 20:1-18, an epiphany is combined with the narrative of the empty tomb.[478]  John 6:16-21 has also been interpreted as an epiphany.[479]

*c) The Passion Narrative* (cf. 4.3.2.c).

### 4.4.3.3  The Johannine Prologue

*Literature*

Bultmann, R., "Der religionsgeschichtliche Hintergrund des Prologs zum Johannesevangelium" (first published in 1923), in his *Exegetica. Aufsätze zur Erforschung des Neuen Testaments,* ed. E. Dinkler (1967), 10-35; "Die Bedeutung der neuerschlossenen mandäischen und manichäischen Quellen für das Verständnis des Johannesevangeliums" (first published in 1925), in *Exegetica,* 55-104. Deichgräber, R., *Gotteshymnus und Christushymnus in der frühen Christenheit. Untersuchungen zu Form, Sprache und Stil der frühchristlichen Hymnen,* SUNT 5 (1967); "Formeln, Liturgische II. Neues Testament und Alte Kirche 1-4," *TRE* 11 (1983): 256-263.    Demke, C., "Der sogennante Logoshymnus im johanneischen Prolog," *ZNW* 58 (1967): 45-68.  Hofius, O., "Struktur und Gedankengang des Logos-Hymnus im Joh 1,1-18," *ZNW* 78 (1987): 1-25.  Hofrichter, P., *Im Anfang war der "Johannesprolog." Das urchristliche Logosbekenntnis – die Basis neutestamentlicher und gnostischer Theologie,* Biblische Untersuchungen 17 (1986). Jeremias, J., *Der Prolog im Johannesevangelium,* Calwer Hefte 88 (1967). Käsemann, E., "Aufbau und Anliegen des johanneischen Prologs" (first published in 1957), in his *Exegetische Versuche und Besinnungen* 1 (⁴1964): 155-180; "The Structure and Purpose of the Prologue to John's Gospel," in *New Testament Questions of Today* (1969), 138-167.    Müller, U.B., *Die Geschichte der Christologie in der johanneischen Gemeinde,* SBS 77 (1975).  Rissi, M., "Die Logoslieder im Prolog des vierten Evangeliums," *TZ* 31 (1975): 321-336.

---

[475] *Das Evangelium des Johannes,* MeyerK 2 (²¹1986), 545f.; *The Gospel of John: a Commentary* (1971), 705.

[476] Cf. earlier W. Bauer, *Das Johannesevangelium,* HNT 6 (³1933), 237.

[477] R. Pesch, "Der reiche Fischfang Lk 5,1-11/Joh 21,1-14. Wundergeschichte – Berufungsgeschichte – Erscheinungsbericht," *Kommentare und Beiträge zum Alten und Neuen Testament* (1969), 103-107, 126f.

[478] R. Bultmann, *Geschichte der synoptischen Tradition,* 313; *History of the Synoptic Tradition,* 288f.

[479] G. Bertram, *Neues Testament und historische Methode. Bedeutung und Grenzen historischer Aufgaben in der neutestamentlichen Forschung,* S a m m l u n g gemeinverständ-licher Vorträge und Schriften 134 (1928), 30.

Theobald, M., *Die Fleischwerdung des Logos. Studien zum Verhältnis des Johannesprologs zum Corpus des Evangeliums und zu 1 Joh,* NTAbh. NF 20 (1988). Wengst, K., *Christologische Formeln und Lieder des Urchristentums,* SNT 7 (1972).

Despite numerous studies,[480] little consensus has been achieved on the Johannine prologue. Questions of its literary unity, written or oral precedents, and religious-historical derivation connect with those of its form and relationship to the whole Fourth Gospel.

The prologue John 1:1-18 according to the NRSV:

1  In the beginning was the Word, and the Word was with God, and the Word was God.
2  He was in the beginning with God.
3  All things came into being through him, and without him not one thing came into being. What has come into being
4  in him was life, and the life was the light of all people.
5  The light shines in the darkness, and the darkness did not overcome it.
6  There was a man sent from God, whose name was John.
7  He came to testify to the light, so that all might believe through him.
8  He himself was not the light, but he came to testify to the light.
9  The true light, which enlightens everyone, was coming into the world.
10  He was in the world, and the world came into being through him; yet the world did not know him.
11  He came to what was his own, and his own people did not accept him.
12  But to all who received him, who believed in his name, he gave power to become children of God,
13  who were born, not of blood or of the will of the flesh or of the will of man, but of God.
14  And the Word became flesh and lived among us, and we have seen his glory, the glory as of a father's only son, full of grace and truth.
15  (John testified to him and cried out, "This was he of whom I said, 'He who comes after me ranks ahead of me because he was before me.'")
16  From his fullness we have all received, grace upon grace.
17  The law indeed was given through Moses; grace and truth came through Jesus Christ.
18  No one has ever seen God. It is God the only Son, who is close to the Father's heart, who has made him known.

It is widely recognized that the first verses of the Gospel cite a "hymn."[481] Whether it is a pre-Christian song[482] or has a Christian precedent[483] is disputed.

---

480 Cf., among others, H. Thyen, "Aus der Literatur zum Johannesevangelium," *TRu* 39 (1974): 53-69, 222-252; J. Becker, "Aus der Literatur zum Johannesevangelium (1978-1980)," *TRu* 47 (1982): 317-321; E. Haenchen, *Das Johannesevangelium.* 112-115, 145-147; *A Commentary on the Gospel of John,* 1: 103-108, 131-135.

481 R. Deichgräber, *Gotteshymnus und Christushymnus,* 118, n. 3. Cf., R. Bultmann, *Johannesevangelium,* 4; *The Gospel of John,* 17: "cultic community hymn;" similarly, K. Wengst, *Christologische Formeln,* 204-206; J. Jeremias, *Der Prolog,* 8: "a psalm." But P. Hofrichter, *Im Anfang,* 41, calls it a "confessional text," basing this on the lack of

Reconstruction of the prologue should begin with the observation that 1:6-8 and 1:15 abruptly present John the Baptist. This is probably to prepare for what follows in 1:19ff. "Has made him known" (ἐξηγήσατο), and indeed all of the present vs. 18, have the same function. Thus the question becomes whether these verses belong to the earliest text. The change from third person plural in vs. 13 to first person plural in 14 offers a further point of approach to reconstructing the pre-Johannine hymn. Disparate judgments about style and metre have led to divergent results.[484]

Certainty is beyond our reach, since the Johannine school tradition had its influence before the final redaction by the Fourth Evangelist. Yet 1:1 and 3-5 appear to be almost a word for word citation, given a secondary interpretation by the Evangelist in 1:6-8. The catchword "light" (φῶς) in 1:9 refers back to 1:5. Details remain uncertain. (For "true" in vs. 9, ἀληθινόν, cf. 1 John 2:8. The participial construction at the end of vs. 9 is especially problematical.) Interruptions in the flow, evident in the interpolations in 1:6-8 as well as elsewhere, show that the Evangelist did not cite a source faithfully. The origin and order of 1:10-12 are unclear; in any case 1:12c must be secondary, as is 1:13. Construction of the earliest form of 1:14-18 is also uncertain.[485] The content of 1:14 and 1:16 (as well as 1:18?[486]), which seems very ancient in terms of wording, have the best claim to belong to a pre-Johannine level. One possibility is that these verses made up a second strophe, in which the community answered the "song of the angels" (= the first strophe[487]).

The earliest form of the prologue represents an early level of Johannine school tradition, as is indicated by comparison with the elder's letters (2 and 3 John) and 1 John. Here are key Johannine concepts, e.g. "truth" (ἀλήθεια, cf. John 1:14, 18; 1 John 1:6, 8, etc.) and "beginning" (ἀρχή, cf. John 1:1f; and not in this absolute sense 2 John 5f.; 1 John 1:1 shows a close relationship to the absolute meaning of the word in the prologue and probably incorporates the same concepts which underlie its earliest level).

---

the "who" (ὅς) and the first person plural style, as compared to hymns found in the NT epistles.

[482] R. Bultmann, "Der religionsgeschichtliche Hintergrund," calls it a hymn of the Baptist community; cf. also J. Becker, *Das Evangelium nach Johannes,* Ökumenischer Taschenbuch-kommentar zum Neuen Testament 4,1 (1979, ²1985): 75, who considers it from the "stream of the Hellenistic Jewish wisdom myth."

[483] E.g., E. Käsemann, "Aufbau," 166, and often; " Structure and Purpose," 150f., and often.

[484] E.g., R. Bultmann, *Johannesevangelium,* 3-5, 18, n. 3, 37, n. 4; *The Gospel of John,* 16-18, 35, n. 3, 59, n. 2, sees as pre-Johannine 1:3-5, 9-12b (without ἐξουσίαν and τοῖς πιστεύουσιν through αὐτοῦ), 14, and 16. E. Käsemann, "Aufbau," 167, " Structure and Purpose," 151, sees two strophes to the original: 1) 1-4 [perhaps without 2] and 2) 5 and 9-12. K Wengst, *Christologische Formeln,* 205, also sees two strophes: 1) 1, 3, 4f., 9-11; and 2) 14, 16.

[485] Separating them as isolated tradition from the pre-Johannine hymn and interpreting them as the choral conclusion of a miracle narrative (cf. U.B. Müller, *Die Geschichte,* 13ff., 41-45) is too hypothetical.

[486] Cf., however, U. Schnelle, *Antidoketische Christologie im Johannesevangelium. Eine Untersuchung zur Stellung des vierten Evangeliums in der johanneischen Schule,* FRLANT 144 (1987), 245, who regards it as a "transitional verse."

[487] C. Demke, "Der sogannante Logoshymnus," 61.

Dualistic trends are more influential in the structural elements visible in the prologue than in 2 and 3 John, and offer insight into the development of early Johannine theology.

The subject of the hymn is the divine Logos. Faith confesses him as the pre-existent mediator of creation (1:1-3, 10) as well as the revealer descended from heaven (1:9-11, 14, 18). That he brings life and light as well as "the glory of God" (δόξα θεου, 1:4, 9, 14) displays his soteriological function.

The history of the Logos concept reaches back to a time well before the origin of the Fourth Gospel. The Hebrew Scriptures have parallels (cf. Genesis 1:1ff., though here it is a creative word rather than a hypostasis), as does Jewish wisdom literature ("Wisdom," חכמה, personified as a mediator, but also identified with the Torah). The interpretation of "mind" (νοῦς, and occasionally also "Word," or λόγος, cf. Irenaeus *adv. haer* I 15, 3 with respect to the Gnosticism of Markus suggests a connection with Christian "gnosis" of the second century.[488] But the Johannine prologue does not contain a systematically worked out symbolism of numbers, nor does it base its soteriology on cosmology. At most, then, it displays an incipient form of Christian gnosticizing. Yet if the concept of a revealer figure is not genuinely Christian, parallels come to mind in the divine Logos especially from the realm of Hellenistic Judaism (cf. the Logos concept of the Alexandrian Philo) and Greek thought. In Neoplatonism, Logos appears with an absolute meaning and portrays the interpretive and formative power which permeates everything (Plotinus, *enn.* III 2, 15). These illustrate how broad was the milieu in which the Johannine Logos concept could arise. First century philosophical and religious syncretism furnished the structural elements out of which the Christ-hymn of the Johannine prologue could be created. Since this occurred before the authorship of the Gospel, the product was a distinctive Christian unit. The Fourth Evangelist was not the first to apply the idea or concept of the Logos to Christ.[489]

Alongside this question is that of the relationship of the prologue to the rest of the Gospel. It is a prelude, in that 1:14 is a key not only to the Christological hymn but also to the whole Fourth Gospel.[490] Yet 1:14 is neither a Docetic point nor anti-Docetic polemic, but a genuine expression of the Fourth Evangelist's theology. In the prologue he not only shifts the "vita Jesu" to the time of creation, but also brings to expression the historical and eschatological dimension which determines the portrayal of Christ all through the Fourth Gospel: the paradox of God and humanity unified in the person of Jesus Christ as the eternal Logos.

---

[488] Cf. R. Bultmann, *Johannesevangelium,* 6, 11-14; *The Gospel of John,* 1: 19, 26-29.

[489] Cf. also O. Hofius, "Struktur," 15, who speaks of the "tradition-context of the Fourth Gospel."

[490] Against, J. Becker, *Das Evangelium nach Johannes,* Ökumenischer Taschenbuch-kommentar zum Neuen Testament 4, Vol. 1 (1979, ²1985), 77f.

# 4.5 The Significance of Rhetoric for the Interpretation of the Gospels

*Literature*

Berger, K. *Exegese des Neuen Testaments. Neue Wege vom Text zur Auslegung.* Uni-Taschenbücher 658 (1977, ²1984), 42-53 and 53-58 (bibliography). Kennedy, G.A. *New Testament Interpretation through Rhetorical Criticism,* Studies in Religion (1984), 73-113.    Klauck, H.-J., "Zur rhetorischen Analyse der Johannesbriefe," *ZNW* 81 (1990): 205-208.    Mack, B.L., *Rhetoric and the New Testament,* Guides to Biblical Scholarship: New Testament Series (1990), 50-56 (on the Jesus tradition), 78-88 (On the redaction of the Gospels).    Standaert, B., *L'Évangile selon Marc. Composition et genre littéraire* (²1984).    Wilder, A.N., Early Christian Rhetoric. The Language of the Gospel (1964).    Wuellner, W., "Where is Rhetorical Criticism Taking Us?" *CBQ* 49 (1987): 448-463.

The question of the Gospels' relationship to ancient rhetoric was raised in connection with Luke's prologue (1:1-4). According to that treatment, the writing of the Gospels has no significant relationship to rhetoric. Thus, rhetorical analysis was first applied to the New Testament letters (cf. 3.2.3), and restricted to the realm classified as *elocutio*[491] in the rhetorical handbooks.[492]

A few older works utilize rhetorical concepts.    Adolf Jülicher's analysis of the parables occasionally refers to Aristotle's *Rhetoric.*[493]

However, contemporary research is devoting more attention to rhetorical issues in examining the Gospels. New Testament genres are being described in light of the rhetorical situation.[494]    Other scholars are examining rhetorical and

---

[491] *Elocutio* (λέξις) includes tropes and figures of style, i.e., verbal ornamentation and images. Cf. M. Fuhrmann, *Die antike Rhetorik. Eine Einführung* (³1990), 114ff.

[492] Cf. H.-J. Klauck, "Zur rhetorischen Analyse," 205; J. Lambrecht, "Rhetorical Critiscism and the New Testament," *Bijdragen* 50 (1989): 244; B.L. Mack, *Rhetoric,* 14f., 19f.

[493] *Die Gleichnisreden Jesu* (reprint, 1976 = ²1910), 52f., 69-73.

[494] K. Berger, *Formgeschichte des Neuen Testaments* (1984). See above, pp. 22f., for specific references to Berger.

argumentative influence on gospel texts.[495]  Thus rhetorical analysis touches on narrative[496] and structuralist work[497] on New Testament texts.

Whether investigation of the argumentative structure of the gospel text should allot "only the role of a model"[498] to ancient rhetoric, or whether it should resort to a "new rhetoric,"[499] it is still questionable that the issue has been formulated correctly for these texts. Even if the application of rhetorical terminology implies no knowledge of educated rhetoric,[500] but simply describes what is found in the New Testament, the synchronic plane of the text still presents an important assignment for exegesis. But this is not the whole task. The text must also be subjected to diachronic analysis. Otherwise the historical dimension of the text, indispensible for understanding the gospel materials as well as the Gospels themselves, is lost. Characterizing the Evangelists as innovative writers with rhetorical or argumentative goals is an incongruous description of how the Gospels came to be.[501]

---

[495] Cf. J. Lambrecht, "Rhetorical Criticism and the New Testament," 244.

[496] Examples of Johannine exegesis: J.L. Staley, *The Prints First Kiss: A Rhetorical Investigation of the Implied Reader in the Fourth Gospel*, SBLDS 82 (1988); R.A. Culpepper, *The Anatomy of the Fourth Gospel. A Study in Literary Design*, Foundations and Facets, New Testament (1983); F. Vouga, "Un exemple de commentaire fondé sur la critique narrative: Jean 5,1-18," in *La communauté johannique et son histoier. La trajectoire de l'évangile de Jean aux deux premiers siècles*, by J.-D. Kaestli/J.-M. Poffet/ J. Zumstein, Le monde de la bible (1990), 135-151; "L'application de la narratologie à l'étude de l'évangile de Jean," in *La communauté johannique*, 97-120.

[497] E.g., B. Olsson, *Structure and Meaning in the Fourth Gospel*, ConBNT Series 6 (1974).

[498] K. Berger, *Exegese des Neuen Testaments. Neue Wege vom Text zur Auslegung.* Uni-Taschenbücher 658 (1977, [2]1984), 55.

[499] C. Perelman and L. Olbrechts-Tyteca, *La nouvelle rhétorique. Traité de l'argumentation* (1958) remains basic.

[500] Hesitation toward such parallels is advisable. Even the question of Paul's specific rhetorical knowledge remains open, deserving restraint in judgment (cf. above, pp. 66f.). Even less clearly does the sociological context of those who shaped and passed on the gospel tradition allow a connection with the rhetoric of the educated *(Hochrhetorik)*. Neither for the historical Jesus himself nor for the early community is there any support for such a supposition. Cf. J. Lambrecht, "Rhetorical Criticism and the New Testament," 246: "It would seem that often too much rhetorical structure is supposed to be present in certain passages of the Bible."

[501] Cf. above, pp. 122f.

# 5 The Acts of the Apostles

*Literature*

Les Actes des Apôtres. Traditions, rédaction, théologie, ed J. Kremer, BETL 48 (1979). Barrett, C.K., *Luke the Historian in Recent Study* (1961). Conzelmann, H., *Die Apostelgeschichte*, HNT 7 (²1972), *Acts of the Apostles*, Hermeneia (1987). Dibelius, M., *Aufsätze zur Apostelgeschichte*, ed. H. Greeven, FRLANT 68 (³1957), *Studies in the Acts of the Apostles* (1956). Grässer, E., "Die Apostelgeschichte in der Forschung der Gegenwart," *TRu* 26 (1960): 93-167; "Acta-Forschung seit 1960," *TRu* 41 (1976): 141-194; 259-290; 42 (1977): 1-68. Haenchen, E., "Das 'Wir' in der Apostelgeschichte und das Itinerar" (first published in 1961), in his *Gott und Mensch. Gesammelte Aufsätze* (1965), 227-264; "'We' in Acts and the Itinerary," in *The Bultmann School of Biblical Interpretation: New Directions*, ed. R.W. Funk and G. Ebeling, *JTC* 1 (1965): 65-99. Hemer, C.J., *The Book of Acts in the Setting of Hellenistic History*, ed. C.H. Gempf, WUNT 49 (1989). Plümacher, E., *Lukas als hellenistischer Schriftsteller. Studien zur Apostelgeschichte*, SUNT 9 (1972); "Lukas als griechischer Historiker," in PWSup 14 (1974): 235-264; "Apostelgeschichte," in *TRE* 3 (1978): 483-528; "Acta-Forschung 1974-1982," *TRu* 48 (1983): 1-56; 49 (1984): 105-169. Radl, W., *Paulus und Jesus im lukanischen Doppelwerk. Untersuchungen zu Parallelmotiven im Lukasevangelium und in der Apostelgeschichte*, Einleitung in die Heilige Schrift XXIII/49 (1975). Schneider, G., *Lukas, Theologe der Heilsgeschichte. Aufsätze zum lukanischen Doppelwerk*, BBB 59 (1985).

## 5.1 The relationship of Acts to Luke

*Literature*

Argyle, A.W., "The Greek of Luke and Acts," *NTS* 20 (1974): 441-445. Beck, B.E., "The Common Authorship of Luke and Acts," *NTS* 23 (1977): 346-352. Cadbury, H.J., *The Book of Acts in History* (1955). Clark, A.C., *The Acts of the Apostles* (1933=1970). Lake, K., "The Preface to Acts and the Composition of Acts," in *The Beginnings of Christianity V. Additional Notes to the Commentary*, ed K. Lake et al. (1933), 1-7. Menoud, P.H., "Remarques sur les textes de l'ascension dans Luc-Actes," in *Neutestamentliche Studien für R. Bultmann*, BZNW 21 (²1957), 148-156. Trocmé, É., *Le "livre des Actes" et l'histoire*, Études d'histoire et de philosophie religieuses 45 (1957). Wilder, A.N., "Variant Traditions of the Resurrection in Acts," *JBL* 62 (1943): 307-318.

Researchers have understood the relationship between Luke and Acts in varied ways. While there are differences between the two works, their linguistic and material resemblances and common outlook on history imply that they have a close connection and should be regarded as from the same author.[1]  This conclusion is significant for exegesis, e.g., in M. Rese's usage of Old Testament citations and motifs for interpreting Lucan Christology[2] or F.W. Horn's study of Lucan ethics.[3] But the literary-historical relationship of the two works demands further clarification.  The solution cannot consist in the attempt to separate Luke from the genre "gospel" through emphasizing its unity with Acts (cf. 5.2).

According to another interpretation, the original unity between Luke and Acts was first dissolved in the arrangement of the canon.[4]  This is evident in the tension between Luke 24:50-53 and Acts 1:1-12.  This tension can be resolved by regarding Luke 24:50-53 and Acts 1:1-5 as interpolations.  Yet both of these passages display a thoroughly Lucan style.  Nor does the textual tradition give any indication that either is a later addition.  Furthermore, ancient techniques of publication would have been overstretched to encompass Luke and Acts in one volume.[5]  Nor would the hypothesis of an interpolator explain the alleged tension between Luke 24:50-53 and Acts 1:1-12.  Lucan intention is the only satisfactory answer, regarding the two works as a unified whole.

## 5.2   The genre of Acts

*Literature*

Balch, D.L., "Acts as Hellenistic Historiography," in SBLSP 24 (1985), 429-432; "Comments on the Genre and a Political Theme of Luke-Acts: A Preliminary Comparison of Hellenistic Historians," in SBLSP 28 (1989), 343-361. Dahl, N. A., "The Story of Abraham in Luke-Acts," in *Studies in Luke-Acts. Essays presented in honor of P. Schubert,* ed. L.E. Keck *et al.* (1966), 139-158. Edwards, D.R., "The Acts of the Apostles and Chariton's Chaereas and Callirhoe. A Literary and Sociohistorical Study," Ph.D. diss., Boston University (1987). Hengel, M., *Zur urchristlichen Geschichtsschreibung* (²1984). Karris, R.J., "Windows and Mirrors: Literary Criticism and Luke's Sitz im Leben," in SBLSP 16, 1 (1979): 47-58. Perrot, C., "Les Actes des Apôtres," in *Introduction à la Bible. Éd. nouvelle III. Introduction critique au Nouveau Testament sous la direction de A. George et P. Grelot* (1976), 239-295 (esp. 255-266). Pervo, R.I., *Profit with Delight. The Literary Genre of the Acts of the Apostles* (1987); "Must Luke and Acts Belong to the Same Genre?" in SBLSP 29 (1989): 453-467. Plümacher, E., "Neues Testament und hellenistische Form. Zur literarischen Gattung der lukanischen Schriften," Theologia viatorum 14 (1977/78): 109-123; "Die Apostelgeschichte als historische Monographie," in *Les Actes des Apôtres.*

---

[1] Cf., e.g., B.E. Beck, "Common Authorship;" E. Plümacher, "Apostelgeschichte," 483f.  For another viewpoint, cf. A.W. Argyle, "The Greek;" A.C. Clark, *The Acts,* 393-408.

[2] M. Rese, *Alttestamentliche Motive in der Christologie des Lukas,* SNT 1 (1969).

[3] F.W. Horn, *Glaube und Handeln in der Theologie des Lukas,* GTA 26 (²1986).

[4] So K. Lake, "Preface," 3f.; P.H. Menoud, "Remarques;" É. Trocmé, "'Livre;'" A.M. Wilder, "Variant Traditions," 311.

[5] Cf. H.J. Cadbury, *The Book of Acts,* 138f.

*Traditions, rédaction théologie,* ed. J. Kremer, BETL 48 (1979), 457-466. Prader, S.M., "Luke-Acts and the Ancient Novel," in SBLSP 20 (1981), 269-292. Richard, E., *Acts 6:1-8:4. The Author's Method of Composition,* SBLDS 41 (1978). Robbins, V.K., "Prefaces in Greco-Roman Biography and Luke-Acts," in SBLSP 14, 2 (1978): 193-207. Schmidt, D., "The Historiography of Acts: Deuteronomistic or Hellenistic?" in SBLSP 24 (1985), 417-427. Schneemelcher, W., "Einleitung zu XV. Apostelgeschichten des 2. und 3. Jahrhunderts," in *Neutestamentliche Apokryphen in deutscher Übersetzung,* ed. Wilhelm Schneemelcher 2 (⁵1989): 71-93; "XV. Second and Third Century Acts of Apostles: Introduction," in New Testament Apocrypha 2 (1992): 75-100. Schneider, G., "Der Zweck des lukanischen Doppelwerkes" (first published in 1977), in his *Lukas, Theologe der Heilsgeschichte. Aufsätze zum lukanischen Doppelwerk,* BBB 59 (1985), 9-30. Sterling, G.E., "Luke-Acts and Apologetic Historiography," in SBLSP 28 (1989), 326-342. Talbert, C.H., *Luke and the Gnostics. An Examination of the Lukan Purpose* (1966); "The Redactional Quest for Luke the Theologian," in *Jesus and Man's Hope,* ed. D.G. Buttrick, A Perspective Book XI (1970), 171-222; *Literary Patterns, Theological Themes and the Genre of Luke-Acts,* SBLMS 20 (1974); *What is a Gospel? The Genre of the Canonical Gospels* (1977); "Once Again: Gospel Genre," in *Semeia* 43 (1988): 53-73. Thornton, C.-J., *Der Zeuge des Zeugen. Lukas als Historiker der Paulusreisen,* WUNT 56 (1991). van Unnik, W.C., "Luke's Second Book and the Rules of Hellenistic Historiography," in *Les Actes des Apôtres. Traditions, rédaction théologie,* ed. J. Kremer, BETL 48 (1979), 37-60. Weiss, J., *Ueber die Absicht und den literarischen Charakter der Apostelgeschichte* (1897).

For a long time it was the opinion of New Testament research that (alongside the Third Gospel as an example of the genre "gospel") in Acts Luke had written a work without analogies in contemporary literature.[6] Yet the prologue, Luke 1:1-4, (and the allusion to it in Acts 1:1) exhibits an acquaintance with contemporary literary and rhetorical techniques, raising the question of analogous ancient genres.

The fictitious apocryphal acts of the second and third centuries furnish no conclusive information as to the genre of canonical Acts,[7] since it remains an open question whether Luke-Acts was the model for these later works.[8]

---

[6] Cf. W.G. Kümmel, *Einleitung in das Neue Testament* (²¹1983), 132; P. Vielhauer, *Geschichte der urchristlichen Literatur* (²1978), 400. Similarly, C.J. Hemer, *The Book of Acts in the Setting of Hellenistic History,* ed. C.H. Gempf, WUNT 49 (1989), 42: "Acts (and its unique relationship with one of the Gospels) is not amenable to close comparisons." Cf. also Hemer, 412, n. 4, 92f., and 220.

[7] On the formal differenciation between Luke's Acts and the apocryphal acts cf. W. Schneemelcher, "Einleitung," and "Introduction;" E. Plümacher, "Lukas als griechischer Historiker," in PWSup 14; 263. For a different view, cf. R.I. Pervo, *Profit with Delight,* 126-131. H. Koester also has a more positive view on the relationship between Acts and apocryphal acts, *Einführung in das Neue Testament im Rahmen der Religionsgeschichte und Kulturgeschichte der hellenistischen und römischen Zeit* (1980), 484; *History and Literature of Early Christianity. Introduction to the New Testament,* 2 (1982): 51f. Cf. also D.E. Aune, *The New Testament in its Literary*

Formal analogies to the whole of Luke-Acts have been suggested. W. Radl refers to parallels in Plutarch's *Parallel Lives*.[9]   C.H. Talbert mentions analogies in the biographies of the philosophers, i.e., in the histories of philosophical schools as found in Diogenes Laertius.[10]   But most parallel biographies conclude with a comparison (cf. the comparative sections in Plutarch's *Lives*), distinguishing them from Luke-Acts.[11] The systematizing tendencies of the philosophical biographies (cf. the succession lists, which are not germane parallels to the presentation in Acts) distinguish them as well.   These preliminary observations indicate that Acts cannot fit without tensions into the context of ancient biography.

That Luke preserves the continuity of church history through a succession of witnesses among whom he includes Paul (Acts 9, 22, 26) provides some resemblance to ancient (philosophical) biography.[12]   Yet Paul is not equated with the other apostles nor expressly designated the "thirteenth witness"[13] (C. Burchard[14]), but is subordinated personally and in his mission to the Jerusalem authorities (cf. Acts 15 and 21).   That Luke makes the effort to give Paul visible status should not mislead us.   Due to the time separating them and Luke's inadequate acquaintance with Paul, his delineation shows important deficiencies compared to the historical Paul.   In understanding apostolicity and justification, Luke is close to the position of Paul's opponents.[15]

---

*Environment* (1987), 152f.: canonical Acts was the literary pattern for the later writing of the apocryphal acts.

[8] I.e., this avoids any judgment as to whether or not canonical Acts was present to the authors of the apocryphal acts.   Cf. W. Schneemelcher, "Einleitung," 78; "Introduction," 82.

[9] *Paulus und Jesus im lukanischen Doppelwerk,* 352f.

[10] C.H. Talbert, *Literary Patterns,* 125-140; cf. pp. 130f. for other comparable examples. See also G. Schneider, "Der Zweck," 27-30. V.K. Robbins refers to "didactic biography" on the grounds of the prologue to the two volume work.

[11] Cf. E. Plümacher, "Neues Testament und hellenistische Form," 111.

[12] As C.H. Talbert affirms in *What is a Gospel?* and in "Once Again: Gospel Genre," 61: "Luke-Acts shares with certain biographies a concern to say where the true tradition is in the present...."

[13] Cf. , on the contrary, P. Vielhauer, "Zum 'Paulinismus' der Apostelgeschichte" (first published in 1950/51), in his *Aufsätze zum Neuen Testament,* Theologische Bücherei 31 (1965), 9-27. [Note that footnotes 13 and 14 are interchanged from their position in the German text.]

[14] C. Burchard, *Der dreizehnte Zeuge. Traditions- und kompositionsgeschichtliche Untersuchungen zu Lukas' Darstellung der Frühzeit des Paulus,* FRLANT 103 (1970).

[15] So H. Koester, "ΓΝΩΜΑΙ ΔΙΑΦΟΡΟΙ. Ursprung und Wesen der Mannigfaltigkeit in der Geschichte des frühen Christentums" (first published in 1968), now in H. Koester and J.M. Robinson, *Entwicklungslinien durch die Welt des frühen Christentums* (1971), 107-146, 142f.; "ΓΝΩΜΑΙ ΔΙΑΦΟΡΟΙ. The Origin and Nature of Diversification in the History of Early Christianity," in Koester and Robinson, *Trajectories through Early Christianity* (1971), 114-157, 153.

Even if there are connections to "historical apologetics,"[16] these occasional apologetic tendencies[17] do not have a determining role. That is given to defining a Christian self-understanding, reflected in the beginnings of the church. Luke's conception is recognizable in the continuing, step-by-step detachment of Christianity from Judaism. Acts 1:8 expresses this programmatically, where through the leading of the Spirit the gospel is disseminated by its witnesses from Jerusalem to the ends of the earth, i.e., Rome. Neither the battle against Gnostic heretics[18] nor opposition to an extreme form of Paulinism or pre-Marcionism[19] located in northern Asia Minor (cf. Acts 16:16ff) can be persuasively shown as influential. Reference to the danger of heresy in Acts 20:29f. is very general and cannot be restricted to a specific heretical group, especially since no new ideas are presented as opposed to the continuity of teaching.[20] The continuity of tradition affirmed here is ecclesiastically rather than dogmatically motivated.

But the reference to Hellenistic tendencies is significant.[21] Luke's primary objective is the presentation of history rather than an invented, but historically possible, story (as in the historical romances[22]).

C. Perrot's characterizing Luke-Acts as "religious history" which stood in a "succession of biblical histories and historical reminiscences known in the synagogues of the first century" agrees with this claim to historicity.[23] But this does not imply a Palestinian and Jewish backdrop. What have been claimed as

---

[16] E.g., G.E. Sterling, "Luke-Acts and Apolgetic Historiography," in SBLSP 28 (1989), 326-342. Cf. also K. Berger *ANRW* II 25.2, 1281.

[17] Cf., e.g., J. Weiss, *Absicht*, 56: "apologia of the Christian religion ... against Jewish attacks."

[18] C.H. Talbert, *Luke and the Gnostics;* "The Redactional Quest;" and *Literary Patterns, passim.* Cf. also G. Klein, *Die zwölf Apostel. Ursprung und Gestalt einer Idee,* FRLANT 77 (1961), 213f; J. Roloff, *Die Apostelgeschichte,* NTD 5 ([17(1)]1981), 303.

[19] W. Schmithals, *Die Apostelgeschichte des Lukas,* Zürcher Bibelkommentar. Neues Testament 3.2 (1982), 12f.; "Die Berichte der Apostelgeschichte über die Bekehrung des Paulus und die 'Tendenz' des Lukas," *Theologia viatorum* 14 (1977/78): 145-165, 160-163. For a critical reaction, cf. E. Plümacher, "Acta-Forschung 1974-1982," *TRu* 48 (1983): 54f.

[20] Against J. Roloff, *Die Apostelgeschichte,* NTD 5 ([17(1)]1981), on Acts 20:20.

[21] Already in W. Radl, *Paulus und Jesus im lukanischen Doppelwerk* (1975) and in C.H. Talbert. Cf. also C.K. Barrett, *Luke the Historian in Recent Study* (1961), 15 ("Hellenistic romance"); and H. Koester in *IDBSup,* 555 and *Einführung,* 755, *Introduction,* 2:316ff.

[22] S.M. Praeder, "Luke-Acts and the Ancient Novel," 269, includes it in the "narrative genres of Greco-Roman antiquity" as an "ancient novel." D.R. Edwards, "Acts of the Apostles," refers to parallels to the structure and literary style of Romans. But R.I. Pervo, *Profit with Delight,* calls it a "historical novel," as does R.J. Karris, "Windows and Mirrors," 53. For a critique, cf. D.E. Aune, *Literary Environment,* 80. P. Gilbert, "L'invention d'un genre littéraire," Lumière et Vie 30 (numbers 153-154, 1981): 19-33, also defends historical interest, and regards Luke as the founder of Christian hagiography. This definition of genre, however, is opposed by the lack of any interest in individual "heroes" in Acts. Luke concentrates not on persons but on an already sketched out conception of history.

[23] C. Perrot, "Les Actes," 260, with reference to the pseudophilonic *antiquitates biblicae.*

Lucan Semitisms[24] are more probably Septuagintalisms[25] than evidence for a Jewish form of spoken Greek.[26] The possible influence of a biblical style of writing history[27] should not be overrated.

It is much more probable that Luke was influenced by Hellenistic conventions and that he knew his way around in the historiographical praxis of his era.[28] E. Plümacher demonstrates this from the manner in which the speeches of Acts fit into the history of literature,[29] Luke's imitation of the Septuagint, his archaic style of speech, his summaries, etc. (cf. 5.5[30]).

---

[24] Cf., e.g., M. Wilcox, *The Semitisms of Acts* (1965). For a different viewpoint, cf. D.L. Mealand, "Hellenistic Historians and the Style of Acts," *ZNW* 82 (1991): 42-66. Mealand shows that some of the expressions claimed as Semitisms (e.g., ἀναστάς + the finite verb, Acts 1:15 and frequently) are found in literary Koine (in Polybius).

[25] Cf., among others, M. Silva, "Semantic Borrowing in the New Testament," *NTS* 22 (1976): 104-110, 108. [Note that footnotes 25 and 26 are interchanged from their position in the German text.]

[26] So N. Turner, "The Relation of Luke I and II to Hebraic Sources and to the Rest of Luke-Acts," *NTS* 2 (1955/56): 100-109.

[27] N.A. Dahl, "The Story of Abraham in Luke-Acts," 152: "The model for his conception of sacred history as a series of predictions and event Luke found, no doubt, in the historical books of Holy Scripture. ... Luke is imitating biblical historiography." Dahl thereby maintains that this occurs in the context of Hellenistic conventions. D. Schmidt, "The Historiography of Acts," refers especially to Deuteronomistic historiography: "...the underlying historiography of Acts is derived from the deuteronomistic historiography." For a critical reaction cf. D.L. Balch, "Acts as Hellenistic Historiography." On Deuteronomistic historiography, cf. M. Noth, *Überlieferungsgeschichtliche Studien. I. Die sammelnden und bearbeitenden Geschichtswerke im Alten Testament*, Schriften der Königsberger Gelehrten Gesellschaft, Geisteswissenschaftliche Klasse 18,2 (1943, [4]1973), *The Deuteronomistic History* (1981); A. Jepsen, *Die Quellen des Königsbuches* (1953, [2]1956); cf. also W. Roth, "Deuteronomistisches Geschichtswerk/Deuteronomistische Schule," in *TRE* 8 (1981): 543-552 (with bibliography); M. Weippert, "Das deuteronomistische Geschichtswerk," *TRu* 50 (1985): 213-249 (with bibliography).

[28] E. Plümacher, "Acta-Forschung 1974-1982," *TRu* 49 (1984): 112, and his *Lukas als hellenistischer Schriftsteller, passim*. For a different viewpoint, cf. J. Wehnert, *Die Wir-Passagen der Apostelgeschichte. Ein lukanisches Stilmittel aus jüdischer Tradition*, GTA 40 (1989), 199 and frequently. On Hellenistic historiography, cf. D.E. Aune, The New Testament in its Literary Environment (1987), 80-96 and 112-114 (bibliography); F. Jacoby, "Über die Entwicklung der griechischen Historiographie und den Plan einer neuen Sammlung der griechischen Historikerfragmente," *Klio* 9 (1909): 80-123; A. Momigliano, "Greek History," *History and Theory* 17 (1978): 1-28; K. Meister, Die griechische Geschichtsschreibung. Von den Anfängen bis zum Ende des Hellenismus (1990) [on Hellenistic historiography, 80ff.]. Lucian the Satirist's "instructional letter" on ΠΩΣ ΔΕΙ ΙΣΤΟΡΙΑΝ ΣΥΓΓΡΑΦΕΙΝ ("How History Should be Written") is informative (cf. K. Wegenast, "Lukianos," in *Der kleine Pauly* 3 (1969): 772-777, 775; for Lucian's text and an English translation, cf. LCL VI, 2-73). Thinking back to Thucydides, Lucian sets himself against the encomiastic historiography of his time.

[29] To be read as a characteristic component of Hellenistic historiography. Cf. also Dibelius, "Die Reden der Apostelgeschichte und die antike Geschichtsschreibung"

Irrespective of historical interest, describing the genre (of Luke as well as Acts) as "general history"[31] or "political historiography"[32] demands caution. It is more correct to say that the author, in light of a (salvation-) historical concept, has written a "historical monograph,"[33] while never disavowing the theological task (see above). The secondary title πράξεις ἀποστόλων, attached to Acts in the second century, alludes to the πράξεις or *res gestae* of persons from antiquity, and thereby in general to ancient historiography. But this provides no closer definition of genre.

Though antiquity recognized doubts about historical tradition, Luke intends no objective history (cf. Thucydides and Tacitus). Luke gives preference to confirming the tradition rather than to critical history. The aim is the believers' assurance (ἀσφάλεια). Luke aims for certainty with respect to what Christians believe, what has happened in history as a basis for their faith, and what is significant for faith's claim to truth.

Luke placed both works, Gospel and Acts, in a single literary association (cf. the reference back to the Gospel as "the first book" [πρῶτος λόγος] in Acts 1:1). His conception of the history of salvation encompasses the whole of Luke and Acts. This is also evident in his inserting the life of Jesus into secular history (cf. Luke 2:1-2 and 3:1-2). Yet interpretation must take account of the fact that the first volume of Luke's historical work was consciously formulated as a gospel.[34] While E. Plümacher strives to apply the category "historical monograph" to both Luke and Acts,[35] this genre identifies Luke only with difficulty. On the contrary, we should take note of the differences between biography and history.[36] While Acts (just as secular historical monographs, e.g., Sallust on Catiline or Jugurtha) places

---

(first published in 1949), in *Aufsätze zur Apostelgeschichte*, ed. H. Greeven, FRLANT 68 (³1957), esp. 120f.; "The Speeches in Acts and Ancient Historiography," *Studies in the Acts of the Apostles* (1956), esp. 138f.; and O. Stählin, "Christliche Schriftsteller," in *Geschichte der griechischen Litteratur. Die nachklassische Periode der griechischen Litteratur von 100 bis 530 nach Christus*, HAW VII/2.2, ⁶1924 (= reprint 1961), 1179.

[30] Cf. also W.C. van Unnik, "Luke's Second Book."

[31] So D.E. Aune, *Literary Environment*, 77, 138-141.

[32] D. L. Balch, "Acts as Hellenistic Historiography." But not for W.C. van Unnik, who maintains that the goal of the author was "decidedly *not political history*."

[33] E. Plümacher, "Apostelgeschichte," in *TRE* 3 (1978): 515 and "Die Apostelgeschichte als historische Monographie," in *Les Actes des Apôtres. Traditions, rédaction théologie*, ed. J. Kremer, BETL 48 (1979), 457-466.; H. Conzelmann, *Die Apostelgeschichte*, HNT 7 (²1972); *Acts of the Apostles*, Hermeneia (1978); M. Hengel, *Zur urchristliche Geschichtsschreibung*, 37; E. Richard, *Acts 6:1-8:4*, 309f.; A. Weiser, *Die Apostelgeschichte*, Ökumenischer Taschenbuchkommentar zum Neuen Testament 5/1 (1981, ²1989), 31. C.J. Thornton, *Der Zeuge des Zeugen*, also refers to Hellenistic historiography; Luke is a subjective, tragic, historian.

[34] See above, p. 101.

[35] "Neues Testament und hellenistische Form," 120; "Die Apostelgeschichte als historische Monographie," 463; "Apostelgeschichte," *TRE* 3 (1978): 515: "However it is substantially more difficult to assign the Lucan work as a whole to an exact location within the traditions of Hellenistic historiography."

[36] See above, p. 112.

persons in the foreground, this is in connection with the theological theme which underlies its conception of historiography (cf. Acts 1:8[37]). Luke's Gospel centers on Jesus in a different way. But Luke and Acts are connected by a salvation-historical design, which also characterizes the other Synoptics, though with a different expression and to a different extent. Mark and Matthew might have written a history of the apostles on the bases of their gospels. Specific to Luke is arranging the history of salvation in periods. The seams which, according to the Lucan conception, mark the era of Jesus as the "center of time" are not clearly determinable. (Is the conclusion the resurrection of Jesus, his ascension, or Pentecost? Is the beginning after John the Baptist? Does the "since then" [ἀπὸ τότε] of Luke 16:16 include John or not?[38]) Yet it is clear that Luke has compiled an exciting *historical* work consisting for one part of the Gospel with its biographical analogies and for the other part of Acts, written with clear theological motivation and objectives by analogy to the historical monographs.[39] Luke-Acts portrays *theological* historiography insofar as the author wants to depict the sort of qualified history in which the influences of the eschaton are verifiable.

## 5.3 The Sources of Acts

*Literature:*

Benoit, P., "La deuxième visite de Saint Paul à Jérusalem," Bib 40 (1959): 778-792. Borse, U., "Lukanische Komposition im Umfeld der ersten Missionsreise," in *Studien zum Neuen Testament und seiner Umwelt,* Serie A 11 (1986): 169-194. Bultmann, R., "Zur Frage nach den Quellen der Apostelgeschichte" (first published in 1959), in his *Exegetica. Aufsätze zur Erforschung des Neuen Testaments,* ed. E. Dinkler (1967), 412-423. Cadbury, H.J., *The Style and Literary Method of Luke.* HTS 6 (1920). Dibelius, M., "Paulus auf dem Areopag" (first published in 1939), in his *Aufsätze zur Apostelgeschichte,* ed. H. Greeven, FRLANT 68 ($^3$1957), 29-70, "Paul on the Areopagus," *Studies in the Acts of the Apostles* (1956), 26-77; "Der erste christliche Historiker" (first published in 1948), in *Aufsätze* 108-119, "The First Christian Historian," in *Studies* 123-137; "Die Apostelgeschichte im Rahmen der urchristlichen Literaturgeschichte," in *Aufsätze* 163-174, "The Acts of the Apostles in the Setting of the History of Early Christian Literature," in *Studies* 192-206. Dupont, J., *Les sources du Livre des Actes. État de la question* (1960). (v.) Harnack, A., *Lukas der Arzt. Der Verfasser des dritten Evangeliums und der Apostelgeschichte. Eine Untersuchung zur Geschichte der Fixiering der*

---

[37] On differentiating between historical monograph and biography, cf. C.H., Talbert, "Once Again: Gospel Genre," 55f.

[38] Cf. H. Conzelmann, Conzelmann, H., *Die Mitte der Zeit. Studien zur Theologie des Lukas,* BHT 17 ($^5$1964, $^6$1977), 12-21, esp. 16-18; *The Theology of St. Luke* (1960), 18-27, esp. 22-24.

[39] Against a common "genre" for Acts and Luke (D.E. Aune, *Literary Environment,* 77, 80), cf. R.I. Pervo, "Must Luke and Acts Belong to the Same Genre?" and J. Roloff, "Neutestamentliche Einleitungswissenschaft. Tendenzen und Entwicklungen," *TRu* 55 (1990): 399.

*urchristlichen Überlieferung,* Beiträge zur Einleitung in das Neue Testament 3 (1908); *Die Apostelgeschichte,* Beiträge zur Einleitung in das Neue Testament 3 (1908). Jeremias, J., "Untersuchungen zum Quellenproblem der Apostelgeschichte" (first published in 1937), in his *Abba. Studien zur neutestamentlichen Theologie und Zeitgeschichte* (1966), 238-255. Schille, G., "Die Leistung des Lukas in der Apostelgeschichte," *Theologische Versuche* 7 (1976): 91-106.

Literary-critical questions furnish an important theme of research on Acts. This becomes especially significant if Luke is regarded not as an eyewitness but as an author dependent on sources. Critical research largely recognizes that the author of Luke-Acts cannot be equated with Luke the Physician[40] nor with one of the other eyewitnesses and companions of Paul; nor is this author[41] identical with whoever wrote the Pastorals.[42]

While the idea of an earlier version has not been widely accepted,[43] the suggestion of an Antiochene source[44] and an earlier account of the journeys of Paul[45] has attained status among researchers.

---

[40] As did the ancient Christian tradition on the basis of Col 4:14; 2 Tim 4:11; Phlm 24: e.g., Irenaeus *adv. haer.* III,10,1; 14,1; the Canon Muratori 2f.. Cf. also A. Harnack, *Lukas,* passim; M. Dibelius, "Historiker," 118f., "Historian," 136f., and frequently elsewhere. This viewpoint is considered again by C.J. Hemer, *The Book of Acts in the Setting of Hellenistic History,* ed. C.H. Gempf, WUNT 49 (1989). C.J. Cadbury decisively contradicted the theory that the author used a medical vocabulary in *Style and Literary Method* 39-64, esp. 50f. Cf. also E. Plümacher, "Lukas als griechischer Historiker," in PWSup 14 (1974): 236f.

[41] On authorship cf. E. Plümacher, "Apostelgeschichte," *TRE* 3 (1978): 521. [Note 42 in the German text.]

[42] So, e.g., S.G. Wilson, "The Portrait of Paul in Acts and the Pastorals," SBLSP 10 (1976): 397-411. Cf. also C.F.D. Moule, "The Problem of the Pastorals: A Reappraisal," *BJRL* 47 (1965): 430-452, where he sees Luke as the author of the Pastorals and as the first collector of the Pauline letters. Cf. also A. Strobel, "Schreiben des Lukas? Zum sprachlichen Problem der Pastoralbriefe," *NTS* 15 (1968/69): 191-210. Against this viewpoint, cf., e.g., N. Brox, "Lukas als Verfasser der Pastoralbriefe," JAC 13 (1970): 62-77; W. Schenk, "Die Pastoralbriefe in der neueren Forschung," in ANRW II.25.4 (1987), 3404-3438, 3421-3423. [Note 41 in the German text.]

[43] Recently again in U. Borse, "Lukanische Komposition."

[44] Cf. A. v. Harnack, *Apostelgeschichte,* 130-158. Harnack assumed an Antioch-Jerusalem source, a Caesarea-Jerusalem source, and as a third source an earlier document (*Vorlage*) comprising legendary materials.

[45] A "we-source," which should be distinguished from the acceptance of an "itinerary." On source theories for Acts, cf. also J. Dupont, *Les sources;* E. Grässer, "Die Apostelgeschichte in der Forschung der Gegenwart," *TRu* 26 (1960): 123ff.; "Acta-Forschung seit 1960," *TRu* 41 (1976): 186-194; E. Plümacher, "Acta-Forschung 1974-1982," *TRu* 49 (1984): 120-138; "Apostelgeschichte," in *TRE* 3 (1978): 491-501; G. Schneider, *Die Apostelgeschichte,* HTKNT 5/1 (1980), 82-103. Schneider also occasionally lists further bibliography for the source theories he discusses.

### 5.3.1  The Question of an "Antiochene Source"

*Literature*

Hahn, F., "Zum Problem der antiochenischen Quelle in der Apostelgeschichte," in *Rudolf Bultmanns Werk und Wirkung*, ed. B. Jaspert (1984), 316-331. Jewett, R., *Paulus-Chronologie. Ein Versuch* (1982).

Several have sought, with various results, to show an *Antiochene Source* in Acts 6-15.[46]  Such attempts are based on the methodological criterion [presupposition] that places and persons involved are originally connected with traditions. Yet the genre is variously defined as either a report[47] or a chronicle.[48] The presumed beginning of the source has not been reconstructed with any certainty. The reconstruction of the source has also been criticized for imprecise methodology.[49]

### 5.3.2  The Hypothesis of a "We Source"

*Literature*

Plümacher, E., "Wirklichkeitserfahrung und Geschichtsbeschreibung bei Lukas. Erwägungen zu den Wir-Stücken der Apostelgeschichte," *ZNW* 68 (1977): 2-22. Robbins, V.K., "The We-Passages in Acts and Ancient Sea Voyages," *BR* 20 (1975): 5-18; "By Land and by Sea: A Study in Acts 13-28m" SBLSP 10 (1976): 381-396. Schmidt, D.D., "Syntactical Style in the 'We'-Sections of Acts: How Lucan Is It?" SBLSP 28 (1989): 300-308. Wehnert, J., *Die Wir-Passagen der Apostelgeschichte. Ein lukanisches Stilmittel aus jüdischer Tradition,* GTA 40 (1989).

The attempt to reconstruct a We-source proceeds on the basis of style criticism. The We-accounts in the second part of Acts begin without introduction and end abruptly (16:10-17; 20:5-8 and 13-18; 21:1-18; 27:1-28:16). Yet the

---

[46] E.g., A. v. Harnack, *Apostelgeschichte*, 130-158; Bultmann, R., "Zur Frage nach den Quellen der Apostelgeschichte" (first published in 1959), in his *Exegetica. Aufsätze zur Erforschung des Neuen Testaments*, ed. E. Dinkler (1967), 412-423, 421-423; J. Jeremias, "Untersuchungen zum Quellenproblem der Apostelgeschichte" (first published in 1937), in his *Abba. Studien zur neutestamentlichen Theologie und Zeitgeschichte* (1966), 238-255; R. Jewett, *Paulus-Chronologie,* 28. The effort is now taken up again by F. Hahn, "Zum Problem," 327f., who includes Acts 6:1-6; 6:8-8:4; 11:19-26; and 13:1-14:27 in his Antiochene source. Later, but still before Luke, 8:5-13 and 26-40 were added.

[47] Hahn, "Zum Problem," 330.

[48] E. Haenchen, *Die Apostelgeschichte*, MeyerK 3 ([7(16)]1977), 95; *The Acts of the Apostles,* Hermeneia (1971), 83f.

[49] Cf. E. Plümacher, "Apostelgeschichte," *TRE* 3 (1978): 293f.

lexical studies of A. von Harnack[50] and the examination of syntactical style by D.D. Schmidt show that the We-passages present shared neither characteristics nor remarkable particularities which cannot be found elsewhere in Acts, so that these materials cannot be distinguished from the remainder of Acts. The We-passages should instead be understood as an instrument of Lucan style.[51]

J. Wehnert also rejects a We-source, and relegates these texts to the redactional activity of Luke. They alternate with "They-passages" from the same hand and are "instruments of Lucan style from the Jewish tradition."[52] While this rightly emphasizes Luke's forceful redactional activity, in tension with this Wehnert sees behind these passages freely adapted oral "narrative reports of a Pauline companion."[53]

The postulated We-source and the hypothesis of an eyewitness author which usually accompanies it are often connected with a confidence in historical accuracy, which accordingly is not to be presupposed for Acts.[54]

### 5.3.3   The Itinerary

*Literature*

Kragerud, A., "Itinerariet i Apostlenes gjerninger," *Norsk teologisk tidsskrift* 56 (1955): 249-272. Larsson, E., "'Vi'-passager och itinerar. Om traditionsunderlaget för Apg.s skildring av Paulus' missionsresor," *SEÅ* 51/52 (1986/87): 127-136. Lüdemann, G., *Das frühe Christentum nach den Traditionen der Apostelgeschichte. Ein Kommentar* (1987). Reumann, J., "The Itinerary as Form in Classical Literature and the Acts of the Apostles," in *To Touch the Text. Biblical and related Studies in Honor of J.A. Fitzmyer,* ed. M. Horgan and P.J. Kobelski (1989), 335-357. Schille, G., "Die Fragwürdigkeit eines Itinerars der Paulusreisen," *TLZ* 84 (1959): 165-174. Vielhauer, P., Review of H. Conzelmann, *Die Apostelgeschichte,* HNT 7, in *Göttingische gelehrte Anzeigen* 221 (1969): 1-19.

In place of previous theories, the possibility of Acts' author having a written *itinerary of the Pauline journeys* is often mentioned.[55]

---

[50] A. V. Harnack, *Lukas der Arzt. Der Verfasser des dritten Evangeliums und der Apostelgeschichte. Eine Untersuchung zur Geschichte der Fixierung der urchristlichen Überlieferung,* Beiträge zur Einleitung in das Neue Testament 3 (1908), 19ff.

[51] E. Plümacher, "Wirklichkeitserfahrung,." According to V.K. Robbins "We" is a stylistic feature of sea voyage accounts ("The We-Passages," 17; "By Land and by Sea," 382-387). D.E. Aune reacts critically to this position, and cites Polybius 36.12 to support the indication of an eyewitness account (*Literary Environment,* 124).

[52] *Die Wir-Passagen,* 197-200, cf. also 184-188.

[53] *Die Wir-Passagen,* 195.

[54] This remains valid against the tendency, now observed to be gaining strength, to rely on Acts' descriptions for relevant and dependable historical information; as, e.g., in C.J. Hemer, *The Book of Acts in the Setting of Hellenistic History,* ed. C.H. Gempf, WUNT 49 (1989), *passim.*

[55] P. Vielhauer, *Geschichte der urchristlichen Literatur* ($^2$1978), 388-390; review of Conzelmann's *Apostelgeschichte,* 6-12; G. Lüdemann, *Das Frühe Christentum,* 28

This hypothesis was founded by M. Dibelius, who expressly opposed interpreting the We-passages on literary-critical grounds as a We-source (cf. 5.3.2).[56] He assigned these to a source which underlay the regularly reappearing notes about stopping places, hosts, preaching and its results, the founding of churches, conflicts, and voluntary or coerced departures in the central portion of Acts.[57] Dibelius explained the *Sitz im Leben* of this account with reference to practical needs, "in making the same trip again, that they might find the way and the former hosts."[58] Thus Dibelius opposed referring such units to local traditions of individual communities, since these texts were "not colorful enough" for that.[59]

Yet significant arguments were also set forth against the hypothesis of an itinerary. The practical needs which Dibelius made responsible for the itinerary are not convincing.[60] And this itinerary is unique in comparison with ancient travel accounts. Since we have no satisfactory answer to the question of *Sitz im Leben* or the genre of the posited oral or written itinerary, its very existence must therefore remain questionable.[61]

According to W. Schmithals,[62] Luke has at his disposal a "Paul source" for Acts 13-28. Despite its brevity, that source provides the narrative framework for this section. Its "(not insignificant) historical character" is compared with the Pastorals. This takes into account the formulations of earlier literary criticism to the extent that, on one hand, the itinerary is assigned to that source, and, on the other hand, it is related to the "We-passages." [63] Beyond this source, Schmithals regards most of the material as from the author of Acts.[64] Schmithals ascribes the source to the Pauline school,[65] and to

---

(with important enlargements). Against the itinerary stand H. Connzelmann, *Die Apostelgeschichte*, HNT 7, 6f.; G. Schille, "Die Fragwürdigkeit," and *Die Apostelgeschichte des Lukas*, THKNT 5 (³1989), 4f.; E. Haenchen, "Das 'Wir' in der Apostelgeschichte und das Itinerar" (first published in 1961), in his *Gott und Mensch. Gesammelte Aufsätze* (1965), 227-264; "'We' in Acts and the Itinerary," in *The Bultmann School of Biblical Interpretation: New Directions*, ed. R.W. Funk and G. Ebeling, *JTC* 1 (1965): 65-99.

[56] Dibelius, "Paulus auf dem Areopag" (first published in 1939), in his *Aufsätze zur Apostelgeschichte*, ed. H. Greeven, FRLANT 68 (³1957), 64f., "Paul on the Areopagus," *Studies in the Acts of the Apostles* (1956), 69f.; cf. also his "Die Apostelgeschichte im Rahmen der urchristlichen Literaturgeschichte," in *Aufsätze* 170, "The Acts of the Apostles in the Setting of the History of Early Christian Literature," in *Studies* 199f.

[57] "Paulus," 64; "Paul," 69f.

[58] Dibelius, "Der erste christliche Historiker" (first published in 1948), in *Aufsätze* 110, "The First Christian Historian," in *Studies* 125f.

[59] "Paulus," 64; "Paul," 69f.

[60] The thesis of A. Kragerud, according to which the itinerary consisted of notes for a mission report about genuine communities, is no more helpful.

[61] For a critique, cf. E. Plümacher, "Apostelgeschichte," in *TRE* 3 (1978): 495.

[62] W. Schmithals, *Die Apostelgeschichte des Lukas*, Zürcher Bibelkommentar. Neues Testament 3.2 (1982).

[63] On the status of the sources presumed by W. Schmithals, cf. E. Plümacher, "Acta-Forschung 1974-1982," *TRu* 49 (1984): 125f.

[64] Schmithals, *Die Apostelgeschichte*, 16.

[65] *Die Apostelgeschichte*, 143.

someone close to the author of the Pastorals.[66]   While admitting the difficulty of reconstructing this source, given Luke's editing, Schmithals connects it with his historical hypotheses.   If vis à vis the idea of a link to the Pauline school,[67] an antiheretical alignment for Acts suggests special reservation,[68] the genre and *Sitz im Leben* of this source remain questionable and accepting it problematical.

### 5.3.4   Luke as Author and Redactor

Instead of attempting to reconstruct additional sources of Acts we should evaluate the compositional–or better the redactional–work of Luke,[69] which unified the circulating written or oral (community-) traditions (e.g., pre-Lucan traditional about Paul).   The classical commentaries of E. Haenchen and H. Conzelmann are marked by a compositional approach.[70] Here, with respect to Acts, Luke can count as "an author of rank."[71]

One cannot refer to the Gospel in arguing against Luke's pronounced redactional activity in Acts.[72] Source material for the Gospel was shaped by its history into determined forms.   Yet the hand of a redactor is even recognizable in the Gospel.

### *Excursus:* Luke and the Pauline Letters

*Literature*

Aejmelaeus, L., *Die Rezeption der Paulusbriefe in der Miletrede (Apg 20:18-35),* Annales Academicae Scientarum Fennicae B. 232 (1987).   Enslin, M.S., "Once Again, Luke and Paul," *ZNW* 61 (1970): 253-271.   Luz, U., "Rechtfertigung bei den Paulusschülern," in *Rechtfertigung. Festschrift E. Käsemann,* ed. J. Friedrich, *et al.* (1976), 365-383.   Müller, P.-G., "Der 'Paulinismus' in der

---

[66] *Die Apostelgeschichte,* 190f.

[67] See above, p. 83.

[68] See above, p. 188.

[69] Cf. M. Dibelius as early as "Zur Formgeschichte des Neuen Testaments (ausserhalb der Evangelien)," *TRu* 3 (1931): 233ff.

[70] So also G. Schille, *Die Apostelgeschichte des Lukas,* THKNT 5 (³1989), 5. Yet R. Pesch again represents another approach in his *Die Apostelgeschichte,* EKKNT V/1 (1980), 45: "It is fundamental to understand that the depiction of Acts is based on sources, even there where they have been so thoroughly reworked that their contour is no longer recognizable." Cf. also P. Benoit, "La deuxième visite de Saint Paul à Jérusalem," Bib 40 (1959), who restricts the "authorial" activity of Luke almost only to redactional rearrangements (779f., 788ff.); and others.

[71] E. Haenchen, "Das 'Wir' in der Apostelgeschichte und das Itinerar" (first published in 1961), in his *Gott und Mensch. Gesammelte Aufsätze* (1965), 256; "'We' in Acts and the Itinerary," in *The Bultmann School of Biblical Interpretation: New Directions,* ed. R.W. Funk and G. Ebeling, *JTC* 1 (1965): 91.

[72] Against J. Jeremias, "Untersuchungen zum Quellenproblem der Apostelgeschichte" (first published in 1937), in his *Abba. Studien zur neutestamentlichen Theologie und Zeitgeschichte* (1966), 253.

Apostelgeschichte. Ein forschungsgeschichtlicher Überblick," in *Paulus in den neutestamentlichen Spätschriften. Zur Paulusrezeption im Neuen Testament,* ed. K. Kertelge, QD 89, 157-201. Schenk, W., "Luke as Reader of Paul: Observations on his Reception," in *Intertextuality in Biblical Writings.* Festschrift B. van Iersel, ed S. Draisma (1989), 127-139. Walker, W.O., "Acts and the Pauline Corpus Reconsidered," JSNT 24 (1985): 3-23.

The negative answer to the question as to whether the author of Luke-Acts was a companion of Paul, and awareness of the distance between the apostle as presented in Acts and the historical Paul, indicates that the author cannot be a disciple of Paul (cf. 3.5). Did the author know and use the Pauline letters in describing Paul? Knowing them would not rule out conscious criticism and alteration.[73]

Such a knowledge is not easily substantiated even where Luke alludes to data also offered by Paul[74] (the apostolic convention of Galatians 2 is without conditions; that of Acts 15 publishes the apostolic decrees, which are probably later, from the time when James was influential in the Jerusalem church). There are also decisive theological differences. Luke is unaware of the problem of Law as Paul dealt with it. Instead he numbers Paul among Jews faithful to the Law (e.g., Acts 21:26; cf. also the description of Timothy's circumcision in Acts 16:3 compared to Galatians 2:3, 6:12ff., etc.). Luke's assimilating a doctrine of justification such as was characteristic of the later Paul is very dubious.[75] Thus, despite the analysis of

---

[73] On the problem of the so-called "Paulinism" of Acts, cf. fht survey of research by P.-G. Müller in QD 89.

[74] For a different viewpoint, cf. L. Aejmelaeus, *Die Rezeption;* G. Klein, *Die zwölf Apostel. Ursprung und Gestalt einer Idee,* FRLANT 77 (1961), 189ff.; M.S. Enslin, "Luke and Paul;" A. Lindemann, *Paulus im ältesten Christentum. Das Bild des Apostels und die Rezeption der paulinischen Theologie in der frühchristlichen Literatur bis Marcion,* BHT 58 (1979), 171; W.O. Walker, "Acts and the Pauline Corpus Reconsidered."

[75] U. Luz, "Rechtfertigung" 366, with reference to Acts 13:38f, thinks that for Luke "obviously the theory of justification was the most important characteristic of Pauline theology." P. Vielhauer, "Zum 'Paulinismus' der Apostelgeschichte" (first published in 1950/51), in his *Aufsätze zum Neuen Testament,* Theologische Bücherei 31 (1965), 18, also maintains that "Acts allows Paul to speak in his own genuine terminology," with the restriction that Luke does not know "its central significance or absolute importance." Yet Acts 13 raises a series of questions. Do the words δικαιόω, νόμος, and πιστεύειν contain Paul's understanding of justification, or reflect a weaker and secondary understanding from the Lucan community? The expression ἄφεσις (τῶν) ἁμαρτιῶν, identified with justification, is found in Acts also in Peter's sermons (2:38; 5:31; 10:43; cf. also 26:18, Jesus' commission to Paul; the proclamation of repentance for the forgiveness of sins in the understanding of Luke is an essential component of apostolic preaching, cf. Luke 24:47) yet is never found in Paul (but in the deutero-Pauline Eph 1:7 and Col 1:14; cf. also Hebrews 9:22 [used absolutely] and 10:18). In Luke's understanding, humanity is called to repentance, proclaimed in light of the eschatological claim of Christ whose messiahship is evidenced in his sufferings and resurrection (cf. Acts 2:29-31, 4:2, 33, etc.). The cross and resurrection are not themselves saving events, so that F.W. Horn, *Glaube und Handeln in der Theologie des*

W. Schenk[76] on Luke's Gospel,[77] the evidence does not support the author's knowing Paul's letters.[78]

## 5.4   The Traditions of Acts

*Literature*

Dibelius, M., "Stilkritisches zur Apostelgeschichte" (first published in 1923), in his *Aufsätze zur Apostelgeschichte,* ed. H. Greeven, FRLANT 68 (³1957), 9-28; "Style Criticism of the Book of Acts," *Studies in the Acts of the Apostles* (1956), 1-25.  Haenchen, E., "Tradition und Komposition in der Apostelgeschichte" (first published in 1955), in his *Gott und Mensch. Gesammelte Aufsätze* (1965), 206-226.   Hahn, F., "Zum Problem der antiochenischen Quelle in der Apostelgeschichte," in *Rudopf Bultmanns Werk und Wirkung,* ed. B. Jaspert (1984), 316-331.  Jervell, J., "Paul in the Acts of the Apostles. Tradition, History, Theology," in *Les Actes des Apôtres. Traditions, rédaction, théologie,* ed J. Kremer, BETL 48 (1979), 297-306.  Neirynck, F., "The Miracle Stories in the Acts of the Apostles. An Introduction," in *Les Actes des Apôtres. Traditions, rédaction, théologie,* ed J. Kremer, BETL 48 (1979), 169-213.  Strecker, G., "Die sogannante Zweite Jerusalmreise des Paulus (Acts 11, 27-30)" (first published in 1962), now in his *Eschaton und Historie. Aufsätze* (1979), 132-141.  Stolle, V., *Der Zeuge als Angeklagter: Untersuchungen zum Paulusbild des Lukas,* BWANT 102 (1973).

Investigating individual oral (and written) traditions behind Acts is more productive than the attempt to reconstruct more or less comprehensive written sources.  While Luke did not have such extensive written sources as he did for his

---

*Lukas,* GTA 26 (²1986), 284, can conclude "in contrast to Paul, the soteriological interpretation of Christ remains undeveloped." As often concluded, Luke describes only "a negative concept of justification = absolution" (as already H.J. Holtzmann put it in *Die Apostelgeschichte,* Hand-Commentar zum Neuen Testament I/2 [³1901], 91).  Luke understood "justification" not as new being in Christ before God, not as the gift of δικαιοσύνη θεοῦ which God graciously transfers to humans.  The Pauline χωρὶς νόμου (Rom 3:21) is also absent from Luke.  His conception of justification first takes hold where the law cannot be fulfilled (Acts 13:38: ἀπὸ πάντων ὧν οὐκ ἠδυνήθητε ἐν νόμῳ Μωϋσέως δικαιωθῆναι).  The Pauline and Lucan understandings of the law display basic differences.

[76] According to Schenk, "Luke as Reader of Paul," 138, etc., Luke offers instructions for reading Paul from Luke's viewpoint, "... a Lukan instruction for reading the Pauline Letters by his code and in its sense."

[77] E.g., Schenk, 134-136, attempts to prove a connection between the sacramental words of 1 Cor 11:23-25 and Luke 22:19f.  The parallel may also be explained without recourse to literary connection.

[78] Cf. also, e.g., J. Becker, *Paulus. Der Apostel der Völker* (1989), 13; *Paul: Apostle to the Gentiles* (1993), 14.

Gospel, he had at his disposal smaller units.[79]   Yet his own formulating of such materials should not be undervalued (cf. Strecker on Acts 11:27-30[80]). Comprehensively organized sections, such as the trial of Paul,[81] or passages lacking an extensive traditional basis, are products of Luke's thorough editing.

Inconsistencies in the text or the narrative presentation are points of departure for the reconstruction of traditions. Disparities in content also suggest that the author is utilizing traditions. In addition, style-critical and form-critical approaches are indicative.[82]

For example, among the traditions used are *name lists* (Acts 1:13, 6:5, 20:4), *miracle narratives* (e.g., Acts 3:1-10, 9:36-43[83]), etc. *Legends* about pious individuals occur in Acts, as the Cornelius episode of Acts 10:1-11:18 indicates. Yet this is not a unity.[84]   The vision of 10:9-16 has probably been expanded by Luke.[85]   Acts 10:27-29 is also secondary,[86] and on the whole the Cornelius account shows marks of heavy Lucan revision.[87]   This tradition may be classified with the *conversion narratives* (e.g., Acts 8:26-39 and 9:1-9), which belong to the class of (personal) legends.[88]   In addition, tradition from outside Christian circles (i.e., Jewish tradition) is evident in Acts. This accounts for the tradition about Herod's death (Acts 12:20-23), presumably condensed by Luke, and also reported in Josephus (*Ant* xix, 343-350). Secular anecdotes such as that about the seven sons of Sceva (Acts 19:14-16) serve "as entertainment rather than any religious or personal interest."[89]   Those short notices which were the point of departure for M. Dibelius's itinerary might likewise go back to individual traditions, since they often suspend the flow of the context and contribute nothing to the action.

---

[79] For a different viewpoint, cf. W. Schmithals, *Die Apostelgeschichte des Lukas,* Zürcher Bibelkommentar. Neues Testament 3.2 (1982), 16, In the course of critiquing the existence of an oral narrative tradition, Schmithals expresses scepticism about the possibility of proving individual traditional units. Against this cf. the viewpoint of M. Hengel, *Zur urchristlichen Geschichtsschreibung* ([2]1984), 17, who holds to the necessity of the author's "reduction and condensation of an originally richer tradition."

[80] "Die sogannante Zweite Jerusalmreise des Paulus (Acts 11, 27-30)."

[81] Cf. Stolle, *Der Zeuge als Angeklagter.*

[82] On distinguishing tradition from redaction, cf. also F. Hahn, "Zum Problem," 321-324.

[83] Cf. F. Neirynck, "The Miracle Stories," 170f.; E. Gräser, "Acta-Forschung seit 1960," *TRu* 42 (1977): 15f.

[84] For another viewpoint, cf. R. Pesch, *Die Apostelgeschichte,* EKKNT V/1 (1980), 333.

[85] E. Haenchen, *Die Apostelgeschichte,* MeyerK 3 ([7(16)]1977), 349; *The Acts of the Apostles* (1971), 361f.

[86] For an analysis, cf. Dibelius, "Stilkritisches," 19; "Style," 13f.

[87] The speeches of 10:34-43 and 11:1-8 are also Lucan. Cf. below, section 5.5.

[88] On all this cf. M. Dibelius, "Stilkritisches," 18-28; "Style," 12-25.

[89] M. Dibelius, "Stilkritisches," 23; "Style," 20. Cf. also Acts 20:7-12; 28:3-6. In Acts 23:6 and 12-21 H. Conzelmann sees "Pauline anecdotes" (*Die Apostelgeschichte,* HNT 7 [[2]1972], 137-139; *Acts of the Apostles,* Hermeneia [1987], 209-211.)

Even if we abandon the attempt to reconstruct longer written sources, we still face the question about possible *collections* of tradition.[90] Not infrequently diverse traditions display a similar outlook. H. Conzelmann suggests that two such collections underlie Acts 1-12, one Hellenistic and another "a collection of reports stemming from Jerusalem."[91] He observes one group of traditions which strongly emphasizes the Twelve, or Peter alone, and another exclusively the "Hellenists." It is uncertain whether these collections were made prior to Luke's work, or by Luke himself from the products of his research.[92] The latter possibility better explains the "redactorial anticipations"[93] and literary character to be seen here and there in the tradition. Yet much remains in the dark, since Luke has given us no account of his editorial activity.

The *tradition about Paul,* by now well established, is a further problem. Since Luke was not a companion of Paul,[94] direct influence of the Pauline school (in the narrow sense) is improbable. There is little historical foundation to the Lucan picture. At most it is secondary or tertiary information which echoes historical events. This is true even of V. Stolle's alleged prison report (Acts 21:1-17, 27-36; 22:23-29; 23:12-35; 24:1-23, 27; and 25:1-12)[95] or of E. Haenchen's supposed eyewitness accounts.[96] It is striking that especially in the trial reports, which deal extensively with Paul, Luke's redactional activity stands out. Independent traditions and personal legends about Paul may have circulated in the Pauline communities, and thus come to Luke's disposal. "Sayings about Paul,"[97] such as may be inferred from Galatians 1:23, imply the existence of such traditions.

---

[90] Cf. F. Hahn, "Zum Problem der antiochenischen Quelle in der Apostelgeschichte," 323.

[91] Conzelmann, *Die Apostelgeschichte,* 6; *Acts of the Apostles,* xxxviii. G. Lüdemann also concluded there were written accounts from the circles of the Hellenists. Cf. his *Das frühe Christentum nach den Traditionen der Apostelgeschichte. Ein Kommentar* (1987), 28 and his *Paulus der Heidenapostel I. Studien zur Chronologie,* FRLANT 123 (1980), 59, where he speaks of a "Hellenist source."

[92] E. Plümacher, "Apostelgeschichte," in *TRE* 3 (1978): 498, 500f.

[93] Conzelmann, *Die Apostelgeschichte*; *Acts of the Apostles;* cf. Acts 8:6f.; 12:3-6; etc.

[94] See above, p. 192.

[95] *Der Zeuge als Angeklagter,* 265-267.

[96] "Das 'Wir' in der Apostelgeschichte und das Itinerar" (first published in 1961), in his *Gott und Mensch. Gesammelte Aufsätze* (1965), 247f., 251. "'We' in Acts and the Itinerary," in *The Bultmann School of Biblical Interpretation: New Directions,* ed. R.W. Funk and G. Ebeling, *JTC* 1 (1965): 83f., 87.

[97] H.-M. Schenke, "Das Weiterwirken des Paulus und die Pflege seines Erbes durch die Paulus-Schule," *NTS* 21 (1975): 505-518, 512. Cf. also C.K. Barrett, "Pauline Controversies in the Post-Pauline Period," NTS 20 (1974): 229-245; J. Becker, *Paulus. Der Apostel der Völker* (1989), 13f.; *Paul: Apostle to the Gentiles* (1993), 14.

## *Excursus:* Tradition and Redaction in Acts 27-28

*Literature*

Dibelius, M., "Paulus in der Apostelgeschichte," in his *Aufsätze zur Apostelgeschichte,* ed. H. Greeven, FRLANT 68 ([3]1957), 175-180, "Paul in the Acts of the Apostles," *Studies in the Acts of the Apostles* (1956), 207-214. Haenchen, E., "Acta 27," in *Zeit und Geschichte. Dankesgabe an R. Bultmann,* ed. E. Dinkler (1964), 235-254. Kratz, R., *Rettungswunder. Motiv-, traditions- und formkritische Aufarbeitung einer biblischen Gattung,* Einleitung in die Heilige Schrift XXIII.123 (1979). Suhl, A., "Gestrandet! Bemerkungen zum Streit über die Romfahrt des Paulus," *ZTK* 88 (1991): 1-28. Wehnert, J., "Gestrandet. Zu einer neuen These über den Schiffbruch des Apostels Paulus auf dem Wege nach Rom (Apg 27-28)," *ZTK* 87 (1990): 67-99. Wellhausen, J., *Kritische Analyse der Apostelgeschichte,* Abhandlungen der Gesellschaft der Wissenschaften zu Göttingen, Philologisch-historische Klasse, Neue Folge 15.2 (1914).

The final two chapters of Acts pose fundamental problems. The cohesive presentation[98] betrays the author's thorough work. The historical veracity of the text is debated: is there behind Acts 27 (and perhaps 28:11-14) the remembrances of an eyewitness[99] or a literary text formulated by analogy to ancient sea voyage accounts and inserted into the narrative about Paul?[100] Did Luke create a miraculous rescue on the basis of some memoranda?[101] Yet the miracle is only one part, albeit the high point, of the legendary sea voyage account. It is wise to withhold judging the account as historical.[102] Luke probably used a secular sea voyage text in his composition. By added comments he adapted the account to the narrative about Paul.

---

[98] Cf. G. Stählin, *Die Apostelgeschichte,* NTD 5 ([1][10]1962, [4][13]1970), 313.

[99] So, e.g., for E. Haenchen (with Lucan insertions of 27:9-11, 20?, 21ff., 33ff., 43). Wellhausen (*Kritische Analyse,* 54) already regarded Acts 27:9-11, 21-26, and 33-36 as Pauline fragments which broke the continuity of the narrative. G. Stählin, *Apostelgeschichte,* also regards the account as based on eyewitness remembrances and E. Plümacher considers this viewpoint in "Apostelgeschichte," *TRE* 3 (1978): 500.

[100] M. Dibelius explained this narrative as a "report about Paul (based on special knowledge?)" inserted into a "secular" sea voyage account which served as "a pattern, model, or source." Cf. his "Die Apostelgeschichte im Rahmen der urchristlichen Literaturgeschichte," in *Aufsätze,* 174; "The Acts of the Apostles in the Setting of History of Early Christian Literature," in *Studies,* 205f. Cf. P. Vielhauer, *Geschichte der urchristlichen Literatur* ([2]1978), 392; D.E. Aune, *Literary Environment* (1987), 129.

[101] R. Kratz, *Rettungswunder,* refers to Acts 27:1-3a and 28:7-16.

[102] But J. Wehnert, "Gestrandet," 89f and 96, sees an apparently authentic report of a journey passed on to and reworked, to which the sections 27:1-8; 28 1[f.], 7, and 10-16 have been adapted.

# 5.5    The Forms in Acts

*Literature*

Bruce, F.F., "The Acts of the Apostles: Historical Record or Theological Reconstruction?" in ANRW II 25.3 (1985): 2569-2603. Dauer, A., "'Ergänzungen' und 'Variationen' in den Reden der Apostelgeschichte gegenüber vorausgegangenen Erzählungen. Beobachtungen zur literarischen Arbeitsweise des Lukas," in *Vom Urchristentum zu Jesus*. Festschrift J. Gnilka, ed. H. Frankemölle, *et al.,* (1989), 307-324. Dibelius, M. "Die Reden der Apostelgeschichte und die antike Geschichtsschreibung" (first published in 1949), in his *Aufsätze zur Apostelgeschichte,* ed. H. Greeven, FRLANT 68 (³1957), 120-162, "The Speeches in Acts and Ancient Historiography," *Studies in the Acts of the Apostles* (1956), 138-185. Gasque, W.W., "The Speeches in Acts: Dibelius Reconsidered," in *New Dimensions in New Testament Study,* ed. R.N. Longenecker *et al.* (1974), 232-250. Schneider, G., "Die Petrusrede vor Kornelius. Das Verhältnis von Tradition und Redaktion in Apg 10,34-43," in his *Lukas, Theologe der Heilsgeschichte. Aufsätze zum lukanischen Doppelwerk,* BBB 59 (1985), 253-279. Schürmann, H., "Das Testament Paulus für Kirche" (first published in 1962), now in his *Traditionsgeschichtliche Untersuchungen zu den synoptischen Evangelien. Beiträge,* Kommentare und Beiträge zum Alten und Neuen Testament (1968), 310-340. Weiser, A., "Tradition und lukanischen Komposition in Apg 10,36-43," in *A cause de l'évangile. Études sur les Synoptiques et les Actes.* Festschrift J. Dupont. Lectio Divina 123 (1985), 757-767. Wilckens, U., Die Missionsreden der Apostelgeschichte. Form- und traditionsgeschichtliche Untersuchungen, WMANT 5 (³1974).

The author is less tied to sources and traditions in Acts than in the Gospel. In distinction to the Third Gospel, Acts reveals an extensive and independent literary activity. This difference between the two works is not difficult to explain. In the first book Luke follows an earlier Christian literary form. In Acts he adopts an ancient genre for his own theological interests.

The following characterize the author's literary procedure: *motifs characteristic of a higher educational level* (e.g., the prologues, Luke 1:1-4 and Acts 1:1-2; the Hellenistic letter formulas in Acts 15:23 and 23:26[103]); *speeches* (e.g., Acts 1:16-22; 2:14-39);[104] *mimesis of the Septuagint,* offering imitation of qualitatively and authoritatively recognized models corresponding to Hellenistic emulation of classic works and giving the subject a certain weight;[105] *archaisms* (using more ancient

---

[103] See above, p. 52.

[104] Cf. also M. Dibelius, "Reden," 120ff.; "Speeches," 138ff.; and above, footnote 29 to this chapter.

[105] E. Plümacher, "Apostelgeschichte," in *TRE* 3 (1978): 507. For the significance of the Septuagint in that era, cf. H. v. Campenhausen, "Das Alte Testament als Bibel der Kirche vom Ausgang des Urchristentums bis zur Entstehung des Neuen Testaments," in his *Aus der Frühzeit des Urchristentums. Studien zur Kirchengeschichte des ersten*

Christological titles such as παῖς θεοῦ in 3:13 and 26, ancient fomulas as at 2:22-23, 2:36, etc. with a function similar to that of mimesis); *"dramatic style"*[106] *and tragic historiography* (inserting individual episodes with important information into the action, e.g., Peter's vision of Acts 10:10-16 which prepares the way for the mission apart from the law to the gentiles; as in tragic historiography Luke is not concerned with historical accuracy but verisimilitude, and thereby persuasion); *summaries* (e.g., 1:14; 2:42-47; 4:32-35; 6:7, where the author generalizes the materials presented in the previous traditions[107]). In addition, letters (see above) and prayers (1:24-25; 4:24-30; cf. 3.3.2) are set into the text. Luke follows ancient conventions through these literary techniques.[108]

On account of strained relationships to their contexts, and of their importance with respect to the narrative framework, the speeches' authenticity was questioned early.[109] Composed speeches give the author opportunity to express that "which has not yet been narrated."[110] More significantly, Luke uses them to clarify decisive moments of his presentation,[111] as do parallels in secular literature.

Yet the so-called missionary speeches (2:14-39; 3:12-26; 4:9-12; 5:29-32; 10:34-43; 13:16-41) have been assessed differently. M. Dibelius explained these speeches, which are always directed to Jewish listeners, on the basis of a schema of contemporary preaching.[112] This was opposed by U. Wilckens, who understands the speeches as preaching which characterizes a specific period in history.[113] For Luke it was not a matter of current preaching, but of speeches from the past seen as moving forces "which themselves cause events and determine their courses."[114]

The structure of these speeches is evident: *a)* a summarizing statement about the kerygma, suffering, death, and resurrection of Jesus; *b)* emphasis on the

---

*und zweiten Jahrhunderts* (1963), 152-196; H. Hübner, *Biblische Theologie des Neuen Testaments. Bd. 1 Prolegomena* (1990), 45f., 63-65.

[106] E. Haenchen, *Die Apostelgeschichte,* MeyerK 3 ([7(16)]1977), 117, n. 1; *The Acts of the Apostles,* Hermeneia (1971), 107, n. 1.

[107] Cf. P. Vielhauer, *Geschichte der urchristlichen Literatur* ([2]1978), 395.

[108] Specific evidence in E. Plümacher, *Lukas als hellenistischer Schriftsteller. Studien zur Apostelgeschichte,* SUNT 9 (1972), 32ff.; also in his "Apostelgeschichte," in *TRE* 3 (1978): 501-513 and "Lukas als griechischer Historiker," in PWSup 14 (1974): 243-261. Cf. also A. Weiser, *Die Apostelgeschichte,* Ökumenischer Taschenbuch-kommentar zum Neuen Testament 5/1 (1981, [2]1989), 30f.

[109] As early as J.G. Eichhorn, *Einleitung in das Neue Testament* II (1810): 35ff., on the basis of his understanding Acts as a composition of Luke. For a different viewpoint, especially in English language research on Acts, cf., e.g., W.W. Gasque, "The Speeches in Acts: Dibelius Reconsidered," 242ff.; F.F. Bruce, "Historical Record or Theological Reconstruction?" 2582-2588.

[110] Cf. H. Schürmann, "Das Testament Paulus für Kirche," 310, n. 3; W. Radl, *Paulus und Jesus im lukanischen Doppelwerk. Untersuchungen zu Parallelmotiven im Lukasevangelium und in der Apostelgeschichte,* Einleitung in die Heilige Schrift XXIII/49 (1975), 133f.; A.Dauer, "'Ergänzungen' und 'Variationen' in der Reden der Apostelgeschichte."

[111] M. Dibelius, "Reden," 151; "Speeches," 176f.

[112] "Reden," 142; "Speeches," 165f.

[113] Wilckens, *Missionsreden,* 72ff.

[114] *Missionsreden,* 96.

disciples as witnesses; *c)* proof from Scripture; and *d)* call to repentance. The relationship of tradition and redaction is uncertain, as the unpersuasive attempt to identify a pre-Lucan gospel structure in Acts 10:36-43 shows.[115]

The objective of Acts complies with Lucan composition. With the help of speeches, Luke shapes a course of action chronologically and geographically complete: the dissemination of the Christian faith from Jerusalem to Rome.

---

[115] See above, pp. 98f. Cf. also A. Weiser, "Tradition und lukanische Komposition;" G. Schneider, "Die Petrusrede vor Kornelius." Further bibliography in A. Dauer, "'Ergänzungen' und 'Variationen'," 311, n. 34 and 312, n. 35.

# 6 The Johannine Apocalypse

*Literature*

*L'Apocalypse johannique et l'Apocalyptique dans le Nouveau Testament*, ed. J. Lambrecht, BETL 53 (1980). *Apocalypticism in the Mediterranean World and the Near East. Proceedings of the International Colloquium on Apocalypticism, Uppsala, August 12-17, 1979*, ed. D. Hellholm (1983). Aune, D.E., "The Apocalypse of John and the Problem of Genre," *Semeia* 36 (1986): 65-96. Berger, K. "Apostelbrief und apostolische Rede/Zum Formular frühchristlicher Briefe," *ZNW* 65 (1974): 190-231. Böcher, O., *Die Johannisapokalypse*, ErFor 41 (³1988). Bousset, W., *Die Offenbarung Johannis*, MeyerK 16 (⁶1906=reprint 1966). Collins, A.Y., *The Combat Myth in the Book of Revelation*, HDR 9 (1976); "Early Christian Apocalyptic Literature," in *ANRW* II 25.6 (1988): 4665-4711. Feuillet, A., *L'Apocalypse, État de question*, StudNeot. Subsidia 3 (1963). Holtz, T., *Die Christologie der Apokalypse*, TU 85 (²1971). Müller, U.B., "Literarische und formgeschichtliche Bestimmung der Apokalypse des Johannes als einem Zeugnis frühchristlicher Apokalyptik," in *Apocalypticism in the Mediterranean World and the Near East. Proceedings of the International Colloquium on Apocalypticism, Uppsala, August 12-17, 1979*, ed. D. Hellholm (1983), 599-619; *Die Offenbarung des Johannes*, Ökumenischer Taschenbuch-kommentar zum Neuen Testament 19 (1984). Schüssler-Fiorenza, E., "Composition and Structure of the Book of Revelation," *CBQ* 39 (1977): 344-366. Strobel, A., "Apokapypse des Johannes," in *TRE* (1978), 174-189. Taeger, J.-W., "Einige neuere Veröffentlichungen zur Apokalypse des Johannes," *VF* 29 (1984): 50-75. Vielhauer, P. and G. Strecker, "Einleitung zu C. Apokalypsen und Verwandtes," in *Neutestamentliche Apokryphen in deutscher Übersetzung*, ed. Wilhelm Schneemelcher II (⁵1989): 491-515; "C. Apocalypses and Related Subjects, Introduction," in *New Testament Apocrypha*, rev. ed. W. Schneemelcher II (1992): 542-568; "Einleitung zu XIX. Apokalyptik des Urchristentums," in *Neutestamentliche Apokryphen in deutscher Übersetzung*, ed. Wilhelm Schneemelcher II (⁵1989): 516-547; "XIX. Apocalyptic in Early Christianity," in *New Testament Apocrypha*, rev. ed. W. Schneemelcher II (1992): 569-602.

## 6.1 The genre of the New Testament Apocalypse

### 6.1.1 Apocalypses and Apocalyptic

Describing the last book of the New Testament as the Apocalypse or Revelation of John[1] fits with the superscription in Rev 1:1-2. Originally ἀποκάλυψις referred not to a literary genre, but to (divine) unveiling of what had been hidden (cf. Gal 1:12, 1 Cor 1:7, etc.). The title "Apocalypse" occurs also in the Christian Shephard of Hermas (Vision, V,1, according to Codex Sinaiticus, is

---

[1] Thus the secondary *inscriptio* ἀποκάλυψις Ἰωάννου; cf. D.E. Aune, *The New Testament in its Literary Environment*, Library of Early Christianity 8 (1987), 226.

"ἀποκάλυψις ϵ'"[2]). Despite this claim, its literary character does not totally coincide with that of an apocalypse.[3]

The concept "Apocalypse" describes not only writings such as the Apocalypse of John. Among the gnostic texts from Nag Hammade are several called apocalypses.[4] Yet the two Apocalypses of James do not fit the genre apocalypse. They are rather to be assigned to the form of the gnostic dialogue.[5] The Mani papyrus from Cologne refers to writings under the names of Adam, Sethel, Enosh, Shem, and Enoch as apocalypses (CMC[6]). Later Jewish works such as the Syriac Apocalypse of Baruch and Greek Apocalypse of Baruch also use the title.

The relationship of the [Johannine] seer to apocalyptic is controversial. It is doubtful that the author refers back directly to Jewish apocalyptic. Early Christian apocalyptic is more likely presupposed (note the expectation of an intermediate messianic kingdom in Paul at 1 Cor. 15:24-28, and see also 1 Cor. 6:2-3, 2 Cor. 5:10, etc.). In addition, apocalyptic influences from the Johannine school may be assumed (cf. 6.4).

---

[2] The number is probably secondary; cf. M. Dibelius, *Der Hirt des Hermas,* HNT Ergänzungsband 4 (1923): 491.

[3] Cf. P. Vielhauer, *Geschichte der urchristlichen Literatur* ([2]1978=1975), 518-520, 522. On other Christian apocalypses and Christian additions to Jewish apocalypses, cf. K. Koester, "Literature, Early Christian," in *IDBSup* (1976), 551-556, 554, and A.Y. Collins, "Early Christian Apocalyptic Literature."

[4] NHC V 2-5; VI 4; VII 1.3 (Apocalypses of James, of Paul, and of Peter, among others). Cf. M. Krause, "Die literarischen Gattungen der Apokalypsen von Nag Hammadi," in *Apocalypticism in the Mediterranean World and the Near East,* ed. D. Hellholm (1983), 621-637, 622. Cf. also P. Vielhauer and G. Strecker, "Einleitung zu C. Apokalypsen und Verwandtes," 507f.; "C. Apocalypses and Related Subjects, Introduction," 559.

[5] K. Rudolph classifies the Apocalypse of Paul also as a gnostic dialogue (cf. "Der gnostische 'Dialog' als literarisches Genus," in *Probleme der koptischen Literatur,* ed. P. Nagel, Wissenschaftliche Beiträge der Martin-Luther-Universität Halle-Wittenberg 1968/1 (K2), 1968, 85-107, 99). P. Vielhauer ("Einleitung zu C. Apokalypsen und Verwandtes," 507; "C. Apocalypses and Related Subjects, Introduction," 559) classifies it with apocalypyses, as do W.-P. Funk ("XXI.1 Koptisch-gnostische Apokalypse des Paulus," in *Neutestamentliche Apokryphen in deutscher Übersetzung,* ed. Wilhelm Schneemelcher II [[5]1989]: 628-633, 629; "The Coptic gnostic Apocalypse of Paul," in *New Testament Apocrypha,* rev. ed. W. Schneemelcher II (1992): 695-700, 696f.) and M. Krause ("Die literarischen Gattungen der Apokalypsen von Nag Hammadi," in *Apocalypticism in the Mediterranean World and the Near East,* ed. D. Hellholm [1983], 621-637, 625-627). On other gnostic apocalypses without the title, cf. Krause, 632-635.

[6] Cf. D.E. Aune, *Literary Environment,* 227. On this manuscript and its significance for the New Testament, cf. G. Strecker, "Der Kölner Mani Kodex, Elkesai und das Neue Testament," in *Oecumenica et Patristica.* Festschrift W. Schneemelcher, ed D. Papandreou *et al.* (1989), 123-134.

## *Excursus:* Was the Author of the Apocalypse an Apocalyptist or a Prophet?

*Literature*

Boring, M.E., "The Apocalypse as Christian Prophecy: A Discussion of the Issue Raised by the Book of Revelation for the Study of Early Christian Prophecy," SBLSP (1974), 2:43-62; *The Continuing Voice of Jesus. Christian Prophecy and the Gospel Tradition* (1991); *Revelation, Interpretation. A Bible Commentary for Teaching and Preaching* (1989), 23-25. Goppelt, L., *Theologie des Neuen Testaments,* ed. J. Roloff. Uni-Taschenbücher 850 (1985=³1980); *Theology of the New Testament,* ed. J. Roloff, 2 vols. (1981, 1982). Schüssler-Fiorenza, E., "Apokalypsis and Propheteia. The Book of Revelation in the Context of Early Christian Prophecy," in *L'Apocalypse johannique et l'Apocalyptique dans le Nouveau Testament,* ed. J. Lambrecht, BETL 53 (1980), 105-128.

The relationship of the seer to prophecy is also signficant. Several have affirmed a positive connection to Christian prophecy.[7] M.E. Boring understands the seer as an "immediately inspired spokesman for the exalted Jesus Christ, who receives intelligible revelation which he is impelled to deliver to the Christian community."[8] It should be noted, however, that the seer himself is never called a prophet (προφήτης),[9] all the more significant, since he refers throughout his book to Christian prophets in the communities.

As early Christianity generally, and Palestinian Christian prophecy specifically, was apocalyptically oriented, so are both the prophetic and apocalyptic combined in this seer. Despite his obvious prophetic consciousness (cf. Rev 1:3; 22:7, 9, 18-19), he is essentially a Christian apocalyptist who distinguishes himself from others named prophets (cf. 11:18; 16:6; 18:20; 22:6, 9) through the book which he writes–an apocalypse (see below, section 6.1.3).

### 6.1.2 The Genre Apocalypse and its Stylistic Characteristics

*Literature*

Betz, H.D., "Zum Problem des religionsgeschichtlichen Verständnisses der Apokalyptik," in his *Hellenismus und Urchristentum. Gesammelte Aufsätze* I

---

[7] Cf. E. Schüssler-Fiorenza, "Apokalypsis and Propheteia.," *passim,* and esp. 113f. L. Goppelt, *Theologie* 510, *Theology* 2:179f. sees the Apocalypse as "the most outstanding example of early Christian prophecy." On the relationship to apocalyptic in the Hebrew Scriptures, cf. below, section 6.2.

[8] "The Apocalypse as Christian Prophecy," 44, in his definition of a Christian prophet, to which the author of the Apocalypse conforms. Cf. also his *The Continuing Voice,* 80.

[9] But M.E. Boring, *Continuing Voice,* 79f., suggests that the seer, in calling himself a "servant" (δοῦλος, Rev 1:1), understands himself as a prophet, in light of the Hebrew Scriptures' use of "the servants, the prophets" (οἱ δοῦλοι οἱ προφῆται).

(1990): 52-71.   Carmignac, Jl, "Qu'est-ce que l'Apocalyptique? Son emploi à Qumran," *RevQ* 10 (1979): 3-33.   Collins, J.J., "Towards the Morphology of a Genre," *Semeia* 14 (1979): 1-20.   Hartman, L, "Survey of the Problem of Apocalyptic Genre," in *Apocalypticism in the Mediterranean World and the Near East. Proceedings of the International Colloquium on Apocalypticism, Uppsala, August 12-17, 1979*, ed. D. Hellholm (1983), 329-343.   Hellholm, D., *Das Visionenbuch des Hermas als Apokalypse. Formgeschichtliche und texttheoretische Studien zu einer literarischen Gattung I. Methodologische Vorüberlegungen und makro-strukturelle Textanalyse*, ConBNT 13:1 (1980); "The Problem of Apocalyptic Genre and the Apocalypse of John," *Semeia* 36 (1986): 13-64.   Pöhlmann, W., "Apokalyptische Geschichtsdeutung und geistiger Widerstand," *KD* 34 (1988): 60-75.   Schüssler-Fiorenza, E., "The Followers of the Lamb: Visionary Rhetoric and Social-Political Situation," *Semeia* 36 (1986): 123-146.   Vorster, W.S., "1 Enoch and the Jewish Literary Setting of the New Testament: A Study in Text Types," *Neot* 17 (1983): 1-14; "'Genre' and the Revelation of John: A Study in Text, Context and Intertext," *Neot* 22 (1988): 103-123.

While it is questionable that any thoroughgoing formal laws can be demonstrated for the literary genre of apocalypse,[10] the following stylistic features are widely recognized.[11]

*a) Pseudonymity.*   Apocalyptists write not under their own names, but remain anonymous or use the names of great persons of the past (e.g., Baruch, Ezra, Enoch).   Along with this come the fictions of earlier dating and the sealing up of the book for posterity.   This latter accounts for why the book first becomes known long after the death of its fictive author.

*b) Visions.*   The apocalyptist usually receives revelation as a vision, either in a dream or in ecstasy, but seldom as an audition.   This revelation, which occurs shortly before the apocalyptists death, may be take the form of a farewell address.

*c) Figurative language.*   Corresponding to the medium of the vision, that which is seen is itself an image descriptive of what is happening, or secretly veiled in the form of symbols and allegories.   The traditional meaning of such images and the intention of the apocalyptist expressed through them is not always the same.

*d) Disclosures.*   Apocalypses often include reflections and clarifications of the images.   Not seldom, these are put forward by one or more interpreting angels *(angelus interpres)* or by God.

*e) Systematizing.*   Frequently the presentation is schematically structured, often with numerical symbolism.   God's wisdom, given the apocalyptist, is reflected in the outward display of the orderly structure which God has given the world.

---

[10] W.G. Kümmel, *Einleitung in das Neue Testament* (²¹1983), 400.

[11] Cf. the survey in P. Vielhauer, *Geschichte der urchristlichen Literatur* (²1978=1975), 487-490.   Cf. also D. Hellholm, "The Problem of Apocalyptic Genre," 22f., and "Methodological Reflections on the Problem of Definition of Generic Texts," in *Mysteries and Revelations. Apocalyptic Studies since the Uppsala Colloquium*, ed J.J. Collins and J.H. Charlesworth. Journal for the Study of the Pseudepigrapha, Supplement Series 9 (1991): 135-163, 149.

*f) Combining minor forms.* Among these are historical surveys of the future, descriptions of the other world, visions of the divine throne room, and the originally non-apocalyptic genres of paraenesis (cf. 3.4), prayers and liturgical texts (requests, laments, thanksgivings and praises, doxologies [cf. 3.3.2], and hymns [cf. 3.3.3]).

Following J.J. Collins[12] and D. Hellholm,[13] D.E. Aune attempts to define the genre "apocalypse" further in terms of form, content, and function.[14]

The *form* is autobiographical prose narrative, though this does not exclude elements of more exalted prose (e.g., Rev 1:1-3) or poetic passages.[15] The "apocalypse" utilizes visions or dreams as media to present this revelation. Its literary high point is a central proclamation. Circumstances which accompany the revelation frame the apocalypse. In D.E. Aune's definition the issue of pseudonymity is understood under the aspect of autobiography. The fictive autobiographical narrative, attributed to a person from the past who gives it authority, necessitates the pseudepigraphical form.[16]

The *content* is a transcending of human experience, usually accompanied by a cosmic or individual eschatological experience.[17]

The *function* of the genre "apocalypse" lies in legitimizing the transcendent authority[18] of its message by means of a revelatory experience. Its goal is to move those

---

[12] Collins sums up the results of the Apocalypse Group of the Society of Biblical Literature: "'Apocalypse' is a genre of revelatory literature with a narrative framework, in which a revelation is mediated by an otherworldly being to a human recipient, disclosing a transcendent reality which is both temporal, insofar as it envisages eschatological salvation, and spatial, insofar as it involves another, supernatural world" ("Towards the Morphology of a Genre," 9). Cf. also D. Hellholm, "Methodological Reflections," in *Mysteries and Revelations. Apocalyptic Studies since the Uppsala Colloquium,* 149. L. Hartman adds to this definition attention to linguistic, semantic and socio-linguistic considerations.

[13] "The Problem of Apocalyptic Genre," cf. also *Das Visionenbuch des Hermas.*

[14] Cf. , "The Apocalypse of John and the Problem of Genre," *Semeia* 36 (1986): 65, 86ff., and his *The New Testament in its Literary Environment* (1987, 230. Though apocalyptic images alone may not be constitutive of a separate genre, this does not justify refusing to characterize writings with a common formal structure such as Ethiopic Enoch (91-105) or the Revelation of John as apocalypses, against W.S. Vorster ("1 Enoch and the Jewish Literary Setting," *passim,* but esp. 11), who appeals to G. von Rad (*Theologie des Alten Testaments II. Die Theologie der prophetischen Überlieferungen Israels* [⁸1984=KT 3 ⁹1987], 331, n. 28, "against ever recurring assertions it must be emphasized that from a literary perspective apocalyptic is no separate genre.") As his own contribution to defining a genre Vorster offers narrative: "a narrative of fantasy, a submode or subgenre of the revelatory writings" ("'Genre' and the Revelation of John," 120, but already in "1 Enoch and the Jewish Literary Setting," 11: "a narrative presented as a circular letter").

[15] E. Schüssler-Fiorenza ("The Followers of the Lamb," 130) describes the Revelation of John differently, as "a poetic-rhetorical work."

[16] According to D.E. Aune, the first person style serves to give life to the depiction of the revelation as if in oral form.

[17] But J. Carmignac ("Qu'est-ce que l'Apocalyptique?" 20) never refers to the eschatological perspective in his definition of the apocalyptic genre.

[18] On authorization as a characteristic function of apocalypse, cf. H. Stegemann, "Die Bedeutung der Qumranfunde für die Erforschung der Apokalyptik," in

addressed to change their thought and behavior in light of the apocalyptic message, through the display of a hope-filled future for those now living under threat to their (religious) existence.[19]

### 6.1.3   The genre of the Johannine Apocalypse

*Literature*

Blevins, J.L., "The Genre of Revelation," *RevExp* 77 (1980): 393-408; *Revelation as Drama* (1984). Bowman, J.W., "The Revelation of John: Its Dramatic Structure and Message," *Int* 9 (1955): 436-453. Collins, J.J., "Pseudonymity, Historical Reviews and the Genre of the Revelation of John," *CBQ* 39 (1977): 327-343. Georgi, D., "Die Visionen vom himmlischen Jerusalem," in *Kirche.* Festschrift G. Bornkamm, ed. D. Lührmann, et al., (1980), 351-372. Hartman, L., "Form and Message. A Preliminary Discussion of 'Partial Tests' in Rev 1-3 and 22:6ff," in *L'Apocalypse johannique et l'Apocalyptique dans le Nouveau Testament,* ed. J. Lambrecht, BETL 53 (1980), 129-149. Kallas, J., "The Apocalypse – an Apocalyptic Book?" *JBL* 86 (1967): 69-80. Karrer, M., *Die Johannesoffenbarung als Brief. Studien zu ihrem literarischen, historischen und theologischen Ort,* FRLANT 140 (1986). Kuykendahl, R.M., "The Literary Genre of the Book of Revelation. A Study of Apocalyptic Research and Its Relationship to John's Apocalypse." Dissertation, Southwestern Baptist Theological Seminary, Fort Worth, TX (1986). Lohse, E., "Wie christlich is die Offenbarung des Johannes?" *NTS* 34 (1988): 321-338. Mazzaferri, F.D., *The Genre of the Book of Revelation from a Source-critical Perspective,* BZNW 54 (1989). Moore, H., "The Book of Revelation," in *International Bibliography of Sociology* ( (1987): 158-174. Palmer, F., *The Drama of the Apocalypse* (1903). Vorster, W.S., "1 Enoch and the Jewish Literary Setting of the New Testament: A Study in Text Types," *Neot* 17 (1983): 1-14.

Some recent researchers have made the epistolary framework (1:4-5 [6]; 22:21[20]) the occasion to explain the Johannine apocalypse as an "encyclical letter"[21] and to contemplate its "actual dispatch."[22] The joining of letter form and

---

*Apocalypticism in the Mediterranean World and the Near East. Proceedings of the International Colloquium on Apocalypticism, Uppsala, August 12-17, 1979,* ed. D. Hellholm (1983), 495-530, 505-507.

[19] Cf. W. Pöhlmann, "Apokalyptische Geschichtsdeutung," 70.

[20] Cf. L. Hartmann, "Form and Message," 135f., 148. D.E. Aune, *Literary Environment,* 240f., attributes 22:10-21 to the epistolary postscript, which in ancient letters summed up the contents of the whole.

[21] Cf. K. Berger, "Apostelbrief und apostolische Rede/Zum Formular frühchristlicher Briefe," *ZNW* 65 (1974): 207; E. Lohse, "Wie christlich ist die Offenbarung des Johannes?" J. Roloff, *Die Offenbarung des Johannes,* Zürcher Bibelkommentar, Neues Testament 18 (1984), 15f. and often; E. Schüssler-Fiorenza, "Composition and Structure of the Book of Revelation," *CBQ* 39 (1977): 358: "early Christian apostolic letter." Cf. also W.S. Vorster, "1 Enoch and the Jewish Literary

apocalypse indicates that the author directs himself to recipients of the Pauline tradition.[23] Yet the epistolary characteristics occur only in the passages which frame Revelation and in the epistles of chapters 2 and 3 (cf. 6.3). Outside of these sections the typical letter format is missing. Since the main part of the book consists of a series of visions, the Apocalypse ought not to be classified with ancient letters.[24]

The Revelation of John can hardly be described as an ancient drama.[25] The presentation is better understood as portraying and explaining history from the perspective of Christian apocalyptic.

Apocalyptic depiction as well as apocalyptic forms are decisive for generic definition.[26] Thus the Revelation of John must be classified as an apocalypse supplied with letter form (its letter framework and epistles).[27] The epistolary framework may have facilitated its being read at worship (cf. Rev 1:3).[28]

Revelation is indisputably a Christian book dominated by the Christ-event.[29]

Thus is is understandable that the work of the seer not only utilizes Christian traditions–alongside others–but shows itself impacted by Christian forms such as that of the letter. Such influence, despite the lack of individual generic elements, does not alter

---

Setting of the New Testament," 11: "a narrative presented as a circular letter;" though for Vorster "narrative" has primary importance.

[22] M. Karrer, *Die Johannesoffenbarung als Brief,* 304, cf. 303f.

[23] Karrer, 306; cf. E. Schüssler-Fiorenza, "The Quest for the Johannine School. The Apocalypse and the Fourth Gospel," *NTS* 23 (1977): 402-427, 425: "... a circular, authoritative pastoral letter which is patterned after the already traditional Pauline letter form."

[24] Cf. also A.Y. Collins, "Early Christian Apocalyptic Literature," in *ANRW* II 25.6 (1988): 4665-4711, 4679f.

[25] Against J.L. Blevins, "The Genre of Revelation," who sees it as a "tragedy;" F. Palmer, The Drama of the Apocalypse; and note also J.W. Bowman "Dramatic Structure and Message."

[26] Against J. Kallas, "The Apocalypse;" H. Koester, *Einführung in das Neue Testament* (1980), 694, *Introduction to the New Testament,* 2 (1982): 248: "a critical discussion of already existing apocalyptic views and speculations;" F.D. Mazzaferri, *The Genre,* 223ff., 382f. D. Georgi, "Die Visionen," 362, feels he has discovered an "anti-apocalypse."

[27] Further, cf. U.B. Müller, "Literarische und formgeschichtliche Bestimmung der Apokalypse des Johannes als einem Zeugnis frühchristlicher Apokalyptik," in *Apocalypticism in the Mediterranean World and the Near East. Proceedings of the International Colloquium on Apocalypticism, Uppsala, August 12-17, 1979,* ed. D. Hellholm (1983), 599-619, 604 and 607: "an apocalypse styled as a letter."

[28] Cf. also Müller, 607 and P. Vielhauer, *Geschichte der urchristlichen Literatur* ([2]1978=1975), 500 and elsewhere.

[29] Cf. E. Lohse, "Wie christlich?" H. Moore, "The Book." But R. Bultmann, *Theologie des Neuen Testaments,* ed. O. Merk ([9]1984), 525; *Theologie of the New Testament* (1951, 1955), 2:175, thinks that the Apocalypse represents "a weakly Christianized Judaism."

basic agreement with the genre "apocalypse."[30]    While the phenomenon of pseudepigraphy is present (cf. 6.4), the elements of *ex-eventu* truth (but cf. 17:3-11) along with pre-dating and sealing are not evident.    Sealing is substantiated through the reference to the one who gives the revelation, Jesus Christ (Rev 1:1), and who still reveals himself to his church in the seer's time.    Any further authorization of the work is unnecessary.    Perhaps the pseudepigraphy of the seer should also be understood in this light.    The motif of contemporaneity corresponds to that of pre-dating in the non-Christian apocalypses, as the warnings in the epistles indicate.    It is the church of the present which the seer encourages to persevere and remember and seeks to comfort with reference to the coming salvation.    The apocalyptic genre also serves the author in propagating his apocalyptic theology.[31]    That revelation occurs not in a dream but in visionary ecstasy indicates a further development in apocalyptic.    Appropriate to the Christian orientation of the work, the *angelus interpres* recedes (only in 17:1ff. and 21:9; cf. 1:1 and 22:1ff.) and Christ himself appears as the revealer.    Correspondingly, most of the visions are not intepreted.

That the work of the seer is not a secret writing, but throughout is based on the Christian community's experiences (of suffering) and aims at wider publication (Rev 1:4, 11, 19; 22:16, 21), shows that the Revelation of John can only be understood as a Christian work.

## 6.2    Sources of the Johannine Apocalypse

*Literature*

Bogaert, P.-M., "Les Apocalypses contemporaires de Baruch, d'Esdras et de Jean," in *L'Apocalypse johannique et l'Apocalyptique dans le Nouveau Testament,* ed. J. Lambrecht, BETL 53 (1980), 47-68. Boismard, M.-É., "L'Apocalypse de Jean," in *Introduction à la Bible,* édition nouvelle III/4, ed A. George *et al.* (1977), 13-55. Bultmann, R. Review of Ernst Lohmeyer, *Die Offenbarung des Johannes,* HNT 16, Tübingen (1926); *Die Offenbarung des Johannes. Übertragen, ibid.* (1926), *TLZ* 52 (1927): 505-512. Ernst, J., *Die eschatologischen Gegenspieler in den Schriften des Neuen Testaments,* Biblische Untersuchungen 3 (1967). Gunkel, H., *Schöpfung und Chaos in Urzeit und Endzeit. Eine religionsgeschichtliche Untersuchung über Gen 1 und Ap-Joh 12* (1895). Hill, d., "Prophecy and Prophets in the Revelation of St. John," *NTS* 18 (1971/72): 401-418. Prigent, P. Apocalypse 12. Historie de l'exégèse, Beiträge zur Geschichte der biblischen Exegese 2 (1959). Wellhausen, J., *Analysen der Offenbarung Johannis,* Abhandlungen der Gesellschaft der Wissenschaften zu Göttingen, Philologisch-historische Klasse, Neue Folge 9.4 (1907).

---

[30] Cf. J.J. Collins, "Pseudonymity, Historical Reviews and the Genre of the Revelation of John."

[31] But H. Koester thinks otherwise, *Einführung in das Neue Testament* (1980), 694, *Introduction to the New Testament,* 2 (1982): 248.

In dealing with the question of sources, we must distinguish between hypotheses about an original version, about sources, and about fragments.[32] W. Bousset's fragment hypothesis begins with an "apocalyptic writer, who in many places is not creating freely but reworking older apocalyptic fragments and traditions of which the transmission still remains largely in the dark."[33] This hypothesis takes precedence over source[34] or original document (*Grundschrift*)[35] hypotheses. It best fits with the book's thorough unity of style and vocabulary, but still takes into account the inconsistencies, doublets, and contradictions which prompt the three literary-critical models.

Proposed as fragments are 7:1-8; 11:1-13; and 12.[36] Fragments are also suggested as present in chapters 13-14, 17-18, and 21-22,[37] although their scope cannot be exactly defined. Nor can we define in detail whether the fragments were transmitted as oral or written tradition.[38]

The content of the fragments is exceptionally varied. It is generally thought that in Rev 11:1-2 the author utilized a Jewish leaflet from the time of the siege of Jerusalem.[39] Traces of a Nero-*redivivus* tradition have been uncovered in chapter 17.[40] Bultmann regarded the Apocalypse as undergoing a redactional reworking, with 21:5-8 as the original conclusion to the book. As in the case of the Gospel of John, the Apocalypse underwent a double redaction. The first redactor added 21:9-22:5 as a doublet to 21:1-4. A second redactor added 22:6-17 (and chapters 1-3 as well).[41] This

---

[32] For surveys, cf. O. Böcher, *Die Johannisapokalpyse,* ErFor 41 ($^3$1988), 11f.; W. Bousset, *Die Offenbarung Johannis,* MeyerK 16 ($^6$1906=reprint 1966), 108ff.; A. Feuillet, *L'Apocalypse, État de question,* Studia neotestamentica. Subsidia 3 (1963), 19ff,; E. Schüssler-Fiorenza, "Composition and Structure of the Book of Revelation," *CBQ* 39 (1977): 346-350.

[33] *Die Offenbarung Johannis,* 129.

[34] M.-É. Boismard, "L'Apocalypse de Jean," suggests two sources from the same author. J. Massyngberde Ford distinguishes three levels: Rev 4-11, revelation to John the Baptist; Rev 12-22, a work of the Baptist's school, with reference to Rev 19:1-7; and Rev 1-3, 22:16-17a, and 20-21, a Christian redaction. Cf. her *Revelation,* AB 38 (1975), 50ff.

[35] H. Kraft, *Die Offenbarung des Johannes,* HNT 16a (1974), 11-15.

[36] H. Gunkel, *Schöpfung und Chaos,* 171ff, who finds parallels to ancient Near Eastern mythology. Cf. P. Prigent, *Apocalypse 12,* 120-135, for a survey of the history of exegesis.

[37] Cf. P. Vielhauer, *Geschichte der urchristlichen Literatur,* 500.

[38] R. Bultmann, in his review of Lohmeyer's commentary, 506, suggests written traditions, but recognizes difficulties: "to me it seems necessary to presuppose written sources for the analysis of the Apocalypse, but without the confidence that we can reconstruct with certainty."

[39] Already suggested by J. Wellhausen, *Analysen,* 15-18. Cf. J. Ernst, *Die eschatologischen Gegenspieler,* 125f.

[40] Cf., e.g., A.Y. Collins, *The Combat Myth in the Book of Revelation,* HDR 9 (1976), 176-183; J. Ernst, *Gegenspieler,* 146-148; U.B. Müller, *Die Offenbarung des Johannes,* Ökumenischer Taschenbuch-kommentar zum Neuen Testament 19 (1984), 297-300. On the Nero legend, cf. also A.Y. Collins, *The Sybylline Oracles of Egyptian Judaism,* SBLDS 13 (9174), 80-87.

[41] Bultmann, review of Lohmeyer, 508.

thesis found little acceptance. It failed to note that 21:1-4 call for an explication such as found in 21:5ff. Chapters 1-3 and 22:6ff. undoubtedly are integral components of the Apocalypse.

The author, writing under the pseudonym "John," used the Hebrew Scriptures as his most important source, as is evident from the numerous allusions as well as the borrowed imagery. But he also used conventional Jewish and Christian apocalyptic traditions. There are striking parallels to the synoptic apocalypse.[42] Accordingly it would be wrong to limit his religious-historical materials solely to the Hebrew Scriptures. The Apocalypse should not be interpreted as a continuation of Old Testament prophecy[43] or an exegesis of the Hebrew Scriptures.[44]

Nor can parallels to Jewish apocalypses support literary dependence on them,[45] for no specific citations from this literature are recognizable.

It is more and more recognized that for determining the orientation of the Apocalypse to theological and religious history and the self-understanding of its author the distinction between tradition and redaction, and therefore redaction-critical methodology, must be utilized.[46]

## *Excursus:* The Composition of the Apocalypse

*Literature*

Bornkamm, G., "Die Komposition der apokalyptischen Visionen in der Offenbarung Johannis," in his *Studien zu Antike und Christentum. Gesammelte Aufsätze II,* BEvT 28 (³1970), 204-222. Hahn, F., "Zum Aufbau der Johannesoffenbarung," in *Kirche und Bibel.* Festgabe E. Schick, ed. by the professors of the Phil.-Theol Hochschule Fulda (1979), 145-154. Lambrecht, J. "A Structuration of Revelation 4,1-22,5," in *L'Apocalypse johannique et l'Apocalyptique dans le Nouveau Testament,* ed. J. Lambrecht, BETL 53 (1980), 77-104. Vanni, U., *La structura letteraria dell'Apocalisse,* Aloisiana 8 (²1980).

---

[42] Cf. E. Schüssler-Fiorenza, "The Quest for the Johannine School. The Apocalypse and the Fourth Gospel," *NTS* 23 (1977): 420-424.

[43] H. Kraft, *Die Offenbarung des Johannes,* HNT 16a (1974), 16, 20.

[44] Against A. Feuillet, *L'Apocalypse, État de question,* StudNeot. Subsidia 3 (1963), 65: "a rereading of the Old Testament;" H. Kraft, "Zur Offenbarung des Johannes," TRu 38 (1974): 81-98, 85. Cf. D. Hill, "Prophecy and Prophets," 417, who connects the seer with Hebrew prophecy (note also p. 414).

[45] Against P.-M. Bogaert, "Les Apocalypses contemporaires," 67, who presupposes a knowledge of Syriac Baruch.

[46] Cf., e.g., J.-W. Taeger, "Einige neuere Veröffentlichungen zur Apokalypse des Johannes," VF 29 (1984): 50-75, 74; O. Böcher, *Die Johannisapokalpyse,* ErFor 41 (³1988), 163; T. Holtz, *Die Christologie der Apokalypse,* TU 85 (²1971), 1-3; U.B. Müller, *Messias und Menschensohn in jüdischen Apokalypsen und in der Offenbarung des Johannes,* SNT 6 (1972).

Hypotheses about sources should not supplant examining the composition of the Apocalypse as a whole. The book is no seriatim arrangement of various sources, but displays a powerful unity and tight composition.

The underlying numerology, most obvious in the septimal organization, is an essential element of structure. Yet it serves less as a key to interpretation than does the "Book with the Seven Seals" (Rev 5:1).[47]

G. Bornkamm's demonstration that in Rev 8:2-14:20 and in 15:1-22:5 the same eschatological events are portrayed–first in anticipation and then with finality–suggests that the composition of the apocalyptic visions foretell the same eschatological era in triplicate. The first time it is summarized in the visions of the seven seals in 6:1-8:1. Secondly it is intimated in fragmentary form in 8:2-14:20. Finally it is fully presented in 15:1-22:5.

Had Bornkamm shown conclusively that "the book" (τὸ βιβλίον) was a bipartite document doubly executed, containing a technical legal text and a corresponding unsealed second text offering insight to the untrained,[48] then Rev 6:1-8:1 could be understood as the table of contents visible on the outside of the document. The sealed contents of the document are portrayed in 8:2-22:5 after the breaking of the seven seals.

The materials of chapters 12-14 and 17-19, resisting incorporation into the context, are supplements.[49]

## 6.3   Forms Utilized in the Apocalypse

*Literature*

Aune, D.E., "The Form and Function of the Proclamation to the Seven Churches (Revelation 2-3)," *NTS* 36 (1990): 182-204. Böcher, O., "Lasterkataloge in der Apokalypse des Johannes," in *Leben lernen im Horizont des Glaubens.* Festschrift S. Wibbing, ed B. Buschbeck. Landauer Schriften zur Theologie und Religionspädagogik 1 (1986): 75-84. Bornkamm, G., "Das Anathema in der urchristlichen Abendmahlsliturgie," (first published in 1950), now in his *Das Ende des Gesetzes. Paulusstudien. Gesammelte Aufsätze I,* BEvT 16 (⁵1966), 123-132. Cullmann, O., *Urchristentum und Gottesdienst,* ATANT 3 (²1950); *Early Christian Worship* (1953). Deichgräber, R. *Gotteshymnus und Christushymnus in der frühen Christenheit. Untersuchungen zu Form, Sprache und Stil der frühchristlichen Hymnen,* SUNT 5 (1967). Farrar, A., *A Rebirth of Images. The Making of St. John's Apocalypse,* Beacon Paperback (²1963). Hahn, F., "Die Sendschreiben der

---

[47] On the composition, cf. G. Bornkamm, "Die Komposition;" and also F. Hahn, "Zum Aufbau;" J. Lambrecht, "A Structure;" E Schüssler-Fiorenza, "Composition and Structure of the Book of Revelation," *CBQ* 39 (1977): 344-366.; Taeger, J.-W., "Einige neuere Veröffentlichungen zur Apokalypse des Johannes," VF 29 (1984): 60-62; U. Vanni, *La structura,* 8; etc.

[48] Bornkamm, "Die Komposition," 205.

[49] Cf. P. Vielhauer and G. Strecker, "Einleitung zu XIX. Apokalyptik des Urchristentums," in *Neutestamentliche Apokryphen in deutscher Übersetzung,* ed. Wilhelm Schneemelcher II (⁵1989): 531; "XIX. Apocalyptic in Early Christianity," in *New Testament Apocrypha,* rev. ed. W. Schneemelcher II (1992): 585.

Johannesapokalypse. Ein Beitrag zur Bestimmung prophetischer Redeformen," in *Tradition und Glaube. Das frühe Christentum in seiner Umwelt.* Festgabe K.G. Kuhn, ed G. Jeremias *et al.* (1971), 357-394; "Die Worte vom lebendigen Wasser im Johannesevangelium. Eigenart und Vorgeschichte von Joh 4,10.13f.; 6,35; 7,37-39," in *God's Christ and His People. Studies in Honour of N.A. Dahl,* ed J. Jervell *et al.* (1977), 51-70; "Liturgische Elemente in den Rahmenstücken der Johannesoffenbarung," in *Kirchengemeinschaft – Anspruch und Wirklichkeit.* Festschrift G. Kretschmar, ed. W.-D. Hauschildt et al. (1986), 43-57. Jörns, K.-P., *Das hymnische Evangelium. Untersuchungen zu Aufbau, Funktion und Herkunft der hymnischen Stücke in der Johannesoffenbarung,* SNT 5 (1971). Koch, K., "Vom profetischen zum apokalyptischen Visionsbericht," in *Apocalypticism in the Mediterranean World and the Near East. Proceedings of the International Colloquium on Apocalypticism, Uppsala, August 12-17, 1979,* ed. D. Hellholm (1983), 413-446. Läuchli, S., "Eine Gottesdienststruktur in der Johannesoffenbarung," *TZ* 16 (1960): 359-378. Müller, H.P., "Die Plagen der Apokalypse. Eine formgeschichtliche Untersuchung," *ZNW* 51 (1960): 268-278. Müller, U.B., *Prophetie und Predigt im Neuen Testament. Formgeschichtliche Untersuchungen zur urchristlichen Prophetie,* SNT 10 (1975). Muse, R.L., "Revelation 2-3. A Critical Analysis of Seven Prophetic Messages," *JETS* 29 (1986): 147-161. O'Rourke, J.J., "The Hymns of the Apocalypse," *CBQ* 30 (1968): 399-409. von der Osten-Sacken, P., "'Christologie, Taufe, Homologie' – Ein Beitrag zu Apc Joh 1,5f.," *ZNW* 58 (1967): 255-266. Popkes, W., "Die Funktion der Sendschreiben in der Johannes-Apokalypse. Zugleich ein Beitrag zur Spätgeschichte der neutestamentlichen Gleichnisse," *ZNW* 74 (1983): 90-107. Prigent, P. *Apocalypse et liturgie,* CahThéol 52 (1964). Robinson, J.A.T., "The Earliest Christian Sequence" (first published in 1953), in his *Twelve New Testament Studies,* SBT 34 (1962), 154-157. Sandvik, B., *Das Kommen des Herrn beim Abendmahl,* ATANT 58 (1970). Schüssler-Fiorenza, E., *Priester für Gott. Studien zum Herrschafts- und Priestermotiv in der Apokalypse,* NTAbh NF 7 (1972); "Redemption as Liberation: Apoc 1:5f. and 5:9f.," *CBQ* 36 (1974): 220-232. Shea, W.H., "The Covenantal Form of the Letters to the Seven Churches," *AUSS* 21 (1983): 71-84. Shepherd, M.H., *The Paschal Liturgy and the Apocalypse,* Ecumenical Studies in Worship 6 (1960). Strand, K.A., "A Further Note on the Covenantal Form in the Book of Revelation," AUSS 21 (1983): 251-264. Vanni, U., "Un esempio di dialogo liturgico in Ap 1,4-8," *Bib* 57 (1976): 453-467.

The author's own creative formulations are hardly to be clouded over. Typical are the *acclamations, doxologies* and *songs* directed to God or to the Lamb, expressing the faith or hope of the threatened community (e.g., 4:8; 5:9-10; 11:15; 12-13; 15:3-4). Being so tightly interwoven with their contexts, the songs of 5:9, 12, 13; 12:10-12; and 19:1-2, 6 cannot be designated as "the oldest of all Christian songs."[50] While it is possible that the seer composed them by analogy

---

[50] As does O. Cullmann, *Urchristentum und Gottesdienst,* 24; *Early Christian Worship,* 21. S. Lauchli, "Ein Gottesdienststruktur," J.J. O'Rourke, "The Hymns," and others refer to numerous liturgical materials. For critiques of these positions, cf. R.

to those used in his community, we cannot get behind the formulations of the author. This applies also to other *liturgical forms.* In Rev 22 there are elements of a eucharistic liturgy, but there is no coherent liturgical sequence.[51] Furthermore, in the Apocalypse drinking the water of life is always conceived as something for the future.[52] It goes along with the emphasis on early Christian liturgy that a "determined, confessional eulogy" has been seen behind Rev 1:5b.[53] The epistolary character of Rev 1:4-6 is certainly underestimated if, along with U. Vanni, we attempt to find in 1:4-8 a fragment of a liturgical dialogue between lector and community. Such hypotheses warn us against overestimating the significance of liturgical forms.[54]

Attempts to derive[55] the structure of the Apocalypse from the Jewish festival calendar[56] or from the eucharistic or paschal liturgies[57] are not persuasive.

Although the forms of early Christian prophetic speech are relatively unknown, some seek to understand the seven letters of Revelation 2-3 against the background of early Christian prophecy. The messenger formula ($\tau\acute{\alpha}\delta\epsilon$ $\lambda\acute{\epsilon}\gamma\epsilon\iota$ $\acute{o}$ + the description of Christ) is the point of departure for these efforts. According to F. Hahn, these letters belong to an individual though inconstant genre consisting of a *messenger formula,* an "I know. . . ($o\hat{\iota}\delta\alpha$)" *section,* a *call to awaken,* and a *saying for those who overcome.*[58] But U.B. Müller assumes two basic forms: call to repentence (2:1-7; 2:12-17, 18-29; 3:14-22) and proclamation of salvation (2:8-11).

---

Deichgräber, *Gotteshymnus und Christushymnus,* 58f.; K.-P. Jörns, *Das hymnische Evangelium,* 178f; D.E. Aune, *Literary Environment,* 243.

[51] Cf. the concluding formula at 22:15; the use of $\mu\alpha\rho\alpha\nu\alpha\theta\acute{\alpha}$ in Greek at 22:20: G. Bornkamm, "Das Anathema in der urchristlichen Abendmahlsliturgie," 166f.; F. Hahn, "Die Worte vom lebendigen Wasser im Johannesevangelium," 56; "Liturgische Elemente in den Rahmenstücken der Johannesoffenbarung," 52-54; J.A.T. Robinson, "The Earliest Christian Sequence."

[52] Cf. U.B. Müller, *Die Offenbarung des Johannes,* Ökumenischer Taschenbuchkommentar zum Neuen Testament 19 (1984), 372; A. Satake, *Die Gemeindeordnung in der Johannesapokalypse,* WMANT 21 (1966), 78f. The reference in Didache 9:2 does not apply here, since in Revelation there is no reference to the vine (= the wine); cf. U.B. Müller, 372.

[53] P. v.d. Osten-Sacken, "'Christologie, Taufe, Homologie';" e. Schüssler-Fiorenza, "Redemption as Liberation," 227; as a confessional formula from the baptismal liturgy: Schüssler-Fiorenze, *Priester für Gott,* 203-212, 212-236.

[54] Cf. J.-W. Taeger, "Einige neuere Veröffentlichungen zur Apokalypse des Johannes," *VF* 29 (1984): 50-75, 67, n. 17, against P. Prigent, "Apocalypse et liturgie," and B. Sandvik, *Das Kommen des Herrn,* 29-34, 114-118.

[55] For a critique, cf. K.P. Jörns, *Das hymnische Evangelium,* 180-184.

[56] e.g., A.M. Farrar, *A Rebirth of Images.*

[57] e.g., M.H. Shepherd, *The Paschal Liturgy;* cf. also P. Prigent, *Apocalypse et liturgie.*

[58] "Die Sendschreiben," 366-391.

For him Rev 3:1-6 joins "exhortation as the preaching of repentence" with the form of a word of salvation, and Rev 3:7-13 represents a word of salvation.[59]

The attempt to explain the structure of these letters on the basis of the Old Testament covenant formulary is questionable.[60]

Beginning with the call to be awake, which is also found in the New Testament parable tradition (Matt. 11:15; 13:9, 43; Mark 4:9, 23; Luke 8:8; 14:35), W. Popkes suggests that the function of the letters is hermeneutical and preparatory.[61] Yet they are scarcely wrapped up in a propaedeutic function so that they could be described as "something of a catalogue of spiritual exercises in preparation for the reception of special knowledge." Since Mark 4's call to be awake is eschatologically oriented, the extensive paraenetic alignment of these letters ought not to be suppressed.

Quite different is D.E. Aune's reference to the form of the "edict." [62] Aune attempts to substantiate the relationship through parallels to the "These are the words . . . (τάδε λέγει)" formula in Roman and Persian edicts. In this he calls attention to the difficulties of classifying these passages as letters.[63] But, in light of the Old Testament stamp on the seer's language, it is more likely that the τάδε λέγει formule is derived from the style of proclamation. Yet Aune's designation of these passages as a "product of the literary artifice of the author rather than the result of the rigid reproduction of the oral style of early Christian prophetic speech,"[64] deserves attention.

In order to characterize those fallen under judgment the seer utilizes a *catalogue of vices* (Rev 21:8; 22:15 is a list of those who practice certain actions; 9:21 names offenses; for the form itself, cf. above, 3.4[65]).

Other forms characteristic of the apocalyptic genre are *visions* (with respect to this form cf. K. Koch and H.P. Müller); *beatitudes* (Rev 1:3; 14:13; 16:15; 19:9; 20:6; 22:7, 14); *paraenesis, prayers,* etc.[66] Käsemann attempts to refer Rev 22:18-

---

[59] U.B. Müller, *Prophetie und Predigt*, 47ff., "Literarische und formgeschichtliche Bestimmung der Apokalypse des Johannes als einem Zeugnis frühchristlicher Apokalyptik," in *Apocalypticism in the Mediterranean World and the Near East. Proceedings of the International Colloquium on Apocalypticism, Uppsala, August 12-17, 1979*, ed. D. Hellholm (1983), 601 with n. 6a. For a different view, i.e., of the epistles as prophetic letters, cf. K. Berger, "Apostelbrief und apostolische Rede/Zum Formular frühchristlicher Briefe," *ZNW* 65 (1974): 214ff.

[60] W.H. Shea, "The Covenantal Form;" K.A. Strand, "A Further Note on the Covenantal Form;" in agreement, O. Böcher, *Die Johannisapokalpyse*, ErFor 41 (³1988), 163. Cf. E. Lohse, *Die Offenbarung des Johannes*, NTD 11 (⁶[13]1983, ⁷[14]1988), 24, who refers to the "schema of the Old Testament covenant admonitions."

[61] "Die Funktion," 106; cf. the interpretation of the letters as hermeneutical preparation for God's revelation in R.L. Muse, "Revelation 2-3."

[62] "Form and Function;" cf. also his *Literary Environment*, 242.

[63] Cf. also L. Hartman, "Form and Message. A Preliminary Discussion of 'Partial Tests' in Rev 1-3 and 22:6ff," in *L'Apocalypse johannique et l'Apocalyptique dans le Nouveau Testament*, ed. J. Lambrecht, BETL 53 (1980), 129-149, 142.

[64] "Form and Function," 198.

[65] O. Böcher, "Lasterkataloge," has studied the relationship to the apostolic decrees and to the Pauline catalogues of vices, but it is improbable that the apostolic decrees are reflected in the Johannine Apocalypse; cf. G. Strecker, "Judenchristentum und Gnosis," in *Altes Testament – Frühjudentum – Gnosis. Neue Studien zu "Gnosis und Bibel,"* ed K.-W. Ströger (1980), 261-282, 275, n. 1.

[66] See above, pp. 208f.

19 to the prophetic form *sentences of holy law* found in the synoptic tradition and the Pauline letters.[67]

## 6.4    The Author of the Apocalypse and the Johannine School

*Literature*

Balz, H.R., "Anonymität und Pseudepigraphie im Urchristentum. Überlegungen zum literarischen und theologischen Problem der urchristlichen und gemeinantiken Pesudepigraphie," *ZTK* 66 (1969): 403-436. Becker, Joachim, "Erwägungen zu Fragen neutestamentlicher Exegese," *BZ* NF13 (1969): 99-102. Böcher, O., "Das Verhältnis der Apokalypse des Johannes zum Evangelium des Johannes," in *L'Apocalypse johannique et l'Apocalyptique dans le Nouveau Testament,* ed. J. Lambrecht, BETL 53 (1980), 289-301; "Johanneisches in der Apokalypse des Johannes" (first published in 1981), now in his *Kirche in Zeit und Endzeit. Aufsätze zur Offenbarung des Johannes* (1983), 1-12. Günther, J.J., "The Elder John, Author of Revelation," *JSNT* 11 (1981): 3-20. Schüssler-Fiorenza, E., "The Quest for the Johannine School. The Apocalypse and the Fourth Gospel," *NTS* 23 (1977): 402-427. Taeger, J.-W., *Johannesapokalypse und johanneischer Kreis. Versuch einer traditionsgeschichtlichen Ortsbestimmung am Paradigma der Lebenswasser-Thematik,* BZNW 51 (1989). Vanni, U., "L'Apocalypse johannique État de la question," in *L'Apocalypse johannique et l'Apocalyptique dans le Nouveau Testament,* ed. J. Lambrecht, BETL 53 (1980), 23-46.

There is wide ranging agreement among researchers that the author of the Apocalypse is not to be equated with the son of Zebedee or with the author of the Fourth Gospel.[68]  Since W. Bousset,[69] the author has often been identified with that John the Elder mentioned by Papias.[70]  In light of its form as an apocalypse, the self-designation of the author as John (1:1, 9) poses the question of authorship in a new way.  Pseudonymity is typical for the genre apocalypse (cf. above, section

---

[67] "Sätze heiligen Rechtes im Neuen Testament" (first published in 1954/55), now in his *Exegetische Versuche und Besinnungen,* II (1964), 69-82, 77f.; "Sentences of Holy Law in the New Testament," in his *New Testament Questions of Today* (1969), 66-81, 76f.

[68] But for a different viewpoint, cf. E. Lohmeyer, *Die Offenbarung des Johannes,* HNT 16 (²1953), 198f., 202f., cf. 194f.

[69] Bousset, W., *Die Offenbarung Johannis,* MeyerK 16 (⁶1906=reprint 1966), 42-45.

[70] E.g., by J.J. Günther, "The Elder John." R.H. Charles, *A Critical and Exegetical Commentary on the Revelation of St. John,* 2 vols. ICC (²1950), rejects identifying the author with this elder or any other known early Christian office, as do U.B. Müller, *Die Offenbarung des Johannes,* Ökumenischer Taschenbuch-kommentar zum Neuen Testament 19 (1984), and others.

6.1.2).[71] Would this not be true also for the Apocalypse?[72] While the question as to whether the seer emphatically identifies himself with John–which would be an argument for pseudonymity[73]–is undecided, the deutero-Pauline letters indicate that an epistolary structure cannot be utilized as an argument for genuineness of attribution.

The question is to which John the pseudonym applies. It could be the presbyter John, to whom Papias testifies as the author of the short Johannine letters, the founder of the Johannine school.[74] It is not impossible that the pseudonym assumes a blending of the traditions of John the son of Zebedee and the presbyter John and the confusion of the two in Asia Minor.[75] Identification with the author of the Fourth Gospel is excluded, since the author of the Apocalypse does not (yet) know that Gospel.

The relationship of the Johannine Apocalypse to the other Johannine writings has not been persuasively described in detail. While numerous likenesses are evident they have differing significance.[76] They must be arranged within the greater framework of the history of the Johannine school tradition.[77] The widely

---

[71] Cf. also P. Vielhauer and G. Strecker, "Einleitung zu C. Apokalypsen und Verwandtes," in *Neutestamentliche Apokryphen in deutscher Übersetzung,* ed. Wilhelm Schneemelcher II ([5]1989): 491-515, 494; "C. Apocalypses and Related Subjects, Introduction," in *New Testament Apocrypha,* rev. ed. W. Schneemelcher II (1992): 542-568, 545; and H.R. Balz, "Anonymität und Pseudepigraphie im Urchristentum," 421-426, although Balz himself does not presume the anonymity of the Johannine Apocalypse (427f.).

[72] Cf. Joachim Becker, "Erwägungen;" U. Vanni, "L'Apocalypse johannique," 28, n. 26: "one may question if there is no pseudonymity when the literary data which suggest pseudonomity are the same in the Johannine Apocalypse as in the other writings (mention of the name of of the detailed circumstances of writing, discourse always in the first person, etc.)."

[73] Already in Erasmus of Rotterdam.

[74] Cf. G. Strecker, "Die Anfänge der johanneischen Schule," *NTS* 32 (9186): 31-47; *Die Johannesbriefe,* MeyerK 14 (1989), 19ff.

[75] Bousset, W., *Die Offenbarung Johannis,* MeyerK 16 ([6]1906=reprint 1966), 46; cf. also 1. John 1:1-4.

[76] Cf. O. Böcher, "Das Verhältnis," and "Johanneisches in der Apokalypse." Cf. also H. Kraft, *Die Offenbarung des Johannes,* HNT 16a (1974), 10. J. Roloff, *Die Offenbarung des Johannes,* Zürcher Bibelkommentar, Neues Testament 18 (1984), 20; E. Schüssler-Fiorenza, "The Quest;" and E. Lohse, "Wie christlich ist die Offenbarung des Johannes?" *NTS* 34 (1988): 321-338, 326 argue against a (literary) relationship. They refer to formal and material contacts with Pauline or post-Pauline tradition. Cf. esp. E. Schüssler-Fiorenza, "Apokalypsis and Propheteia. The Book of Revelation in the Context of Early Christian Prophecy," in *L'Apocalypse johannique et l'Apocalyptique dans le Nouveau Testament,* ed. J. Lambrecht, BETL 53 (1980), 105-128, 121-128.

[77] J.-W. Taeger is not persuasive in his argument that the Apocalypse may be regarded simply as witness to the "later history of Johannine verbal images," i.e., the water of life, *Johannesapokalypse,* 82. For a different outlook, cf. F. Hahn, "Die Worte vom lebendigen Wasser im Johannesevangelium. Eigenart und Vorgeschichte von Joh 4,10.13f.; 6,35; 7,37-39," in *God's Christ and His People. Studies in Honour of N.A. Dahl,* ed. J. Jervell *et al.* (1977), 51-70.

held consensus with respect to dating the Apocalypse in the time of Domitian[78] is by no means conclusive. On the contrary, scant concrete allusions to official persecutions under the Caesars do not permit an exact dating. It is more significant that there are original apocalyptic expressions in the letters of the elder (esp. 2 John 7), in 1 John, and in the Fourth Gospel. Attributing these motifs to an ecclesiastical redactor as assumed by R. Bultmann undervalues the continuity of tradition in the Johannine school and, in general, the significance of apocalyptic in the history of early Christianity.

---

[78] Cf. O. Böcher, *Die Johannisapokalpyse,* ErFor 41 ($^3$1988), 36-41; A.Y. Collins, "Dating the Apocalypse of John," BR 26 (1981): 33-45; H.W. Günther, *Der Nah- und Enderwartungshorizont in der Apocalypse des heiligen Johannes,* FB 41 (1980), 100-148; A. Strobel, "Apokapypse des Johannes," in *TRE* (1978), 174-189, 187.

# 7 The Canon of the New Testament – Epilogue

*Literature*

von Campenhausen, H., "Die Entstehung des Neuen Testaments" (first published in 1963), in *Das Neue Testament als Kanon. Dokumentation und kritische Analyse zur gegenwärtigen Diskussion,* ed. E. Käsemann (1970), 109-123; *Die Entstehung der christlichen Bibel,* BHT 39 (1968); *The Formation of the Christian Bible* (1972). Dassman, E., "Wer schuf den Kanon des Neuen Testaments? Zum neuesten Buch von Bruce M. Metzger," *Jahrbuch für biblische Theologie* 3 (1988): 275-283. Gamble, H.V., *The New Testament. Its Making and Meaning.* Guides for Biblical Scholarship: New Testament Series (1985). Hahn, F., "Die Heilige Schrift als älteste christliche Tradition und als Kanon" (first published in 1980), in his *Exegetische Beiträge zum ökumenischen Gespräch. Gesammelte Aufsätze* 1 (1986), 29-39. (von) Harnack, A., *Das Neue Testament um das Jahr 200* (1889); *Lehrbuch der Dogmengeschichte* I (⁴1909=1990); *History of Christian Dogma,* vol. 2 (1897); *Die Entstehung des Neuen Testaments und die wichtigsten Folgen der neuen Schöpfung,* Beiträge zur Einleitung in das Neue Testament 6 (1914); *Marcion: Das Evangelium vom fremden Gott. Eine Monographie zur Geschichte der Grundlegung der katholischen Kirche,* TU 45 (²1924). Jülicher, A., *Einleitung in das Neue Testament.* Grundriss der theologischen Wissenschaft 3.1 (¹,²1894, ⁵,⁶1906), neubearbeitet in Verbindung mit E. Fascher (⁷1931), 450-558. Knox, J., *Marcion and the New Testament. An Essay in the Early History of the Canon* (1942). Kümmel, W.G., "Notwendigkeit und Grenze des neutestamentlichen Kanons" (first published in 1950), in *Das Neue Testament als Kanon. Dokumentation und kritische Analyse zur gegenwärtigen Diskussion,* ed. E. Käsemann (1970), 62-97; *Einleitung in das Neue Testament* (²¹1983), 420-451, 585-587; *Introduction to the New Testament,* rev. ed. (1975), 475-510. Leipoldt, J., *Geschichte des neutestamentlishen Kanons,* 2 vols. (1907-1908). Lietzmann, H., *Wie wurden die Bücher des Neuen Testaments heilige Schrift?* (1907). Lührmann, D., "Gal 2,9 und die katholischen Briefe. Bemerkungen zum Kanon und zur regula fidei," *ZNW* 72 (1981): 65-87. Merk, O., "Bibelkanon 2. Nt.licher Kanon," in *EKL*³ 1 (1986): 470-474. Metzger, B.M., *The Canon of the New Testament. Its Origin, Development, and Significance* (1987). *Das Neue Testament als Kanon. Dokumentation und kritische Analyse zur gegenwärtigen Diskussion,* ed. E. Käsemann (1970). Overbeck, F., *Zur Geschichte des Kanons,* Libelli 154 (1965=1880). Paulsen, H., "Die Bedeutung des Montanismus für die Herausbildung des Kanons," *VC* 32 (1978): 19-52. Ritter, A.M., "Die Entstehung des neutestamentlichen Kanons," in *Selbstdurchsetzung oder autoritative Entscheidung?: Kanon und Zensur. Archäologie der literarischen Kommunikation* II, ed. A. and J. Assmann (1987), 93-99. Sand, A., Kanon. *Von den Anfängen bis zum Fragmentum Muratorianum,* Handbuch der Dogmengeschichte 1, 3a (1974). Schneemelcher, W., "Bibel. III. Die Entstehung des Kanons des Neuen Testaments und der christlichen Bibel," in *TRE* 6 (1980): 22-48. Zahn, T., *Geschichte des* *neutestamentlichen Kanons.* 2 vols. (1888-1892); *Grundriss der Geschichte des neutestamentlichen Kanons* ($^2$1904).

The writings treated above were joined together into a New Testament canon through a process which lasted until the middle of the fourth century C.E. The beginnings of this process which reach back into the first century[1] remain largely in the dark, despite various suggestions of a four gospel canon[2] or Pauline corpus (cf. above, section 3. 6) emerging. Nor is there yet any consensus about further development of the canon.[3] The attempt to originate canonical development with Marcion[4] is not persuasive in light of pre-Marcionite developments.[5] Yet this association with Marcion correctly notes that the struggle over orthodoxy, carried on in the second century especially with gnosticism (and possibly including the ecclesiastical confrontation with Montanism[6]), was influential for the development of the canon. This holds true even if only partial proofs can be furnished and the account leaves many possibilities open.[7] It is wise therefore to reserve judgment on the classical thesis that, in facing the threat of heresy, the early catholic church was established by means of hierarchy, creed, and canon.[8] This thesis needs to be modified considering the extennsive history of early Christian tradition, without implying that the canon can be understood only on the basis of developments within the church.[9] Alongside widely proclaimed apostolic derivation, considerations of dissemination and even chance may be responsible for the recognition of a writing as canonical.

While the origin and development of the canon are unrecoverable in detail, it is nevertheless certain that the essential portion of the New Testament canon was recognized by the end of the second century. The Muratorian Canon, the oldest list of Christian scripture, and the early church fathers (e.g., Irenaeus) witness to this.

A few writings were long disputed (esp. James, 2 Peter, 2 and 3 John,[10] Hebrews, and the Apocalypse). To a great extent, the four gospels and letters of Paul had a firm position from the early period.

---

[1] W. Schneemelcher, "Die Entstehung," 26.

[2] H. Von Campenhausen, *Die Entstehung der christlichen Bibel,* 201-207; *The Formation of the Christian Bible,* 171-176.

[3] B.M. Metzger, *The Canon,* 11-36, gives a survey of research on the canon.

[4] As by A. von Harnack, *Marcion;* J. Knox, *Marcion;* and once again by H. von Campenhausen, *Die Entstehung,* 174; *The Formation,* 148. Cf. P. Vielhauer, *Geschichte der urchristlichen Literatur* ($^2$1978=1975), 785.

[5] For a critique, cf. W. Schneemelcher, "Die Entstehung," 37f.

[6] Cf. H. Paulsen, "Die Bedeutung," 22.

[7] On this cf. W. Bauer, *Rechtgläubigkeit und Ketzerei im ältesten Christentum,* mit einem Nachtrag ed. G. Strecker, BHT 10 ($^2$1964); *Orthodoxy and Heresy in Earliest Christianity* (1971).

[8] A. von Harnack, *Dogmengeschichte* 1:353-425, *History of Dogma,* 2:18-93.

[9] So W.G. Kümmel, "Notwendigkeit," 69f.

[10] As in the Muratorian fragment, which apparently knew 1-3 John. Cf. G. Strecker, *Die Johannesbriefe,* MeyerK 14 (1989), 12f.

The fourth century saw a provisional conclusion to canonical development.[11]

* * *

The writings of the New Testament canon are one part of early Christian literature. The special significance they possess for the church's message to this day accounts for the separate treatment of their literary history. Yet the history of early Christian literature should not be restricted in principle to discussing the canonical writings of the New Testament. Since the second century shaping the canon has drawn an artificial boundary between writings similar in nature, a boundary which we must transcend. The demand made long ago by G. Krüger and W. Wrede that the boundary of the canon must be overstepped in New Testament interpretation[12] is being realized in various newer works.[13] In raising questions of literary history, slighting extra-canonical writings[14] is misguided, for historical interpretation is compelled on grounds of form and content to include this wider circle of writings in its purview.

The theologically decisive criterion is the proclamation of the gospel of Jesus Christ. This is the early Christian authors' central concern. The theological statements in the early Christian writings can be evaluated in accordance with their testimony, thus posing the question of the unity and diversity of the New Testament canon.

---

[11] Cf., e.g., the 39th Festal Letter of Athanasius, which found its way into Greek canonical collections.    On this cf. W. Schneemelcher, "Haupteinleitung," in *Neutestamentliche Apokryphen in deutscher Übersetzung,* ed. W. Schneemelcher, I[6] (1990), 25 (translation: 39f.); "General Introduction," in *New Testament Apocrypha,* rev. ed. W. Schneemelcher I (1991), 31, (translation: 49f.). Cf. also the decisions of the synods of Hippo Regius in 393 and of Carthage in 397 and 419.

[12] Cf. above, pp. 9 and 10.

[13] E.g., P. Vielhauer, *Geschichte der urchristlichen Literatur.*

[14] As, e.g., in B.M. Metzger, *The Canon,* 271, 287.

# Index of Texts

## 1. Hebrew Bible

## 2. New Testament

## 3.    Other Texts

# Index of Subjects and Names